THE HEART OF A
Religion

MW00682737

Scott Mann has taught philosophy and social theory at the universities of
Sussex, Sydney and Western Sydney. He was a lecturer and director of the
Centre for Liberal and General Studies at the University of New South
Wales, and is currently teaching in the University of Western Sydney. His
previous book was *Psychoanalysis and Society: An Introduction* and he has
just written a book on analogical reasoning in natural science. He lives in
the Blue Mountains.

SCOTT MANN

The Heart of
a Heartless World

Religion as Ideology

BLACK
ROSE
BOOKS

Montréal/New York
London

Copyright © 1999 BLACK ROSE BOOKS

No part of this book may be reproduced or transmitted in any form, by any means electronic or mechanical, including photocopying and recording, or by any information storage or retrieval system—without written permission from the publisher, or, in the case of photocopying or other reprographic copying, a license from the Canadian Reprography Collective, with the exception of brief passages quoted by a reviewer in a newspaper or magazine.

Black Rose Books No. CC272
Hardcover ISBN: 1-55164-127-5 (bound)
Paperback ISBN: 1-55164-126-7 (pbk.)

Canadian Cataloguing in Publication Data

Mann, Scott
Heart of a heartless world : religion as ideology

Includes bibliographical references and index.
Hardcover ISBN: 1-55164-127-5 (bound)
Paperback ISBN: 1-55164-126-7 (pbk.)

1. Religion–Controversal literature. 2. Ideology–Religious aspects.
3. Religion and sociology. 4. Psychoanalysis and religion.
5. Philosophy, Marxist. I. Title.

BL2775.2.M35 1998   200   C98-901071-6

Cover Design by Associés libres, Montréal

**BLACK
ROSE
BOOKS**

C.P. 1258	2250 Military Road	99 Wallis Road
Succ. Place du Parc	Tonawanda, New York	London, E9 5LN
Montréal, H2W 2R3	14150	England
Canada	USA	UK

To order books in North America: (phone) 1-800-565-9523 (fax) 1-800-221-9985
In Europe: (phone) 0181-986-4854 (fax) 0181-533-5821

Our Web Site address: http://www.web.net/blackrosebooks

A publication of the Institute of Policy Alternatives of Montréal (IPAM)
Printed in Canada

CONTENTS

CHAPTER TEN / Catholicism, Oedipus and Sexual Guilt

CHAPTER ELEVEN / Catholicism *cont.*

CHAPTER TWELVE / Protestantism and Obsessional Neurosis

CHAPTER THIRTEEN / Protestantism *cont.*

CHAPTER FOURTEEN / Womb Envy, Creation and the
                  Copenhagen Interpretation

MENENIUS. I tell you, friends, most charitable care
Have the patricians of you. For your wants,
Your suffering in this dearth, you may as well
Strike at the heaven with your staves as lift them
Against the Roman state, whose course will on
The way it takes, cracking ten thousand curbs
Of more strong link asunder than can ever
Appear in your impediment. For the dearth,
The gods, not the patricians, make it, and
Your knees to them, not arms, must help. Alack
You are transported by calamity
Thither where more attends you; and you slander
The helms o' the state, who care for you like fathers,
When you curse them as enemies.

SHAKESPEARE, CORIOLANUS, ACT I, SCENE 1

PREFACE

RELIGION AS IDEOLOGY

It is easy to get lost in arguments about the precise nature and definition of religious – or, more broadly, mythico-religious – thought and practice. For present purposes I use the term 'religion' to refer to belief systems which centre upon, presume the existence of – and involve a direct and personal relationship with – higher 'spiritual' forces and powers, gods and demons, angels and guardian spirits, heavens or hells, with some bearing upon human 'earthly' life, and practices thought to mediate between the 'earthly' and 'heavenly' worlds – including prayer and sacrifice. It includes belief systems focussed upon the supposed 'immaterial' souls or spirits of humans, or animals, and their continued existence after the bodily death of the individuals concerned, as well as alleged (personal) 'souls' or spirits of material objects, including natural forces, the earth or, indeed, the universe as a whole. And it includes reference to 'otherworldly' sanctions for earthly beliefs and values.

One interesting and important fact about all of these sorts of beliefs is the apparent lack of any sort of empirical evidence for any of them. Nor has any logical argument for the existence of any such forces, entities or processes stood the test of rigorous analysis. Indeed, these days, proponents of these sorts of ideas seldom bother to try to construct any such empirical or logical justification. These are the sorts of ideas you take on trust – through a leap of 'faith', rather than seeking to 'test' or 'justify'.

The question therefore arises of why such ideas have not only persisted from stone age times right through to the present, but have also continued to profoundly influence all aspects of human life, in public and private, in sickness and health, in war and peace, in politics, work and culture.

Even as particular political ideas and forms, particular systems of economic organisation, particular movements in art and philosophy have come and gone, major religious traditions have persisted, expanded, developed, adapted, reasserted themselves – with incredible tenacity and resilience. Today, even amongst highly educated, supposedly secular populations, outside of any particular organised religious tradition, vague ideas of benevolent deities, guardian spirits, re-incarnation and life after death remain very widespread. Nor are these populations immune from outbreaks of radical fundamentalist zeal, overriding all vestiges of human intelligence and decency; sweeping away hundreds of years of (apparent) progress in scientific, moral and political enlightenment.

These developments require some sort of rational explanation – in terms of actual physical, psychological or social forces – rather than imaginary, supernatural ones. And, apparently, we do not have to look too far for at least the beginnings of such an explanation.

We know that human beings are very much products of their social circumstances. They come to see the world and relate to the world through the particular beliefs and practices provided by the social situation in which they grow up. And if those beliefs and practices are religious, so do they come to see themselves and their world in religious terms.

But this, of course, does not explain where such ideas came from in the first place, or why people have stuck with particular ideas despite the availability of serious alternatives. Social circumstances and traditions are never entirely homogenous, and they never entirely negate human powers of rational thought and action. So there are always alternatives of some kind. Nor does it explain why individuals and groups have enthusiastically seized upon 'new' religious ideas and movements, apparently radically at odds with their earlier life experience.

We know that humans have a tendency to cope with life's problems by retreating into wish-fulfilling fantasy. And sometimes such fantasy gets mixed up with reality. As children we were looked after

and cared for by bigger, stronger, cleverer adults. As adults its difficult to take responsibility for our own lives in a complex and hostile
world, and tempting to imagine that there is still some good parent
figure – bigger and stronger and cleverer than ordinary humans –
available to help us along.

It is difficult to cope with the realisation of the inevitability of
death – as the total disintegration of body and mind, and the
breaking of deep emotional bonds that goes along with it. It is
tempting to imagine that something of ourselves and of our loved
ones survives – some souls or astral bodies, floating through new –
otherworldly – dimensions, maintaining such loving bonds forever.

It is difficult to accept the arbitrariness and unfairness of a world
that punishes the virtuous as often as – or more often than – the
selfish, the evil and the cruel (with sickness, persecution, exploitation). It is tempting to imagine some broader scheme of things in
which all wrongs will be redressed, wickedness punished and virtue
rewarded.

But if this were really all there is to it then it is difficult to see
how such fantasies have persisted for so long; how they have been,
and continue to be, taken entirely seriously by honest, sincere,
intelligent and highly educated human beings. Apparently there are
other forces at work here, beyond mere individual wish-fulfilling
fantasy.

Another consideration is the human propensity for altered states
of consciousness above and beyond such creative imaginings. Every
night every human dreams, and thereby (apparently) undergoes all
sorts of fantastic experiences. And in ages past it has been far from
self-evident that such dreams are 'merely' extensions of waking
fantasy.

Not everyone has a so called 'near death' or 'out of body' experience, providing apparently direct evidence for the existence of
immaterial souls, angels, heaven and hell. But some do, and those
around them can be profoundly impressed by their accounts of
such experiences and by the changes they undergo as a result of
such experiences. This last area of 'out of body' experiences has

been subject to intensive interest and investigation in recent years. And it continues to sustain serious argument in support of religious belief (in the sense I have defined it above).

But it is still far from clear that these considerations are alone adequate to explain the persistence, intensity and particular character of religious belief. There are, after all, other possible explanations of the nature of dreaming than those that make reference to out of body experiences and communication with spirits. And there are better explanations of 'near death' experiences than those that make reference to 'minds' and 'souls' existing 'outside' the body. We have no good reason to suppose that anyone ever does better than 'seem' to have 'out of body' perceptions. Furthermore, "even if we did apparently encounter a case of thoroughly reliable perception of events from a point of view remote from the body, this still would not conclusively demonstrate that a person had left her body" (SMITH AND JONES 1986, p. 23). The same goes for telepathy and other 'paranormal' phenomena; – they need not be seen to imply the existence of immaterial souls, spirits, gods etc.

Of course, religion is not just about belief. There is, typically, also a social dimension of acceptance, support and love from a community of believers. Locating oneself within such a community provides a clear social identity and role, as well – in some cases – as concrete emotional, political or even financial support. But we have still got to explain why individuals feel the need for support of this kind, why such a group should define itself in specifically religious terms, and how it should come to be in a position to offer particular 'material' benefits to its members.

It seems that something more is required in the way of a proper explanation of the persistence of religious belief. We need to refer to real social and psychological forces over and above socialisation and the inertia of established tradition, over and above mere wish-fulfilling fantasies, altered states of consciousness or social support.

Amongst the human sciences, those that have gone furthest in exploring some of these other forces are historical materialism and psychoanalysis, the former focusing upon the role of economic and social power relations, the latter upon the role of individual emotional development and the dynamics of unconscious mental life in contributing to the generation and maintenance of religious ideas and practices.

Both provide coherent, productive and well-established frameworks for exploring the causes and consequences of belief systems in general – including specifically religious belief systems. Both have sustained long and fruitful traditions of research in this area. And many who have not explicitly recognised or acknowledged any particular commitment to either tradition have, nonetheless, utilised ideas drawn from one or both of them in casting light upon the 'true' nature of religious belief.

The key concept here is that of ideology as a system of ideas which is false (or largely false), but which nonetheless, for various reasons, appears appealing and correct, and functions as a real historical force insofar as individuals and groups see themselves and the world through such ideas. Ideologies are products of the interaction of previous beliefs with changing social and psychological circumstances. They answer or respond to various pressing needs while at the same time limiting and constraining individual perception and action by systematically misrepresenting true social relations and possibilities.

This book provides an introduction to the analysis of religious ideas in terms of these traditions; an introduction to the analysis of religions as ideologies. I aim to show how these two different approaches – from the perspective of materialist social science and of the psychoanalytic theory of individual personality formation – can usefully complement one another in providing explanation and understanding of particular religious ideas and practices.

Throughout the book I have been guided by 'classic' materialist and psychoanalytic writings in the area – including (on the materialist side) Marx and Engels's pioneering writings on religion and ideology, Kautsky's wonderful *Foundations of Christianity* and Siegel's recent synthesis – *The Meek and the Militant;* and (on the psychoanalytic side) Freud's own writings on religion, Melanie

Klein's fruitful extensions of the Freudian scheme, Roheim's psychoanalytic anthropology, Bettelheim's study of *Sacred Wounds*, and Melford Spiro's exemplary studies of psychoanalysis and culture.

But so too have I drawn extensively upon a number of outstanding recent works from outside of either such tradition, including Uta Ranke-Heinemann's work upon Catholicism and sexuality, Gimbutas, Downing and Eisler's writings on the religion of the Goddess, Henry Frankfort's studies of ancient Egyptian and Mesopotamian religions, Carolyn Merchants writings on the Protestant Reformation and the Scientific Revolution and studies of the life and times of Jesus by Morton Smith, Ian Wilson, John Riches, Domenic Crossan, Bishop Spong, Ranke-Heinemann and others.

Following a brief Introduction dealing with the scientific status of materialist and psychoanalytic theory, Chapter One begins to apply these theories to general questions of the origin and nature of religious belief. Thereafter I have organised the material in a roughly chronological sequence, starting with the religious ideas of Palaeolithic peoples. Thus Chapters Two and Three consider ideas in pre-agricultural tribal societies; Chapters Four and Five take us from Neolithic Goddess worship up to the origins of the patriarchal Indo-European religions that carried through to the Roman Empire; Chapters Six and Seven consider the first development of class society, the state and state religion – with particular reference to ancient Egyptian society; Chapters Eight and Nine look at the early development of Christianity within Roman occupied Palestine; and Chapters Ten and Eleven focus upon aspects of the early development of Catholic Christianity in Europe; Chapters Twelve and Thirteen consider the Protestant Reformation and Chapter Fourteen looks at certain trends in the development of modern science permeated by magical and mythological ideas.

This book is in no way intended as any kind of comprehensive history of religious ideas, nor even any kind of comprehensive survey of any particular religious tradition or traditions. Rather, it aims simply to cast some light upon specific elements of a range of particular – largely western – religious traditions by reference to considerations of the social and psychological contexts of production of such ideas. I have aimed for (a certain amount of) historical continuity mainly for the purposes of considering the longer term historical forces involved.

I am quite sure that the same explanatory ideas and principles, here applied principally to developments in Europe and the Middle East, are directly transferable to eastern religions, as e.g. Melford Spiro's brilliant psychoanalytic studies of Burmese religion indicate. However, I could not begin to do justice to other major traditions while keeping the book of manageable length.

Each chapter – or pair of connected chapters – is basically a separate essay on a particular aspect of a particular religious tradition. The topics have been specifically chosen so as to cover as wide a range of explanatory ideas and principles as possible. So that, while the book does not provide an introduction to comparative religion or religious history, it does provide an introduction to the sociological and psychological study of religion.

INTRODUCTION

Three people stand out as having contributed more than any others to revolutionising ideas of human nature and human social life in the late nineteenth and early twentieth century; English geologist, traveller and biologist, Charles Darwin (1809-1882), German philosopher, economist and revolutionary, Karl Marx (1818-1883) and Austrian medical researcher, doctor and psychotherapist Sigmund Freud (1856-1939).

Each of them started out in a field of study characterised by a considerable accumulation of data, observations and provisional classifications, but also considerable confusion and conflict. There was very little in the way of explanatory theory, with which to make sense of such data. They provided such theory, and in the process laid the foundations for a range of new scientific disciplines – in biology, social theory and psychology. And through so doing, they also radically changed ideas of what it is to be human.

All three shared a fundamentally materialist approach, and provided materialist models or mechanisms of the nature, origin and development of living systems, of human societies and of the human psyche. Before their contribution, ideas of divine creation of living things, of a spiritual force distinguishing living from non-living matter, of humans as a combination of corruptible material body and immortal spiritual soul, and of the soul as vehicle of free will and insight into higher spiritual realities were intellectually respectable and nearly universal.

After Darwin, Marx and Freud, these sorts of ideas lost most of their remaining intellectual appeal. There were now clear, coherent and comprehensive alternative explanations for the relevant facts, making it much more difficult to continue to seriously entertain ideas of gods and spirits.

DARWIN

Darwin layed the foundations for a new science of living things, with no place for 'vital spirits', divine interventions or divine plans. And he did so by creating a model of a living organism as a purely physical system, produced by physical processes. At the same time, he identified new, key 'emergent' properties which distinguished this particular sort of physical system from all others.

Living systems are specific sorts of organisations of material parts (systems and sub-systems) characterised by the properties of multiplication, heredity and variation (in fitness). Multiplication means that one such system can give rise to two or more such systems – it can reproduce itself. Heredity means that like begets like; the reproduction process is basically a 'copying' process. But it is not always a 'perfect' copying. Variation means that not all such entities are identical. In particular, not all are identical in their powers to survive and reproduce – in the particular circumstances in which they find themselves.

These (new, higher-order) properties are products of the particular structural organisation of the material components of the entities concerned, rather than the intervention of any kind of non-material forces. And in the years since Darwin's day there has been substantial progress in understanding the physical organisations in question (in particular, the relation of genotype to phenotype, the genetic code, processes of meiosis and mitosis, protein synthesis and mutation).

Given a population of entities of this kind, a process of evolution by natural selection becomes inevitable. And in the course of time, "the population will come to consist of entities with properties which help them to survive and reproduce" (MAYNARD-SMITH 1986, p. 4).

Thus, given that the organisms in a population differ in their abilities to survive and reproduce, and given that such differences are handed on to their offspring, then, in time, that population will exhibit an increasing proportion of 'fitter' individuals.

To take a simple example, consider a herd of kangaroos in which there is variation in hopping speed; suppose that faster kangaroos are better able to survive because they are better able to escape from predators (SOBER 1993, p. 9). If such hopping speed is inherited, then, gradually, the average hopping speed of the herd will increase, as 'natural selection' favours faster kangaroos over slower ones; the faster survive to produce more descendants.

Of course, the continued operation of evolutionary forces in the longer term presupposes continued variability, as well as heredity. As Maynard-Smith says, "if heredity were exact, evolutionary change would eventually slow down and stop; continuing evolution requires that heredity is inexact, so that new variants arise from time to time" (MAYNARD-SMITH 1986, p. 4).

Darwin argued that this sort of process could explain the great diversity of past and present species on earth as branches of a single 'tree of life'. According to this idea, the different species that now populate the earth derive from common ancestors – human beings and chimpanzees, e.g., derive from a (relatively recent) common ancestor. But more than this, the idea of a single tree of terrestrial life implies that for any two current species there is a species that is their common ancestor – not only are we related to chimpanzees and gorillas, we are also related to all other animals and plants.

It has sometimes been said that Darwin's evolutionary theory is untestable and therefore non-scientific. The contention is that it merely provides a definition of life from which a pattern of development follows logically – without reference to empirical observation. At the same time, it is often said that the concept of fitness has no independent reference. "Who survives? Those who are fittest. And who are the fittest? Those who survive. Given this definition, it cannot fail to be true that the organisms we presently observe survived because they were the fittest" (SOBER 1993, p. 69).

In fact, such claims of untestability are thoroughly misguided. Implicit in the idea of survival of the fittest is the idea of descent from ancestral populations with different attributes. Such an idea is potentially falsifiable. And the same goes – to a much greater extent

– for the idea of a single tree of life. As Maynard-Smith points out, "a single fossil rabbit in Cambrian rocks would be sufficient, because the first fossil mammals are found in rocks some 400 million years later than the Cambrian" (MAYNARD-SMITH 1986, p. 5). Even more so, a single living creature with a different genetic code – with different nucleotide triplets coding for the different amino acids – would radically undermine the idea of a common origin.

Another consideration is that natural selection is only one possible cause of currently observable traits in living populations, along with genetic drift, mutation and migration. Fitness therefore has substantial meaning over and above the mere fact of survival. Most important of all, the original model of 'life' upon which the whole theory hangs is itself testable; we can always ask whether any thing in the world really does exhibit the defining properties of life in the Darwinian model (including all of those things identified as alive before Darwin).

In practice, over the years, these ideas have been massively confirmed by geological, paleontological, microbiological, biochemical and many others sorts of investigations. And such confirmation has radically undermined alternative – mythico-religious – explanations for biological phenomena.

In providing a purely materialistic explanation for biological teleology, for specialisation and integration of functions in living organisms, so do such ideas undermine 'natural theological' arguments for the intervention of a creator god. As Maynard-Smith says, "we expect organisms which have evolved by natural selection to have organs which help them to survive and reproduce; that is, we expect them to have parts with functions" (op. cit.).

At the same time, these ideas clearly imply a fundamental continuity between human and animal life which radically undermines any notion of a specifically human 'immortal soul' or spirit.

MARX

Karl Marx, a great admirer of Darwin's work, aimed to take this process of 'materialisation' a stage further. He aimed to lay the foundations for a new science of society and history, in some respects parallel to Darwin's biological science. As noted above, Darwin had showed how biological systems were purely 'natural', physical systems with new emergent properties deriving from the particular organisation of their material constituents. In the same way, so did Marx show how social systems are material and biological systems with further new and emergent properties in virtue of the organisation of their constituent material components.

At the same time, whereas Darwin had undermined the idea of higher, spiritual realities, Marx took the next step of beginning to explain where such ideas came from in the first place and how they have been able to persist despite the lack of evidence for them – even after the Darwinian revolution itself.

According to Marx, social systems are characterised by three major sorts of emergent properties or functions – material (or economic), ideological and political. The material function is concerned with the reproduction of human material life through the production and distribution of material goods. And the institutions and practises through which such ongoing material reproduction is achieved are called the 'economic base' of society.

There are two sides to such production and distribution. On the one hand, a technological side, called by Marx the 'forces of material production', and including developing human knowledge, strength, skills, tools, machines, infrastructure and raw materials utilised in production. On the other, a social side, called by Marx the 'social relations of production', as the specific structures of ownership, power and control over productive forces, the social division of labour through which material production and distribution are organised.

Particular sorts of productive forces are said to 'correspond' to particular sorts of production relations, in the sense that particular production relations can accommodate only a limited range of types of productive technology. And particular stable – self-reproducing – totalities of relations and forces of material production are called 'modes of production',

The ideological function is concerned with the mental reproduction of human life through the production and distribution of ideas. These are not just any old ideas, but rather those most fundamental sets of ideas through which people come to identify themselves and to make sense of they world they inhabit, through which they perceive and give meaning to the world. Specifically, they are ideas which answer fundamental questions of what exists in the world (factual knowledge or belief about society, nature, identity), what are the 'good' or 'right' things for people to do (morals, ethics and priorities), and what is it possible for human beings to achieve. People are not born with such ideas and, like material goods, they have to be produced and distributed – through specific sorts of social practices and institutions.

The political function is concerned with overall social integration through dispute regulation, adjudication, law and defence, ultimately grounded in the use of means of coercion and violence. In some societies such a function is concentrated in a state which effectively monopolises such means of coercion and uses them to ensure its own maintenance. Together, those institutions and practises specifically concerned with ideological and political functions constitute what Marx calls the social 'superstructure' or 'superstructures'.

The basic thesis of Marx's materialist theory of history concerns the 'determination' of superstructural functions by the economic base of society. What this means is that the economic base has a much higher degree of autonomy in ensuring its own self-reproduction than do institutions and practises specialising in ideological and political functions.

When forces and relations of material production are in balance and harmony then they tend to promote the stabilisation of ideological and political practices in harmony with them. Where such forces and relations are in contradiction, this instability is also reflected in ideology and politics.

Such 'contradiction' can arise from a number of different sources. On the technological side, new innovations can outstrip the powers of existing production relations to control them, or the application of technology can generate ecological crisis – leading to underproduction and social breakdown. In particular, such developments can exacerbate already existing social conflicts within the relations of production.

Where a particular social group maintains a monopoly of effective control over major means of material production – and uses such monopoly power to dominate and exploit the rest of the population, there will always be conflict between the different 'class' groups, In 'normal' circumstances, such monopoly economic power allows the rulers to maintain control of the work force through manipulation of ideological and political, as well as economic forces. But in situations of economic crisis, such power is undermined, opening the way for possible social revolution and the creation of qualitatively new social forms.

Here we can begin to see how Marx explains the generation and persistence of religious ideas. On the one hand such ideas are tools of oppression and control, created and disseminated by the rulers to keep the exploited workers quiet – living in obedient passivity or fear. On the other, such ideas are products of the workers own experience of exploitation and misery, dreams of a better life in another world.

Here, of course, we begin to see how we might test the materialist theory. For, given particular sorts of economic relations, so should we be able to predict the general form of the corresponding ideological and political relations (and vice versa). Instances of ideas or political arrangements radically out of kilter with economic relations – or instances of radical new ideas preceding and causing qualitative economic change (rather than vice versa) would create serious problems for the theory.

Because of the primacy of the base function, Marx and his collaborator Friedrich Engels identify specific societies as specific modes of production (corresponding roughly to the 'species' concept – as interbreeding population – in Darwinian theory). Thus, they distinguish tribal societies – as societies characterised by kin-corporate or collective control of the technology of hunting and gathering or horticulture, societies based upon extended patriarchal family production units, Asiatic societies with central state control of intensive agricultural technology, slave, feudal and capitalistic societies with different degrees and forms of private property in major (and increasingly sophisticated) productive technology, and corresponding forms and degrees of exploitation and class conflict.

Like biological populations and species, such modes of production are subject to evolutionary change. We have already considered some of the 'internal' driving forces of such change – in the form of technology, ecology and class conflict. But these are complemented by interaction with 'external' forces in the form of other societies – through trade, competition for resources, piracy, warfare, imperialism etc.

Here is another area where the theory can be empirically tested insofar as it predicts particular trajectories of development within and between particular social forms. For example, Marx and Engels made a number of predictions about the future of industrial capitalist society which can be tested by reference to events since their deaths.

FREUD

Sigmund Freud, medical researcher, doctor and psychotherapist, working in Vienna at the beginning of the twentieth century, was also an admirer of Darwin and a committed materialist. In his new science of human personality there is no place for immortal 'souls', spirits or divine interventions. On the contrary, he associated 'mental' states and operations directly with physico-chemical states of the brain and perceptual systems, and sought to explain the nature and generation of personality through the interaction of innate – biologically based – and external social forces.

Furthermore, like Marx before him, he saw himself as carrying forward Darwin's original assault upon religious illusion through uncovering the real forces that sustained such illusion. Only, in this case, he focused rather upon individual, psychological considerations than upon broader social ones. In particular, he argued that unconscious mental forces and infantile 'fixations' played a major role in the process.

Here again, Freud developed a tripartite scheme of new, emergent properties or functions as the foundation of his new science. But, in this case, these are the emergent properties that define the human mind or personality, associated with the three functions of (1) rational thought and decision making, (2) conscience and the so called 'ego-defences', including repression and (3) instinctual desire.

Thus, the ego is identified with the conscious rational 'self', in touch with reality via veridical perception and logical reasoning. The ego is the vehicle of rational thought and action, in conscious touch with beliefs and desires via exercise of normal deliberation and memory.

The 'super-ego' is the agency of conscience, 'monitoring' thoughts and actions and responding with psychological rewards (pride) and punishments (guilt) in the service of particular 'moral' values, norms or rules. Closely associated with it are various so-called – unconscious – defence mechanisms, functioning to 'protect' the ego from external or internal (super-egoic) threat through 'distorting' or otherwise influencing conscious awareness in various ways – including the 'repression' – or exclusion from conscious awareness – of unacceptable desires, thoughts and feelings.

The 'id' is the source of instinctual desires, and repository for repressed materials. 'Energised' by such instinctual desires, repressed materials struggle to find their way back into consciousness – and control of conscious action, coming out in dreams (when the barriers of repression are relaxed in sleep), but also in slips, neurotic symptoms and in a range of waking beliefs and actions.

These, and other related ideas, provide the basis for a typology of human personality – including obsessive-compulsive, depressive, hysterical, psychopathic, schizoid and various other types. In particular, Freud argued that the nature and extent of repressed ideas played a crucial role in determining personality, along with the 'strength' of the super-ego and conscious rational ego.

Freud traced the development of these different components of personality through a series of stages, from early infancy through to adulthood, through the interplay of constitutional tendencies and social contingencies – particularly the dynamics of early family life. He maintained that different sorts of early childhood experiences – particularly traumatic experiences and excessive or inadequate gratification of desire – could lead to what he called 'fixation' at a particular developmental stage. Such fixation played a central role in determining adult personality types.

Here we can see how we might – in principle at least – go about testing the theory – checking to see whether the various defining features of these different personality types are indeed correlated, and whether particular sorts of child-rearing practises are indeed correlated with the predicted outcomes in terms of adult personality.

Freud's theories complement Darwin and Marx's contributions in further undermining the explanatory status of religious notions of soul, spirit or divinity. Not only does he explain the generation of personality – and morality – without any reference to such ideas, he also explains where such ideas themselves come from, as symptoms of psychoneurosis or psychosis. He shows how such ideas are products of fantasy wish-fulfilment and of the operation of unconscious defence mechanisms, rather than of conscious rational thought.

In particular, Freud carried forward the process of de-sanctification by arguing that far from being some direct link to God, the super-ego or conscience is merely a child's eye view of parental authority – a fantasy parent figure, threatening abandonment and bodily mutilation as punishments for socially unacceptable thoughts – especially sexual thoughts. As such, it is a thoroughly 'historically conditioned' sort of phenomenon, reflecting the prejudices of the age, rather than insight into eternal or universal truths and values.

ASSESSMENTS

Darwin's ideas met with massive hostility and rejection at the time of their first appearance – precisely because of their obvious threat to established religious doctrine. But evidence and rational argument eventually won the day – at least within the scientific community. And today, Darwin remains secure as the founder of modern biology – despite continuing attacks by religious fundamentalists. Some of his ideas about the nature of inheritance have fallen by the wayside, but all serious scientists still subscribe to the basic elements of the theory as outlined above.

Darwin's ideas are taught in schools and universities around the world. They remain the orthodox line and the foundation of contemporary biological science, and while there are still lively debates about some crucial elements of the theory (including the major 'units of selection' – genes, organisms or groups) natural selection is now an accepted fact – rather than a provisional theory.

Things are very different in respect of Marx and Freud's contribution, however. The great majority of the supposed experts in social and psychological theory – inside the universities and elsewhere – now explicitly criticise and reject their ideas as untestable – and hence unscientific – or as decisively refuted by empirical testing, or both. Indeed, hardly a week goes by without some public attack upon either or both of them, supposedly driving the final nails into their respective coffins.

Most of those studying social science or psychology at a university will find very little time devoted to serious consideration of their ideas. And if their names do come up their ideas are usually treated as of largely 'historical' or 'philosophical' significance; meaning they started the ball rolling, or produced ideas reasonable in their day, but such ideas have no significant bearing upon contemporary reality and contemporary scholarship. At best, they are seen as providing some sort of vague 'world-view' or general guide to life and morality, rather than any concrete explanation of specific facts.

Students referring to Marx or Freud's work in their own writing, particularly students quoting from them, are likely to find such quotes branded as 'polemical' – no matter what they happen to say. And students pursuing higher research degrees are actively encouraged – 'in their own interests' to avoid explicit mention of Marx and Freud, if they want to get work in the academic community in the future.

In light of these judgements it might seem reasonable to go with the flow and pass on to better things. Why bother with materialist or psychoanalytic theory at the end of the twentieth century?

Well, one good reason is that every major development that has come after Marx in economic theory, political theory, sociological theory and anthropological theory has been either a critical response to, or development of his ideas (typically without acknowledgment). At the same time, his ideas – or at least others ideas of his ideas – have profoundly influenced the practical political and economic life of the late nineteenth and twentieth centuries; – more so than those of any other individual.

Major developments in psychology after Freud have also, in many cases, been critical responses to – or developments of his ideas (again, often without acknowledgment). Freud's ideas have profoundly influenced the arts (painting, novel-writing, poetry, movie making etc.) and art criticism throughout the twentieth century, along with ideas and practices of child care, and, most significantly, of practical psychotherapy.

In many areas, in fact, the 'experts' continue to develop and use Marx and Freud's ideas for both theoretical and practical purposes, without acknowledging – in some cases without realising – that they are doing so. You cannot properly understand subsequent developments in most areas of the human sciences without a proper understanding of Marx and Freud's contribution.

Another consideration is the frequent misunderstanding and misrepresentation of Marx and Freud's ideas when their names appear in the educational system or the media. Generally speaking, they have been very poorly served by 'standard' textbooks (in psychology, economics, anthropology etc.) and by 'standard' authorities in general.

It is not difficult to see some possible reasons for this. Darwin's ideas apparently no longer pose any serious threat to the prevailing status quo of industrial capitalist economic relations and liberal democratic ideology and politics. On the contrary, on some interpretations, as in the case of the 'selfish gene' idea, and of some strains of 'sociobiology', they have been taken to provide solid support for such institutions and practices. Marx's ideas, by contrast, are much more unsettling for supporters of this status quo insofar as they provide the basis for damning practical and moral indictments of such a system, as exploitative, prone to deepening crisis and degeneration into fascist totalitarianism.

We are supposed to have taken Freud's ideas of infantile sexuality, repression and neurosis in our stride and moved on to more 'balanced' perspectives. In fact, some of his major insights remain just as troubling – just as threatening – to many people today as they were when they first appeared, seventy years or more ago. It is still supremely difficult for many to seriously entertain ideas of the family as a psychological and sexual battleground, of widespread child abuse, of young children as creatures with an active aggressive and sexual fantasy life, of some human actions and some of the deepest human thoughts and feelings as products of forces outside of conscious awareness, including murderous rage, love, homosexual feelings, infantile dependence or a desire to wallow in dirt.

Certainly we can see how these sorts of (political and emotional) considerations might get in the way of a proper rational assessment of the ideas in question, just as religious prejudices once made it difficult for many to seriously consider the pros and cons of Darwin's evolutionary theory.

I believe that these considerations, on their own, provide ample reason for continued serious study of materialist and psychoanalytic theory, and ample reason for considering some of the current treatment of Marx and Freud's ideas by the intellectual establishment as nothing short of scandalous. But there remain other, and still better reasons for such study.

First of all there is the fact that even if Marx and Freud are completely wrong in all of their major ideas, they are still wrong in interesting and important ways. Their theories still remain the most comprehensive and wide ranging currently available to make sense of and explain the great diversity of phenomena of human social life. Each provides a different prism through which such phenomena can be viewed, highlighting different aspects, different connections and different dimensions. You cannot study either one without thereby immediately confronting major questions of the nature and meaning of human life.

Secondly, and despite apparent contradictions between these two different explanatory schemes, there is always the possibility that their ideas are actually largely correct. There is always the possibility that their theories do indeed provide reasonably accurate models of specific areas of human social life and personality from which accurate predictions and explanations can be derived.

I have already indicated some of the reasons for rejecting the charge of untestability so often levelled at materialist and psychoanalytic theory. I think that the situation here very closely parallels that in respect of Darwinian evolutionary theory. Just as such charges are misguided in that case, so are they equally misguided in respect of Marxian and Freudian theory.

Indeed, there are good grounds for arguing that the latter two theories have sustained quite healthy and 'progressive' research traditions – continuing to deliver a range of new predictions and insights, confirmed by new observations over long periods of time, as others have worked upon, developed and modified the original theories.

There is also the possibility that when the ideas of Marxist materialism and Freudian psychoanalysis are brought together, rather than pursued separately, then qualitatively new insights might emerge. Here again, biology provides a useful analogy in the modern synthesis of Darwinian evolutionary theory with Mendelian genetics. Initially developed in isolation, each later came to be seen as crucially complimenting, correcting, clarifying and extending the other to provide a comprehensive picture of the nature of life on earth.

I think that many exciting and fruitful ideas have emerged from the attempt to achieve a similar synthesis of Marxian and Freudian ideas – through the efforts of Reich, Marcuse, Althusser and others. I aim to continue this tradition in this book, bringing together the analytical tools of both Marxist materialism and Freudian psychoanalysis to try to cast light upon a range of issues in the sociology and psychology of religion.

CHAPTER ONE
MATERIALISM, PSYCHOANALYSIS AND RELIGION

Part One
RELIGION AS IDEOLOGY

Karl Marx's pithy aphorisms on religion as 'the opium of the people' and 'the heart of a heartless world' (from his *Contribution to the Critique of Hegel's Philosophy of Right*, first published in 1844) are widely known. But the theory behind such ideas, and the full breadth of Marx and Engels's thinking about religious ideas and practices are much less widely appreciated.

It is often assumed that the originators and leading theorists of historical materialism were wholly and completely 'negative' in their judgements about the historical role of religious ideas and practices. Religion is, after all, primarily concerned with supernatural – i.e. non-material – and, in particular, divine forces of various kinds. It supposedly concerns the interaction of human individuals and human society with such supernatural forces. According to materialist theory, no such supernatural forces actually exist.

Religious ideas and practices (rituals, worship etc.) have therefore had quite a different significance and have functioned in ways quite different from those attributed to them by the true believers themselves. And materialists, who are also socialists are primarily concerned with the objective role of such ideas and practices in challenging or supporting social inequality and exploitation (ultimately with their role in fostering or thwarting socialist revolutionary transformation).

In terms of the classical materialist model of society as 'economic base' and 'ideological (and political) superstructures' religion is clearly located in the superstructure. While religious belief systems and practices, like other superstructural elements (literature, art, politics, philosophy and science etc.), develop according to their own internal traditions and dynamics, and register effects both upon other such elements and upon the economic base itself (e.g. encouraging hard work, renunciation, accumulation etc.), nonetheless, they remain only relatively autonomous and independent.

All such superstructural elements are really "different manifestations of a unified process of social development from which they have evolved" (SIEGEL 1986, pp. 23-4). It is the underlying economic movement, the life of the economic base, that is most powerful in shaping this overall development, that is ultimately 'determinant' of this total process.

There are two principle dimensions of such 'determination'. On the one hand is the idea that the economic life circumstances of individuals and groups – their position within the social division of labour and of power – profoundly influence the ways in which they respond to, interpret and develop the ideas available to them. Those in a position of wealth and privilege, tend to 'see the world' in a different sort of way from those experiencing poverty or exploitation.

Ideas which endorse the existing status quo are rather more likely to 'make sense' to the former sorts of groups than the latter. Concomitantly, the latter are more likely to endorse or develop ideas – and practices – which actually challenge such established inequality and exploitation. Such dissatisfaction poses an ever present threat to the power and privilege of the rulers.

On the other hand there is the parallel concept of a 'dominant' ideology – functioning to ongoingly 'counteract' any such ideological threat to the established status quo 'from below'.

Since control of major material productive forces (of land, raw materials, tools and skills etc.) within the base gives control of the systematic (specialised, superstructural) production (and distribution) of ideas also, the dominant religious ideas of a particular epoch or territory will tend to be those of the class that controls such material productive forces. And where such economic relations are characterised by radical inequality (in such control) and exploitation, such ideas typically serve to legitimate and sanctify such inequality and exploitation.

The key concept here is that of the economic (material) surplus; the material wealth generated over and above that required to maintain (and ongoingly reproduce) the productive forces (the workers, their tools, the fertility of the land etc.). For substantial surplus is required in order to sustain such specialised institutions of ideas-production and distribution as civil service bureaucracies, temples, churches, religious schools, universities, newspapers, TV stations etc. The rulers are able to use their monopoly power over the means of production to force the producers to hand over such surplus to them as rent, taxes or whatever. And such surplus can then be used to finance the production and distribution of ideas which reflect and support the interests of the rulers.

On the one hand the stability of class power depends on the provision of ideas to the rulers themselves which function to integrate and mobilise them in the effective maintenance and extension of their power. Such ideas must themselves, to some extent, accurately reflect the reality of their situation. And such reality as these ideas do have presumably reflects their origin in the real life circumstances of the ruling groups. At the same time, so must such ideas (generally) facilitate conflict resolution amongst such rulers, harden them to the suffering of the victims of their exploitation (assuage their guilt) and flatter and re-assure them as to the legitimacy and value of their lifestyle and purpose.

It is easy to see how religious ideas might accommodate these latter demands, at least, in providing a framework of divine rules and sanctions for dispute regulation, and some sense of divine purpose – of pursuit of higher 'spiritual' goals underlying the reality of domination, privilege and exploitation. Any crime is acceptable if it is done in god's name, and anything is possible to those convinced they have god's protection and support.

On the other hand, we can see how the stability of such class rule could also depend upon providing an appropriately docile, accepting, and/or enthusiastically hard-working sort of mentality on the part of the labouring majority. And here again, religious ideas seem ideally adapted to this purpose.

The ruling class – or their representatives in the priesthood – threaten divine retribution for any challenge to the existing status quo, or promise divine recompense or reward – in the afterlife (or in a future 'earthly' incarnation) for uncomplaining acceptance of the existing situation by the exploited masses. Their rule receives God's blessing as 'natural', 'ideal', 'eternal', and ultimately beneficial to all. Any challenge to their 'law' is a 'sin' against God.

In the broader scheme of things (in the context of 'eternity' and the 'hereafter') there is no such thing as inequality or unfairness. Everything is balanced, all crimes punished, all suffering recompensed. Alternatively, there is no inequality, only 'different', interlocking and mutually dependent social roles and responsibilities; everyone has their own part to play in fulfilling God's glorious plan.

Or again, inequality and the suffering of the exploited are acknowledged, but they are assimilated to natural phenomena, beyond all scope of change. Some are 'born' to suffer (by a mysterious but inexorable divine purpose etc). Perhaps, indeed, exploitation and inequality actually have a positive role – restricting the slaves opportunity to sin, and thereby saving their immortal souls (as some of the early Christian fathers suggested), punishing sins or stimulating obedience and effort.

In some cases the same religious ideas can serve in both of the above noted roles – of mobilising the rulers and mentally enslaving the rest. Though, clearly, the same set of ideas need not be used for both purposes. On the contrary, different sets of ideas – not necessarily closely related – can be 'tailored' to these different functions (the esoteric and the exoteric, the higher and the lower vehicles).

Ideally, these ideas are 'programmed' into each new generation (through appropriate 'moral education') prior to any significant development of the individuals critical faculties. The 'life process' of the exploited masses is thereafter 'tailored' towards continuous and active deployment and re-enforcement of such ideas, without (opportunities for) any sort of critical examination, questioning or challenge.

As Maurice Godelier says,

> "For the installation and maintenance in power of part of society (the male sex, an estate, a caste or class) repression is less effective than adherence, and physical or psychological violence counts for less than intellectual conviction which brings with it acquiescence, the acceptance, if not the co-operation, of the dominated" (GODELIER 1988, p. 156).

The corollary of the idea of religion as a superstructure is that economic crises of underproduction – which erode the material surplus available to the rulers – thereby also erode the rulers' effective power over such specialised ideas production and distribution. For it seems reasonable to assume that the satisfaction of the rulers own material wants and needs and the maintenance of their military power (also sustained by such material surplus) would take precedence over such specialised ideas production when it comes to necessary 'cut-backs'. Such crises therefore 'weaken' the rulers' ideological power over the exploited majority (and over their own cohesion and integration).

For now it becomes possible for the material life circumstances of the oppressed to increasingly predominate in shaping their ideas.

Now radical 'counter' ideologies can emerge from the periphery – from being largely ignored or ridiculed or neglected – to 'speak' to an increasingly wider audience. The realities of inequality and exploitation thus stand increasingly clearly revealed to the victims themselves. The veils of religious mystification are finally torn away to reveal the true material reality.

These developments are, of course, significantly re-inforced by inevitably worsening conditions of poverty and exploitation – as the rulers attempt to pass on the costs of the crisis to the working population – in terms of increased labour demands, reduced wages etc. Certainly, the workers can no longer be 'bought off' with consumer durables, job security, a substantial social wage etc.

In fact, as Godelier points out, it is perfectly in keeping with the 'internal logic' of Marx's theory that religious ideas and practices (i.e. ideas and practices ostensibly concerned to mediate between natural and supernatural forces) could also become integral to the production relations of the economic base – rather than merely 'reflecting', endorsing or legitimating such relations.

In many societies, 'sacred' organisations of one sort or another have been major owners and controllers of (material) productive forces. Property relations and appropriation of material resources – including appropriation of the surplus labour of the mass of the population – have been organised and expressed directly in terms of religious ideas and practices. Here, for example, the land has been regarded as the property of a god, and this god has been kept happy or healthy and well disposed to the human population, (maintaining the fertility of the land) through payment of rent by peasant farmers to the god's earthly representatives (the priestly bureaucrats etc.).

But the basic principle remains that religious ideas in this case still function to organise, stabilise and legitimate inequality and exploitation by presenting what is in fact the unrequited handover of hard-won resources from workers to parasitic ruling groups as an exchange of services.

As Godelier says,

> 'the fact that the services rendered by the dominant have been predominantly concerned with the invisible (i.e. divine) forces (supposedly) controlling the reproduction of the universe (rain gods etc.) has always been crucial' [in perpetuating inequality and oppression]. "For the terms of the balance which is established between the services exchanged, those rendered by the dominant seem all the more fundamental for being the more imaginary, whereas those rendered by the dominated seem all the more trivial for being the more material, since they only concern the universally visible conditions needed for the society's reproduction" (GODELIER 1988, p. 161).

Part Two
THE PROGRESSIVE ROLE OF RELIGIOUS IDEAS

However, if we consider the specific details of Marx and Engels own comments on the subject we find that there is actually rather more to their ideas of religion than this. In particular, we find that their analysis is far from completely or straightforwardly negative.

In the first instance we must consider Marx and Engels's ideas of 'primitive communism' in small scale hunting-gathering and horticultural tribal societies. Here, they followed American ethnographer Lewis Morgan in identifying the 'gens' or extended (originally) matrilineal descent group as the basic unit of 'primitive' tribal organisation. And most importantly, they identified it as the fundamental unit of collective ownership, control and appropriation of material resources in such tribal society – with such resources (equally) available to all the members of the group in response to need.

Certainly, they believed that such 'primitive' communism fell far short of the communism that is possible on the basis of modern science, culture, education and technology. It remained radically restricted by the low level of development of the material (and mental) productive forces. But it did anticipate some of the basic principles of such future communist society in terms of collective ownership and control and planned redistribution of material goods within the 'gens'.

Furthermore, since religious ideas of various kinds were probably integral to the maintenance of such 'gens' structures, so were they therefore also integral to the maintenance of such collective owner-ship, and planned production for need. Here, we think of kinship structures, roles and responsibilities built around ideas of (common) dreamtime ('totemic') ancestors for all the members of the group, and of divine sanctions supporting mutual aid and mutual respect within and between groups.

Nor must we forget the role of what we today tend to classify as 'religious' ideas in providing explanations for phenomena inex-plicable in terms of everyday perception. 'Origin myths', e.g. often provide perfectly coherent explanations for the origin of the world, of human and animal life, specific social institutions and practices etc. And in so doing, so do they serve the same human 'need for meaning' that animates modern scientific research.

Certainly, the 'animistic' explanatory theories of tribal peoples have been refuted by the advance of modern science. But, in many cases, such theories were probably the best available at the time – in situations where the low level of technological development actually precluded the development and testing of better ones.

There is substantial evidence indicating that the 'religious' beliefs and practices of tribal peoples can have 'useful' individual and social 'functions' in promoting mental and physical health, ecologically sustainable production etc. And, in some cases (e.g. the Iroquois Indian dream theory) we see remarkable 'anticipations' of more recent ideas, embedded within such religious and animistic world-views.

No materialist would go too far with trendy New Age preoccu-pations with the 'Wisdom of the Ancients'. Suggestions of palaeo-lithic anticipations of modern particle physics are clearly ludicrous. But pre-industrial technology need not preclude significant progress in ecology, ethology, practical pharmacology and psychology. On the contrary, in many cases the absence of sophisticated technology will tend to promote advance in these sorts of areas. (Who would claim that the behaviourisms of Watson or Skinner offer more real psychological insights than the 'mythology' of the classical Greeks?)

As far as later, class-divided societies are concerned, it is true, as Siegel points out, that Marx and Engels argued that the primary social function of religion has, indeed, been to 'sanctify exploitative and repressive institutions'. Nonetheless, the situation is still a complex one.

There are the problems associated with the classical materialist idea of 'linear' historical progress towards the true proletarian socialism of the future. Given that such a 'developed' communism – of 'plenty' – was not possible prior to the development of an industrial capitalist world economy, the question arises of how we assess the role of those exploitative religious elites of the past who have (for limited periods, at least) actually fostered the development of material and mental productive forces (in ways which Marx and Engels themselves believed were not possible on the basis of a more equitable distribution of – very – scarce resources). Presumably, in overseeing agricultural and architectural innovation, the expansion of markets, literacy, numeracy etc., such elites (in the early states of Sumer, Egypt, India, China, Peru and Central America e.g.) had a positive historical role. While certain 'reforms' might have been both desirable and possible, within such a context, more radical social liberation struggles by the oppressed masses could have been retrograde steps – away from 'civilisation' and back to 'barbarism'.

This sort of idea is not necessarily quite so cynical as it might sound at first and has relevance for contemporary debates about ecology and the calls of the Greens for the 'developed' societies of the world to return to a smaller scale, simpler sort of lifestyle. Marx and Engels believed that the ancient theocracies of Sumer, Egypt, China etc., typically relied upon strong central state power to oversee and co-ordinate production and distribution so as to sustain very substantial populations (far in excess of any that could be maintained by earlier, tribal technologies) in relative peace and security. They believed that in such a context – of 'Asiatic Despotism' – the destruction of such central power was likely to produce widespread social chaos, violence, misery and famine, and a regression back to some sort of primitive feudal isolation, chronic conflict and instability, rather than a communistic utopia. There is substantial historical evidence (from China and Egypt e.g.) to support this conclusion.

This is clearly relevant to the contemporary world situation insofar as the developed capitalist states have the material and mental resources to sustain expanded world population levels while extending the mental, material and political freedoms and opportunities of all in and through the operation of a planned world economy. But without the benefits of such sophisticated technology and large scale planning, there is a very real danger that a precisely similar regression to (or extension of existing) feudal poverty, chaos and misery is the only other alternative.

More obviously (and closely related to this first point) there is the area of the spontaneous generation of revolutionary class consciousness from the immediate life experience of oppression. As Siegel says, precisely because ideas of supernatural forces bearing upon human life have – in past ages – so "dominated peoples thinking about the world and society around them, rebellious moods and movements amongst the oppressed in pre(modern) times – and even after – tended spontaneously to acquire a religious colouration and heretical cast. The aims and aspirations of social agitators were expressed through traditional religious ideas adapted to the needs and demands of the insurgent masses" (SIEGEL 1986, p. 26).

Nor is this merely a matter of 'radical' ideas and practices being 'influenced' and 'directed' by pre-existing modes of thought. Pre-existing religious ideas have themselves on occasions played a significant role in stimulating and directing such radicalism. For while material conditions of exploitation, oppression and inequality might themselves have been sufficient to directly generate anger and a will for social change, it has often been religious ideas that have provided the blueprint for the actual form of such change (a 'vision' of a better world), and, through so doing, provided the spark that stimulated united action to try to achieve it.

Religious ideas have provided a framework of common identity and common commitment which have contributed crucially to the integration and cohesion of groups engaged in revolutionary struggle. This has been particularly the case in respect of some national liberation movements, struggling to escape from the domination by expansionary imperialist powers, where ideas of religious and national identity have become intimately intertwined.

So have such ideas contributed to the 'confidence' or faith which have sustained revolutionary struggles, despite the threat of injury or death. Here we think particularly of the promise of martyrdom and direct passage to heaven for Jewish Zealots challenging Roman imperial rule or radical Circumcellians, challenging the power of Augustine's Roman soldiers.

In this connection, Siegel quotes Engels comments in *The Peasant War in Germany* relating to the stimulus provided for peasant revolt against feudal oppression by Luther's translation of the Bible. "Through the Bible he (Luther) contrasted the feudalised Christianity of his day with the unassuming Christianity of the first century, and the decaying feudal society with a picture of a society that knew nothing of the complex and artificial hierarchy" (SIEGEL 1986, p. 27).

Nor was German Anabaptism a special exception. As Engels says, "throughout the Middle Ages (the) chiliastic dream visions of Christianity – the idea of the second coming of Christ, which would bring a thousand years of the kingdom of God on Earth – inspired... the revolutionary struggles of the poor and the oppressed". And indeed, after the Middle Ages, in the first great revolutionary struggles of the modern epoch, communist theory and practice underwent very significant development amongst the radical dissenting Protestant sects of the English Revolution.

As Siegel says,

"this sheds a new light upon Marx's [famous phrase] 'Religion is the opium of the people'. This is generally taken to mean that religion is a drug which enables the masses to bear their misery by losing themselves in dreams that deprive them of the capacity to revolt... This is undoubtedly a good deal of what Marx meant, but it is not all he meant. Immediately preceding this famous sentence is the sentence 'Religious distress is at the same time the expression of real distress and the protest against real distress'. Opium dreams can rouse to protest and struggle, can stimulate as well as stupefy" (SIEGEL 1986, p. 28).

But he adds the important Marxist proviso:

"Opium however, is never conducive to realistic perception, and it is precisely because communism could not be achieved (until the development of modern industrial capitalism), because the struggle for it could only be an anticipation of the future, that the yearning for it took the form of fantasy." (op. cit.)

This raises a number of problems. If we see that religions exist as complex belief systems, then it far from clear that they are always completely false.

Part Three
GOD AND HEAVEN

The whole question of the historical role of religious ideologies is further complicated by other considerations. We saw earlier how the 'orthodox' Marxist assumption was that underproductive crises would tend to undermine the power of the 'ruling ideology' by eroding the material surplus necessary to sustain specialised ideological productive forces (of Church, State, mass communications etc.). It would then become possible for less mystificatory and potentially revolutionary ideas – arising out of the real life circumstances of the oppressed majority – to develop and spread amongst such people.

There is no doubt that the development of revolutionary class consciousness is possible in such a situation (whether or not such ideas remain cloaked in religious forms). But the lessons of history indicate that such a result is very far from necessary – even when the real material pre-requisites of socialist transformation are well established. On the contrary, there is plenty of evidence to suggest that such situations are just as likely to call forth new and 'radical' ideologies all too easily subverted by other class groups, struggling to impose new forms of domination with the support of the disaffected masses themselves. Or we see the spread of 'fundamentalist' and fascist ideologies even more personally and socially regressive and destructive than the old ruling ideas – promoting hatred, prejudice, scapegoating, genocide and mass destruction amongst the working people themselves – leaving the way clear for the ascent of new oppressors and exploiters, for the resurgence of the power of the old rulers or for general social regression and ruin.

In face of these sorts of developments, socialists like Reich, Fromm, Marcuse, Althusser and others have turned to psychological theory to try to explain this failure. In particular, they have turned to variants of Freudian psychoanalytic theory to explain how 'irrational' unconscious forces can still isolate and alienate individuals and groups from a 'true' perception of their situation, interests and possibilities – despite the 'relaxation' of the ideological – and economic – power of the ruling class.

Here, the child rearing practices of the previous generation become another crucial element in the equation of social determination – alongside of pre-existing ideological, political and economic circumstances. For, according to psychoanalytic theory, it is these practices that shape the personality structure of the generation concerned, including the extent to which their perceptions and actions are distorted by so-called 'ego defence mechanisms' of projection, splitting, fixation, repression and fantasy. Such 'regressive' modes of mental activity undermine the development of revolutionary class consciousness and the pursuit of class interest by the oppressed masses.

From a psychoanalytic point of view, we can see how the relaxation of economic determination associated with the crisis (the relaxation of ruling class control) throws into sharp relief forces which have actually been operative all along; influencing thought, perception and action. And here too we begin to explain some of the characteristic forms of religious ideas and feelings in a way that the materialist account conspicuously fails to do.

Thus, materialism has little to contribute when it comes to explaining the ubiquity of ideas of a perfect heavenly realm, counterbalanced by a hell of eternal torment, of faith in the love of divine super-human parent figures and fear of demons, of desperate placation and appeasement of such beings through sacrifice and prayer, of angels, guardians, magical substances, powers and fluids of various kinds. In terms of psychoanalytic theory, by contrast, such ideas (or at least the tendency to make sense of such ideas and take them very seriously) are seen to derive directly from universal experiences of early childhood.

As far as (orthodox) Freudian theory is concerned, two key concepts here are those of the oral phase of development and the Oedipus complex. The former refers to the earliest stage of psychic life outside the womb, when it is assumed that the child's emotional and perceptual life is very much focussed upon their mouth, as the primary means of satisfaction of desire and contact with the parent. The latter refers to a later stage of emotional development – round about the ages of three to six or seven, when the child entertains fantasies of sex and violence directed towards the parents, but is subsequently forced to abandon or 'repress' such fantasies under threat of punishment.

It is in the earliest oral phase of the first year of life that the child moves from a state of 'primary narcissism' (deriving originally from symbiosis with the body of the mother in the womb) – in which they feel in perfect harmony with the universe, without frustration, pain or limitation – to a first awareness of their own existence as a separate – limited and suffering – individual, profoundly dependent upon adult love and care for their survival. The parents or guardians now become the bearers of the perfect happiness (love, food, protection and power) of the primary narcissistic state. The child's attitude now oscillates between the desire to regain such lost perfection through 'fusing' once again with the body of the parent, and the desire to be an autonomous individual in their own right, no longer dependent upon such external resources for survival and the maintenance of self esteem. The former is associated with clinging tight to the body of the parent and fantasies of oral re-incorporation. The latter is concerned, rather, with boldly venturing out to explore and master the external world.

We naturally and correctly associate maturation with reduced dependence and increased real autonomy. But there are obvious limits upon how far any human can 'transcend' their dependence upon their fellows, and ultimately, both absolute autonomy and absolute dependence are 'unrealistic' aims for a human being. The individual can neither return to the womb nor can they entirely free themselves from dependence upon other human beings – for emotional as well as material support. And 'normal' growth and maturation is supposed to involve an increasing understanding and acceptance of the true state of affairs.

But where an individual becomes fixated in the oral phase of development, due to 'excessive' or 'inadequate' fulfilment or major trauma (including too early or insensitive weaning) then they remain, forever after, trapped in or liable to regress back to the perceptions, priorities and problems of the oral phase. They feel a deep need for continuous support from external sources, in particular, from parent figures (or parent substitutes) of some sort. The individual either takes for granted the provision of such resources or else desperately fears that they will not be available or will be withdrawn at any moment. They respond to the latter fears by fantasies of angry oral attack upon the objects of such desire and frustration, desperate subordination to, or attempted control of such 'necessary others', or with a regressive retreat into a private fantasy, 'womb', world of their own. At a later stage of psychological development, the 'resolution' of the Oedipus complex marks the point at which the child massively introjects and identifies with the authority, values and demands of the parents or parental generation. Many cultures, in attempting to achieve a final Oedipal resolution in adolescence, demand that any such dependent feelings – towards other human beings – be radically suppressed or repressed.

Adolescent boys, in particular, are supposed to turn their backs upon their mothers and upon the women's world and prepare to become fearless – and independent – warriors. Where they have spent all of their previous lives in intimate association with the body of the mother, however, such suppression becomes all the more difficult. But the transition is often facilated by the provision of appropriate religious ideologies. Thus, it can be quite acceptable for such individuals to displace such feelings of dependence onto divine forces of various kinds (guardian spirits, the Virgin Mary etc.) as substitutes for the earthly mother.

Here, the macho identity typically masks a frozen core of infantile dependence – a continued need for mothering that is thrown into sharp relief in the modern western world by men's generally greater problems (than women) in coping effectively with divorce and bereavement. Less suppression of dependent feelings has generally been demanded of girls than of boys. In the interests of patriarchy, at least, it has been seen as desirable that women remain 'bound' in 'dependent relationships' – devoted to parents, grand-parents, husbands, children and other relations. In practice, precisely because they have not been called upon to repress such feelings so early and so powerfully, women have typically been in a better position to come to terms with them, and transcend their more debilitating consequences.

But individuals of both sexes, 'let down', as they believe, by their real human love objects (because such love objects fail to live up to their insatiable 'oral' demands) can turn to fantasies of the infinite powers of divine, super-human forces – totally devoted to themselves – for the necessary love and care they crave.

In contrast to the Marxist concept of ideology explored hitherto, the psychoanalytic tradition has used the term 'ideology' to refer to just those belief systems that 're-inforce' such infantile fixation through continuing to foster the illusion that such a return to primary narcissistic fusion with the body of the mother really is possible; the illusion of 'perfect' all powerful and all loving parents, always available to care for the individual, or of the possibility of 'absolute' autonomy and freedom from any necessary dependence upon others. This tends to place religious beliefs (along with 'manic' Nietzscheian 'anti-religions' and extreme 'liberal' individualism), once again, at the top of the list.

This relation is re-inforced when we consider the integrally oral dimension of so many religious beliefs and practices, from food sacrifices (including human sacrifices to feed the gods), and cannibalisation of sacred ancestors to Jesus account of God's kingdom (centred upon feasting to feed the hungry) and the Catholic mass.

Here we can clearly see how fixation in the oral phase of development can render individuals particularly vulnerable to religious credulity, blackmail and control. A childlike faith in the ongoing provision of parental love or low self-esteem and a desperate need for such love, can mean that orally fixated individuals all too easily 'accept' such regressive ideologies and are prepared to pay a very high price (in money, time, devotion, efforts etc.) for their promised forgiveness and 'salvation' – without asking too many difficult questions.

Part Four
THE DEVIL AND HELL

More recently, Melanie Klein and her followers have gone much further in exploring the 'fine structure' of the oral phase of development – and its implications for later life – through detailed investigations of the play and fantasy life of young children. In particular,

Klein has developed the ideas of what she calls the 'paranoid-schizoid' and 'depressive' positions as developmental phases of the first year of life which nonetheless continue to influence thought and action throughout the human lifespan.

Klein argues that in order to generate the image of the parent as all good, all loving and caring – while maintaining contact with the real parent, the early oral infant actually employs the defence of splitting the real parent into two separate beings – the ideal good and the bad. So while the parent in their nurturing, loving aspect becomes the perfect good parent or good breast, the parent in their frustrating, non-gratifying aspect becomes another – different – perfectly evil bad parent or bad breast. The child can then fantasise the complete destruction of the bad parent (e.g. through using their teeth in chewing and biting) so as to be left only with the perfect, good parent. Once the interference of the bad is ended only the good is left, devoted completely to the child.

Just as they split their objects, so too does the young child split themselves, projecting their bad feelings (of pain, anger, discomfort etc.) into other objects – parents, siblings and the world at large. Because of the predominance of such splitting and projection in this phase of development, leading in turn to paranoid fears of persecution, Klein calls it the 'paranoid schizoid position'.

Here we can see how Klein clarifies the origins of ideas of demonic persecution – as well as divine redemption. For having thus created a perfectly evil bad breast – and other monsters – and attempted to destroy them in fantasy, so does the child fear terrible revenge persecution by their own creations (according to the 'talion' principle of 'an eye for an eye'). Any and every frustration comes to be experienced as an unmoderated attack – or threat of attack – by such evil demons – motivating a retreat back to fusion with the ideal 'good' parent.

Klein argues that the situation is further complicated by the child's envy of the ideal good parent. For in idealising the good parent as repository of all power and perfection, so does the child deprive themselves of any such goodness. This can provoke feelings of envy and resentment towards – and fantasies of greedy oral attack upon – that good parent. And as even the good parent is turned bad or hostile by such attacks, so is the child left in a hostile and terrifying world (a vision of hell).

In the 'normal' course of events, however, the provision of consistent adult love and care allows for a gradual synthesis of the good and bad elements of the parental objects and of the self. The parent is now seen as a person-in-their-own-right, with a life of their own, separate from that of the child. Similarly, with the recognition of the unitary other comes the first stabilised recognition by the child of their own existence as a unitary self – reclaiming their 'bad' feelings from the outside world.

Klein speaks, in this connection, of entry into the 'depressive position', because, with the beginnings of a true recognition of the differentiation of the self and other comes recognition of the child's massive dependence upon such an external other. With this recognition comes the fear that the child has damaged and alienated that other with their own hostile attacks and bad feelings. The child fears loss of the necessary life-giving love and care of the other through their own hostility and inadequacy.

There are three possible types of response by the infant to such depressive guilt or fear. Firstly, the child can simply regress directly back to paranoid schizoid splitting and projection. Secondly, the child can embark upon attempts to repair the damage they imagine they have themselves inflicted upon the parent (and the relationship) through their own hostility and aggression. Through their play and their real relations with that parent they can try to 'rebuild' the loving bond (trying to be a 'good' and loving child etc.). Klein calls this reparation. Thirdly, they can respond with what Klein calls manic defences.

Because in the depressive position it is the experience of dependence that is associated with fear of loss, mourning, pining and guilt, manic defences are directed against any feelings of dependence, which will be obviated, denied or reversed. As Klein says, the key feelings here are control, triumph and contempt. Ideally, primarily through reparation, the child is able to develop their own powers of thought and action and their own self-esteem in such a way as to significantly attenuate depressive guilt and dependence. However, where such a development is undermined by a failure of proper parental love and care in either paranoid schizoid or depressive positions, there is a danger of fixation – leading to the persistence of paranoid schizoid and depressive fears and fantasies into later life.

In particular, we can see how parents who give love to their children only on a conditional basis, who demand impossibly high standards of 'good' behaviour, could contribute to a deep depressive fixation on the part of those children, leaving them trapped in a spiral of depressive guilt, low self esteem and endless reparation.

These ideas offer the clearest insight into the psychological obstacles to the development of revolutionary class consciousness in an economic crisis situation. For in such a situation, individuals fixated in a depressive relation to established authority (on account of problems in early childhood resolution of paranoid-schizoid and depressive fears) will tend to blame themselves for the reverses they suffer as primary victims of the crisis. As the bosses try to make them bear the costs of the crisis – in more and harder work for subsistence wages, in unemployment, poverty, removal of social welfare provision, war, insecurity and famine – they are all too amenable to ideologies of guilt and self-blame. They willingly rush into wage cuts and hand-backs (crusades and other wars of aggression etc.) to assuage their own depressive guilt and try to 'win back' the favour of the lords, bosses or gods.

If the self hatred and pain becomes too much, or if early childhood abuse has promoted particularly intense paranoid schizoid fixation, they are all the more prone to radical regression back to paranoid schizoid modes of perception and action. Now they are easy prey to the fundamentalist demagogues who promise eternal happiness through a renewed fusion with the body of the ideal 'good parent' – purchased at the expense merely of the total destruction of some scapegoat group which has become the repository for projection of the bad parent and the bad self.

Here, the hatred and anger and fear are deflected away from the self and onto some 'appropriate' external object with consequent powerful feelings of release and relief. Through paranoid schizoid regression both the parent and the self can be loved and idealised at the expense of the external scapegoat.

Of course, the problem here lies not so much with the demagogues themselves (wrestling with their own inner demons), not with 'fundamentalist' ideologies *per se* – which always hover around the periphery of society. But rather with the brutal or uncaring or inconsiderate and inconsistent child rearing practices that render significant numbers of people amenable to embracing such demagogues as leaders and such ideas as truths – and acting upon their dictates, bringing such individuals and ideas out of the periphery and into the mainstream.

The problem lies with those members of the old ruling class – or of new ascendant, exploiting groups, who encourage and sustain pre-existing ideologies of racism, sexism etc. which pave the way for such paranoid projection, who provide the necessary financial support to bring these marginal characters and their ideas to such a receptive audience (in the interests of deflecting revolutionary class consciousness and dividing the workers amongst themselves to maintain class rule). They always imagine they can control the forces they thus unleash – but all too often they are wrong, and such forces bring massive random destruction onto the heads of all concerned.

Part Five

IMPLICATIONS

So what is the final verdict on the social role of religion as an ideology? Clearly this is a deep and difficult question – especially in light of the complex interdependence of religious and progressive revolutionary ideas and practices in past ages and the continued relevance of religious self consciousness for some oppressed minorities struggling against imperialistic domination.

In future chapters I will explore this question by reference to more detailed and concrete studies of a number of different religious traditions. But one thing that does seem to be quite clear (already) is the crucial importance – for socialists – of striving to further the rights – and improve the situation of – young children and those caring for them in the period before the development of any potentially revolutionary situation. This has been an area neglected by some socialists in the past. But the sorts of psychological considerations adduced above indicate that – quite apart from their intrinsic significance as basic humanitarian reforms – progress in this area is absolutely fundamental in laying the foundations for any future socialist transformation.

Furthermore these considerations suggest that it is surely true that religious ideas have – for the most part – long outlived their usefulness as (necessary) guides or inspirations to progressive social transformation. With the advance of natural and social science – including historical materialist and psychoanalytic theory – we no longer require religious myths, dreams and fantasies to understand the world – or to change it.

On the contrary, just as capitalism has long outlived its usefulness as a force for progress in human life, and now threatens to destroy the very conditions that make human life possible on the planet, so do religious ideas now serve predominantly to obstruct true perceptions, sanctify exploitative social relations and nurture false hopes.

Wherever you look in the modern world, the fight for humane reforms – for the rights of women and children, ethnic minorities etc. – is a fight against religious institutions and religious ideas. And the same is very much more the case in respect of more fundamental social transformation towards socialist democracy, equality and freedom.

Over the years it has been fashionable for liberals to criticise Marxist socialists for elevating historical materialism itself to the status of a religious doctrine; with its own prophets (Marx, Engels, Lenin, Trotsky, Gramsci) its own creed, and its own idea of socialism as the coming of the kingdom of God. And there is no doubt that some have embraced the leading theorists and their ideas with a fervour and a blind faith very reminiscent of religious fundamentalism.

But the fact remains that as far as those leading theorists themselves were concerned, neither historical materialism nor psychoanalysis have any place for divine or supernatural forces – or supernatural guarantees – of any kind.

And both of these systems of ideas can properly contribute to the construction of a better world only when they are purged of all such mystificatory religious notions.

CHAPTER TWO
**ANIMISM AND MAGIC AMONGST
HUNTER-GATHERERS**

Part One
SOCIAL SCIENCE

In the last chapter I considered two major sorts of influence upon the development of religious beliefs and practices. On the one hand I concentrated upon the role of the social relations of material production, of class inequality and class conflict. And on the other I touched upon the role of infantile emotional experience, psychic fixation, repression and the unconscious mind.

In this and subsequent chapters I want to move on to begin to further develop and illustrate these ideas by reference to the details of the belief systems of certain specific human societies. I want to show how these different forces have actually interacted in practice to generate, maintain or transform specific, historically known systems of thought or ideologies.

As has frequently been pointed out, human social organisation cannot be isolated in a laboratory and subjected to systematic experimental investigation. We cannot isolate a specific human society and "hold the class structure constant, while systematically varying child-rearing practices" (or vice versa) to see how ideology changes in consequence.

But of course the same applies also to many sorts of natural systems also; we have no power to isolate and control them. This has by no means precluded scientific theorising about such systems – including empirical testing of such theories.

This is because the natural world itself provides relatively isolated systems, in which the more-or-less constant operation of certain, predominant forces is expressed or manifested in relatively straightforwardly perceivable regularities of various kinds. Or where quantitative or qualitative changes in the operation of a particular force stand out against a background of otherwise relatively constant forces. Observations of certain parts or states of such systems can serve as the basis for (improbable) predictions about other such (observable) parts or states. Understanding of such relatively simple and isolated systems can then guide and direct the approach to more complex natural systems – on a solid foundation of verified predictions about the life of (elements of) the simpler systems.

The same considerations apply to social life. It is true that contemporary industrial societies (and, indeed, most contemporary pre-industrial societies also) – anywhere in the world – are far from simple and isolated (characterised as they are by participation in a capitalist world market, and world-wide communications systems, by diverse cultural and class groupings, social subcultures, families, schools, peer groups, religious congregations, developed mass communications etc.). But history provides evidence of earlier social forms approximating much more closely to this sort of ideal.

Archaeological evidence indicates that – after 45,000 years ago, as fully modern human forms (homo sapiens sapiens) became established throughout most of the habitable world, all such early human social forms were organised as semi-nomadic hunting-gathering bands, operating with so-called Palaeolithic (or Old Stone Age) material technology – such as digging sticks, wooden spears, carrier bags, fire and fire sticks, stone cutting and scaping tools etc.

Such archaeological evidence goes some way towards indicating the sorts of social organisation involved here – both directly, in terms of the details of campsites, and less directly in terms of the restrictions imposed upon such organisation by such – limited – material technology.

Furthermore we know that in some relatively isolated and inhospitable parts of the world, up until quite recent times, small numbers of people continued to live as hunter gatherers, on the basis of palaeolithic technology, fundamentally unchanged for thousands of years. Traditionally, direct historical experience of the lifeways of these groups has been utilised as a guide to the interpretation of such archaeological data (relating to earlier hunting-gathering populations).

It is true that such experience demonstrates considerable diversity of social organisation and belief amongst societies with fundamentally the same – palaeolithic – technology. In particular, we see different sorts and degrees of sexual division of labour in material production and childcare, and of social hierarchy and inequality amongst historically known hunter-gatherers. However, there do seem to be certain fundamental social structural features shared by all historically known hunting gathering groups, with good evidence for taking such features to be common to all such human societies in pre-historic times also (after 45,000 years ago).

Within these parameters, the diversity of historically known hunting gathering groups can actually serve as the basis for testing the different theories of religious ideology outlined in the first chapter. For we can see that such societies exhibit a range of differences in just those dimensions most relevant to the psychoanalytic and materialist analyses. Which is to say, they differ in respect of early child-rearing practices, and of inequality and contradiction in the relations of material production, as well as in respect of adult personality and ideology.

By first considering the former sorts of differences we can generate predictions about the sorts of ideological differences we might expect to be correlated with them, on the basis of materialist and psychoanalytic theory. We can then consider the currently available information about the belief systems of such groups to see how such predictions actually fare in practice.

Certainly there are limitations to this sort of approach. But I think that it has been used quite successfully in the past, at least to test certain aspects of psychoanalytic theory. Thus Stephens's classic study of menstrual taboos (STEPHENS 1962), Slater's study of maternal ambivalence and narcissism (SLATER 1968), the various studies of Beatrice Whiting, J.W.M. Whiting and I.L. Child and other works, have provided substantial verification for important elements of theory.

Such studies have typically involved statistical analysis of large amounts of available data – concerning a range of other sorts of societies, apart from those of hunter-gatherers. And they provide crucial background and support for the sort of ideas I am considering here.

But rather than providing any further such statistical analysis, my aim here is simply to concentrate upon certain paradigm cases, certain specific hunting gathering groups that cover the range of variation in respect of particular social structures and practices, most relevant to testing the materialist and psychoanalytic theories of ideology.

Part Two
GENERAL FEATURES OF
HUNTING-GATHERING SOCIETIES

Considering first the similarities, the things which all or most such hunter-gatherers had in common, we see that the great majority of them lived for most of the time in small groups or bands of two to fifty or so individuals – typically somewhere between. Such individual bands were united over large areas – of hundreds to tens of thousands of square miles – by relations of kinship and co-opera-tion, into wider tribal organisations of five-hundred or more. Often, the members of the tribe would see themselves united by descent from a common ancestor back in the dreamtime at the beginning of the world.

In some cases, there were significant social divisions and groupings intermediate between band and tribe, such as the territorial subdivi-sions of Australian tribes, sometimes called 'countries' functioning as typically exogamous, patrilocal, collective – property – controlling and political units.

The different bands and tribal subdivisions would remain in contact via periodic marital exchanges, with girls or boys from one group marrying – and moving – into another, and various forms of mutual aid and exchange of goods and services along kinship lines – with individuals and groups redistributing necessary resources to look after their relatives both in and outside the group.

In times of extreme economic stress, such bands would break down into individual family groups – of parents, children, and pos-sibly one or more grandparents – as minimal dispersal units, spread-ing out to exploit widely distributed food resources. At other times (in some cases) the whole tribe – sometimes more than one such tribe – or some substantial sub-groups of it (e.g. the territorial divisi-ons of Australian Aboriginal tribes) would assemble together for lesser or greater periods of time – to engage in religious ceremonial, or exploit particularly abundant seasonal food supplies, for example.

Individual bands were in more or less continuous movement typically over very large land areas (except in situations of unique natural fertility, with available means for prolonged food storage) so as to be able to continue to maintain themselves without destroying the delicate ecological balances upon which their life depended. There were fairly regular exchanges of personnel between bands in response to changing ecological conditions (local shortage or abun-dance etc.) and personal relations (friendships, squabbles etc.).

Each band would have its own extended territory, around which it would move – seen as the collective property of the group (of the band itself or tribal subdivision), rather than as the private property of any individual. So that, from the point of view of historical materialist theory, such societies, and, indeed, tribal societies in general are communist societies.

The resources of this land would be seen as (more or less) freely available to any and every member of the band or extended kinship group, and arrangements would exist for sharing of territory and resources with other such bands (or tribal subdivisions) when this was seen as necessary. Or, in some cases, (again, typically amongst Australian Aboriginal groups) such collective property ownership was divided along sexual lines, with certain tracks, areas, sacred sites closed to men or to women.

Such groups generally lacked any kind of institutionalised leadership or power hierarchy, though the older people and others with greater knowledge or experience (generally, or in specific areas), or greater (supposed) magical powers would be respected – or feared – and deferred to, by all the rest.

Compared to other, later and more complex social forms, such hunting gathering societies were generally characterised by a relatively low level of division of labour and high levels of general co-operation within and between groups, in material production, distribution and reproduction, including the care of young children.

It seems to have been virtually impossible for nursing mothers to carry more than one young child around with them in course of the food quest. All such societies seem to have relied on infanticide as a necessary population regulation mechanism – where prolonged lactation, low body fat, tabooed separation of the sexes failed to provide adequate birth spacing.

As far as surviving children were concerned, such societies seem, generally to have been characterised by particularly intense and prolonged 'maternal' care and nurturance; with prolonged holding and carrying of young children, children sleeping in close proximity to adults, breast feeding for years rather than weeks or months (with children left to wean themselves) and relatively late and gentle toilet training.

Very often, orthodox psychoanalytic investigators have tended to assume that such considerations suggest the likelihood of predominant oral dependent and erotic fixations and personality types in such groups. As Borneman says,

> "the more undisturbed, the more pleasurable the sucking stage of individuals, the stronger their later conviction that things will always turn out for them. They confront life with an unshakeable optimism which often does in fact help them ...to cope with life's problems and setbacks" (BORNEMAN 1976, p. 13).

At the same time, "since they live under the illusion that the world is their mother," they work only when they have to, i.e. they do not struggle and strive for success in their work, since "they believe the mothers breast will always flow for them. They neither despise nor respect property and possessions because they do not perceive these things as objects in the first place" (ibid).

While generally endorsing this sort of idea, others have, quite correctly, raised crucial questions of the point at which particularly intense parental love and care – fostering self-confidence, optimism and self-esteem, – turn into intrusion and abuse – undermining such confidence and self-esteem. And, of course, an infant's experience of parents killing young siblings – as a means of population control – might be expected to have a profoundly traumatic quality, with serious consequences for later life. Clearly, these are crucial questions to be addressed in considering specific cases.

Where there was a significant division of labour amongst the adults of hunting-gathering societies it was typically a sexual division of labour. Here, the men took control of hunting large game animals, of conducting ocean going fishing trips and other, more dangerous, or longer distance collecting expeditions, and of distributing the raw materials provided by such ventures. The women, by contrast, took primary responsibility for the care of young children and for gathering vegetables and small animals (eggs, insects, shellfish etc.) in closer proximity to the groups central base camp. So too did they tend to perform the bulk of necessary processing of such hunted and gathered materials – cooking food, making clothes etc.

This division of labour, apparently based upon the biological fact of women's pregnancy and the need for prolonged breast feeding (with all or most women of childbearing age necessarily occupied in one or other of these processes to allow for group survival – in terms of population replacement, required mobility etc.), could become a source of greater male (economic, political, ideological) power within the group. For pregnancy and childcare actually prevented women from hunting large game – and from fighting effectively to defend themselves from the men of their own group or other (hostile) groups. As long as they had foetuses and young babies to look after, they could only gather and process plant and animal materials within a limited area, whereas men could gather and hunt and wage war over long distances – or threaten violent action against the women and children of their own group.

The meat of larger game animals tended to be more highly valued than vegetable materials amongst hunter-gatherers (possibly, in part, because of its greater rarity and the greater time and danger involved in procuring useful amounts of it). So male control of hunting and military organisation were both (potentially) sources of differential power over the female population.

There seems to have been quite wide variation in the frequency and intensity of warfare amongst different hunting-gathering populations. In some cases (particularly amongst some Australian Aboriginal groups), warfare between (and sometimes within) different tribes (associated with, e.g. 'women stealing raids', revenge expeditions – for actual or magical attacks – or disputes over territory etc.) seems to have been a fairly frequent occurrence – and could have played a significant part in population regulation.

More generally, though, hunting-gathering groups seem to have been characterised by relatively low levels of warfare, compared to later sorts of social organisation. In most cases, male hunting itself depended upon a systematic exchange of meat for gathered foods within the family. Hunting was not (generally) a reliable source of food and could only be maintained so long as the women's gathering continued to supply food to the hunters (as well as to the women themselves, children, the old, the sick etc.) on a regular, everyday basis.

Child rearing women could thus, in theory, survive for prolonged periods without any contact with the men if they so chose – in sharp contrast to some later social forms where childrearing was – and is – simply not compatible with economic autonomy in this sense, and therefore provides a solid foundation for male blackmail and control of the female population.

So it seems that in most hunting-gathering societies the women generally still retained considerable power and autonomy compared to the women of later societies. The men could not (e.g.) supervise and control the women's everyday productive activities (as in the case of some settled, agricultural societies) without destroying the substantial benefits of the division of labour to themselves – in the form of time free for the interest and excitement of the hunt, control of its products etc. And the women were able to retain a space for articulating their own thoughts and feelings, developing their own ideological and political practices etc.

Nonetheless, to the extent that the exchange between women and men was sometimes a very unequal one – in respect of labour time and effort – we can see here the beginnings of a sex-class system in materialist terms. Through gaining differential control of major material productive resources (i.e. the means of hunting larger game etc.) – and of the means of violence (in this case, pretty much the same thing) – men were able to gain control of women's labour. They were able to enforce the production of a (kind of) surplus (of gathered and processed materials) by such labour, for appropriation by themselves (without recompense). As materialist theory predicts, so does the control of material surplus (in this sense) provide the means for control of mental production, in allowing the men extra time free for the production and distribution of ideas.

In groups with such a sexual division of labour – and of power – prolonged mothering of the young boys was sometimes more or less rudely interrupted by adolescent male initiation ceremonies, seen as effecting or aiding the transition from childhood to adult masculinity. In a number of North American hunting-gathering groups, e.g., such initiation took the form of a vision quest in which the young boy (at or immediately before puberty) was required to seek the assistance of a guardian spirit to help him withstand the trials of existence and promote luck in hunting, warfare, love and so on. The parents or elders sent him out, usually together with other boys, into the forest or mountains to fast and suffer from the cold and attacks by dangerous wild animals. In this weakened state he would sometimes have visions of spirits – frequently in animal form – that henceforth became his guardian spirits – speaking to him, guiding and assisting him, particularly in times of stress.

Needless to say, all such adolescent initiation ceremonies – involving some kind of major trauma inflicted on the young by the older generation of same-sex parents – have always been a major focus of interest for psychoanalytic investigators, insofar as they are seen to be associated with the transition from childhood desire to adult discipline through final (or delayed) Oedipal resolution. The traumas of initiation are typically associated with final imposition of parental authority – and repression of incestuous and aggressive Oedipal desires. Through initiation, the child introjects and identifies with parental authority, with an idealised image of the parent, with parental goals and values.

The association of prolonged and sympathetic mothering, male initiation, male hunting and warring, and the acquisition of the guardian spirit is particularly interesting in this connection. We can see how a major component of such Oedipal resolution in this context involves the boy's repression of massive oral dependence upon the mother, in favour of adult male autonomy, independence, bravery etc. The guardian spirit clearly takes the place of the mother as lost love object, protecting, nourishing, loving and guiding the individual thereafter. With such a spirit – as disguised mother-figure – always available to them, boys no longer need a real mother to look after them.

Girls, by contrast, remain close to mothers (their own or others) and to the earth, thought of as nurturer of all life, in a community of women, committed directly to nurturance, rather than autonomy and war. They therefore require no such (disguised) supernatural assistance. Here, less elaborate initiations sometimes prepare the girl for adult sexuality and motherhood – celebrating specifically female powers of procreation and nurturance.

But such adolescent male initiation rites are also interesting from a materialist point of view insofar as they were sometimes very lengthy and elaborate procedures, playing a central role in regenerating the traditional ideologies of the societies in question, and sustained by 'surplus' material produce supplied by the women. The women supplied the food, and the adolescent boys. The older men then took over the ideological processing of this new generation of males, and, in some cases, also thereafter gained access to surplus material labour performed by this younger generation.

Part Three
BELIEF SYSTEMS

As far as the ideas or belief systems of such hunting-gathering groups are concerned, we must carefully distinguish two different sorts of thing. On the one hand, all hunting gathering groups were distinguished by a very highly developed practical 'cookbook' kind of knowledge of the world they lived in, insofar as it was relevant to their survival. They had a detailed knowledge of the geography of the lands they inhabited, of the location of useful water and mineral-sources, ocean currents, weather patterns etc. They knew of the appearance, distribution, behaviour and practical uses of thousands of sorts of animal and plant species – where to find them, how to collect them, how to process them into useful finished products – such as foods, clothes, tools, boats, traps, nets, bags, medicines, artists materials etc. They knew how to regulate their own populations and those of other species, about the cycles of the seasons and the delicate ecological interdependencies upon which their life depended.

As Geoffrey Blainey points out, even 40,000 years ago, the ancestors of the Australian Aboriginals;

> "imported botanical and zoological knowledge – practical lore about plants and animals of which the average educated Australian is now ignorant. They made stone and wooden tools for the hunting, digging or preparing of food. They almost certainly possessed a variety of skills for catching fish and many techniques of tracking and hunting animals and birds. They knew how to make fire. They probably had considerable knowledge of plants with medical properties and they probably knew how to harness certain poisons for their own use and to rid some toxic plants of poison. They must also have had impressive knowledge of how to build simple craft that could cross wide rivers and narrow seas. It is probable that they possessed all these skills before they reached Australia, and that in their long history in this land they increased some skills and allowed others to vanish" (BLAINEY 1991, p. 84).

But when it comes to the world beyond such immediate perception and control (and immediate material need satisfaction), to the formulation of explanations for those elements of everyday experience which could not be explained in terms of immediately perceptible causes or forces, hunters and gatherers relied upon what we would today call mythico-religious – rather than philosophical or scientific – theories.

That is to say, speculative models of possible unperceived forces or mechanisms at work in the world were constructed, modified and transmitted through the generations, without rigorous ongoing logical and empirical criticism and testing. Very limited access to material technology not only radically restricted the stock of ideas available for constructing such models (by analogy) but also prevented any real scientific experimentation to actually test such theories. They were therefore chosen and developed for reasons other than their predictive power, empirical verification or correspondence-to-the-facts.

There were, of course, many things in the experience of hunting-gathering peoples – as of all peoples – for which immediate perception provided no explanation. Here, I refer to the perennial questions. What is the nature, origin and destiny of the cosmos as a whole? Where did the human species (the tribe etc.) come from in the first place? How did humans originally acquire all of their unique abilities and power? Why do people dream, and what exactly are dreams? Why do people and animals live and die, while the mountains, the stars, the sun seem never to change? Why earthquakes, storms, floods?

For hunter-gatherers, as for all humans, some such questions were rather more pressing than others. Some appeared to be matters of much more than merely intellectual significance. Why do some people get sick? Why do all people die? And what happens to them when they do? Can anything be done about sickness, pain and death?

For hunter-gatherers, particularly, questions of fertility – of how precisely each new human and animal and plant life is produced, of the nature of the magical gestation processes taking place within the human or animal or earth mother, were very much in this sort of category. For it was clear to all concerned how crucially dependant was the day-to-day survival of the group – and the year to year survival of all human society – upon the maintenance of such fertility in people and in nature.

At the same time, the pain, the magic, the danger, the mystery and the joy of the birth process made it an absolutely central life experience for all concerned. This was especially so in a society without hospitals, machine technology and science to compete with, negate or conceal such magic and mystery.

Here, of course. we see a first and most obvious level of determination of ideas by the material base of society. Major problems and preoccupations of the material labour process motivate and direct the search for 'higher' or 'deeper' knowledge of causes and mechanisms. In the absence of any very significant division of labour (particularly any significant division of mental and manual labour) – with all of the adult population more or less directly involved in the same sort of material labour activities (of hunting, gathering and processing natural resources, producing and caring for children etc.) – all share the same sorts of explanatory preoccupations and concerns.

Whenever any human group seeks to provide 'deeper' explanations of such natural or social phenomena – going beyond any causes or forces that can be directly perceived in the world – they can only start out with the explanatory concepts they already have available. It is in the nature of explanation that it is always, in some sense, reduction of the unknown to the known. So that all such deeper explanation can, in the first instance, operate only by extrapolating into the unknown the forms and mechanisms of 'everyday' explanation – in terms of the directly perceived 'natures', powers and causal relations of 'everyday' objects.

All such deeper explanation always makes use of the process of analogy (and analogical reasoning). Our incomplete 'direct' knowledge of the forces and powers at work in the world (deriving ultimately from perception directed by innate powers of discrimination and classification) is supplemented by our imagining things analogous to the forces and powers we know, which could, perhaps, exist (beyond the world of perception) and be responsible – through their actions – for the phenomena we observe.

Up until quite recent times, people's immediate experience of themselves – and other humans as causal agents (interacting with each other and with material nature), has provided the basis for such analogical model building. We know why we (and others like us) acted as we did because we know the felt need or want and/or reasoning process that motivated our action. We know how we are able to act thus, because we understand the particular productive powers (of knowledge, strength, tools, social assistance etc.) available to us to do so. And we know how (at least some) such powers are created and maintained through processes of learning, nourishment, practise or exercise – because we have directly experienced such processes. This can easily lead us to believe that perhaps other things – perhaps everything – can be explained in the same sort of way – in terms of the desires, knowledge, action, or situation of conscious agency.

These considerations are particularly relevant to the case of hunting-gathering tribes, which seem to have been characterised by so-called 'animistic' and 'organic' world-views. For here, everything in the world – both perceived and non-perceived – is seen either as itself endowed with its own thoughts and feelings, needs and powers of conscious action and/or as a structural element or product of or adjunct to the body or action of some larger powerful living entity, endowed with such thoughts, feelings and active life process.

The animistic world is a world of spirits or souls, animating the earthly bodies of material objects of all kinds, as well as existing in their own right as gods, demons, ghosts etc. But in addition to such supernatural personalities, so is it also a world of more impersonal, but still, to some degree 'animate' supernatural objects, fluids and powers, thought of as inhabiting, flowing through, or passing between individuals.

In this latter sort of category are ideas of 'mana' as mystic power, life, will or soul-fluid residing in specific individuals, objects or places, and the mystic quartz crystal or pointing bone of the Australian sorcerer, thought of as inhabiting and 'empowering' the body, but also capable of leaving it under certain circumstances. In particular, we can see how magic powers are associated with blood, breath, milk and other bodily fluids, thought of as capable of creating life, curing sickness and bringing death.

The idea of an organic world view is that of the universe as an integrated, living, metabolising totality. People, society, nature are all seen as interconnected and interdependent elements of the metabolic life process of the cosmos as a vast living system. In particular, such organic thinking very often involves the idea of the earth as a nurturing mother-figure; an all-powerful parent who provides for the needs of humankind (through supplying her plant and animal children etc.), but who also sometimes turns against them, inflicting upon them storms, droughts, scarcity etc.

These two sorts of ideas can be quite compatible – and, indeed, complementary – with individual spirits and magical substances seen as elements, children or manifestations of the higher world-spirits.

As far as hunter-gatherers are concerned, we generally find – not surprisingly – a significant pre-occupation with animal and plant spirits or spirit animals. This includes the appearance of spirits in animal form, the spirits or souls of animals, and the identification of some animals as 'spirits' rather than 'real' or 'ordinary' animals. Generally, for hunter-gatherers, the boundaries between 'ordinary' animals and spirits were rather vague. As Hultkranz observes;

> "hunter-gatherers think of animals as by nature mysterious since their behaviour is both similar and different to that of humans. Such a tension between known and understood and unknown and not understood creates a sentiment of something uncanny, something not quite belonging to normal reality" (HULTKRANZ 1987, pp. 22-3).

Similarly hunter-gatherers generally recognised a close affinity between people and animals; they were brothers and sisters, and it was people's task to respect and be in harmony with the animals. Such affinity was integral to beliefs about the origins of the human and natural world.

Thus, in Australia we encounter 'totemic' dreamtime ancestors in both animal and human form; and those who were capable of assuming both animal and human form. It was these 'animal' ancestors that created mountains, creeks and other natural features. They filled the environment with human and animal 'souls' and instructed people in practical and spiritual knowledge, including (sometimes complex) marriage rules which maintained tribal structure and identity.

In North America the dreamtime ancestors were generally thought of as originally more or less human, but a change later took place that turned many such primeval beings into animals and birds. This close kinship between humans and animals expressed itself in tendencies for hunter-gatherers to imitate the animals in dress, action and thought, and through so doing, acquire various animal 'powers'.

I have already mentioned the North American guardian spirit quest, with such spirits frequently taking animal form. And here the individual was seen to acquire some of the special abilities or powers of the animal species concerned. For example an individual might acquire strength from a bear guardian, or skills of speech or song from a bird guardian. The bonds between humans and animals were also expressed in ritual activities, for example where men imitated the movements of game animals or wore their horns or skins and engaged in dances which were supposed to 'bring forth' the game for the hunters to capture.

I have also touched upon the crucial importance of the fertility of animal and plant species to hunter gatherers. And in a number of groups so-called 'increase' ceremonies, aimed at stimulating the fertility of animal or plant species, multiplying their numbers or summoning the souls of a new generation into the wombs of the adult females, are of particular significance.

We can refer, in this connection, to the 'bear ceremonialism' of Northern hunting peoples, involving the ritual appeasement and ceremonial disposal of a particular bear, so that other bears will feel honoured and allow themselves to be caught as well.

Each animal species was seen as having its master or lord or father, often in the form of a mysterious animal spirit, larger than ordinary animals of the same kind. Or else the earth itself was seen as (or as containing), the mother of all animal and plant species. Various ceremonies, including bear ceremonialism amongst the Japanese Ainu people e.g., aimed to appease or placate these animal parents, so that they would continue to provide their animal children for people to hunt and gather.

For hunter-gatherers the world was typically divided into three levels: heaven, earth and the underworld. The various worlds were often united through a world tree with its roots in the underworld, its trunk stretching through the world of humans and animals, and its crown in the sky world. There was usually a heavenly god who ruled over the sky, a host of spirits that controlled atmospheric phenomena such as wind, rain etc. There was as well a huge group of spirits who influenced human life on earth and some beings, including Mother Earth (as source of vegetable life) who travelled about in the world below.

With institutions like that of the guardian spirit quest, and other special initiation procedures, large numbers of ordinary tribes people, usually men, but sometimes women as well, acquired special spiritual powers, bestowed by their guardian animal spirits, by elders re-incarnating totemic ancestors etc. Acquisition of such powers was frequently associated with the 'introjection' of magical objects or substances of various kinds.

In some groups there were also 'medicine men' or women who had more spirits than most, and whose spirits specialised in helping to cure the diseases of their clients. The medicine man or woman received their mission to cure from the spirits that came to them, and in their visions they received instructions in the ways of healing.

Typically disease was seen as caused by the intrusion of hostile spirits or magic substances into the human body (in some cases, projected into the victim by hostile sorcerers or witches) or by 'loss' of the soul or spirit guardian. The most common therapeutic procedure was to remove the agent of the disease – whether it was an object or a spirit. Sucking, blowing and drawing it out with a fan were common techniques.

In some cases the medicine man or woman would fall into a trance or altered state of consciousness to enable their spirit or soul to transcend the boundaries of the other worlds. In their trance they gathered information from the spirits of the dead or stole away the souls of patients that that gone to the realm of the dead during fever or coma. The medicine man or woman then brought the soul back to the sick person, often by pressing their hands against the latter's head. Such specialised medical practitioners, regularly falling into deep trance states, are known as shamans.

But shamans were not only doctors. They were able to use their special powers to discover the location of game and of missing persons, the perpetrators of crimes and the course of future events. Their power derived from spiritual revelations in visions and dreams, which were seen as providing direct contact with the supernatural world. And they sometimes employed powerful psychotropic drugs to facilitate such contact.

Because of their supposedly greater spiritual powers, shamans could acquire considerable social power and privilege – in contrast to the generally egalitarian tendencies of hunting-gathering social organisation.

Hunter-gatherers generally seem to have conceived time in a cyclical, rather than linear form; an eternally recurring cycle of events and years. The cyclical time concept applied not only to the macrocosmic world (of the seasons etc.) but also to the microcosm of the human individual. Each person was seen as following a cycle of time from birth to death. Rituals marked the important changes of life; birth ceremonies, puberty rituals, initiations into specific tribal societies and death rituals. Death was typically seen as the beginning of a new life, either on this earth through re-incarnation as another human, or transmigration into some animal, or in a transcendent heaven. (As Hultkrantz points out, very often the individual or the social group might hold several different ideas about the dead at the same time; the dead as residing in the other world, the dead as re-incarnated in other people and the dead as haunting ghosts.)

Part Four
THE PSYCHOANALYTIC PERSPECTIVE

How and why did people come to take these sorts of ideas seriously? How and why did they come to participate in these sorts of institutions and practices?

In the first instance, of course, this is what they were taught as children, and it was what others – including adult authority figures – already believed. Established ideas have a profound inertia just because they are established ideas. And if such ideas are 'transmitted' to the new generation in the right sort of way – in vivid and terrifying initiation ceremonies which function to 'anchor' them to the social super-ego e.g. – then they could, thereafter, remain highly recalcitrant to change through experience or logical criticism.

But this does not explain the initial creation and appeal of such ideas. Nor is it really enough to explain their persistence. After all, ideas do change radically on occasions. Many people in the modern world no longer take seriously any such organic or animistic sorts of ideas, despite the fact that their parents or grand parents still did so.

Presumably such – animistic – mythico-religious ideas persisted, amongst hunter-gatherers – also because they satisfied some powerful human needs, or served the interests of some powerful humans (in a position to continuously re-inforce the effects of early training).

In this connection a number of investigators have argued for the likelihood of a universal human need for meaning – transcending immediate awareness of the objects of perception. So too have Freud, Weber and others argued that all religion serves two universal social-psychological functions in relation to the problem of human suffering. First of all, it provides answers to intellectual problems of the existence of suffering and its seemingly unfair and unequal distribution. (Virtue will be rewarded in the end; evil will be punished, etc.) Secondly, it provides means for (apparently) overcoming such suffering, both in respect of specific life problems and in the form of ultimate salvation.

We have already seen how animism fulfils all of these three sorts of function. It provides some general meaning, structure and explanation of human life, nature and the cosmos. It offers explanations for the problems of human life. And it offers various – magical – ways of supposedly overcoming such problems. It offers magical powers of control of natural forces through ritual activity – ensuring the food supply, curing illness, achieving success in love and war and promising eternal life, etc.

But powerful as these motivations may have been, they are really not a sufficient explanation for the belief in the reality of the mythico-religious world. In particular, they do not adequately explain why such beliefs took the particular forms they did. And this, of course, is where psychoanalytic and materialist theory come into the picture.

As far as psychoanalytic considerations are concerned, the argument is that such beliefs persisted also because human individuals and groups were pre-adapted cognitively – as well as motivationally – to believe in their reality. This cognitive pre-adaptation derives from the prolonged helplessness and extended dependency of the human infant and from the psychological consequences of these phenomena in terms of the young child's first conception of the world – prior to the acquisition of language and culturally constituted conceptions of reality.

Long before children were taught about the magical substances and powers of the mythico-religious world, they were dealing with the magical substances and powers of their own and others' bodies, – milk, lactation, breath, crying, urine, faeces, excretion, blood – in situations of intense feelings of joy, hatred, fear, awe, envy etc.

Long before they were taught about the powerful spirit beings who inhabit the mythico-religious world, they had continuous and prolonged experience – also accompanied and shaped by very intense feelings – of those powerful super-beings who inhabit the family world – i.e. parents, older siblings etc.

As touched upon in the last chapter, psychoanalytic investigators have shown how, entirely helpless from birth, and absolutely dependent on these other beings, young children form highly distorted, exaggerated and bizarre representations of these bodily products, powers and parenting figures. Certainly, as they grow older, most children relinquish these representations – though only after considerable struggle – in favour of more realistic conceptions. At first, however, these bizarre and distorted images, the products of what Freud called 'primary process' cognition, are unconstrained by the – rational – 'secondary process' cognition characteristic of mature ego functioning.

Normal development in a modern society supposedly involves relinquishing or transcending such primary process modes of thought – splitting and reification of early parental images etc. But they may, instead, merely undergo a certain sort of transformation.

As Melford Spiro points out, if a society offers the young child a mythico-religious belief system full of culturally constituted images – of gods and demons, saviours and satans, magical substances and fluids – highly similar to their own individually (psychically) constituted images of the powerful forces and beings of their own family world, then the former may be directly merged or identified with the latter. Such a merging provides very strong grounds for taking seriously the external reality of the various gods and spirits of the mythico-religious system, because the individual has themselves directly experienced the reality of the forces in question in the course of their own childhood. (See SPIRO 1987, Ch. 7.)

Chapter Three
HUNTER-GATHERERS *cont.*

Part One
PARANOID SCHIZOID THOUGHT

As we saw in Chapter One, psychoanalysis envisions life in the womb generally experienced as perfect contentment – a blissful feeling of 'oceanic' peace and union – undisturbed by desire (since desire presupposes frustration).

As Lasch says,

"the transposition of bodily needs into the register of desire... begins only with birth, when we begin to experience instinctual demands... as a clamorous assault on the lost equilibrium we seek to restore. The womb gave us an unforgettable experience of absolute oneness with the world – the basis of all our intimations of immortality and of the infinite, subsequently reformulated as religion. At the same time it gave us a taste of complete self-sufficiency and omnipotence" (LASCH 1985, pp. 166-7).

Birth puts an end to the experience of narcissistic self-sufficiency and union with the world, even though most parents manage to recreate something of the safety and contentment of the womb for their babies. The newborn experiences hunger and separation for the first time and senses their helpless, inferior and dependent position in the world, so different from their former omnipotence.

As they are forced to acknowledge their own limitation and dependence, the illusion of perfect happiness is preserved by projection of the lost perfection onto the body of the parent – or, initially, onto those parts of the parent's body most directly concerned with the gratification of the child's desires – particularly the mother's breasts. Thus, the child 'idealises' the mother – or the parts of her body – as a source of unending, unambiguous gratification. They can then strive to regain the lost perfection through, once again, fusing with the maternal body.

Here is the ultimate foundation for belief in an 'organic' world system, like that of hunting-gathering tribes, as such lost perfection – now associated with maternal love and care – is projected out also into the wider world, as a fantasy defence against the harsh indifference of material reality. The world itself comes to be perceived on the pattern of the mother's body, as the extended – nourishing, loving, protective – womb for living humans and animals.

'Assailed by excitation' – and frustration – the infant seeks to restore the lost illusion of self sufficiency. And, to the extent that parents or guardians strive to keep the child safe, warm, well-fed and happy, they can help to restore the illusion for a while. To the extent that parents respond immediately and effectively to the child's expressions of desire, indeed, successfully anticipate such expressions, they can re-inforce the child's defensive fantasy of the 'omnipotence of their thoughts' – the idea that the child's own wishes actually control the world.

As Freud says, it is this fantasy of the 'omnipotence of thoughts' – the idea that wishing makes it so – that is the foundation of all magical beliefs and practices, in childhood and in later life. While young infants have initially limited co-ordinated control of their arms and legs – and little idea of using them as adults do, to gain control of the world, they spontaneously express their feelings of need and frustration by screaming. And such screams, typically, magically and instantaneously bring about the presence of adult 'gods' available to satisfy the child's every need.

The scream 'automatically' recreates the magical fusion with the body of the parent; it brings the nipple when they are hungry and drives it away when they have indigestion. Thus the crying function acquires a magical efficacy. The scream is a magical invocation or exorcism – the first magical spell.

But, in order to maintain the illusion of parental perfection in face of the reality of frustration – without completely withdrawing from that reality – the child has to 'split' their perception of the parent – or the parent's body-parts – into the idealised 'good' and the frustrating 'bad' parent – or bad breast. They can then fantasise the destruction of the bad, so as to be left only with good – which they strive to incorporate into themselves – or 'introject'.

As Roger Money-Kyrle says;

> "the conscious experience of the infant initially centres around two primary metabolic functions; incorporation and ejection. They incorporate the nipple, milk and air, and eject faeces, urine – unwonted food, sick and breath, sometimes in the form of screams. They soon distinguish between these two functions, and between their objects, dividing their world of good and bad objects into things that go into and things that come out of their body. But as they make little or no distinction between fantasy and fact, imaginary acts of incorporation or ejection are equivalent to real ones. They fantasise taking in good things and expelling bad things as a defence against the limitations of a less than perfectly satisfying world." (MONEY-KYRLE 1950, p. 83.)

Money-Kyrle further notes that the child can "incorporate or eject any object in fantasy if not in fact. Both these functions can be used aggressively, [they] can eat or bite to destroy bad objects as well as to incorporate good ones. [They] can eject good objects as gifts (or protectors) or bad ones as aggressive projectiles" (ibid., p. 84).

The child fantasises oral and other attacks upon the bad object – chewing it up and spitting it out – so as to try to completely destroy it – and leave the way free for uninterrupted love and gratification from the good object. But they never can completely escape the reality of frustration and through their own anger and aggression they thereby turn such bad objects into angry vengeful monsters – threatening to launch the same kind of hostile attacks upon themselves.

Even the good breast itself can be turned bad by the child's insatiable demands (including fantasies of forcibly entering the mother's body to steal the good things not immediately given) and by their envy of the mother's powers to give and withhold life. And these fantasies of attack upon the body of the mother can produce fears in the child of both their own destructive powers and of vengeful persecution by fierce maternal demons of various sorts.

At the same time as the infant thus splits its objects (in fantasy) so does it split itself in an effort to renounce or deny any unpleasant or scary feelings. Such split-off 'bad' parts of the self can also be projected into the parent.

As Melanie Klein says,

"the phantasied onslaughts on the mother follow two main lines; one is the predominantly oral impulse to suck dry, bite up, scoop out and rob the mothers body of its good contents... The other line of attack derives from the anal and urethral impulses and implies expelling dangerous substances (excrements) out of the self and into the mother. Together with these harmful excrements, expelled in hatred, split-off parts of the ego are also projected... into the mother. These excrements and bad parts of the self are meant not only to injure but also to control and take possession of the object. Insofar as the mother comes to contain bad parts of the self, she is not felt to be a separate individual but is felt to be the bad self... Much of the hatred against parts of the self is now directed towards the mother. This leads to a particular form of identification which establishes the prototype of an aggressive object-relation" (KLEIN 1975, pp. 68-9).

Because of the predominance of such splitting, projection and persecutory anxiety, Klein calls this kind of thinking and feeling the 'paranoid-schizoid position'. She sees it as serving a crucial developmental function in clarifying the distinction between good and bad. As Julia Segal says, there are serious dangers associated with muddling of the two. "Without this splitting the baby may not be able to distinguish fully between love and cruelty and to feed trustingly... Where this process has failed, any expression of love may have concealed within some form of cruelty. Child abuse seems to involve this confusion between love and cruelty" (SEGAL 1992, p. 33).

However, such paranoid schizoid splitting clearly has its own problems. As Segal acknowledges, deeply splitting a mother or father into a fairy god-mother and a wicked step-mother is a distortion of reality, and it is important that the child fairly quickly moves on to more balanced and realistic modes of thought and perception.

Normally, in the course of time, repeated experiences of gratification and the experience of their return give the infant the inner confidence to tolerate hunger, discomfort and emotional pain without recourse to such intensive splitting, projection and fantasised aggression, They increasingly integrate rather that split their perceptions – and their objects.

As Segal says,

"Awareness of objects as more whole, with both loved and hated characteristics, begins. This has considerable consequences. Awareness of the self as a more whole, loving and hating being can also begin. Conflicts between different parts of the self are no longer solved by splitting and pushing those parts into others, including the good object itself, but by holding them within the self" (SEGAL 1992, p. 38).

"With a fairly well-established idea of the distinction between goodness and badness, the baby can begin to see both in the same mother/breast without one destroying the other and the mother/breast with it. Disappointment with the mother does not turn her into something wholly bad and dangerous; damage is no longer feared as total destruction. A good experience does not mean heaven forever; its loss is not the end of the world but is real, manageable grief mitigated by hope for good experiences in the future" (ibid.).

But these same experiences also reinforce the child's awareness of separation and helplessness. "They make it clear that the source of nourishment, love and gratification lies outside the child, while the need or desire is within." As the child comes to see the various good and bad part-objects as really different sides of the 'whole' parent (and the self) so do they come to see that their own happiness – their own survival – depends upon the continuous love and care provided by an autonomous 'other' – whom they cannot control simply through their own magical wishes.

With such recognition comes the fear that they have damaged and alienated that other through their own hostile attacks and bad feelings. The child is faced with the prospect of total abandonment, loneliness and destruction in a hostile world, as a result of their own limitations and inadequacies.

Klein refers to these sorts of feelings as feelings of depressive guilt, characteristic of the depressive position, as against the persecutory guilt of the paranoid schizoid position. The latter is merely a fear of vengeful persecution by the objects of one's own aggression. The former, by contrast, is grounded in the ability to empathise and sympathise with such victims – to feel for them and with them.

While splitting and projection are thus reduced in the depressive position, other sorts of defences become more significant – including repression, as the fearful child seeks to 'shut-out' all of those thoughts and feelings deemed unacceptable or hostile to the parent, and identification with the aggressor, as a form of 'manic defence', mobilised to protect the child from a hostile and aggressive parent.

As Melanie Klein argues, in the life world of the infant, all of these defence mechanisms – of splitting, projection, repression etc. are associated with thoroughly 'concrete' fantasy perceptions. The child's own projected hostility e.g. can be experienced as a fierce snake or alligator attacking others or turning back upon themselves, trying to burrow into their body, etc.

In the fantasies of the child,

> "people and parts of people live and die inside and outside the self; move around; give rise to enormous gratification and equally enormous fear, jealousy or envy; are pushed from one person to another, either regardless of behaviour or in accordance with subtle or less subtle behaviour. Reality testing involves examining the results of such phantasy operations (e.g. of destructive attack) upon others as well as discovering the limits of the effectiveness of such phantasies. In this way phantasies strongly influence expectations and interpretations of real events in the world" (SEGAL 1992, p. 31).

When such fantasies are at their height – particularly in the throes of the paranoid schizoid position – the child is clearly in an animistic world of split off spirit beings of various kinds – good and bad. Bad spirits can enter the child's own body – or the bodies of others – to cause damage or disease; while good spirits can cause health and happiness. So here too we see the origins of hunter-gatherers ideas of magical techniques for the production and cure of disease.

We saw earlier how in fantasy the child can eat or bite or destroy bad objects as well as incorporate good ones; how they can eject good objects as gifts or bad ones as aggressive projectiles, while the good and bad objects they incorporate and eject become endowed with magical powers for good and evil. As Money-Kyrle points out, "these objects then are the infantile equivalents of the supernatural fluids, substances and creatures which play so large a role in the delusions of psychosis and of superstition".

> "The prototypes of supernatural creatures are to be found in those parts of the human body (such as the breasts, the nipple and the penis) which attract the child's attention in the early period before he has learned to distinguish personalities as a whole. For in his fantasy, these so called part-objects are animate beings capable of an independent existence both inside and outside himself. Some superstitions are almost undisguised variants of such infantile ideas..." (MONEY-KYRLE 1950, pp. 85-6).

As we have seen, the mothers breast, as the baby's original love object is one such paradigm part object, endowed with all kinds of properties which go far beyond those of a mammary gland providing milk and warmth and skin contact. As Segal says,

> "on the one hand it is seen as the source of all life, love, and hope, of babies and good things, of comfort, peace and serenity... the child fantasises getting inside it or taking it in and fusing with it in a blissful state... However they also fantasise being eaten up by it, torn apart or threatened by it, they fantasise the breast being damaged or dangerously bad, inside or outside themselves" (SEGAL 1992, p. 41).

These considerations cast light upon a number of aspects of animism and magic in hunting-gathering societies. Here, in particular, we think of the activities of shamans, finding the lost souls of the sick, expelling the evil spirits sent by other tribes or other shamans, sucking out such evil spirits, or putting good objects into the bodies of their clients to drive out the bad ones. "The Central Australian medicine man e.g. has magical bones, sticks, snakes or stones which he may keep in his own body. He can use them to kill or cure. He may project his snake into a patient to drive out the evil, or to produce evil of its own" (MONEY-KYRLE 1950, p. 101).

Part Two
FREUDIAN PREOCCUPATIONS

It is true that from the depressive position onwards (already established in the course of the first year of life) 'normal perception' becomes increasingly less distorted by such defensive fantasies. But in times of extreme stress (according to Klein) everyone goes back to the spirit world of the paranoid schizoid position. And those who have encountered problems in their earliest months – and have consequently become to some extent 'fixated' in the paranoid schizoid position, are particularly prone to such 'regression'. Such regression is clearly all the more likely if it is actively supported by powerful social traditions, ideologies and imperatives – such as appear to be characteristic of many hunting gathering societies – with no clear alternative answers to fundamental existential questions.

As Segal says,

"paranoid schizoid mechanisms and relationships may be used in any situation where life and death anxieties abound... Under the pressure of frustrations of various kinds, the attacks of the paranoid schizoid position continue throughout life, though mitigated more and more by a sense of love and reality which can no longer be totally denied" (SEGAL 1992, p. 39).

Furthermore, fantasies continue to play a central role in later stages of emotional life and development, particularly in relation to sibling rivalry, and so-called anal and phallic phases of development and the Oedipus complex, and particularly where manic defences are to the fore. As Lasch notes,

"early fantasies of reunion centre upon the incorporation of external goods on which the infant depends, in other words on oral desires associated with the experience of sucking, biting and swallowing. As the child begins to discover other parts of their body, oral fantasies come to be overlaid with anal and genital fantasies, in which e.g. the child repossesses the mother and thus restores the sense of primal oneness through the agency of the phallus" (LASCH 1985, pp. 170-1).

"The failure of oral fantasies to sustain the illusion of self-sufficiency causes the child to take a livelier interest in the rest of their body, while the conflicts that grow out of the fantasy of sexual intercourse with the mother precipitate the Oedipus complex – an event which has to be understood, accordingly, as another variation of the underlying themes of separation, dependence, inferiority and reunion" (ibid., p. 171).

Thus, as the child begins to discover their own sexual feelings and possibilities – and those of the parents – they fantasise intercourse with the mother as a means to return to primary narcissistic perfection through symbiotic fusion with the maternal body. Such 'mature' sexuality is also equated with adult self sufficiency and autonomy – as against childhood dependence.

But just as other fantasies break down in the face of experience (surviving thereafter only in the unconscious) so does the child also discover that their genital equipment is inadequate to the task of seduction of the adult. And in this context, Freud's notorious idea of 'penis envy' makes perfect sense – as a wish to steal the 'larger' and more 'potent' penis of the father.

As Lasch points out,

"it occurs in boys as well as in girls and signifies not a shocking recognition of the biological and social inferiority of women, as Freud thought, but an intensified awareness on the part of the child that his grandiose fantasies of sexual union with the mother, constructed in the first place as a defence against feelings of helplessness, are completely unrealistic after all, and that the child continues to occupy a dependent, inferior position in relation to his parents" (ibid., p. 172).

The magical penis of the father – as the means to re-establish the primal fusion with the body of the mother – is readily recognisable in many beliefs and rituals of hunter-gatherers. Here in particular, we think of magic wands and of the sacred poles (planted in the navel of the earth) as the means whereby dreamtime ancestors ascended to heaven or returned into the earth in Australian Aboriginal myth and ritual.

Another such Oedipal fantasy is that of the phallic mother – or mother with a penis – which serves fundamentally the same need as penis envy. "By equipping the mother with a phallus, the child unconsciously denies knowledge that she needs that of her husband... The fantasy of the phallic mother announces, in effect, it is not true (that) the sexes are different; my father is of no importance either to me or to my mother. I have nothing to fear from him and besides my mother only loves me" (ibid., p. 173). And the phallic mother also makes fairly frequent appearances in myth and folklore.

As with the earlier oral phase of attack upon bad objects, Oedipal fantasies of mutilating, killing or displacing the father engender corresponding fears and fantasies of paternal retribution. Boys, in particular, fear castration by the father as punishment for their incestuous and patricidal desires. And such fear can motivate repression of the desires in question.

Freud sees the 'super-ego' as heir to such Oedipal conflicts. The super-ego is a model of the persecutory, 'bad' parent, introjected so as to 'oversee' and control the individuals thoughts and feelings – 'nipping in the bud' or shutting out of conscious awareness thoughts or feelings deemed 'unacceptable', as a defence against punishment or rejection by the real parent. Such 'unacceptable' thoughts include regressive oral desires for fusion with the maternal body, as well as the later Oedipal – 'phallic' desires that have become the 'last hope' of such re-union. In this sense, acquisition of the super-ego is equated with the destruction of the illusion of infantile omnipotence and acceptance of reality and the social status quo.

Thereafter, the super-ego functions to generate anxiety and guilt, whenever repressed Oedipal desires threaten to surface once again into consciousness. It thereby motivates retreat from social situations likely to bring such ideas to the surface – including situations which involve symbolic substitutes for the aims or objects of such desires.

Freud refers to these sorts of desires and defences in explaining the phenomena of totems and taboos in tribal societies – including the societies of hunters and gatherers. The tabooed act arouses anxiety because it is associated with a repressed desire. Thus, to take a classic case, the tribesman experiences anxiety in contemplating killing the totem animal – equated with the dreamtime ancestor of the group – because, from the point of view of the unconscious, this is equated with killing the father (as Oedipal rival). Similarly, they experience anxiety in contemplating sexual relations with a woman of the same totemic kinship group, insofar as this is unconsciously equated with incest with the mother or sister. In both cases, such desires arouse the threat of punitive castration or death at the hands of the paternal super-ego.

Here we can understand the meaning of phallic emblems as protective talismans, and of the phallic devils that can make the individual sick by stealing their soul or entering their body. We can begin to understand much of the elaborate ceremonial of some hunter-gatherers initiation ceremonies as mechanisms for – delayed – Oedipal resolution (with threats of bodily mutilation by the older generation underpinning adherence to relevant taboos on incest and endogamy). And we can see how such – comparatively late and potentially ineffective – male Oedipal resolution ties up with the widespread belief amongst hunter-gatherers and others that death is always a result of witchcraft perpetrated by hostile sorcerers, usually in other groups. It will, after all, typically be the older members of the group who die first, and in such a situation – of death of a father – such magical killing represents the jealous patricidal fantasy of the sons (of the younger generation) projected outside of the group as a protective psychic defence mechanism.

Here is a major cause of in – group solidarity (in face of a common enemy) and out – group hostility and warfare amongst tribes people, as the sons appease the paternal super-ego by leading revenge expeditions that set in train prolonged vendettas or cycles of blood vengeance.

Part Three
KLEINIAN CONSIDERATIONS

Melanie Klein found that, initially, sexuality is conceived by the young child by analogy with oral feelings and actions, with the genitals of both sexes equated with mouths and breasts, and intercourse with a process of feeding and nourishment. As Segal notes, where the experience of feeding – and corresponding "feeding fantasies have been predominantly good, the (corresponding) fantasies governing sexual relationships will be predominantly good" (SEGAL 1992, p. 45).

With the persistence of paranoid schizoid splitting, however, such 'oral' fantasies of genital sex will also include bad ones. Here, we see the origins of those 'negative' fantasies of the dangerous (as opposed to the consoling) phallic woman; the devouring witch or demon who steals men's – or boys' – penises. And clearly, such fantasies will tend to be encouraged by a mothers own ambivalence towards the masculine identity of her son, smothering him with seductive demands, showing signs of envy or jealousy in relation to his male body, threatening him with castration as a punishment for masturbation, etc.

Insofar as entry into the vagina of the mother is equated with a return to the perfection of the primary narcissistic state, so do the female genitalia, and symbolic substitutes for them in the wider world (woods, caves, grottos, cairns etc.) acquire a profound significance as gateways to higher realms. Concomitantly, paranoid schizoid splitting gives them the significance of gateways to death, destruction and hell.

Here again, we can see how these sorts of ideas influence many aspects of belief and perception amongst hunter-gatherers – insofar as the natural world is equated with the body of the mother, and specific natural features' take on the magical powers and possibilities of that body – as conceived in primal fantasy. Specific sacred sites, e.g., mark the boundaries between the worlds of heaven and earth, past and present.

Another very important dimension of the maternal body for the young child is its magical power for producing new life – new babies. For this function also becomes bound up with a constellation of powerful and ambivalent feelings on the part of the young child.

In the paranoid schizoid position, babies, still inside the body of the mother, are likely to be the objects of fantasies of violent attack upon the mothers body by the child. Envious of the mothers powers to create new life, the child seeks to steal or destroy her unborn children. Or jealous of such children as sibling rivals, the child fantasises destroying them before they are born.

Such attacks will, in turn, produce paranoid fears of vengeful persecution by the spirits of the dead babies or by the mother herself. Later, they will give rise to depressive guilt for having damaged the mothers body and her – most valuable – babies – and a corresponding need to 'make good' or repair such damage.

For the little girl, such early envy of the maternal womb – and its powers for the creation of new life – will later be significantly mitigated by socially sanctioned play with dolls and the knowledge that she will ultimately be able to produce 'real' babies of her own.

As Segal says,

> [young girls, and later women,] "under the influence of the depressive position, want babies because in fantasy they want to restore to their mothers the babies they damaged in her in fantasy when they were small... They want a baby as part of a loving relationship, confirming the goodness of the bond between two different people, representing on a deep level baby-self and breast-mother; and their own self in relation to their loved parents" (ibid., p. 51).

Little boys, however, can get quite a different social message. And recognition of their biological inability to produce babies of their own can perpetuate such womb envy – and its corresponding paranoid schizoid fantasies of attack upon the female body – into later life.

Insofar as the earth itself has – in fantasy – the significance of an extended maternal body, so do the living things that grow out of it and move upon it acquire the significance of children of that maternal body. Entry into the body of the earth – to collect roots, or tubers, or mineral ores – thus acquires the significance of entry into the body of the mother to steal or destroy her gestating babies. And the harvest and consumption of animals and plants on the surface of the earth similarly comes to be associated with cannibalistic consumption of the earth mothers children.

Such actions are therefore likely also to generate paranoid fears of maternal persecution and depressive fears of having damaged the body of the mother and her babies (and the consequent threat of abandonment by her). And these considerations lie behind various ceremonies of appeasement, placation, reparation and thanks to the earth goddess and her animal and plant spirit children in relation to hunting and gathering. So too have they been implicated in early steps towards cultivation and domestication of wild species – giving back the seeds of food plants to mother earth to replace those taken from her; carefully tending and nurturing them, raising animals whose parents have been killed, etc.

From Klein's point of view, the re-direction of affection – and Oedipal fantasy – from mother to father is typically a very early development. Partly, it results from a general 'spilling over' of love for the breast, and a natural response to the loving care provided by the father. Partly it is a response to feelings of being let down and frustrated by the mother (and as Freud would say, to fear of paternal retribution for incestuous desires for the mother). And partly the father is welcomed as a barrier between the child and the overwhelming intensity of (both positive and negative) feelings in relation to the mother.

As Segal says,

> "Fathers are... felt to come between the baby and the breast, separating them and destroying fantasies of fusion with an internal and external mother/breast. This may be a source of frustration and anger but ultimately it also helps to establish a sense of separateness and space for the baby as well as for the mother, keeping them from becoming too close and too muddled up and trapped in each other" (ibid., p. 49).

As Freud says, the turn towards the father can stimulate jealous hostility towards the mother, leading, in turn, to fear of maternal retribution. And maternal images (as well as paternal ones) can thus be taken up into the punitive super-ego – in boys as well as girls.

Its true that various factors militate towards this (Oedipal) shift to the father being greater in the case of girls than of boys; the likely heterosexuality of the mother, her possibly greater ambivalence in relation to the daughter, the fathers 'prioritisation' of the daughter and powerful social pressures of various kinds. But as Freud points out also, for both sexes the desires of the Oedipus complex are essentially bisexual, and final sexual orientation depends upon the relative strength – and the degree of repression – of the different desires concerned.

Melanie Klein emphasises the continuity of the Oedipal super-ego as heir both to the vengeful bad mother of the paranoid schizoid position and to the empathetic identification with the suffering victim (and corresponding guilty reparation) of the depressive position. To the extent that paranoid schizoid splitting is still to the fore, the super ego is no more than (as Lasch says) "the individuals own aggressive impulses, directed initially against the parents or parent surrogates, projected onto them, re-interpreted as aggressive and domineering images of authority, and finally redirected in this form against the self".

It is thus far removed from any genuine social conscience or agency of moral intuition. Though clearly, fear of such an agency could function effectively to 'enforce' conformity to certain simple social norms or prohibitions.

However, there will normally also be an important depressive dimension to the resolution of the Oedipus complex – based upon sympathetic identification with the loving parent (as innocent victim of the child's fantasised attacks) and a realistic appreciation of the child's own potentialities and limitations.

Just how all of these different developments and forces balance up, which sorts of fantasies predominate and for how long, depends crucially upon the nature of childcare in the societies concerned.

Part Four
SOCIAL DIVISIONS

Now, clearly this is only a first step towards understanding the animistic beliefs and practices of hunter-gatherers. And I will move on shortly to begin to consider how specific sorts of child-rearing practices influenced and shaped such beliefs in specific hunting-gathering groups.

Before that, however, it is important to see how, in considering the general nature of such beliefs and practices, so can we see their potential for sustaining social power relations. If particular individuals or groups were able to convince others that they had special magical/spiritual abilities – privileged access to spiritual forces – then this meant also that they had ultimate control of the food supply, of war and peace, sickness and health for the rest of the group. And presumably, differential control of the production and distribution of ideas could put particular individuals or groups in a position to be able to do this.

Similarly, if different sorts of childhood experience rendered particular individuals or groups liable to higher levels of splitting, anxiety, depression, guilt then clearly, this would tend to render such belief systems all the more vivid and significant for them. And so would it tend to leave them particularly open to social control via such belief systems.

We have already seen how the relatively low level of development of material technology amongst hunter-gatherers could have put women at a distinct 'economic' disadvantage compared to men. With such limited technology a division of labour along sexual lines, with women caring for young children and gathering (mainly) vegetable foods and men hunting larger game animals might have been a 'logical' development (of potential benefit to all concerned). It might even have been necessary for survival. But such a division of labour would also have given the men a monopoly of direct access to highly valued animal products.

Obviously this was all the more significant where hunting played a major role in group subsistence (as e.g. in frozen Arctic regions). And in face of other hostile human groupings the men's hunting organisation could function also as a defensive force – able to engage in effective military action of a kind quite impossible for nursing mothers and children.

This kind of imbalance could (though obviously need not) have been used by the men to gain greater time free from 'necessary' material productive activity – for leisure activities or for the creation, development and transmission of ideas. And if men – as men – were thus in a better position to develop and propagate belief systems or ideologies so were they in a position to use such belief systems to still further increase their advantages – through legitimising male superiority – male 'spiritual' power, etc. In practice, indeed. there is likely to have been a feedback process in operation here, with boys brought up on such ideologies much more likely to take advantage of their material position, etc.

Amongst the men themselves, I have already considered the special case of the shaman. There are good grounds for identifying shamans as individuals who suffer the general psychic traumas of the population more intensely than most, who are therefore under greater pressure than most to find a means of coming to terms with them. These are individuals who, in coming to terms with their own problems, thereby acquires power over others.

Similarly, in societies characterised by relatively high levels of intra-psychic ambivalence and conflict, and particularly in situations of social disruption, stress and rapid change, there will be other individuals – prophets, charismatic figures etc. whose psychic and social situation enables them to become group leaders – activating in the rest of the group the powerful, regressive desires for a radical return to the primary narcissistic state of ecstatic fusion with the body of the mother and the world.

Such individuals can become the bearers of ideologies which function to direct the projection of all of those attributes ('bad' parts of the self, persecutory super-egoic elements etc.) which stand in the way of such idealisation of the ego. Along with such projection goes regression and loss of ego boundaries. And as vehicle of such narcissistic 'liberation', so does the leader become all the more powerful as they take over the ego's reality testing function for the whole group.

Here again, we can see the operation of a positive feedback, whereby such individuals can turn their power into time free for the further elaboration – development, adaptation – of the ideologies in question. And this can, in turn, provide materials for further consolidating, maintaining or extending their power.

It is important to recognise that we are concerned here with individuals or groups psychically predisposed to embrace ideologies and practices of significant power inequalities based upon (supposed) privileged access to divine forces or spirits. We are concerned with individuals who seek to come to terms with or compensate for their own insecurities through the exercise of (supposed) magical powers, through bending others to their will and indulging the material benefits which such powers can confer or subordinating themselves to such power. Without such psychic predisposition, those concerned would not be expected to take advantage of their particular economic or psychic situation in this way. Nor would inherited ideologies of power and domination sit so well with them.

So we can see how material and ideological production and power thus interact and re-inforce one another in quite complex ways – even in such relatively 'simple' and small scale societies as these. However, to see precisely what this means in more concrete terms, I will now move on to consider some specific cases.

Part Five
THE MBUTI PEOPLE

Considering first the Mbuti pygmy people whose hunting gathering band culture survived until recent times, isolated from outside influences in the tropical rain forests of Zaire in Central Africa, we see a situation of relatively undeveloped division of labour between the sexes in material production – and correspondingly undeveloped differential male economic power over the female population.

As amongst all known hunter-gatherers, the men did take charge of bigger game hunting while the women shouldered the major burden of gathering and childrearing. But Mbuti society was distinguished by the fact that there was actually very little in the way of 'big' game hunting – at least at the time of Colin Turnbull's classic studies. Men and women (and children) worked together in cooperative net hunting of smaller and medium sized animals and had equal rights to the products of such hunting. And when not involved in such hunting activities, the men of the band worked alongside the women in gathering and in nurturing and caring for the young children from birth onwards. (TURNBULL 1961, 1965)

In terms of the materialist thesis of economic determinism, we should expect that such basic equality of economic power would be reflected in a corresponding equality of political power. And this does indeed seem to have been the case. Mbuti society seems to have been distinguished by a general absence of institutionalised 'political' leadership and inequality within and between the sexes, as well as only very limited development of autonomous male hunting-political organisation, separate from the home world of the women and

children. Politics essentially involved ongoing and free discussion
and debate amongst all adult members of the band, with age, experience and special abilities being recognised and respected, without
conferring any 'automatic' power or privilege.

Particularly important here was the fact that Mbuti bands were
never involved in warfare so that the men had no monopoly of military organisation, necessary to protect pregnant or nursing mothers.
Their dense forest homeland protected them from warlike agrarian
neighbours, and continuous friendly interchange of personnel between bands, along with well worked out procedures for sharing
scarce resources, eliminated the threat of war between the different
Mbuti bands themselves.

As noted above, all the adult members of the community were
actively involved in childcare. And such childcare was characterised
by consistent warmth, love, and respect, recognising and responding to the needs of the children, at their particular stage of development of mind and body, rather than seeking to impose the needs of
the adults through emotional blackmail or physical abuse.

In terms of orthodox psychoanalytic theory, we should expect
that such sympathetic, indulgent and prolonged childcare (with
children left to wean and toilet train themselves, with guidance,
rather than discipline from the parents), would tend to foster significant oral erotic and dependant fixation, associated with high levels
of trust, self-esteem and optimism. But such self-esteem and optimism would remain dependant upon appropriate ongoing affirmation and feedback from the community, and would be incompatible
with long term, isolated struggle in pursuit of fixed goals in a hostile,
unsupportive environment.

From a Kleinian perspective, it would be expected to facilitate
relatively speedy and successful resolution of the paranoid-schizoid
position, without excessive splitting, idealisation, or projection,
while in the depressive position the child would tend to move very
much in the direction of reparation rather than manic defence and
regression. Individuals would quickly develop a capacity for sympathetic identification with others, and their sense of self esteem

would remain bound up with the feelings of the significant others in their environment.

Here, the active involvement of the fathers, alongside of the mothers, in such sympathetic and loving child care could be expected to have been particularly significant. For not only would such collective childcare have generally reduced the infants pain, frustration and ambivalence, and thereby strengthened the external and internal 'good' object. So would it have ensured that from the beginning that good object included both masculine and feminine dimensions; from the start, the infant would have identified with both sexes, rather than with the mother alone, thereby avoiding the manifold psychic and social problems associated with such a purely maternal infantile identification.

Instead of making all of their massive infantile demands upon a single harassed and frustrated mother figure – or upon a single (female) sex – and therefore directing all of their frustrated anger at her as well, while idealising the absent father (as perfect good mother), such demands and frustrations would have been directed upon the fathers as well, thereby humanising both parents and radically reducing splitting and idealisation.

The absence of patriarchal domination in social relations generally, the relative equality of men and women in economics, politics, childcare and (as we shall see also) ideology, would have radically reduced the parents ambivalence towards their own children – in terms of jealousy, envy or resentment of their infantile or later adult (e.g. male) prerogatives. Indeed, it is this absence of splitting, idealisation and projection on the part of the parents (in relation to their children) that makes it possible for the children themselves to work through the paranoid schizoid and depressive defences of infancy without serious fixation or regression.

Certainly 'phallic' Oedipal feelings and fantasies – in relation to both mothers and fathers, and siblings – could be expected to have developed on the part of both young girls and boys. And despite the active involvement of fathers in the care of young children, the mother would still have tended to be the primary love object for both girls and boys, on account of her prolonged breast feeding and greater involvement in care of the young child in the first years of life.

The young girl – in the 'phallic' phase – would still tend to turn to the father in response to her developing awareness of sexual difference and parental heterosexuality. So that both sexes would ultimately come into Oedipal conflict with the same sex parents, in the sort of way mapped out by Freud.

But the continuous, active and loving involvement of both parents in the life of the young child (of three to seven years old), along with the relatively low levels of paranoid-schizoid fixation already considered, would tend to have ensured that such conflicts were relatively quickly and realistically resolved, with comparatively low levels of repression and subsequent mental conflict and instability.

A general absence of repression, envy and resentment amongst the adult generation would have facilitated rich and fulfilling sexual relations between adults, and thereby radically reduced the likelihood of them relating to their children as sexual objects (expecting them to take the place of absent, unloving or hostile spouses), and thus intensifying, encouraging and prolonging the Oedipal fantasies of those children.

For the boys, the presence of the real father, as good lover of the mother, would have precluded extended fantasies of taking his place as the mothers lover, with a corresponding splitting of the image of the father – on the one hand built up as ultimate enemy, on the other as ultimate ego-ideal to be unconditionally emulated and identified with (at the expense of identification with the mother and things female).

For the girls, similarly, the presence of the real father, as well as the mother, would have precluded the extended idealisation of an absent fantasy father, at the expense of the mother.

It is true that the presence of loving, caring parents does not preclude the development of Oedipal aggression and hostility, and corresponding guilt and repression. On the contrary, the more loving the parent, the worse the child feels about their own jealous hostility towards them. And the greater the pressure to transcend such hostility – along with the other unacceptable desires associated with it – so as to protect the loving parent and retain their love and approval.

Nonetheless, the sort of ideal child-rearing environment apparently provided in Mbuti society would presumably have minimised repression and the aggressive power of the super-ego, through minimising the aggressive feelings of the Oedipal child. And perhaps it would have allowed for something approximating Freud's ideal 'dissolution' of the Oedipus complex, where the child identifies readily with (the values of) the loving parent(s) and incestuous and murderous desires are renounced with a minimum of anxiety and repression.

Certainly, we can see how Mbuti-style child rearing could facilitate effective working through, sublimation and integration of the polymorphous desires and possibilities of infantile sexuality into something approaching Freud's 'genital' adult personality structure (capable of 'mature' and realistic perceptions and relationships), rather than massive repression of such desires, with subsequent distortion of perception, thought and action by super-egoic persecution and – fantasy – ego-defence. And, in fact, the empirical evidence seems to support this sort of analysis, with Mbuti adults still very much in touch with childhood spontaneity and the pleasure potentials of their bodies, while also exhibiting developed adult powers of reality testing and sympathetic understanding of others.

As far as ideology is concerned, we can see little opportunity or motive for the sort of male domination considered earlier as characteristic of some hunting-gathering groups. So that we should not expect Mbuti mythology or cosmology to be constructed in such a way as to legitimate or perpetuate radical inequality between the sexes. On the contrary, it might rather be expected to involve substantial affirmation of solidarity and equality within and between the sexes, as a crucial element in maintaining such solidarity and equality in real social relations.

Nor should we expect that Mbuti mythology or cosmology to be heavily burdened by primitive (paranoid schizoid) defensive functions and the distortions of primary process thought, by repetition of unresolved Oedipal conflicts or appeasement of the social super-ego. Though, clearly, oral erotic or depressive fixation could be expected to be reflected in a major focus upon integration, parental love and care and separation anxiety.

And, indeed, these sorts of expectations are broadly confirmed in practice. In sharp contrast to the mythico-religious ideas which have dominated western history from classical times, the Mbuti world-view apparently does not include super masculine or feminine 'heroes' or villains, gods or demons, dominating, struggling, fighting, mutilating and killing one another. It is not about begging or stealing special 'spiritual' or magic powers from such super-beings, or playing them off against each other. Nor is it about pursuing 'spiritual' liberation in transcendent realms beyond earthly reality.

Turnbull maintains that, unlike the ancient Greeks and other highly patriarchal cultures, the Mbuti have no creation myth as such (in which some sky father god imposes 'order' upon a chaotic female earth). For them the forest they inhabit is the heaven and the earth; it is the cosmos – or, at least, the central 'node' of the cosmos. As they say, the forest is everything. It is the totality of all inanimate and animate being; it is a higher ('divine') reality that exists as a person, a 'god' to whom the Mbuti speak as a mother, father, lover or friend. At the same time, they are a part of it; and "each person and animal is endowed with some spiritual power that derives from the forest itself".

The forest insulates and protects the Mbuti from their warlike and demon-haunted Bantu neighbours; it provides them with abundant gifts of food, shelter, warmth, clothing and affection. It scares away illness and punishes the guilty. It is Life. And as such it is celebrated, depended upon, trusted, respected, obeyed and loved.

"The forest is the ultimate authority. It expresses its feelings through storms, falling trees, poor hunting – all of which are taken as signs of its displeasure. But often the forest remains silent, and this is when the people must sound out its feelings through discussion. Diversity of opinion may be expressed, but prolonged disagreement is considered to be noise and offensive to the forest. Certain individuals may be recognised as having the right and the ability to interpret the pleasure of the forest. In this sense there is individual authority, which simply means effective participation in discussions. The three major areas for discussion are economic, ritual, and legal matters having to do with dispute settlement. Participation in discussions is evenly divided between the sexes and amongst all adult age levels." (SANDAY 1981, p. 22)

"Death overtakes humans and other living things because the forest goes to sleep. And in such circumstances it must therefore be awakened to persuade it to carry on providing nourishment, health, goodwill – in short, happiness and social harmony for all the Mbuti people." (op. cit.)

To awaken the forest the Mbuti instituted a 'molimo' festival; – over a period of as long as a month the band spends every day hunting and gathering with extra special effort. An abundance of captured game and other foods is then shared out and eaten at a feast which is followed by dancing and singing almost till dawn, and in the morning the voice of the forest summons the Mbuti to fresh hunting and more dancing. Thus life triumphs again over death.

But the forest cult – the celebration of the love and bounty of the forest – is observed not just on special ritual occasions but every day and in all the Mbuti's actions; in the morning, before leaving for hunting or gathering, in the evening when they return and prior to dividing up the proceeds, as well as on all special occasions, the Mbuti turn to the forest and worship it – which is to say, they dance and especially sing in its honour.

Here, we see evidence of a classically organic and animistic world view. Clearly, human attributes are projected onto the forest as a whole, and onto its various living constituent parts. So too do we see evidence of oral dependant optimism and enthusiasm, in the assumption that the home world of the Mbuti is the centre or pivot of the human cosmos, and that the forest must only be woken up from time to time in order to continue to nurture its human children. At the same time, the greater part of Mbuti ceremonial seems to fulfil the role of 'reparation' in relation to the forest-parent – indicating an underlying depressive fixation.

However, what is most striking about the Mbuti forest ideology, compared with the beliefs of other hunting gathering peoples, operating with similar sorts of material technology, is its essential realism; the comparatively low levels of 'primary process distortion' apparently involved. There does indeed seem to be very little paranoid schizoid splitting, projection and idealisation involved, very little wish-fulfilling fantasy (to produce gods and demons, heavens and hells), compared to other, pre-scientific belief systems.

The 'divine' cosmic forest seems to be, to a great extent, the real forest, recognised as a complex ecosystem of integrally interdependent parts, with all of its actual characteristics and productive possibilities. The 'organic' features of this world-view seem to be grounded in genuinely organic natural and social relations and interdependencies, rather than in fantasy wish-fulfilment or the requirements of social domination and control. And despite their, in some ways, child-like behaviour, the Mbuti seem to be quite grown-up in the sense of thinking logically and rationally and remaining in close touch with their own true feelings, rather than being dominated by irrational fears, hatreds and fantasies.

Part Six
THE INUIT PEOPLE

We now move on to consider a hunting-gathering population which seems to be the antithesis of the Mbuti, specifically the Inuit or Eskimo people of the northern Arctic coastlands.

Compared to the comparatively benign and uniform environment of Central Africa, the home of the Inuit people is particularly harsh and difficult, with enormous differences between summer and winter conditions. In order to survive in this difficult environment, the Inuit developed the most sophisticated technology of all hunter-gatherers including igloos, kayaks, dog-sleds, harpoons, snow goggles and fur clothing with water proof seams. And these were all produced from a very small number of locally available raw materials – ice, animal skins, bone, stone and drift wood.

Most important for present purposes is the very low level of vegetable gathering activities amongst the Inuit compared to other hunting-gathering populations (and the comparative difficulty and danger of hunting in the Arctic environment). In some cases, indeed, Eskimo groups managed without any plant food whatever by eating at least half of their meat raw – including fat and internal organs to supply necessary vitamins and minerals.

Given the general rules concerning the sexual division of material labour amongst hunter-gatherers, noted earlier, we should expect that this would mean that the men provided the great bulk of subsistence food supply in such groups – with the women 'dependent' upon them for survival. And this does indeed seem to have been the case (with certain provisos – see below).

Thus, the Netsilik Eskimos, north-west of Hudson Bay, e.g., followed a regular annual migration circuit determined by the hunting activities of the men. In the winter the men from several family groups would come together in co-operative seal hunting on the ice flows. In the summer smaller groups would move inland with the men fishing and hunting caribou with bows and arrows.

Now its certainly true that in this hostile environment, continued male hunting depended crucially upon provision of appropriate clothes, tools and housing. And the women seem to have played a crucial role in providing such things.

However, the fact remains that insofar as the women took the prime responsibility for the care of young children (including prolonged carrying and breast feeding) they were quite simply not in a position (for much of the time) to hunt seals, whales, walrus or caribou with harpoons or bows. This put them into a vulnerable and economically dependent position – compared with the women of other hunting-gathering groups, who, as we have seen, could generally combine childcare with subsistence food gathering. And it seems that the men took full advantage of their economic dominion, forcing women into a subservient role of household servants and sexual objects. So that while there was little in the way of institutionalised leadership amongst the family groups, all of the men seem to have exercised political power over all of the women – as a sort of sex-class in materialist terms.

Women were forced to marry at an early age (often before puberty or to already married older men) so as to have a man to hunt for them – the alternative being begging for food. Men married so as to have a woman (or women) to make their clothes and cook for them, as well as catering to their sexual needs. And men seem to have treated their wives (and older children) very much as their own private property – to deal with as they saw fit.

In particular, Eskimo culture is well known for regular 'wife-lending' as a means of forming alliances and exchanging services amongst the men. Such wives were 'given' by their husbands to other men for lesser or greater periods of time – to provide sexual and other services – including cooking and cleaning – for those men.

The women themselves appear to have had no say in the process and to have been violently beaten by their husbands for taking any initiatives of their own in the area of extra-marital relationships.

As Farb points out, such wife-lending seems to have played an important role in all Eskimo groups as a means of creating alliances and bonds of reciprocity between different (family) groups. In this role it was supplemented by a range of other sorts of alliances including betrothal, adoption, trading partnerships, meat-sharing, ritual feasts and wrestling partnerships. Male ownership of women was also integral to another dimension of Inuit society radically different from anything in Mbuti society – in the form of periodic violent conflicts between the men – usually resulting in the death of one party. For in most cases such conflicts were motivated by adultery – in the sense of men 'appropriating' the wives of others without the consent of those other husbands.

There does not seem to have been any organised warfare between different Eskimo groups (though there were wars between Eskimos and other groups for control of territory). But such individual violence seems to have been very widespread.

As Farb points out,

> "when the Arctic explorer Knud Rasmussen visited a community of fifteen Eskimo families in the early 1920's, he found that every one of the adult males had committed homicide at least once, and in every case the apparent motive had been a quarrel about a woman" (FARB 1978, p. 53).

With kinsmen of the victims obliged to seek blood vengeance, such murders could provoke cycles of repeated violence. And short of murder, 'might' seems to have been 'right' in Eskimo society, with the victors of wrestling and other (dispute-resolving) competitions cheered by the rest of the community, no matter how the dispute might have started originally.

As noted above, there seems to have been only limited development of institutionalised leadership roles in Inuit society. But senior male hunters were recognised as – temporary – group leaders on the basis of their skill, experience and prestige. And, as we shall see below, shamans seem to have been able to exercise considerable political power (and gain significant material advantages) through their magical abilities in relation to physical and mental illness and control of the food supply.

As far as childcare is concerned, there was apparently a significant dichotomy between early indulgence and later discipline. Early on, babies were never left alone (to the mercy of hungry dogs) but carried close to the mothers body, and children were not fully weaned from the breast till about five years old. As Lisitsky says, "children were not merely loved, they were even respected as being under the special guardianship of the wise spirits of the ancestors". Parents made toys for their children and the young children played together in the snow and in the warmth indoors.

But some accounts indicate deep parental ambivalence in relation to the young child.

> "A woman who has an infant puts a small piece of meat to the child's mouth and then places it in a bag. This is believed to please the child's guardian spirit (tornaq). At night a piece of meat is placed in a dish near the child. If the child's guardian spirit should visit at night, he would look for food and if he should not find any would eat first the mothers vital organs, then the fathers, and then those of the other natives." (Lantis, quoted in G. ROHEIM, *The Gates of the Dream* 1952, p. 192.)

Here we see a particularly vivid representation of the angry, hungry child of the paranoid schizoid position, entering into the body of the parent to eat or destroy its contents, as considered earlier. Presumably the parent here projects the angry hungry child inside themselves into their own child, and then strives to appease that child in the interests of self-protection.

Another relevant consideration here is the requirement for men to raise the families of others they had killed as their own. For in some cases this meant that they were raising step sons who would later try to kill them in blood vengeance for their original fathers. Presumably this encouraged some degree of ambivalence in relation to such sons on the part of such step-fathers.

After the age of seven the parents began to 'discipline' their children. And by age ten it was thought that the children no longer needed – or no longer possessed – the special protection of the guardian ancestral spirits, and should rapidly learn their adult responsibilities.

As Lisitsky says,

"the new strict discipline from hitherto easygoing parents often came as a disagreeable shock, though the child had had warning from seeing the same sudden change happen to all (their) older playmates" (LISITSKY 1976, p. 123).

Not only did the child now become subject to strict parental discipline in the interests of learning their adult role requirements. It seems that young girls, in particular, now became subject to patriarchal domination and abuse. As Rasmussen found, young girls could now be regularly assaulted by boys and older men without any protection from their parents.

From a psychoanalytic point of view, in such a situation of male jealousy, aggression and domination, we might anticipate substantial ambivalence on the part of mothers towards their children – as both emotional substitutes for aggressive patriarchal husbands, and embryonic patriarchs – or the helpless victims of such patriarchs – themselves. Along with relatively 'distant' father figures in the early years, this might, in turn, be expected to encourage a corresponding ambivalence on the part of the children towards their mothers and fathers.

On the one hand they are likely to remain bound to the mother by powerful oral and Oedipal bonds of affection and desire; on the other, they could well feel stifled and overwhelmed by the powerful emotional bond to the mother. Both sorts of feelings could encourage hostility towards the father as rival for the mothers love and for his failure to come between mother and child – so as allow a space for increasing autonomy on the part of the child.

The sudden switch from (relative) indulgence to strict discipline could be expected to exacerbate hostile feelings towards the parents, while also intensifying fears of parental retribution. So too would we expect envious hostility on the part of the older children for their 'indulged' younger siblings. Here we might expect strong – but not necessarily effective – efforts to suppress hostile feelings, leading to powerful intra-psychic contradictions and struggles – associated with obvious symptoms of (obsessional) neurosis or even psychosis.

All of these considerations – both social and psychological – are apparently reflected in the mythico-religious 'world-view' of the Inuit, characterised by both patriarchal hostility towards femininity, by paranoid schizoid splitting and by intense obsession and anxiety.

As with the Mbuti, the 'animistic' religion of the Inuit is characterised by extreme simplicity – without the revelations, redeemers, priesthood, orthodox rituals or articles of faith of more complex societies. However, in sharp contrast to the general optimism and realism of the Mbuti belief system, Inuit beliefs were characterised by deep pessimism and fear in relation to nature 'spirits' and by an elaborate system of taboos or injunctions regulating the relations between humans and the natural world which had to be precisely observed in order to avoid sickness, starvation and suffering.

In a famous and much quoted passage, Rasmussen records one Eskimo's summing up of their traditional religion and ethos,

> "we fear the Weather Spirit of earth, that we must fight against to wrest our food from land and sea. We fear Sila (the Weather Spirit). We fear death and hunger in the cold snow huts. We fear Tak anakapsaluk, the Great Woman down at the bottom of the sea that rules over all the beasts of the sea. We fear the sickness that we meet with daily around us; not death, but the suffering. We fear the evil spirits of life; those of the air, of the sea, and the earth that can help wicked shamans to harm their fellow men. We fear the souls of dead human beings and of the animals we have killed." (Lewis 1976, p. 163)

As Lewis comments,

> "The final phrase of this baleful catalogue touches on the most crucial theme of all for understanding of Eskimo conceptions of sin and taboo. For, as Rasmussen's informant continues; 'the

greatest peril of life lies in the fact that human food consists entirely of souls. All the creatures which we kill and eat, all those that
we have to strike down and destroy to make clothes for ourselves, have souls, as we have, souls that do not perish with the
body and which therefore must be propitiated lest they revenge
themselves on us for taking away their bodies'." (ibid., p. 164)

Here is one of the downsides of an animistic perspective. But,
as we saw earlier, the idea of animal spirits need not necessarily lead
to such pessimism and fear. It really depends upon the attitude
presumed to exist on the part of the parent of the animals – the
relevant mother or father of the animals. And this, in turn, depends
upon the prevailing attitudes (both conscious and unconscious)
towards the human parent and, in particular, the human mother.
For the Mbuti, the predominant attitude (of the forest-mother) is
assumed to be love for her human children. But for the Inuit the attitude of Sedna – the mother of the sea animals – is altogether much
more ambivalent, as we might expect from earlier observations.

As Roheim points out, Sedna, the mother of the sea animals is
the principle deity of the Central Eskimo peoples. She has total
power over the destinies of humans and almost all the 'religious'
observances of these tribes aim to try to retain her good will or to
propitiate her if she has suffered some offence. She is believed to
live in a lower world in a house built of stone and whale ribs. The
souls of seals, sealions and whales are believed to come from her
house. After one of these animals has been killed, its soul stays with
the body for three days. Then it goes back to Sedna's house, to be
sent out again by her. If any taboo or prescribed custom is violated
during the three days that the animal soul stays with its body, the
'violation' ('pitsse'te') becomes attached to the animals soul and
causes it pain. The soul strives in vain to free itself from these
attachments but is forced to take them down to Sedna. Somehow,
they make her hands sore and she punishes the people who are the
cause of her pains by sending them sickness, bad weather, and
starvation. But if all appropriate taboos have been observed, the sea

animals will allow themselves to be caught, 'they will even come to meet the hunter'. The object of the many taboos that are in force after the killing of the sea animals, therefore, is to keep their souls free from attachments that would hurt Sedna as well as themselves. (See ROHEIM 1945)

The pain in Sedna's hands is connected to the myth of Sedna – dealing with her early life. She lived together with her father and rejected all suitors till a fulmar wooed her with his song. He promised her a comfortable life, but he lied and she suffered cold and hunger when she lived with him. The father later killed the fulmar and rescued the daughter but other fulmars chased after his boat and made a heavy storm. In order to escape himself he threw Sedna overboard.

> "She clung to the edge of the boat with a death grip. The cruel father then took a knife and cut off the first joints of her fingers. They fell into the sea and became whales. Sedna held onto the boat more tightly, the second finger joints fell away under the sharp knife and swam away as seals... The fulmars thought Sedna had drowned and the storm subsided. The father let her back into the boat, She swore revenge. After they had gone ashore she called her dogs and let them gnaw off the feet and hands of her father while he was asleep. He cursed himself, his daughter and the dogs." And then they were all swallowed up under the earth where they have lived ever since. (See ROHEIM 1952, p. 183.)

Roheim interprets this as a symbolic representation of the father coming between the mother (represented by the boat) and the daughter. Here, perhaps, is the father enforcing the loss of the original narcissistic fusion of the daughter with the body of the mother – and the world; the loss of the 'indulged' childhood and the forced entry into a harsh world of adult responsibilities. Such a separation is necessary for the creation of new life (represented by the sea animals). But there is also the danger that it incurs the anger of the daughter against the (quite possibly also abusive, authoritarian) father figure. More broadly, the imposition of male 'authority' inevitably generates female anger and the threat of female retribution (the symbolic castration of the father). And this, in turn, necessitates further male 'defences' of control and domination of the female population.

But it seems that it is not just sea animals that carry taboo violations as painful objects clinging to their bodies. Such violations also materialise in the form of vapours or miasmas attached to the body of the transgressor themselves. The nature of these attachments differs depending upon the particular taboo that has been transgressed. But they are visible only to the shaman – who is able to see them with the aid of his guardian spirits – and to the sea animals – who are repelled by them (fearing they too will become infected), and refuse to let themselves be caught.

"In many cases the transgressions become fastened also to persons who come into contact with the transgressor. This is especially true of children to whose souls the sins of their parents, particularly their mothers, become readily attached" (ROHEIM 1945, p. 114). If the shaman does not free the soul of the original sinner from such attachments then they will die. But once the sinner acknowledges the relevant violation to the shaman – in a special seance situation – they can free themselves and those they have infected.

While for men one of the most heinous of crimes is sex with an animal, for women concealment of a still birth is equally bad. Unless it is made known, and appropriate steps taken, such a crime infects those around the woman with bad hunting, sickness etc.

Here again we get an insight into the true origin of Inuit religious belief. For such aborted foetuses are said to cling to Sedna's hair, causing her pain and discomfort. Once again they are hungry, angry, greedy children; – attacking the mother of the animals because they have been 'rejected' or 'cut-off' by their earthly mothers.

As a child the individual feared they had turned their mother bad through their own badness – their greedy, angry attacks upon her body contents – including her unborn children – (in fantasy) thus stimulating talion persecution by a mother and her babies turned into avenging demons. Now, as an adult in a situation of stress, they are overwhelmed by the same paranoid fears – projected onto the broader canvas of an animistic world-view. But now also the men displace the angry child inside themselves into the aborted foetus of the woman; they shift the 'blame' onto the women. And they deflect the angry foetus – as sibling-object of their own hostility – away from themselves, to get its revenge, instead, upon the mother, Sedna.

Lewis maintains that the whole intricate taboo system

> "turns on the principle that those animals and pursuits with which the Eskimos are concerned in the winter months must not be brought into direct contact or mixed with those of the summer season. Thus the produce of the sea and of the land must be kept separate and not brought together unless special precautions are taken. Seals (winter game) and everything pertaining to them must be insulated from all contact or association with caribou (summer game)" (LEWIS 1971, p. 164).

But Roheim highlights a whole series of taboos that seem rather to be about avoiding all

> "cuttings, cleavings or separations in certain situations. It is forbidden to remove oil drippings from under the lamp, to scrape hair from skins, to cut snow for the purpose of melting it, to work on iron, wood, stone or ivory at a time when the soul of a human being or a sea animal is about to be separated from the body. The taboo is on separation but when this taboo is violated and the separation takes place, this separation becomes a cleaving, an attachment in another sphere, in the sub-aquatic realm of the goddess" (ROHEIM 1945, p. 113).

We can see how these ideas tie in with the myth of Sedna considered earlier. For such cuttings and cleavings remind the woman of the fathers role in cutting her off from her own mother. They remind the man of the woman's revenge – Sedna's castration of the father – as her dogs ate his hands and feet, and the revenge of the angry unborn children, as objects of his greedy, oral aggressive infantile fantasies.

Farb argues that such taboos "promote co-operation because all members of the group are made to suffer together. In the simple society of the Eskimos, the sharing of fears and the scrupulous attention to details of conduct create a social bond... a unifying social mechanism". But as Lewis points out, "it is above all women whose lives are taboo-ridden, who are the commonest offenders and sources of danger". So that such taboos seem to be as much to do with male control (and projection of male guilt) as with social 'unification'.

Certainly the taboo system provides a significant part of the power-base of the shaman in Inuit society. For it is only the shaman who can properly diagnose and treat the taboo violations supposedly responsible for physical or mental sickness, poor hunting, bad weather etc. As noted earlier, such magic 'spiritual' power can be turned into real material advantage by the shaman – claiming food, wives and other property (and therefore also time free from necessary productive work) as payment And the great majority of powerful shamans in traditional Inuit society seem to have been men.

On the one hand, the shaman – sometimes 'possessed' by the spirit of Sedna (who has been summoned up through a hole in the ground) oversees the interrogation of the individual identified as a taboo violator and forces confession and penance from the 'guilty' party – typically a woman. "He writhes and moans with pain. As long as the sins of the people are not confessed her hair is in the wildest disorder." As Lewis says, "all those present are now under strong pressure to confess any taboo violations which they might have committed. Some offences are readily acknowledged; others are only reluctantly divulged as the shaman insistently presses his audience to reveal their misdeeds."

"The seance group, and especially women whose taboo infrac-
tions have generally more serious consequences, desperately
search their consciences and denounce their neighbours in the
concerted quest for the uncovering of sins which will account for
the present distress. Women named by others are led guiltily
forward, shamefaced and weeping and urged to repentance by the
shamans own cries of self-reproach... Under this barrage of exhor-
tations, a woman will confess some misdeed. For example, she
had a miscarriage but, living in a house containing many other
people, concealed the fact because she was afraid of the consequences. Her dissembling, though condemned, is readily understood, for had she revealed her condition, custom would have
obliged her to have thrown away all the soft skins in the igloo,
including the huts complete internal skin lining. Such is the incon-
venience of ritual purification required that the temptation to conceal a miscarriage is evidently very strong" (LEWIS 1971, pp. 165-6).

As Lewis points out, "in the treatment of the sick at public shamanic seances it is generally the patient who is thus ceaselessly
harangued". It is typically the patient, or someone close to them that
is blamed for their own illness – as resulting from taboo violation.

On the other, the shaman's 'soul' leaves their body in trance to
journey down to the house at the bottom of the sea and do battle
with Sedna in order to get her to release the sea animals for the men
to hunt. Here again the shaman's journey – recounted to his fasci-
nated audience, provides clear evidence of the men's deep ambivalence towards the mother and women in general.

He sees Sedna as a castrating, phallic woman with a huge single
pigtail (where Eskimo women usually wear two) – 'twice the length
of her arm'. His interaction with her takes the form of a rape – he
penetrates her house and her body (he stabs her with a knife or
harpoon) to assert his superiority. He cuts off her fingers – as in the
Sedna myth – to release the sea and land animals for men to hunt.

At the same time, there is also the idea that he pleases Sedna,
and makes her feel good by combing her hair and removing the

aborted foetuses that cause her pain. He is also actually doing her a favour in cutting her fingers and spilling her blood, for she experiences this also as a relief. Perhaps, after all, she is too powerful for him to overcome by force.

Problems not attributed to Sedna are typically attributed to the spells of hostile shamans or to the intervention of capricious evil spirits And, here again, the only defence is to hire a shaman of your own to 'save' your soul or engage in spiritual combat with the hostile shaman or spirit. "With the aid of his helping spirits, the shaman entreats, cajoles, threatens and even does battle, in the most dramatically charged seances, with these constantly menacing powers which he alone has the skill to influence and control." (ibid., pp. 167-8)

Potential future shamans seem to be precisely those individuals least able to cope with the contradictory psychological and social pressures of Inuit society. They typically show signs of their future calling in adolescence – in the form of persecution by demons, confusion, visions, hallucinations, possession etc. But they are able to overcome their problems to some extent – and turn them to positive account – through shamanic initiation. This is closely similar to the typical North American spirit quest, considered in the last chapter. But in this case it is only the aspiring shaman – rather than all male adolescents – who secludes themself in a lonely spot to await the appearance of a guardian spirit.

Presumably, his guardian spirit, as good mother, protects him from persecution by bad maternal elements that previously threatened to overwhelm him. He has somehow found a way to segregate his good and bad objects – or his persecuted and persecutory selves – so as to prevent the destruction of the good by the bad and escape some of the paranoid fears that continue to afflict others.

And while other men might resent the power of the shaman, they presumably appreciate his regular reassertion of male victory over the mother and of a taboo system that 'keeps women in their place'. They can identify with his colourful stories of victory over Sedna and magical journeys to the moon, as well as relying upon him to solve problems of sickness, bad weather etc.

CHAPTER FOUR
RETURNING TO THE GODDESS

Part One
MYTHOLOGY

In 1971, when feminist Elizabeth Gould Davis wrote about the superiority of women, and the recognition of such superiority in a Goddess-centred religion of Neolithic times, the idea that 'God was once a woman' was controversial, novel and strange to many. Since that time the situation has changed dramatically with a great out-pouring of material on the Goddess and Goddess worship. And today, the resurrection of the Goddess, in practice as well as theory, is in full swing, with some feminists and Greens arguing that a return to worship of an Earth mother goddess is a necessary condition for women's liberation and for the regeneration of the earth's ecology.

Dozens of feminist publications articulate and endorse such a Goddess religion and there are magazines such as *Sage Woman* and *Crone Chronicles* devoted wholly to such ideas. At the same time, feminist groups in England, Canada, Germany, Australia, the US and elsewhere call upon the goddess in meetings and utilise witch-craft rituals as (supposed) forms of social activism.

In fact, in recent history, the idea that God was once a woman goes back to J.J. Bachofen's studies of classical Greek mythology. For here is substantial evidence of a patriarchal challenge to previously dominant female divinities, resulting in an – uneasy – victory for the men, with continued tension and conflict between the sexes.

As Downing points out, the majority of the classical myths exhibit 'a deep suspicion of female power',

> "they seem concerned to validate the priority of the social over the natural order, and to record the establishment of a 'rationally based' polity in which rulership is no longer to be determined matri-linearly... The goddesses are not only subordinated to the god [Zeus], they are defined as being in their very essence related to men, each in a very particular way; Hera is wife, Athene is fathers daughter, Aphrodite is the responsive beloved, Artemis is she who shuns men. Thus they are represented from the perspective of male psychology, and consequently both sentimentalised and denigrated" (OLSON 1985, p. 55).

But, at the same time, so do numerous tensions and inconsistencies point to an earlier period when things were very different; when goddesses ruled supreme; in particular the ancient goddess Gaia as earth mother and creator of all things. Even in classical times she is equated with the earth itself, as source of all life and home of the dead. She is the earth as it is in itself – "not the earth as subdued by humankind".

Gaia's special place was also the major 'sacred site' of Greece, the oracle at Delphi, seen as the 'omphalos' or navel of the earth. This was where the earth had first come into being, and remained the place of direct contact with higher, divine powers. Such powers were the source of oracular visions – "probably originally in the form of prophetic dreams". And though, in classical times, the Delphic oracle was seen as having been usurped by the misogynistic god Apollo, Gaia was still seen as the giver of dreams and oracles, the source of secret knowledge emerging from the unconscious.

Her first creations are the natural features of the earth – sea and mountains and sky – born from her body parthenogenetically. Later she couples with the god of the sky to produce the second generation of divine beings – the Titans, and later still she intervenes to allow the birth of further gods when her son, Chronos, tries to prevent this.

As Downing argues, amongst the pre-Homeric 'offshoots' or children of Gaia, those which point most directly to earlier – matricentric – beliefs and values are Themis, the Erinyes, Demeter and Persephone. "Each reflects a different aspect of Earth. Themis… is the mother of Justice and the Fates… She comes particularly to be associated with righteousness… in the sense of harmony with the natural order…"

The Erinyes or Furies also represent the forces that insist upon such 'right ordering', in tune with natural forces – and emerge to reestablish such natural order when it is challenged. "They appear especially to exact retribution for the most heinous crimes, of matricide and oath breaking. But the Erinyes are… also the Eumenides, the consoling ones, associated with marriage and children and a gentle death (as of Oedipus)" (OLSON 1985, p. 53).

Demeter is the corn mother – goddess of cultivation, but she is also a model of a human mothers love for her daughter, and of the grief of bereavement. Persephone (the daughter) is the goddess of the underworld and of renewed life in Spring.

Most probably, the other major goddesses were originally pre-Helladic local earth goddesses, as local manifestations, expressions or children of Gaia; Hera in Argos, Athene in Attica, Artemis and Aphrodite in the Near East. As Downing argues, "to remember Gaia's relation to these later goddesses is not to say that they are nothing but Gaia herself under other names, but rather that she is the ground out of which their figures emerge" (ibid., p. 54). At the same time, "all humans have their source in Gaia. (And) Pandora, the first woman, is Gaia in human form" (ibid., p. 56).

It is true that in classical times Gaia has been to some extent pushed into the background. As Downing says, "In Homer, though ...Gaia... is more than a vague and inchoate conception of the whole earth as animate and conscious, she is not as concrete and personal as her Olympian offspring and not personally active" (ibid., p. 51). But there are clear indications that this had not been without a profound struggle.

"The establishment of the Olympian order was a revolution, as is made plain in Hesiod's Theogeny in the account of Zeus's battle against all the generations of divine beings who had preceded him (including Gaia, the mother who had first encouraged him against his father)." Zeus established his ascendancy – and the ascendancy of the Olympian order over the older Ouranian Titans, only through defeating the fearsome dragon Typhoeus, created by Gaia to protect the older order.

Here too we clearly see some re-writing of history in favour of patriarchy. "Aphrodite, who in Hesiod is recognised to be generations older than Zeus is in the Odyssey represented as the daughter of Zeus and Diane." Hera, originally Zeus's older sister, becomes in Homer, "not only a needy, dependent spouse but (also) a younger sibling. Even Athene, whose stature is less diminished, is made into a goddess entirely dependent upon male power, proud to be motherless, Zeus's parthenogenetic creation" (ibid., p. 55).

Similarly, Apollo has to fight the female monster Python, created by Gaia as guardian of the shrine, to gain possession of the Delphic oracle. And even after he has killed Python with an arrow (and punished the spring nymph Telphusa) Gaia continues to oppose him by sending pre-emptive oracular dreams to potential visitors to Delphi.

Apollo is indeed the epitome of (insecure) patriarchy, with strenuous efforts made to deny his dependence upon, or connection to, any sort of female (and, in particular, maternal) principle. And he is involved also in the struggle with the Erinyes (portrayed in Aeschylus's *Oresteia*) which is probably the most direct – mythological – representation of the struggle between the old divine, matriarchal order and the new patriarchal one.

The key development here is the murder by the Greek leader Agamemnon of the daughter, Iphiginia, from his marriage with Clytemnestra, to appease the anger of Artemis and permit the Greek fleet to sail against Troy. This motivated Clytemnestra to plot together with a lover, Aigisthes, to murder Agamemnon upon his return from Troy. Some years later, Apollo, via his oracle at Delphi, commands Orestes, Iphigenias brother, to avenge his father's murder. Apollo threatens that if he does not kill his mother, his soul will receive no sustenance after death. And with the assistance of his surviving sister, Electra, Orestes kills both his mother and her lover.

Pursued by his mothers avenging spirits, the Erinyes, Orestes flees to Delphi, where he is purified by Apollo. Still pursued by the Erinyes, as devouring, castrating, maternal serpent monsters, – who refuse to recognise the validity of the purification – Orestes continues his wanderings until at last he is tried on the charge of matricide at the Athenian court of the Areopagus, created for this purpose by Athene.

At the trial the argument revolves around the question of whether Clytemnestra's murder of Agamemnon or her own death at the hands of her son is the more serious crime. But this is generally taken to represent the conflict of the life and values of the old matriarchal system with the new patriarchy. And, once again, Apollo plays a key role, arguing against the Erinyes that only the male is the true parent, with no 'real' connection between mother and child.

Despite the pathetic weakness of his arguments, despite the weakness, vanity, selfishness, stupidity and cruelty of Agamemnon – including his murder of his own daughter – Apollo wins the day, clearly indicating the radical shift in values and power from women to men.

Bachofen and other nineteenth century theorists saw these stories as representing, not just a change of religious ideology, but a pervasive change in the whole social order at some stage in pre-history, from a 'static', materialistic, nature-oriented matrilineal and matriarchal culture, to a new, dynamic, innovatory, human, social and spirit oriented patriarchal order. In this connection, Bachofen speaks of mythological traces of an earlier 'gynaeocratic' social organisation, characterised by 'tradition, generation and living interconnection through blood and procreation' being replaced by the 'male Apollonian' culture of 'conscious deliberated action' in Archaic and classical times.

More specifically, in his major work, *Das Mutterrecht*, Bachofen distinguishes three different stages of historical development. The first stage of human society, with Bachofen associates with hunting and gathering, is characterised by what he calls 'hetaerism', or sexual activity 'unregulated' by marital relations. In the absence of recognised paternity, descent is recognised only in the female line, although men may hold political power. This phase is succeeded by 'Demetrian matriarchy', a social system based on the institution of monogamous marriage which coincides with the first development of agriculture by the women. Here women dominate and the principle of maternity is honoured by the worship of a female deity. Only with the overthrow of 'mother-right' and the mother goddess, along with a recognition of paternity, does the modern form of patriarchy – and patriarchal property – emerge.

Bachofen sees Mother right, or inheritance in the female line, as grounded in the 'obvious' and directly perceptible physical connection between mother and child. And he sees the 'material' primacy of motherhood in this sense (reflected particularly in the myth of Demeter and Kore) as 'naturally' leading to 'a primacy of the mortal woman' or real social power for women.

At the same time, he sees the discovery of paternity as a significant advance in abstract thinking, leading 'logically' on to patriarchy, to all of the unique accomplishments of classical Greek civilisation – in politics, economics, art, philosophy and science – and ultimately to modern western 'civilisation'. As he says, the father as 'promoting cause' of gestation represents a higher principle of spirituality in contrast to the material contribution of the mother.

On the one hand, as Bachofen says, "the mothers free giving is the exalted hope of the Demeter mystery, which is preceived in the fate of the grain seed". On the other,

"Helladic man, wants to win everything, even the most exalted heights, on his own. In struggle, he becomes aware of his fatherly nature, and raises himself above materialism to which he had once completely belonged, and struggles towards his own divination. No longer does he look for the spring of immortality in the child-bearing woman; now he looks for it in the male creative principle, on which he bestows the divinity that was once accorded only to motherhood."

Later on, on the basis of linguistic, mythological and archaeological evidence, a number of authorities came to associate this – supposed – qualitative leap forward in spirituality and culture with the intrusion of vigorous, patriarchal Indo-European speaking pastoralists into the ancient, settled horticultural matriarchal societies of the Greek peninsula.

And, of course, in a later climate of racism, totalitarianism and misogyny this idea became the basis for racist and fascist ideologies extolling the continued superiority of the 'Aryan' master race, as 'bearers of civilisation' and 'natural victors' in an endless evolutionary struggle for survival or domination.

Part Two
PRIMITIVE COMMUNISM

Later in the nineteenth century, Karl Marx and Friedrich Engels took up and developed these ideas of a primordial matriarchy. But, for them, the ideas had quite a different sort of primary significance. In particular, for them it was the egalitarian and communistic organisation of this hypothetical matriarchal society that was most significant. For it vindicated their belief, as revolutionary communists, that such communistic social organisation was possible and viable.

In this case, however, they had much more than merely hypothetical mythological evidence to go on. They were able to refer also to substantial ethnological data drawn from societies which had retained such 'primitive communistic' modes of social organisation into recent times.

In particular, they relied heavily upon studies of the Iroquois Indians of North America, a society apparently only one stage removed from semi-nomadic hunting and gathering – corresponding to Bachofen's second stage of 'Demetrian matriarchy'. The Iroquois were a group of tribes sharing a common language and culture, occupying a series of villages – sometimes numbering several hundred people – in forested territory centred upon what is now New York state. Such villages were constructed on flat land alongside streams or lakes and protected by log palisades, with the forest around them cleared to make space for 'garden' cultivation of food crops. Inside the palisade were large rectangular longhouses made of elm bark on a wood frame, each containing many compartments that were occupied by several related families.

Major means of production amongst the Iroquois, including the land itself, the tools and crops, were collectively owned by specific kin-corporations and inalienable, rather than being the saleable private property of individuals. All members of the groups in question co-operated together in production, and shared the fruits of their collective labour, with resources regularly re-distributed in response to need.

But there was also a very strongly matriarchal dimension to such primitive communism. Property and goods were effectively controlled by, and inherited entirely through, the female line. The women owned the longhouses, the garden plots, the stored grain and the tools used to cultivate the land – though the forests were originally cleared and burned by the men. Disputes were adjudicated and peace and order maintained in the village and the longhouse by the senior women. Husbands came and went, either through losses in warfare or through a simple process of divorce, by the free choice of either party, and the children of these unions belonged to the mothers lineage and were cared for within the extended matrilineal family.

"In the political sphere, women not only appointed the *sachems* (the male war chiefs – without jurisdiction in the affairs of the village) and named their successors when they died; women might also act as regent for a *sachem* too young to rule. In warfare, they had the power of life and death over prisoners. They also helped to select the religious practitioners known as 'keepers of the faith' and half of these had to be females." (FARB 1978, p. 102)

Early on, Europeans had been struck by close parallels between Iroquois beliefs concerning an Earth Mother and Corn Goddess etc., and the classical Greek myths of Gaia and Demeter considered earlier. In Iroquois mythology corn, and the particular skills of planting and harvesting it, were introduced into the world by a earth goddess called the Ancient-Bodied. In some stories the corn plant is seen to have sprung from the bosom of the earth mother. And generally the spirit of the corn itself is represented as a young woman, a corn goddess, daughter of the earth mother.

This idea extends to the myth of the three sisters, the spirits of corn, beans and squash – each clothed in the plant they guard and decorated with flowers. They like to be together, in friendly mutual assistance – as expression of the fact that at one time all three crops were planted together on the same hills, and presumably also of the fact of extended matrilineal, matrilocal solidarity in the settled, farming village. The sisters come to live amongst the ripening plants in the growing season.

Here too we find the idea that the new crops are the children of the corn goddess – every spring she returns down into the earth where her children cry for her. The cycle of the plant – growth, death, new life, is thus mirrored in the fate of the corn goddess. She is at once the corn itself, its spiritual protector, and the patron of the human women who cultivate the corn.

In cult she is represented by a young virgin – needing no male assistance in her creative endeavours – who scatters grains of corn on the earth before the first day of planting. And at the harvest festival and the midwinter feast the three sisters receive the thanks of the people. On the latter occasion, the earth mother is thanked for her willingness 'to yield plentifully of her fruits' and the three sisters for being 'the main supporters of human life'.

Compare this with the Demeter-Kore story in Greek mythology. As noted earlier, Gaia is the earth as it is in itself, rather than the earth as subdued and subordinated to human needs. Thus, she is responsible for the fertility of wild plants (and animals) – at the foundation of the (women's) gathering economy, rather than of domesticated plants. Through her daughter Rhea she gives birth, first to Hestia, the protectress of hearth and home – of the woman's world – completely committed to peace, harmony and constructive mediation of disputes. It is Hestia who teaches humans to build permanent houses – as basic units of the first – permanent – matrilocal settlements (following earlier hunting-gathering wanderings). Her second daughter is Demeter, the gentle goddess of the corn and of sexual initiation. It is Demeter who teaches humans – in particular, the women – how to cultivate corn, as the economic foundation of such permanent settlements.

Demeter gives birth to Core, identified with the green corn, and afterwards called Persephone, identified with the ripe ear of corn – and taken down into the underworld to become queen of the dead. While Demeter search's for her daughter the earth is barren of crops. But ultimately she is re-united with Core and a compromise reached whereby Core spends nine months of the year in the upper world and three months in the lower – reflecting the yearly cycle of planting, growth, harvesting etc.

Downing argues that in their essential loving bond with one another Demeter and Persephone are two aspects of Gaia – the fertile, vegetative, conscious, this worldly side, and the destructive, unconscious, otherworldly side. Demeter is the human side of Gaia – in her love for her daughter and in her bereavement and grief. But Persephone is also the goddess of spring and rebirth, as well as death and the underworld.

The parallels between the two systems of thought are clear. And the fact that the Iroquois are also close to being a truly matriarchal society – as well as sharing such mythico-religious conceptions with the pre-classical Greeks – seemed to confirm Bachofen's speculations about Greek matriarchy. It seemed, indeed, to Marx and Engels, to support the idea of a 'universal' (or at least very widely distributed) evolutionary stage of human social development.

To understand why such a stage should have developed or persisted so much later in the new world as compared to the old (where it was already long gone before the dawn of recorded history), however, we must consider the material foundations of such a society.

Thus it is, first of all, crucial to recognise that as far as Marx and Engels were concerned, the ideology of the goddess was an effect rather than (as Bachofen believed) a cause of matriarchal organisation of material production. And to understand such organisation we must see it in its historical context as the next step from semi-nomadic hunting and gathering.

Marx and Engels believed that women's power in Iroquois society developed from the fact that it was the women who had pioneered the new 'horticultural' technology and settled village life (as an extension of their earlier vegetable gathering activities) at a time when hunting was in decline (due to human population expansion and other factors). At the same time the men continued to live a semi-nomadic lifestyle of hunting and gathering.

As Farb points out, the men were "nearly always away (from the villages) making war, hunting, trapping and trading. So, by default, the males had allowed the females to become economically self-sufficient" (FARB 1978, p. 103). In fact, the men failed to generate sufficient material wealth to support themselves, and remained dependent upon the women for the continued privilege of maintaining their macho hunting and warring lifestyle.

"Iroquois women not only totally controlled the lands they cultivated, the implements they used, and the seed supply, they also
maintained the right to distribute all food, even that obtained by the
males through hunting. The females could thus prevent the forma-

tion of a war party, if they disagreed with the action, by withholding supplies of dried corn needed for the expedition. In other words, the unusually high status of (women) is not explainable as some historical curiosity, but rather as a direct result of controlling the economic foundation of the tribe" (op. cit.).

It was this economic power – and autonomy – that allowed the women the scope to develop new religious ideologies of their own, reflecting and articulating their particular roles, priorities and preoccupations, rather than simply reproducing earlier hunting and gathering based ideas – of 'masters of the animals', 'animal spirits' etc.

Not surprisingly, therefore, Marx and Engels also refer to changing economic circumstances as the major driving forces behind the collapse of such matriarchal social organisation, and its replacement by patriarchy. Specifically, they consider what happens when the men are finally forced to abandon their nomadic hunting – through depletion of wild game resources or other considerations – and develop some new productive techniques of their own.

Thus, Engels argues that in the old world, early male control of hunting and warfare logically extended, first into control of domesticated animal herds and of the new wealth in ploughed fields and milk, wool, and meat products generated by such animals, and later into control of human slaves, (captured in war) to work the increasingly productive farmlands. And the men were able to utilise this new found wealth and power to overthrow 'mother-right' and ensure that a patriarchal law of inheritance began to prevail.

Engels explains that "as wealth increased, it, on the one hand, gave the man a more important status in the family than the woman and, on the other, created a stimulus to utilise this strengthened position in order to overthrow the traditional order in favour of his (male) children" (ENGELS 1977, p. 56). The new 'patriarchal' family resulting from this prehistoric social revolution involved "the mans absolute power over the woman, with a view to guaranteeing her fidelity, and thus the paternity of the children". As Engels says, "the overthrow of mother-right was the world historic defeat of the female sex". For, having overthrown the right of inheritance through the mother, the man "seized the reins in the house also, the woman was degraded, enthralled, a slave to the man's lusts, a mere instrument for breeding children" (ibid., p. 57).

This development was delayed or avoided in the new world because of limited resources of readily domesticable plant and animal species which severely restricted the opportunities for male technological innovation.

As Engels says, at this point,

> "we reach a stage (of cultural evolution) where the differences in natural endowment of the two great continents begins to assert itself... Now the Eastern continent – there so called Old World – contained almost all the animals suitable for domestication and all the cultivable cereals with one exception, while the western, America, contained only one domesticable mammal, the llama, and that only in part of the south, and only one cereal fit for cultivation, but that the best, maize. The effect of these different natural conditions was that from now on the populations of each hemisphere went its own special way, and the landmarks on the border lines between the various stages (of development) are different in the two cases" (ibid., p. 25).

But it is important to note that, when the Europeans deprived the Iroquois of their traditional hunting territories, forced the men back into the villages and offered them access to the technology of plough agriculture, here too the men wasted little time in instituting a parallel subordination of the female population.

In relation to earlier observations upon the destruction of Greek matriarchy by Indo-European speaking invaders, possibly migrating down from Southern Russia, we can see how such an eventuality is by no means excluded by the Marx-Engels's account. Indeed, if Southern Russia provided opportunities for marginalised men to domesticate wild horses at an early period, to serve as the basis for new, increasingly mobile, pastoral modes of social organisation, then its easy to see how they could have come to pose a serious threat to settled agrarian matriarchies thousands of miles away.

Here, indeed, we can see how something like the hunting and warring lifestyle of the Iroquois males could have been given a new lease of life by such an innovation – as happened on the North American Great Plains, when a number of tribes gained access to horses from the Spanish, and became long distance raiders and buffalo hunters. But the Indo-Europeans faced no such opposition from European settlers with guns.

Before leaving Marx and Engels's studies in this area, it is important to consider some of the implications of these idea for contemporary developments. In particular it is worth emphasising the fact that Marx and Engels believed that the foundations of women's oppression remain just as fundamentally materially grounded in modern industrial society as they were in pre-historic times. The difference is that it is no longer the individual patriarchal household that is the primary unit of control of productive technology, but rather the capitalist business.

Marxist feminists see power as still residing essentially in control of major material productive forces, and today, such power is denied to the great majority of men as it is to women. The foundation of women's oppression is the same as that of men; the fact that women constitute the majority of wage workers who create all the wealth of society but get back only enough to survive.

Certainly women are typically worse off than men, getting only three quarters of the wages of men for the same work, concentrated in less skilled, and poorly paid, part-time and ununionised areas of employment. They continue to bear a double burden of work both inside and outside the family. The continued existence of the privatised, nuclear family provides the foundation for the perpetuation of ideas about women that portray them – primarily – as wives and mothers. This, in turn, sustains a situation in which women take primary responsibility for the needs of every family member – including children and old people. As well as working for pay, they perform masses of unpaid housework.

But it is not the men of the working class who really benefit from this situation, rather it is the capitalist class. The more unpaid housework that women perform the less the bosses have to pay out in wages to all family members – and the more they can run down basic social services. The less wages they pay unorganised, ununionised women workers, the less they have to pay men – for the weaker the working class as a whole is – and the bigger the bosses' profits. And if they can divide working class men and women along gender lines – with women blaming men for oppressing them, and men blaming women for taking their jobs, the weaker that class is in confronting the real enemy – capitalism.

In this context, we can see the development of the new ideologies of women's liberation from the 60's onwards as very much the product of changing economic circumstances – specifically the culmination of the postwar boom of the developed western economies, drawing increasing numbers of women into the workforce, and into higher education, and the subsequent collapse of that boom with corresponding efforts to undermine all the gains made by working people when labour was in demand.

Part Three
ARCHAEOLOGICAL CONSIDERATIONS

Subsequent research has gone a long way towards confirming this basic Bachofen-Marx-Engels scheme of historical development – at least in respect of the Old World. James Mellaarts excavations of the two important neolithic sites in Turkey, at Catal Huyuk and Hacilar, have been particularly important in this regard.

Not surprisingly, the original scheme needs some modification in the light of more recent data. In particular, Engels seems to have been wrong in assuming that domestication of sheep, goats or cattle by the men necessarily undermined the original Neolithic matriarchy. And had he considered other North American groups – like the Hopi or Zuni Pueblo peoples – instead of focussing exclusively upon the Iroquois, he probably would have modified his views in this area.

On the other hand, domestication of horses by the men – as means of long distance transport – does indeed seem to have played a crucial role in the destruction of matriarchy. And the broad outlines of Engels account remain applicable.

Generally, the origin of the Neolithic or agricultural revolution is now traced back to the end of the last Ice Age, when a combination of environmental change (including global warming and loss of land area) and hunting overkill led to the extinction of many species of large game animals that had been the preferred prey of human hunter-gatherers. In many areas, people compensated for these extinctions by foraging for a 'broader spectrum' of plants and animals – including the wild ancestors of what were later to become domesticated species.

From about 11,000 BCE, in the Middle East, some hunting-gathering populations became increasingly reliant upon wild wheat and barley stands. And such reliance went along with a shift from semi-nomadic wandering to settled village life – with these first villages centred around wild seed storage facilities. As Marvin Harris points out,

> "It was a relatively short step from settling down near wild stands of wheat and barley to propagating the plants whose seeds were bigger and did not fall off at the slightest touch. And as the wild stands gave way to cultivated fields, they attracted animals like sheep and goats into close association with humans, who soon found it was more practical to put these animals in pens, feed them, and breed the ones with the most desirable characteristics rather than simply hunt them all to extinction" (HARRIS 1990, pp. 392-3).

There are good grounds for seeing the agricultural revolution as the single most important technological innovation in human history – leading to radical changes in all areas of human life. Most obviously, the change from a semi-nomadic lifestyle to settled village life was associated with significant increases in population, and villages evolved into the first sizeable towns.

"Here hundreds, sometimes thousands of people lived and worked, tilling and in many places also irrigating the land. Technological specialisation as well as trade accelerated in the neolithic. And, as agriculture freed human energy and imagination, such crafts as pottery and basket making, textile weaving and leather crafting, jewellery making and wood carving, and such arts as painting, clay modelling and stone carving flourished" (EISLER 1990, p. 16).

The idea that it was women who pioneered the development of agriculture – at least in the case of the original, smaller scale, garden cultivation or horticulture – has been strongly supported by a mass of anthropological material relating to historically known human societies. Amongst hunter-gatherers it is found to be women who have taken the first steps towards active cultivation of plant species – removing weeds from stands of wild food plants etc. And there have been a number of cases of direct historical evidence of the actual transition from women's gathering to settled horticulture while the men continued to hunt – as e.g. with groups of Shoshone Indians in Utah and Nevada.

Furthermore, there is now substantial evidence that the religion of the earliest neolithic communities centred upon worship of an earth-mother goddess – just as Bachofen and others had suggested. At Catal Huyuk, e.g., the largest known neolithic site in the Near East, a flourishing town for at least 800 years (from about 6250 to 5400 BCE) there are sophisticated wall paintings, plaster reliefs, stone sculptures and large quantities of figurines made of clay "All focussed upon the worship of a female deity," – associated with fertility, birth, life and death. And as Eisler points out,

"while the excavations carried out at Catal Huyuk, as well as at nearby Hacilar (inhabited from approx 5700 to 5000 BCE) have yielded some of the richest data about this early civilisation, the Southern Anatolian plain is only one of several areas where settled agricultural societies worshipping the goddess have been archae-ologically documented" (ibid., p. 11).

In fact, by c. 6000 BCE "fully agricultural societies began expanding into hitherto marginal territories such as the alluvial plains of Mesopotamia, Transcaucasia, and Transcaspia on the one hand, and into South-Eastern Europe on the other". Moreover, "some of this contact, as in Crete and Cyprus, definitely went by sea" and in each case "the newcomers arrived with a fully fledged neolithic economy" (op. cit.).

At the same time,

"Goddess figures are characteristic of the neolithic art (through-out) the near and Middle East, e.g. in the middle eastern neolithic site of Jericho, where back in 7000 BCE people were already living in plastered brick houses – some with clay ovens with chim-neys and even sockets for door posts – clay goddess figurines have been found. At Tell-Es-Sawwan a site on the banks of the Tigris distinguished by early irrigation farming and the striking geometrically decorated pottery known as Samarra, a variety of figurines, among them a cache of highly sophisticated painted female sculptures, have been unearthed. In Cayonu, a neolithic site in Northern Syria, where we find the earliest use of ham-mered native copper and the first use of clay bricks, similar female figurines have been excavated, some of then dating to the sites earliest levels. These small goddess figurines have later parallels at Jarmo, and even as far west as Aceramic Sesklo, where they were manufactured even before ceramic pottery was introduced" (ibid., p. 8).

Maritza Gimbutas, in particular, has charted similar develop-ments in neolithic-chalcolithic South-Eastern Europe, in an area extending roughly northward from the Aegean and Adriatic (including the islands) all the way up into Czech Republic, Southern Poland, and the Western Ukraine. As she notes,

> "during the millennia of agricultural stability, the material welfare of the villages of South-Eastern Europe had been persistently improved by the increasingly efficient exploitation of the fertile river valleys... wheat, barley, vetch, peas and other legumes were cultivated, and all the domesticated animals present in the Balkans today, except for the horse, were bred. Pottery technology and bone and stone working technologies had advanced, and copper metallurgy was introduced into East Central Europe by 5500 BCE. Trade and communications which had expanded through the millennia, must have provided a tremendous cross-fertilising impetus to cultural growth... the use of sailing boats is attested from the sixth millennium onwards by their incised depictions on ceramics" (quoted in EISLER 1990, p. 13).

Between c. 7000 and 3500 BCE these early Europeans developed a complex social organisation involving significant craft specialisation. They apparently maintained complex religious and governmental institutions.

> "They used metals such as copper and gold for ornaments and tools. They even evolved what appears to be a rudimentary script. In Gimbutas's words, 'if one defines civilisation as the ability of a given people to adjust to its environment and to develop adequate arts, technology, script and social relationships, it is evident that Old Europe achieved a marked degree of success' " (ibid., p. 13).

And here again are many indications of a goddess-based religion. As Eisler says, "everywhere, in murals, statues and votive figurines – we find images of the goddess. In the various incarnations of maiden, ancestress, or creatrix, she is the lady of the waters, the birds and the underworld, or simply the divine mother cradling her divine child in her arms" (ibid.).

Such a religion seems to have permeated all aspects of social life, and women seem to have been largely responsible for its major rites and observances. As Gimbutas says,

> "In the models of house shrines and temples, and in actual temple remains, females are shown supervising the preparation and performance of rituals dedicated to the various aspects and functions of the goddess. Enormous energy was expended in the production of cult equipment and votive gifts. Temple models show the grinding of grain and the baking of sacred bread... In the temple workshops – which usually constitute half the building or occupy the floor below the temple proper, females made and decorated quantities of various pots, appropriate to different rites... the most sophisticated creations of Old Europe – the most exquisite vases, sculptures etc. now extant were women's work" (ibid., p. 14).

Not only are there strong indications of a general equality between the sexes in these early neolithic cultures, but there are signs also of a general equality, and a general absence of internal hierarchy and privilege, supporting Marx and Engels's ideas of primitive communism. As Gimbutas says,

> "a division of labour between the sexes is indicated, but not a superiority of either... In the 53 grave cemetery at Vinca (e.g.) hardly any difference in wealth or equipment was discernible between male and female graves... In respect of the role of women in the society, the Vinca evidence suggests an equalitarian and clearly non-patriarchal society. The same can be adduced of the Varna society; I can see no ranking along a patriarchal-masculine value scale" (ibid., p. 14).

Particularly important here is a general absence of any signs of warfare and aggression – as a foundation for male domination and a hierarchy of male power (the 'chain' of command) such as we see in the archaeological remains of later cultures. As Eisler says,

"in sharp contrast to later art, a theme notable for its absence
from neolithic art is imagery idealising armed might, cruelty and
violence based power. There are no images of 'noble warriors' or
scenes of battles. Nor are there any signs of 'heroic conquerors'
dragging captives around in chains or other evidence of slavery...
What we do find everywhere – in shrines and houses, in the dec-
orative motifs of vases, in sculptures in the round, clay figurines,
and bas reliefs – is a rich array of symbols from nature. Associated
with the worship of the Goddess, they attest to awe and wonder
at the beauty and mystery of life" (ibid., p. 17).

In later periods we find lavish burials of tribal chieftains or petty
kings, often including elaborate weaponry and sometimes also the
bodies of wives and retainers, sacrificed to accompany the chief to
the afterlife. But such things are completely absent from neolithic
remains. Indeed, there are no signs of any significant deployment of
material resources into the manufacture of arms.

As Gimbutas sums up,

"during the early agricultural period women reached the apex
of their influence in farming, arts and crafts, and social functions.
The matriclan with collectivist principles continued... There is no
evidence in all of Old Europe of a (hierarchical) patriarchal chief-
tainate of the Indo-European type, There are no royal tombs and no
residences in megarons or hill forts. The burial rites and settlement
patterns reflect a matrilineal structure, whereas the distribution of
wealth in graves speaks of an economic egalitarianism" (GIMBUTAS
1991, p. 324).

So too have more recent investigations generally confirmed the
idea of the destruction of these early neolithic civilisations by nomadic
patriarchal pastoralists, migrating from peripheral steppe areas, with
the benefit of superior military technology and mobility. Though, in
this case, there is substantial disagreement about precise dates and
routes (of migration) and about the identity of the peoples concerned.

Gimbutas argues for a number of 'waves' of migration of Indo-European or Aryan speaking peoples originally from the arid steppe regions north of the Black Sea, moving into Europe, disrupting and subordinating the goddess-worshipping neolithic societies of the region. As she says, "thanks to the growing number of carbon dates, it is now possible to trace several migration waves of steppe pastoralists or 'kurgan' peoples that swept across prehistoric Europe". These repeated incursions and ensuing cultural shocks and population shifts were concentrated in three major thrusts, wave No. 1 at c. 4300-4200 BCE, No. 2 c. 3400-3200 BCE and wave No. 3 c. 3000-2800 BCE.

Not only were these people equipped with horses – and ultimately chariots – unavailable to the settled horticulturalists, they also had hard bronze weapons; in the form of daggers and halberds, thin and sharp axes, maces and battleaxes – along with bows, while the defenders had only softer copper axes, for chopping and shaping wood. As Gimbutas says, "probably by no later than 3500 BCE the kurgans had (learned the relevant) metallurgical technology from the Transcaucasians, and soon afterwards they were forging lethally effective weapons out of metal".

These military advantages allowed the Indo-European invaders to conquer and subjugate indigenous neolithic populations, quite possibly killing the men and children and sparing some of the women "whom they took for themselves as concubines, wives or slaves". As Eisler points out, we have relevant evidence from the Old Testament of precisely this sort of behaviour by the patriarchal pastoral Jewish tribes in the course of their own migrations.

The Indo-Europeans brought with them their own patriarchal warrior gods, which became the foundation for the classical Greek pantheon – considered earlier – as well as parallel religious systems in Persia, India, Turkey and elsewhere. Originally such gods appear to have been specifically associated with the sorts of natural phenomena of relevance to migratory pastoralists – a sky father, a sun god (or goddess), a thunder or rain god, and deities of the moon and dawn.

So too do they seem to have been connected with certain hierarchical divisions within Indo-European society. As Mallory points out, "among the earliest attested (of such divisions) is the familiar division of Vedic India into the Brahmans (priests), Ksatriyas (warriors) and Vaisyas (herder-cultivators) – with the Sudras – the lowest group, outside the Aryan community and composed of the suppressed indigenous population" (MALLORY 1989).

That these divisions were quite possibly already established amongst the Indo-Europeans before their conquests, and corresponded to a fundamental division of their religious pantheon is suggested by an ancient treaty (found in Turkey) dating back to 1380 BCE. Here, the King of Mitanni, in Northern Syria, evokes the names of the Indic gods Mitra, Varuna, Indra and the Nasatyas.

> "The first two names are characteristically found co-joined in [the earliest Indian sacred texts] the Vedas, ie Mitra-Varuna, and they represent two main aspects of Indic sovereignty. Mitra personifies the concept of contract, and governs the legislative aspects of sovereignty while Varunas domain pertains more appropriately to the magical or the religious. The god Indra is the warrior god par excellence while the Nasatyas are twins, associated closely with horses, and find their clearest roles in the maintenance of health of both livestock and people" (ibid., p. 131).

We cannot here consider the steps whereby these or other proto-Indo-European deities became transformed into the specific classical Greek deities considered earlier (e.g. Zeus and Apollo). But we can already see how very different is this new scheme from that of the neolithic mother goddess – with its new emphasis upon masculinity, upon hierarchy, upon war and aggression, and upon air and sky, rather than the fertile earth.

And, of course the conquerors sought to impose their warlike patriarchal values and social hierarchy upon the conquered territories which they settled, as reflected in radical changes in the archaeological and historical record thereafter. Though there are signs – such as those considered earlier from classical mythology – that they were less than entirely successful in crushing all opposition and totally replacing earlier ideas and practices.

In light of these exciting new discoveries, it is not surprising that feminists – and socialists – should have developed a new interest in the Goddess of the ancient neolithic. For the worship of the goddess was clearly an integral part of a viable, and apparently in many ways admirable pattern of life now long gone. It seems perfectly reasonable to suggest – as did Marx and Engels – that we can learn something from neolithic society of value for us today.

But some have gone very much further than this. They have argued that the actual resurrection of neolithic religion and/or neolithic technological and social organisation offers a solution to pressing problems of the modern age. It is to these sorts of ideas that we turn in the next chapter.

CHAPTER FIVE
THE GODDESS *cont.*

Part One
PSYCHOLOGICAL CONSIDERATIONS

There is actually a considerable diversity of different views and approaches within the current movement of return to the Goddess, ranging from the sane and the sensible to the hopelessly regressive and silly. At one pole are those who wish to rehabilitate the Goddess – or Goddesses – essentially as a metaphor for female identity, and a vehicle for psychological insight and liberation. In particular, consideration of Goddess mythology is seen as a useful step towards women's psychic liberation.

For example, Christine Downing, in her classic study of *The Goddess (Mythological Images of the Feminine)* – examining a range of different female deities of Homeric mythology, notes that a diet of purely male images of divinity leads to severe spiritual 'malnourishment'.

"We are starved for images which recognise the sacredness of the feminine and the complexity, richness and nurturing power of female energy. We hunger for images of human creativity and love inspired by the capacity of female bodies to give birth and nourish, for images of how humankind participates in the natural world suggested by reflection on the correspondences between menstrual rhythms and the moons waxing and waning. We seek images that affirm that the love women receive from women, from mother, sister, daughter, lover, friend, reaches as deep and is as trustworthy, necessary and sustaining as is the love symbolised by father, brother, son or husband. We long for images which name as authentically feminine courage, creativity, loyalty and self-confidence, resilience and steadfastness, capacity for clear insight, inclination for solitude, and the intensity of passion. We need images, we also need myths – for myths make concrete and particular; they give us situations, plots, relationships. We need the goddess and we need the goddesses" (DOWNING 1984, p. 5).

It is important to see that for here, such myths are primarily a means to the end of overcoming the psychic alienation of women in a patriarchal society, putting them in touch with their own suppressed or repressed feelings and potentialities. As she says,

"Patriarchy is active not just in the external social world but also in our unconscious – even amongst those of us who have tried to free ourselves from patriarchy's values and assumptions. Freud and Jung have taught us how deeply our thoughts, feelings and modes of response are informed by mythic prototypes of which we may have no conscious cognisance. To know who we are means knowing who they are. If we ignore them, they act on us and in us in ways we fail to recognise. They act as delimiting stereotypes. It is only as we recognise their presence and seek to know them as fully as possible, to re-imagine them, that their power to open up new dimensions of feminine life is released. Only then can they become life-giving archetypes" (ibid., p. 23).

To this end, Downing highlights the usefulness of the diversity of the classical Greek goddesses as projections or externalisations of different dimensions of female identity. As she says,

> "The very differentiation we may first experience as diminution may help us sort through the various aspects of our femaleness in a way that the undifferentiated wholeness of the archaic mother-goddess cannot do... The differentiation helps us to comprehend ways in which each of us differs from other women and to celebrate our variety. It may help us to understand (and perhaps overcome) differences with other women that are experienced as difficulties. The differentiation also provides us with a language for understanding some of the stages of our own lives and some of the particular inner conflicts we feel at a given time" (ibid., p. 23).

Demeter e.g., "exemplifies the mother's own experience of motherhood... From the maternal side we are brought in touch with how much of motherhood is loss..." (ibid., p. 39). Ariadne represents a progress from relations with men who need women to supply them with the "strength, the courage, the insight, the readiness to risk the exploration of their soul", to relations with men "in touch with the feminine in themselves" – so that they do not 'need' a woman to "supply it for them". In this latter regard, Ariadne represents female bisexuality, as Dionysus (her divine partner) represents male bisexuality.

Hera offers insights into the intrinsic limitations of marriage relations with men, Athene insight into women's creative and intellectual potential, their courage and self-sufficiency, their power also to "bring men into touch with their own highest creative potentiality".

Artemis is about re-birth or the birth of the true self, about women forming deep relations with women, coming to terms with independence, solitude and death. And Aphrodite is about "the sensual dimension underlying all... important relationships", including therapeutic and educational relationships.

There are certainly problems with these sorts of ideas. It is not clear how far Downing wants to go in subscribing to the Jungian idea of the archetypes of the collective unconscious which is basically a religious idea (of super-human deities etc.). There is also some possible suggestion that it is patriarchal religious ideas which are most important in maintaining patriarchal social relations and that a new – feminist – religion is a necessary condition for overcoming such patriarchal social relations.

But without endorsing any such idea as these we can still see the general wisdom and value of this sort of approach – assuming that genuine insights into female psychology really are to be found in the work of Homer and other Greek mythologists. And Downing presents a good argument that this is indeed the case.

At the opposite end of the spectrum, however, are those who go for a much more literal, objective, fully theistic interpretation of the Goddess idea; those who really do want to establish a new religion – or at least resurrect an old one – with its own rites, prayers, priesthood etc. And, typically, the emphasis here is very much upon an undifferentiated, primordial neolithic Earth Mother Goddess, rather than upon the diversified pantheon of Classical Greece.

Included in this group are feminists who definitely do see religion as the ultimate foundation of patriarchy – and a new religion as a necessary condition for its overthrow. Here too are some Greens who see such a new religion as a necessary condition for ecological survival; only through a new attitude of 'respect' and humility and love in relation to mother nature can current trends of ecological destruction be reversed. Included in this group are also those so-called 'deep-ecologists' who identify the ecosphere of the earth – not including human beings – with such a divine force – the Earth Goddess – and who identify the autonomous life and survival of this force as the ultimate value.

New Age bookshops now provide dozens of texts detailing appropriate observances and techniques for contacting the Goddess without and within, including accounts of established communities seeking to spread the word and change the world. And beside such texts are dozens of others about tuning in to the cosmic forces that supposedly regulate all human, animal and plant life on the planet earth – but which are threatened or undermined by 'masculine', 'western' science and technology.

Here, the principal psychological driving force seems to be precisely that attempt to return to primary narcissistic perfection which is arguably the ultimate foundation of all religious belief. Only here we see it in particularly clear, primal and unmitigated form. This is not so much an attempt to liberate or extend the powers of the self (of the conscious rational ego) as to escape from the burdens and responsibilities of selfhood altogether.

As such it is one amongst many contemporary religious movements, 'therapeutic cults, experiments in psychic healing' and 'self-proclaimed counterculture's' which, as Christopher Lasch says, "seek the shortest road to nirvana".

> "Whereas the worlds great religions have always emphasised the obstacles to salvation, [such contemporary cults – including the worship of the goddess –] promise immediate release from the burden of selfhood. Instead of seeking to reconcile the ego and its environment (through constructive development of both) the new cults deny the very distance between them. Though they claim to extend consciousness into areas hitherto unexplored (or not explored since ancient times) they promote a radical contraction of consciousness. They are founded on the need not to know" (LASCH 1985, pp. 165-6).

A number of feminists with a background in psychoanalytic ideas have explicitly endorsed the regression to the primary narcissistic state clearly involved here. They see this as a necessary escape from the 'instrumental', objectifying rationality of patriarchy, which equates freedom with isolation and control and which threatens to destroy the world through its endless pursuit of profit and power.

But as Lasch points out, this sort of position – equating narcissistic fusion with femininity and egoic (or super-egoic) instrumental rationality and control with masculinity, radically distorts the fundamental insights of psychoanalytic theory.

"That kind of argument dissolves the contradiction held in tension by the psychoanalytic theory of narcissism; namely, that all of us, men and women alike, experience the pain of separation and simultaneously long for a restoration of the original sense of union. Narcissism originates in the infant's symbiotic fusion with the mother, but the desire to return to this blissful state cannot be identified with 'feminine mutuality' without obscuring both its universality and the illusion of 'radical autonomy' to which it also gives rise, in women as well as in men."

"The desire for complete self-sufficiency is just as much a legacy of primary narcissism as the desire for mutuality and relatedness. Because narcissism knows no distinction between the self and others, it expresses itself in later life both in the desire for instant union with others – as in romantic love [and in symbiosis with the body of the earth mother] and in the desire for absolute independence from others, by means of which we seek to revive the original illusion of omnipotence and to deny our dependence upon external sources of nourishment and gratification. The technological project of achieving independence from nature embodies the solipsistic side of narcissism, just as the desire for mystic union with nature embodies its symbiotic and self obliterating side. Since both spring from the same source, the need to deny the fact of dependence, it can only cause confusion to call the dream of technological omnipotence a masculine obsession, while extolling the hope of a more loving relation with nature as a characteristically feminine preoccupation. Both originate in the undifferentiated equilibrium of the prenatal state and both, moreover, reject psychological maturation in favour of regression, the 'feminine' longing for symbiosis no less than the solipsistic 'masculine' drive for absolute mastery" (ibid., p. 245-6).

"With their fear of 'masculine' rationality and their exaggerated admiration for the narcissistic ego ideal, which embodies an allegedly feminine counterweight to the rational ego, the advocates of cultural revolution [including those who wish to resurrect the neolithic earth goddess] hold up narcissism as the cure for a disease that [actually] springs from the same source. They recommend a narcissistic symbiosis with nature as the cure for technological solipsism, itself narcissistic in origin. This kind of thinking shorn of its psychoanalytic subtleties and reduced to a handful of shopworn slogans and platitudes now permeates not only the women's movement but also the environmental movement and the peace movement as well, whose adherents blindly follow feminists in conceiving of 'feminine' virtues as the remedy for environmental devastation, imperialism and war" (ibid., p. 248).

As Lasch points out, it is perfectly possible to reject these sorts of ideas without also rejecting feminism, environmentalism or the pursuit of peace. As he says,

"It is precisely because the party of narcissism... has gone so much further than others in calling attention to the dangers of 'instrumental reason' and (capitalist) industrial technology that its ideas need to be subjected to careful scrutiny. A new politics of conservation has to rest on a solid philosophical foundation, not on a critique of instrumental reason that extends to every form of purposeful activity. It has to rest upon a respect for nature, not a mystical adoration of nature. It has to rest on a firm conception of selfhood, not on a belief that the 'separate self is an illusion'" (ibid., p. 253).

Part Two
ECOLOGICAL CONSIDERATIONS

There is no doubt of the seriousness of the environmental crisis now facing the human species. In particular, the pollution of the atmosphere with carbon dioxide, released from the burning of fossil fuels and the destruction of trees is producing a cumulative greenhouse effect whereby the suns heat is trapped after being radiated back by the earth. Even the apparently minimal increases in global temperature caused by this process could be sufficient to melt the polar ice sheets, radically change the world's weather patterns, flood low lying lands and literally drown entire nations.

Other greenhouse gases such as methane, nitrous oxide and chlorofluorocarbons (CFCs) are destroying the stratospheric ozone layer that protects living organisms from the effects of ultraviolet radiation. The widening of holes in the ozone layer over the poles generates increased risk of skin cancers, damage to crops and fisheries and further disturbances of temperature levels.

Such chronic problems are complimented by those acute ecological disasters and horrors that sometimes find there way into the newspaper headlines. The explosion of the Chernobyl reactor in the Ukraine, sending radioactive clouds around the world, three thousand people killed and hundreds of thousands injured by the release of toxic dioxin gas from the Union Carbide plant at Bhopal in India, a hundred thousand tonnes of crude oil spilled on the shores of Alaska from the supertanker Exxon Valdez, vast spills from leaking oil pipelines in Siberia, disintegrating nuclear submarines pouring radioactive waste into the sea, massive floods in Bangladesh, increased levels of rainforest destruction around the world, all seem to portend immanent disaster for the whole planet.

> "These are just the ones that hit the headlines. Pollutants are tipped into rivers and spewed out of factory and power plant chimneys every day in every country. Ten million tonnes of toxins are released every year from the US alone. Forests and lakes in Central Europe, Scandinavia and Canada are wilting under the combined pressure of these poisons. Public water supplies are becoming increasingly polluted... major cities are grinding to a halt under the weight of public transport... Around the world hundreds of millions of people are an inch away from starvation. Millions succumb to famine and disease" (BLACKIE 1990, p. 5).

However, it is far from time to succumb to total despair. It is vital not to see current developments as indications of an immanent apocalypse, whose cause and outcome lie beyond all possibility of rational control by human beings.

It is this sort of attitude, I think, which promotes a desperate search for some sort of super-human agency which might be able to intervene to reverse such an inevitable plunge into ecological destruction. This, in turn, encourages a 'blind' religious faith in any promising – effectively promoted – candidates, in place of rational understanding of the problem – and appropriate political-economic, scientific-technological action to improve the situation.

This is probably a major factor in the current vogue for re-discovering Gaia, the Earth Mother Goddess. It is hoped that, somehow, an appropriately 'respectful' attitude towards the goddess will 'win her over', once again, to the cause of loving and caring for her human children. Renewed worship of the Mother Goddess will somehow restore her – the earth – to health, in the sense of restoring an optimum environment for human health and well-being.

Frequently, this sort of idea goes along with a radical rejection of modern industry as irremediably destructive and polluting. As a leading British Green activist, Jonathan Porritt says, "it is industrialism itself – a 'super ideology' embraced by socialist countries as well as by the capitalist west – which threatens us". And the implication is that we must return to the sort of small scale, handicraft-based self-sufficiency of pre-industrial times if we are to respect the goddess appropriately and save the earth.

Alternatively (for deep ecologists e.g.) the earth as a whole is treated as a super-organism which will ultimately survive precisely through freeing itself of its human 'parasites'. And in this case, the worshippers escape the problems of the moment by identifying with this all-powerful – near-immortal – super-being.

The problem is, of course, that there is no Mother Goddess and even if there were, its far from clear that a new 'cult' of the Mother Goddess would do anything for the environmental health of the earth, furthermore, to go down this path is to obscure the true causes and consequences of environmental problems – and therefore obstruct appropriate action to address such problems.

There can be no return to the social organisation and technology of the earlier neolithic period, such as is advocated by some Greens. Most obviously, all talk of a return to small-scale self sufficiency or a rejection of modern industry, ignores the massive growth in world population since neolithic times – sustained by modern high intensity agriculture and a complex world wide division of labour. As James Lovelock says, "this flood of righteous wrath (directed against industry per se – as irremediably harmful and polluting) ignores the certainty that if we gave up our industrial civilisation only a few of us would survive".

It ignores the fact of guns and bombs also – suggesting that the sort of massive social chaos and disintegration of contemporary culture (with massive destruction of population) implicit in such a 'return' to local self-sufficiency would be more likely to lead to a new feudalism (of local armed warlords controlling and exploiting unarmed peasant drudges) than a new (primitive) communism. And it ignores the fact that the neolithic economy was not, itself, stable in the longer term – but subject to change due to the sorts of social forces considered earlier (of population expansion, sexual division of labour, competition, warfare etc.).

It is certainly true that from the start of the industrial revolution the development of the factory system brought appalling conditions for the mass of the working population. And that even those gains in wages and conditions achieved in the first world (through working class struggle and changing conditions in the labour market) seem to have been bought at the expense of exporting the horrors of the early industrial revolution to the 'newly developing' territories of the world.

As Duncan Blackie says,

"Today all over the world chemical plants spew out deadly poison and factory workers know the crushing monotony and dangers to health that go with their work... In the newly industrialising

areas of the world huge modern industries are developed at break-
neck pace with even less concern for the people who work in
them. Breathing the air in Mexico City is the equivalent of smoking
sixty cigarettes a day" (BLACKIE 1990, p. 26).

But as Blackie points out,

> "This is just one side of the story. Industry has made possible a
> massive improvement in living standards for many people, creating
> better housing and massively reducing necessary housework...
> Modern means of transport allow for the distribution of goods around
> the world; putting iron ore in the same place as coal; putting food in
> the same place as people, putting petrochemicals in the same place
> as plastics industries, all depend upon modern transport" (ibid., p. 28).

As noted earlier, the production and distribution of food on the
present scale would simply not be possible without the development of industrial processes, and modern means of communication. Similarly, the provision of relatively cheap, mass-produced
shoes and clothing depends upon technology which simply did not
exist two centuries ago.

This sort of technology potentially frees all human beings from
a life of drudgery devoted simply to the production of the necessities of life. At the same time, modern technology opens up educational and cultural possibilities for all, undreamt of by previous
generations. Popular access to the accumulated knowledge and
cultural heritage of the human race, – in books, tapes, CD's, films,
galleries, databases etc., and the opportunity to build upon and
extend that heritage massively enriches human life compared to
that of earlier, pre-industrial periods.

It is no longer necessary for any of the world's population to go
without the basic necessities of life – in the form of adequate food,
shelter, rest, exercise, education, leisure and worthwhile and stimulating work. Modern technology generates a massive surplus of the
materials necessary to sustain such a lifestyle.

Of course, this by no means implies that everyone has access to such necessary resources. On the contrary, the capitalist organisation of production ensures that massive greed, wastage and over consumption on the part of the few co-exists with massive poverty, misery and starvation for many. But the problem here is capitalism rather then modern industry *per se.*

> "Neither is it the crude size of industrial undertakings that leads to ecological damage. Small is not beautiful under capitalism. In practice no one, given the choice, would decide to work in a sweat-shop instead of a large textile factory. The wages are worse and it is much more difficult to organise to improve working conditions, Neither is it the case that small production units are more ecologically sound, In capitalism's competitive world they are more likely to be forced to cut corners" (BLACKIE 1990, p. 26).
>
> "The tyranny of the factory comes not from the factory itself, but from the class divisions within it, from the relations between those who produce the wealth and those who own it. The people who suffer the most from uncontrolled industrial processes, from the chemical worker breathing toxic fumes to the building workers falling off shoddy scaffolding, are also those who are denied control over production in our society" (op. cit.). [And the solution is, rather, safer factories, not no factories.]

We cannot go back to, neither should we want to put our faith in, either the ideology or the politics, economics or technology of neolithic times (though we can, perhaps, learn something from all of these). On the contrary, we require all of the resources of contemporary knowledge and technology to begin to solve contemporary problems of pollution, environmental degradation, poverty, inequality and exploitation.

Of course, more sophisticated thinkers have tried to resurrect the Goddess in a radically new form, grounded in modern science rather than ancient mythology. James Lovelock, in particular, has become well-known for his so-called Gaia hypothesis – in which the whole planet is seen as a single, metabolising, self-regulating, living organism. As he says, "the Gaia hypothesis was first described in terms of life shaping the environment, rather than the other way round. Life, or the biosphere, regulates or maintains the climate and the atmospheric composition at an optimum for itself" (LOVELOCK 1991, p. 25).

"As understanding of Gaia grew, however, we realised that it was not life or the biosphere that did the regulating, but the whole system. We now have Gaia theory, which sees the evolution of organisms as so closely coupled with the evolution of their physical and chemical environment that together they constitute a single evolutionary process, which is self-regulating. Thus the climate, the composition of the rocks, the air, and the oceans are not just given by geology; they are also the consequences of life" (ibid.).

He further clarifies,

"Through the ceaseless activity of living organisms, conditions on the planet have been kept favourable for life's occupancy for the past 3.6 billion years (e.g. temperatures have remained relatively constant despite an increase in solar output by 25% and the level of oxygen has remained constant for hundreds of millions of years despite its highly reactive character). Any species that adversely affects the environment, making it less favourable for its progeny, will ultimately be cast out, just as surely as will those weaker members of a species who fail to pass the evolutionary fitness test" (ibid.).

This idea has generated intense debate. Biologists Doolittle and Dawkins, e.g., have argued that there is no way that the diverse living organisms of the earth could act in symbiosis (to their mutual advantage) to regulate the planetary environment (ibid., p. 62). And it is difficult to see why the 'offending' species should be singled out for extinction – while others survive – in the manner suggested by Lovelock.

The issue is by no means resolved. Certainly Lovelock has produced a spirited defence of the idea that living organisms could have played a central role in maintaining an earthly environment appropriate to life for millions of years. In particular, he has constructed some suggestive models of major feedback processes operating over very long times scales, both to maintain and to introduce qualitative change in the earthly environment, and some quite specific predictions about such feedbacks currently in operation which has been substantially confirmed by subsequent empirical observation (e.g. predictions relating to the transfer of dimethyl sulphide and methyl iodide from the oceans to land surfaces, as part of a crucial rainfall regulating mechanism).

Some such feedbacks have, of course, been recognised as of absolutely crucial significance long before the Gaia hypothesis. As Lovelock points out, photosynthesisers use the energy of sunlight to fix carbon dioxide and water to make sugar and release oxygen to the air. By removing carbon dioxide from the atmosphere they tend to cool the planet by removing some of its greenhouse effect. Consumers gain energy by reacting oxygen and organic matter made by the photosynthesisers. Some of this organic matter escapes oxidation and sinks into the sediments of the soil where fermenters digest it and convert it to carbon dioxide and methane. And a small residue of indigestible organic matter always escapes and is buries in the earths crust. "This burial of a small amount of carbon made by the photosynthesisers is what sustains the oxygen in the air."

Clearly there are many other such complex feedbacks in operation. So that what is really at stake is the nature and degree of interdependence between them in maintaining a stable earthly environment, rather than the existence of such mechanisms. Lovelock implies a very high degree of interdependence with living systems involved at all levels. Others deny such interdependence and play down the role of living systems.

However, either way, these considerations have no real relevance to the idea of faith in the Mother Goddess. Even if Lovelock is entirely correct, 'personification' of the earth as Mother Goddess remains wholly inappropriate, and 'faith' in such a goddess wholly misguided. In no way will the regulatory systems in question respond to 'good will' or 'sacrifice' or 'prayer'. On the other hand, Lovelock is quite explicit in recognising that 'real' human actions could radically disrupt such natural processes. As he says in respect of the greenhouse effect, e.g., "with Gaia present the system might react to oppose heating and sustain the current temperatures... But even if such a system response does occur, it may be temporary. As more greenhouse gases are added to the air, and more damage is done by farming to natural ecosystems, eventually the system could well become overloaded and fail" (ibid., p. 168).

Rather than a God, we are here simply concerned with a highly complex natural system. And to reverse or slow down the destructive effects of pollution requires an appropriate – scientific – understanding of the system in question, and appropriate technology based upon such understanding. Rather than a new religion, Lovelock urges e.g. adoption of new means of electrical power generation. As he says,

> "Fossil fuel burning power stations are amongst the principal atmospheric sources of CO_2, SO_2 and nitrogen oxides. They are at best only forty percent efficient and waste the rest of the energy of the fuel... in cooling towers. There is no reason on scientific and engineering grounds why coal should not be burned so that most of the energy is made usefully available, and so that the pollutant emissions are gathered and either used profitably or stored where they will do no harm. Pilot plants in which coal can be converted to hydrogen and CO_2 already exist. In these plants, the hydrogen could be the fuel of gas turbine power stations, and the CO_2 could be collected and disposed of underground or in the ocean" (ibid., pp. 180-1).

It is true that Lovelock has encouraged a certain amount of anti-humanist, 'deep-ecological' earth worship by comparing humans to 'pathogenic microorganisms or tumour cells' disrupting the 'normal' metabolism of the Gaia organism. And on occasions he treats human history as only a brief and insignificant moment in the life history of this super-creature.

However, the fact remains that there is nothing in this model of a self-regulating ecosphere that implies any such anti-humanist scheme of values. And it provides no support for religious faith of any kind – whether in the good and loving earth mother, who nurtures her human infants, or a bad one who shakes them off without a second thought.

Part Three
OTHER CANDIDATES

The Mother Goddess, and the self-regulation of the ecosphere, are by no means the only candidates for divine intervention to save the world from environmental catastrophe. In recent years vast resources have been put into promoting major transnational corporations as such benign, super-human saviours.

Since the 70's, one transnational conglomerate after another has embarked upon extensive publicity campaigns of self-promotion as the environmentally enlightened visionaries of the business world. And in the Business Council for Sustainable Development they have worked together to lobby national and international government bodies, conferences and regulatory authorities in pursuit of the freedom to develop their own policies of responsible environmental action. Amongst the six hundred or so transnational corporations belonging to the BCSD, which between them account for a third of global GDP and seventy per cent of world trade, are such pioneers of sustainable development as Du Pont, Unilever, Shell and Rio Tinto Zinc.

The extensive advertising campaigns instituted by these corporations aim to convince the world that they are, indeed, deeply committed to maintaining or restoring the environmental health of the earth; that we have nothing to worry about if we simply put our faith in them to do the right thing. At the same time, they rush to our supermarket shelves new 'green' products (or at least re-package old ones in such a way as to make us better informed about their green credentials) so as to provide consumers with the opportunity to do the right thing too.

Certainly such corporations seem well ahead of the earth goddess as candidates for our 'faith' and our 'allegiance'. Unlike the Earth Goddess, they do actually exist in reality, rather than in wish-fulfilling fantasy, and they can indeed command super-human resources and powers, capable of re-shaping the world. Indeed, such corporations dominate the 'commanding heights' of the world capitalist economy – particularly in the most technologically advanced sectors – in a number of cases, rivalling medium sized nation states in their economic power.

However, there are good grounds for arguing that they actually do not exist in anything like the form presented by their propaganda. They are very far from being benign deities. And as far as ecological responsibility is concerned, 'faith' in the transnationals is just as misplaced as faith in the Mother Goddess.

Such corporations are, in fact, highly stratified business operations, ultimately under the control of relatively small groups of – all too human – managers and directors, who have effective power over major investment decisions. Such decisions are themselves ultimately dictated by considerations of (short or medium term) profitability and success in a competitive (world) market – rather than by considerations of human needs or well being, or of the long term health of the environment. As long as competitive market forces rule, things could be no different. Companies that take the 'longer' view or the more 'responsible' view could simply not survive in the competitive struggle with quick profit (and power) seekers.

It is true that transnational corporations do have clear advantages over their single nation competitors when it comes to price fixing. Where the same organisation is both buyer and seller of particular commodities, with branches in different countries, it is possible to shift profits to where taxes are lowest, by over-invoicing imports or under invoicing exports from high tax countries, and inflate costs where they sell on a costs plus fixed profit basis to governments. They can make profits from currency fluctuations, avoid exchange controls, circumvent tariffs and ease repatriation of profits.

They also get the benefits of monopoly pricing agreements in particular territories, arranging amongst themselves to avoid price competition and sell at a fixed optimum price (determined by market research) competing instead through advertising and pro-ductivity gains. This typically allows for a higher rate of profit in the monopolised sector – at the expense of the non-monopoly sector.

But all of these operations still remain 'market driven' to the extent that they are motivated by the very attempt to escape the 'normal' constraints of the market (with equalisation of profit rates). Nor do they involve any final transcendence of market competition; no monopolies are absolute, with greater super-profits attracting others to challenge them; pricing agreements are temporary and dependent upon a balance of economic power; and competition continues on a world scale.

Future success is still dependent upon present profits; it is profits which determine the scope of action available to a corpora-tion to pursue such transnational expansion and price-fixing. And it is therefore a vain hope that such operations could somehow come to serve 'higher' environmental goals, rather than further profit maximisation.

One of the major motivations for initially nationally based com-panies to enter into transnational operations has been and remains the desire to escape from any sort of effective regulation by nation states – including legal pollution control measures and taxation which could provide nation states with the resources to clean-up the local environment.

With nation states access to world resources increasingly depen-dent upon investment by transnationals, and transnationals ability to shift such investments around on a world scale, such corporations are in a position to force nation states to exempt them from such control and such taxation – through the threat of moving 'offshore' to territories with more 'liberal' business regimes (instead they demand direct and indirect subsidies, including appropriate infrastructure etc.).

And, of course, access to such 'liberal' business regimes – often in less developed areas of the world, is itself another major motivation for going transnational in the first place. For clearly, businesses can get away with much reduced labour – and other – costs in territories with very high levels of unemployment (often created by forcing traditional producers off the land in favour of agribusiness monocultures), with little history of trade unionism, with police-military governments actively involved in suppression of workers rights and organisation. And the shift of investment away from previously 'developed' areas, in turn, increases unemployment, weakens unions and reduces wage-costs there also.

Low wages and lack of political rights hardly puts the workers in a position to 'insist' upon environmental responsibility in their working and living conditions and consumption patterns. And, indeed, even the best paid consumers exercise very little real control over production. Power over such matters lies much higher up in society – with those who really control production – including the managers and directors of the transnationals. And profitability still remains the ultimate consideration in deciding just what 'choices' the consumers are actually to be offered.

At the United Nations Conference on Environment and Development – the Earth Summit – in June 1992, the transnationals (via the BCSD) lobbied vigorously and effectively to ensure that they were absolved from any general legal responsibility for environmental degradation in exchange for a promise of self-regulation. They ensured also that the conferences non-binding 'action plan' for sustainable development had no bearing upon the crucially important GATT, that, in other words, there should be absolutely no environmental restrictions upon 'free' world trade.

The past behaviour of the transnationals and big corporations generally gives little ground for faith in any such self-regulation. On the contrary, far from being pioneers in ecological responsibility, it is the transnationals themselves that are most directly to blame for producing the current crisis in the first place. And their actions continue to exacerbate – rather than improve – the situation.

Du Pont, e.g., one corporation currently most actively involved in self-promotion as environmental saviour, has been described as the company most directly responsible for the hole in the ozone layer.

> "If Du Pont is a pioneer, it is in the development and production of CFCs. Since the company first marketed them in 1931, it has enjoyed a near monopoly of the trade in many of the compounds used in aerosol sprays, insulating foams, cleaning agents, chillers and automobile air conditioners, controlling as much as a quarter of the global market... When the impact of these compounds on ozone depletion was first revealed in 1974, the company vigorously fought a US ban on aerosol sprays and argued for non-regulation of the industry. In the 1980's Reagan's anti-regulatory policies removed any incentive to research into alternatives and Du Pont instead expanded its CFC production facilities in Japan in response to increased demand for non-aerosol products. The company's decision" – in 1988 – "to shift to CFC like substitutes (HCFCs and HFCs, which will themselves continue to contribute to global warming and ozone degradation, if at lower levels) [was] a strategic move to ensure its monopoly of a new market in advance of its competitors. Part of its strategy (was) to buy time for itself, convincing the Bush administration that its products (were) the only viable alternatives to CFCs and ensuring that the 190 Clean Air Act amendments postponed the phasing out of HCFCs and HFCs to the year 2040" (TREECE 1993, p. 70).

Du Pont certainly seems to one of the worst, with a notorious record of falsifying information concerning its toxic emissions and failing to uphold safety standards. US government statistics identify it as the single largest corporate polluter in the country, with total reported pollution fourteen times that of Dow Chemicals, and thirty times that of Mobil Oil. But similar stories could be told about virtually all of the major transnationals.

And in face of this sort of reality – of a world production system dominated by such amoral and unscrupulous monsters it is probably not surprising that New Agers and others should retreat into a fantasy of a benign Earth Mother Goddess and local self-sufficiency; or even the massive denial that turns the transnationals themselves into benign saviours (as their managers take up tai chi etc.). However, for most people, particularly in the 'newly industrialising areas', the facts of massive exploitation and environmental destruction by such corporations are all too real and obvious.

So if the Mother Goddess is not going to save us from the transnationals (and the nationals for that matter) – and they are not going to save us from the consequences of their own actions – where do we turn? The usual answer (provided by the media, politicians etc.), is to the nation state – or its leaders – and to those super-national organs of collective state power like the United Nations, the International Monetary Fund, and the World Bank, etc.

Surely they have the power to repair the damage and issue in a new and ecologically responsible era of sustainable technology? Is it not, after all, only such global collaboration of political authorities that is capable of solving what are clearly global environmental problems, as most authorities would agree? Here again, we are urged to 'have faith' in our elected representatives, and others not so elected, to do what has to be done to regulate and control the greedy and unscrupulous corporations – in the 'public interest'.

Unfortunately, there is once again little evidence for believing that salvation lies in this quarter either. As noted earlier, the very forces that give the transnationals their unique powers simultaneously undermine the power of nation states to regulate and control them and reduce the resources available to such nation states to 'clean up' their territories and the world. And, given the power that such corporations have to influence the membership and actions of governments and civil service authorities, we should not normally expect very much serious opposition to them from such authorities anyway.

In practice, this expectation is strongly born out by the relevant empirical data. Considering the example of the United States government, as the economically and militarily most powerful state structure in the world today, we note, e.g., the US presidents reluctance even to attend the Earth Summit in 1992 – seen by many as the last opportunity to embark upon a commonly agreed global program of 'sustainable development'. We note also his refusal to sign key, binding agreements in biodiversity protection and atmospheric emissions involving significant financial commitments and compliance with specific timescales.

While the world's scientific community called for a sixty per cent reduction in atmospheric emissions of green house gases immediately, the most that was agreed at the conference was an open-ended, non-legally binding statement of 'intent' to hold emissions to 1990 levels. The US representative – whose industries are responsible for twenty-five per cent of the relevant world emissions, managed to delete the specific target date of 2000 from the treaty, previously agreed by 110 countries.

A biodiversity agreement aimed at protecting the worlds stocks of plant and animal species was similarly undermined by the US's refusal to sign or commit significant resources to aiding developing countries in the task. If, as a result, current rates of tropical deforestation continue, some fifteen to twenty per cent of the worlds estimated 3.5 to 10 million plant and animal species may become extinct by the year 2000, though they have tremendous future potential as renewable sources of energy, industrial products, medications, genetic inputs to agriculture and applied biological research, if they are not exterminated first. Such destruction

"will gravely jeopardise our capacity to meet future global needs for the diversification and substitution of food crops, given that ninety percent of the world's current food production is dependent

upon just sixteen of the potentially 80,000 edible plant species, all
(the rest) of which are located in the tropics. At the same time, a
wealth of medicinal resources and expertise, much of it accumulated by the forests indigenous inhabitants will be sacrificed and
with it the potential to control diseases such as Aids and various
forms of cancer" (ibid.).

Nor does the destruction of the forests provide any useful agricultural land in the longer term. As Lovelock points out,

"the wet and cloudy tropics are not a given state of the Earth.
The trees themselves keep things this way, by evapotranspiring
huge volumes of water through their leaves. The rising vapour
condenses to form clouds, the rain falls, the trees grow, and their
roots bind the shallow soil and leaf litter, where nutrients are
rapidly recycled by bacteria".

[At the same time] "through their capacity to evaporate vast
volumes of water vapour, trees serve to keep the ecosystems of
the humid tropics and the planet cool by providing a sunshade of
white reflecting clouds".

"Take away the trees, and the rain will cease. Trees and rain go
together; without one there cannot be the other. Without rain, the
soil will begin to die, too, as the bacterial ecosystems that sustain it
are exposed to harsh conditions and erosion. The forest will not
return – and the land will turn to scrub or desert" (LOVELOCK 1991,
p. 157).

On the basis of a number of computer models of environmental regulation by living systems, Lovelock argues that biodiversity is
actually integral to the stability of the complex feedback processes
that maintain conditions suitable for life on earth.
Furthermore,

"The rate of forest clearance is now so great that if it continues, by the year 2000, sixty-five percent of the forests will have

gone. Numerical models based on Gaia theory... predict that once more than this proportion of a self-regulating ecosystem dies, then it can no longer sustain its climate and total collapse takes place" (op. cit., p. 158).

Lovelock suggests that

"If we delay our decision to stop felling the trees until seventy percent are gone it might be too late; the rest would die anyway. It we let deforestation continue we may soon reach the day when at least a billion people are living in these once forested regions but in a hostile climate, hot and arid If it should happen, we shall be faced with the problems of the South Saharan drought multiplied a hundredfold" (op. cit., p. 158).

The only significant decision to emerge from the UN conference actually served to strengthen the ability of institutions already dominated by the more advanced economies – such as the World Bank – to dictate the priorities of development within the societies of the third world. And all the indications are that these priorities involve sacrificing the interests of the world's dispossessed majority to the destructive dynamic of global capital accumulation and market competition.

Certainly they involve continued pillaging of the raw materials of the third world in the interests of profit and debt servicing – with monocultures, cash cropping, open cast mining, deforestation etc. As Ticknell and Hildyard point out,

"By designating the atmosphere and biodiversity as 'global commons' the (Global Environment Facility scheme – devised by the major economic powers) implicitly suggests that everyone has a right to access and that local people have no more claim to them than a corporation based on the other side of the globe. Pressing problems with a direct impact on local peoples – desertification, toxic waste pollution, landlessness, pesticide pollution and the like, all of which occur throughout the globe and could therefore be judged as being of 'global concern' – are pushed to one side whilst the local environment is sized up for its potential benefit to the North and its allies in the South" (TICKNELL AND HILDYARD 1992, p. 823).

But this does not mean that those third world state powers that seek to expand their national economies beyond such dependent status are necessarily environmental saviours – struggling for ecological responsibility and sustainable growth. On the contrary, throughout the third world, local ruling capitalist classes push through ruthless programs of 'modernisation' that are conspicuous in their massive disregard for environmental considerations and values.

As Treece points out, the last quarter century has seen the emergence of new centres of capitalist production, in particular in Mexico, Brazil, South Korea, Taiwan and Indonesia – as well as in Hong Kong and Singapore,

> "which have rendered the term 'Third World' obsolete as a description of the major economies of Latin America and South East Asia. Like others before them in the post war period, such as India, these newly industrialising countries managed, through massive state intervention, to raise their export of manufactured goods above that of raw materials, often involving regional, sub-imperialist spheres of influence in the process" (TREECE 1993, p. 74).

These development strategies have frequently involved the "incorporation of the most remote rural regions and their populations into the national market structure and into the process of industrialisation", typically with extreme brutality and massive social and environmental disruption. Indigenous cultures – integrated with local ecosystems through centuries of adaption – are destroyed overnight, their members murdered, forced to work as semi-slave labour in appalling conditions, or reduced to begging on the outskirts of the new industrial areas.

But as Marx and Engels argued, the very process of industrial expansion generally also expands the one force really capable of qualitative and progressive social change – the industrial proletariat or working class. Previously isolated politically and economically undeveloped populations are increasingly brought together in large-scale industrial operations in ways which ultimately promote the development of socialist ideologies and socialist political struggles.

Clearly there are massive obstacles to be overcome, obstacles of political and economic intimidation, unemployment and demora-lisation produced by appalling working and living conditions. There are the distractions of religion, drugs and 'entertainment'. But capi-talist industrialisation has its own dynamic towards increasing education, solidarity and power on the part of the workforce. The power to produce the necessities of life – and wealth – is also the power to bring such production to a halt and ultimately to take democratic control of the production process and of social life in general, including the vital process of restoring the environmental health of the planet.

CHAPTER SIX
CLASS, STATE AND RELIGION

Part One
MATERIALISM AND POLITICS

Historical materialist social science distinguishes three essential dimensions or functional requirements of any human society. First of all there is the material dimension or function; the provision of appropriate relations or institutions for the production and distribution of material goods – including necessary food, clothing and shelter, and the tools and machines necessary for producing and distributing such material goods. People are material beings and their material needs have to be satisfied on a regular – ongoing – basis if they, and society, are going to continue to exist. And the institutions and practises through which such needs are satisfied are identified as the material base of society.

Secondly there is the ideological dimension or function – the provision of appropriate relations or institutions for the production and distribution of beliefs and values; of particular systems of philosophical, religious, moral, political, legal ideas or 'world-views'. For people do not live by bread alone – they also need to be able to make some sense of their lives in a broader context of history, cosmology, destiny – to find some deeper meaning for human existence. These institutions and practices are a major component of the superstructure of society.

But in addition to these two functions there is another – of vital importance to the successful operation of the other two – particularly in times of unforeseen emergency. This is the political function, concerned with organising and integrating the operations of society as a whole.

When we think about politics in the modern world we probably think of a whole constellation of specialised parliamentary, judicial, bureaucratic, managerial, police-military structures which go to make up the modern state. But the state is actually a very recent development, absent for most of human history or pre-history. The sorts of tribal societies we have examined hitherto are essentially stateless societies, lacking all – or most – such specialised institutions and practices. But though they lacked apparatuses of state this does not mean that they lacked all political integration or government. On the contrary, it was still necessary for the operation of the community to be organised as a whole; for the activities of all members to be co-ordinated and integrated in the struggle against natural forces, the defence of the community against hostile neighbours or raiders, the adjudication of disputes and the punishment – or control – of miscreants.

There would always be unforeseen economic emergencies – such as fire or flood – requiring decision and concerted action. So would there inevitably be internal disputes and antisocial actions requiring swift response in order to maintain social stability. And virtually all tribal societies appear to have been involved in warfare at some stage, fighting over resources or other issues.

The majority of these functions are distinguished by the necessity of application of some kind of coercive constraint or compulsion as ultimate sanction for the maintenance of social order and harmony. And in the Marxian scheme this is a central defining feature of the political dimension of social life; the conscious, overt and immediate use of forcible coercion in order to enforce particular 'norms' or 'rules' or 'laws' of social integration.

Coercion in this sense is distinguishable from the coercion of natural laws and forces – of wind and rain, flood and drought, – 'forcing' humans to take shelter, to migrate etc. It is distinguishable from the 'moral' coercion of the social super-ego – functioning 'automatically' within the psyche to mobilise guilt and self-hatred in the service of particular norms and values. So is it distinguishable from the power of tradition and public opinion, or of the social 'ego-ideal' – similarly 'shaping' human behaviour largely independent of any conscious decision to do so.

Hal Draper identifies all of the latter forms of coercion as 'blind' coercion; "the characteristic of blind coercion is that the individual 'wants' to do what he has to do. The characteristic of outside coercion [or political coercion] is that the individual acts as he is supposed to act under threat of force, expressed or implied" (DRAPER 1977, p. 241).

Blind coercion in this sense plays an important part in the life of all tribal societies. In this connection Draper quotes Southall to the effect that, "in stateless societies every man grows up with a practical and intuitive sense of his responsibility to maintain constantly throughout his life that part of the fabric of society in which at any time he is involved..." (ibid., p. 238).

The small scale and low level of technological development of such societies render such 'moral' constraint both possible and necessary – because of the crucial mutual day-to-day dependence of all members of the group and because of the delicate ecological balance that must be maintained between society and nature if the former is to survive. As we have seen, in such societies it is kinship that provides the framework of reciprocal responsibilities and obligations in terms of which life is organised. "The lack of specialised roles and the resulting multiplex quality of social networks means that neither economic nor political ends can be exclusively pursued by anyone to the detriment of society, because those ends are intertwined with each other and further channelled by ritual and controlled by the beliefs which ritual expresses." (op. cit.)

This does not mean that it was never necessary to make conscious – collective – decisions about future policy and the specifically political application of coercive force. But it does mean that the agency of such decision – and such action – was likely to be a council or public meeting of all adult members of the community striving to achieve consensus through free discussion and debate.

As Engels says, "in primitive times, the whole public authority in time of peace was exclusively judicial and vested in the popular assembly" (quoted in DRAPER 1977, p. 243). And where such assemblies saw it necessary to impose coercive sanctions it was the whole – armed – community that was the agency for enforcing such decision – typically in the form of ostracism or banishment of the serious wrongdoer. Similarly, all would participate in communal defence against hostile aliens and the adjudication of disputes. Thus, political power in this sense was exercised by the whole group against those who challenged the interests of the whole group.

In materialist terms, such collective control of political power directly reflects collective control of major productive resources in tribal society. Because there is no minority monopoly of such resources, neither can there be any such monopoly of political power.

But things change drastically with the emergence of class divisions within the economic base of society. As Draper says, "the organising authority which regulates the common affairs of the social group can now function no longer as an arm of the community as a whole, for the interests of the new classes are irreconcilable" (ibid., p. 244). With the division of society into a class of rulers, who control the major productive forces (the land and its resources), and a class of ruled who are forced to labour to generate a surplus for those rulers – there is always the possibility of rebellion by the exploited groups. This necessitates the creation of specialised institutions of coercive control available to the rulers (police forces, pris-

ons, torture chambers etc.) to keep the dispossessed in their place –
through threat or practice of physical violence.

The simplest case of class formation imaginable here would be
conquest of a substantial population of settled agricultural tribespeople – perhaps occupying neolithic villages or towns over a large
area, by a much smaller tribal population, perhaps a group of –
highly mobile – nomadic pastoralists, in possession of some superior
military innovation (horses, chariots, bronze weapons, guns etc.).
Here, indeed, we are reminded of earlier comments concerning migration and conquest by Indo-European speaking tribes travelling
down from Southern Russia, and of the Spartans of the classical
period. Such military superiority would enable this much smaller
population to establish itself as a ruling class – appropriating surplus
produced by the much larger subject population (there probably
would not – initially – be surplus sufficient to sustain a larger population of non-labouring conquerors without substantial intensification of production). But continued appropriation could well depend
upon constant mobilisation of the rulers as an armed force, super-
vising and directing the labour of the majority.

Here direct coercion remains integral to the economic base of
society. But the more such direct coercion is removed from the base
and concentrated within specialised institutions of the superstructure, the closer we approach to the origin of the state. As Draper
says, "the state is the institutionalised instrument of direct coercion,
and of forcible coercion as necessary, even though it too utilises less
direct forms of coercion as much as possible" (ibid., p. 242).

There are other, perhaps more likely, ways in which class and
state forms can emerge. Marx and Engels are particularly interested
in a process which we might call 'transformation of a (useful) social
function'. The key idea here is the emergence of the state out of a
division of labour in a society. As Engels says, even in primitive –
tribal – communities "there were from the beginning certain common interests the safeguarding of which had to be handed over to
certain individuals [*albeit*, originally] under the control of the community as a whole" (ibid., p. 246).

In this case, perhaps the obvious example would be the appointment of a temporary 'war chief' to organise the defence of the community from external raiders or invaders of the kind considered in the previous example. Perhaps one village of a tribal group is then developed as a military training camp and garrison – a base for a specialised (full-time) military force organised by the new war chief.

Another sort of case, of particular interest to Marx and Engels, is the appointment of a 'water control officer' to organise large scale irrigation projects for the community as a whole. For in dry and desert environments such projects can acquire particular importance as the community becomes more and more dependent upon the proper working of increasingly elaborate systems of dams, sluices and canals. And with such increasing dependence goes increasing power for the person 'in control'.

Such a water control officer could be seen as a special case of what today is sometimes called the 'big-man intensifier' – the individual (in a tribal society) who takes the lead in mobilising their close kin – and others – in projects of productive intensification which increase their prestige in the shorter term and in the longer term allow or encourage expansion of population. Such population expansion, in turn, creates increasing dependence upon, and further encouragement to, such intensificatory activities (especially where they involve increasing regional specialisation – and a corresponding reduction of regional self-sufficiency). And, of course, we can see how such intensification and such population expansion could become tied in with the organisation of specialised military defensive programs of the kind considered above (more population means more soldiers, more surplus means more resources for warfare etc.).

Here, modern anthropology identifies a particular form of social organisation intermediate between tribe and state known as a 'chiefdom'. A chiefdom is a form of social organisation still essentially based upon kinship and collective property, but with different kinship groups now 'ranked' – and perhaps fulfilling particular functionally specialised tasks – within a hierarchical system under the domination of a hereditary chief. Although resources are still collectively owned, groups higher in the hierarchy now have more power over such resources and privileged access to their fruits.

The crucial point of these developments for the generation of class and state structures is their relation to control of social surplus. For at some point, control of surplus for use in the common interest can turn into control of surplus to sustain a specialised police-military force which can be used against the rest of the community. Such a 'Praetorian guard' can be used to enforce further surplus appropriation to sustain an increasingly privileged lifestyle for their masters and for themselves, further and further removed from that of the rest of the population.

In the cases just considered, the formation of class inequality and the formation of the state are one and the same process, with the state power of chiefs, kings, high priests and military leaders, as effective owners and controllers of the land and its resources, while the rest of the population are increasingly reduced to peasant serfs working long hours for bare subsistence and delivering their surplus product to the state as tax or forced labour.

But the principle is the same as in the case where class formation precedes such state formation. The state is still the institution, "or complex of institutions, which bases itself on the availability of forcible coercion by special agencies of society in order to maintain the domination of a ruling class, preserve existing property relations from basic change, and keep all other classes in subjection" (ibid., p. 251).

The state exercises power over a particular territory, maintaining borders, determining the movement of people, goods and ideas in and out of the territory. In particular, it defends such a territory against foreign invasion and prevents the subject population escaping to other lands. Territory in this sense replaces kinship in tribal society as the foundation of social organisation. Indeed, the growth of state power inevitably dissolves the wider kinship bonds and responsibilities of tribal society, as specialised institutions of state power increasingly usurp the former – military, religious, adjudicative – functions of kinship.

The state levies taxes on those living within its territories – often on the basis of land use; people (or family units) pay rents or dues for the continued privilege of subsistence farming – in proportion to the amount of land they work. And, of course, states are soon also into the business of creating or borrowing money to finance their expanding operations.

An increasing amount of the funds collected as taxes go towards supporting an expanding bureaucracy; – a new organisation of individuals superimposed upon a tribal, familial or other 'customary' sort of organisation amongst the primary producers, and specifically devoted to taking over the mental side of work, so as to leave only the manual or material side of labour for those below them.

As political philosopher John Burnheim points out, a bureaucracy is a permanent organisation of professional officials directed by a central authority, governed by specific operational procedures and a hierarchical chain of command, to ensure implementation of policy from the top. The officials are generally full-timers, with specialised – mental – abilities and functions, centring upon literacy and numeracy, record keeping and information processing. (See BURNHEIM 1985, Ch. 2.)

It would seem that literacy and numeracy were first developed as accounting tools, to keep track of the increasingly vast wealth obtained by the rulers of the early states of Mesopotamia and Egypt as taxes or tribute. Secondarily they became tools of production, facilitating the increasingly vast and diverse construction projects instituted by the rulers for civil, religious and military purposes.

As Sohn Rethel says,

> "intellectual in separation from manual labour arose as a means of the appropriation of products of labour by non-labourers – not originally as an aid to production. It served the calculation of tributes, the accounting of credits and repayments in the relations

between the temple authorities or officials of the Pharaoh and their debtors, the storing and listing of appropriated products, the recording of the volume of incoming or outgoing supplies and other similar operations" (SOHN RETHEL 1978, p. 90).

Sohn Rethel goes on to describe the activities of the harpedonapts, stretchers of the rope in ancient Egypt. Assigned in pairs to high officials of the pharaoh, such experts took measurements for the building of temples and pyramids, the laying down and paving of dams, the construction of granaries and the measurement of their volume. But most important, they were employed in parcelling out the soil as it re-emerged from the yearly floods of the Nile. "This partition of the soil was done for the purpose of re-assessing the peasants tributes for the coming year" (ibid., p. 91).

Bureaucracies have achieved great things. They have presided over incredible productivity increases to support very substantial populations and have supervised incredible feats of architecture, art and town planning, including the construction of the pyramids of Egypt and Mexico. And stable bureaucratic structures have been integral to particular state forms (in Egypt and China e.g.) which have persisted, essentially unchanged for thousands of years. As Burnheim points out, their operation on the basis of established rules makes them predictable and reliable, without arbitrary decisions. Their hierarchical and professional structure allows general policy to be translated into specific directives by experts. The hierarchy allows for permanent monitoring of policy and action and masses of information from the base can be centralised for policy review. Large size allows for economies of scale and concentration of resources for large scale projects and for accumulation and cross-referencing of information.

The problem is, of course, that they have traditionally served ruling tyrannies or oligarchies, enforcing the will of absolute monarchs, or of the elite groups of church and state. As Burnheim says, they are major obstacles to creative thought and action, to innovation, progress and efficiency. Diversity, experimentation and flexibility are sacrificed to uniformity and avoidance of risk and predictability. (BURNHEIM 1985, pp. 52-4.)

A limited and entrenched repertoire of rules and roles means inflexibility of thought and action. The long chain of command can distort the flow of information – through bias, short-sightedness, vested interests, and inertia at every level. It can inhibit novel understanding of problems, novel choices or novel actions and it can create problems for monitoring performance effectively. Bureaucracies tend to reduce everything to quantitative rather than qualitative considerations – with quality suffering accordingly, With each office at each level of the hierarchy generally engaged in routine work, there is a tendency for each to pursue operational self-sufficiency. This leads to wasted resources, reduplication of services, hoarding of resources, local empire building and lack of accountability.

At the same time, they are insatiable in their demands for taxation to support their expanded operations. As bureaucracies expand, taking over more and more of what used to be communal or individual processes of decision making and initiative, ordinary people feel increasingly helpless and alienated. "Bureaucratic regulation homogenises and atomises social relationships." (op. cit.) Bureaucratic organisation becomes a major block to creative work and thought – both within the bureaucracy itself and outside it. Tasks simplified, subdivided, broken down into mechanical steps and procedures become boring, repetitive and ultimately meaningless.

The state, including the bureaucracy, organises the provision of infrastructures (roads, docks, bridges, dams etc.) sanitation and welfare – perhaps opening state granaries to the public in times of famine. It also regulates trade with other states, the search for raw materials in other territories, and generally seeks to advance the interests of its own ruling class against those of other such states.

It continues to organise communal defence and 'enforce' laws and norms within its territories. With the expansion of the ruling class it becomes increasingly important to find ways to deal with developing antagonisms amongst individuals and groups within that class. Thus we see the provision of special parliaments and courts to allow for the articulation and integration of competing ideas and interests and resolve disputes with minimum disturbance to the system as a whole.

All of these tasks remain subordinated to the crucial requirement of continued military suppression of the subject classes – representing the ruling class as a whole in confrontation with the whole of the (more or less organised) working class. And, as Draper points out, state officials "will conspire with the national enemy if [their] own working class threatens [their] rear" (DRAPER 1977, p. 259).

Part Two

STATE, IDEOLOGY AND RELIGION

However, there are obvious problems in relying upon the continuous threat of violence to maintain social order. Forcing people to work at the point of a spear or gun is likely to add significantly to the resentment they feel towards a system that exploits and controls them. It is costly and dangerous and relies very heavily upon the continued loyalty of the guards – quite possibly recruited from amongst the working class themselves. Much better to find other means of keeping the workers under control, with forcible coercion by specialised police-military personnel kept as a technique of last resort, when all else fails. And here, of course, from the time of their first appearance, state powers have employed a variety of other techniques to ensure the compliance of the subject population. They have, e.g., created and encouraged specific racial, tribal or caste divisions through privileging certain groups – as officials in the lower reaches of the state hierarchy, as privileged suppliers of goods etc. – to the detriment of others. Thus they have divided the subject population against itself and thereby deflected hostility away from the ruling state and economic power.

So too have they sought to co-opt potentially dangerous elements of the subject classes – buying their loyalty or integrating them as new members of the ruling elite. Marx speaks of this as an index of the continued strength and viability of ruling class power, and this can clearly be a source of new ideas and new initiatives.

But the most important substitute for violence or the threat of violence as a means of social control is ideology. To the extent that the state controls the flow of information within its territories it is able to systematically falsify and distort the facts of its own oppressive domination and close off possible avenues of dissent – in thought and in action. It can, e.g., present a picture of chaos and horror beyond its boundaries, from which only state power protects its own citizens. All episodes of rebellion, of initiatives by the working population, of breakdown of social order and mass misery under the present regime can simply be written out of the history books. In their place are put harmony, order, progress, stability and happiness – orchestrated by that regime.

Throughout the whole history of the state, the most important alternative to direct coercion has always been religious belief and religious ritual, organised and perpetuated by specialised institutions of state. From the beginning, secular and sacred authorities, chiefs and shamans, kings and priests, have worked closely together to try to control the thoughts and feelings of the working population through ideas of gods and demons, ghosts and spirits, heavens and hells. As Engels says, "now, if ever, the people must be kept in order by moral means, and the first and foremost of all moral means of action upon the masses is and remains – religion" (quoted in DRAPER 1977, p. 264).

It clearly helps if the big-man intensifier in a tribal society also has supernatural powers or gains the support of the local shaman. As we have seen, shamanism is the first – specialised – profession amongst hunter-gatherers, and frequently the shamans special access to supernatural forces is as much a source of fear as of reassurance amongst their fellow tribespeople. We saw also how, in some hunting gathering societies, shamans would function as judge and jury, identifying wrongdoers – rule breakers – and imposing punishments of various kinds. And the first (institutionalised, hereditary) chiefs typically worked hand in glove with shamans, medicine men or witches in maintaining and extending their power over the rest of the community. (See e.g., P. RADIN 1957, Ch. 3.)

In most – perhaps all – cases of pristine state formation, the temple is close to the core of the emerging state structure, with high priests as central agents of state power. As Roux says, in reference to the earliest known state forms, in ancient Mesopotamia,

> "the fact that the Sumerian society crystallised around temples and was first organised on a theocratic basis had deep and lasting consequences. In theory, e.g., the land never ceased to belong to the gods, and the mighty Assyrian monarchs whose empire stretched from the Nile to the Caspian Sea were the humble servants of the god Assur, just as the governors of [the early city state of] Lagash, who ruled over a few square miles of Sumer, were those of their god Ningirsu" (ROUX 1980, p. 90-1).

This, of course, created a nice illusion of equality in subservience to the gods which masked the increasingly radical differences of wealth and power amongst human groups on earth, and absolved the leaders of personal responsibility for exploitation and war insofar as they sought only to do as the gods required.

Its quite possible that the incipient priesthood had taken an active role in the ('intensificatory') hydraulic engineering projects necessary for rendering harsh deserty areas of Sumer fertile and capable of supporting substantial populations. So that here, real earthly knowledge and expertise could go hand in glove with ideas of direct access to divine forces whose aid was necessary in maintaining the fertility of the land. In such a context it perhaps made perfect sense that the gods should own the land.

Insofar as the land belonged to the gods – or most especially the particular 'city-god' of the particular temple city in question – it was to the gods that rents and tributes were payed by the working population. And, of course, the priests, as the gods representatives on earth, were the immediate recipients of such offerings, taking charge of their disposition as the gods saw fit.

It seems that in the early days,

> "the land owned by the community (in the guise of its god)
> was divided into three parts. Some of it, the kur land, was parcell-
> ed out to provide sustenance for the members of the community
> who cultivated it... Another part of the land – in one case e.g. one
> fourth of the total – was reserved for the god. This was called
> nigenna land, and its produce was stored in the temple... [while] a
> third type of temple land was rented out for cultivation by indivi-
> duals... All members of the community... were obliged to culti-
> vate [the negenna] land and to undertake corvee on the dikes and
> canals insuring its irrigation. ...Not only the produce of the fields,
> but implements, ritual equipment, and animals needed for sacri-
> fices or rations for the people were likewise temple property. Fur-
> thermore [specialised craftspersons] acknowledged the obligation
> to exercise their special skills in the service of the god" (FRANKFORT
> 1978, p. 222).

These early Mesopotamian states also set the pattern for things
to come in modelling the supernatural world directly upon the
earthly hierarchy of state power. As Roux points out,

> "the divine society was conceived as a replica of the human
> society of Sumer and organised accordingly. The heavens were
> populated with hundreds of supremely powerful manlike beings,
> and each of these gods was assigned to a particular task or a
> particular sphere of activity. One god e.g. had charge of the sky,
> another of the air, a third one of the sweet waters and so forth,
> down to the humble deities responsible for the plough, the brick,
> the flint or the pickaxe... the gods of Mesopotamia were not of
> equal status... [at the pinnacle of the hierarchy] were An, Enlil and
> Enki... they ruled the world through authority, force and wisdom
> as it should be ruled and formed the supreme triad responsible
> not only for the regular functioning of the cosmos but also... for its
> creation" (ROUX 1980, p. 95-6).

This divine triumvirate presumably corresponded to the earthly power of the (originally elected) king or lugal, high priest or sangu mah and governor of the city state or ensi. And it is easy to see how this close association between heaven and earth would lend support to this earthly authority, as the gods representation on earth.

In Egypt this process went a step further with the actual deification of the earthly king or queen. Here, the whole universe was conceived on the pattern of a monarchy. The first king of Egypt had also been first divine-king of the world – including the world of the dead. And this role was seen as handed on to his successors, the pharaohs.

Not only was the pharaoh themself accorded divinity in their lifetime, they were specifically identified as the earthly incarnation of the supreme god, Horus. As Frankfort says, "the throne was always occupied by Horus, son of Osiris – from another viewpoint, by the son of Re… Pharaoh… shared permanence with the divinely ordered universe and was truly superhuman" (FRANKFORT 1961, p. 88-9).

If the ordinary people could be persuaded to accept this sort of idea then it could clearly become a major foundation for the stability of the hierarchical state structure; how futile to challenge the power of a god, how dangerous to challenge a power that can judge and control you after death as well as during life. And, in this context, resources devoted to the creation of massive pyramids and temples and elaborate rituals and festivals were resources well spent insofar as they re-inforced this idea in the minds of ordinary people, of the superhuman powers of their rulers.

On a more mundane level, the Chinese state had the power to deify any appropriately law-abiding citizen after their death as a reward – for loyal service to the state, so that they could take their place within a divine – bureaucratic – hierarchy that mirrored that state hierarchy on earth. As Ahern points out, zealous soldiers, upright officials, or citizens who died defending their country, when thus deified, provided models "of obvious value for the state" (AHERN 1981, p. 79-80).

Ahern also highlights a range of other ways in which religious ritual and belief helped to bolster state power in China.

"When they performed rituals entreating the gods help in time of need [state officials showed] citizens that the state had the peoples welfare at heart" (ibid., p. 81). "Whereas involvement in a magistrates court would be assiduously avoided [by ordinary people] because of the enormous cost of customary fees at every step of the way, and the uncertainty of the outcome, a god could be asked for help or advice at little cost with nothing to lose; whereas the range of things officials would even consider dealing with was narrow (legal infringements, gross suffering as from a natural disaster) the gods would consider any request, concerning anything from a suitable mate for ones daughter to rain for ones crop" (ibid., p. 82).

Thus, the gods provided a useful safety valve, taking pressure off the state. Furthermore "by placing blame for misfortune on the gods, the government may have sought to strengthen its own legitimacy" (op. cit.). Finally, as Ahern says,

"one could argue that the religious system did not open the possibility of a more even distribution of power and resources; it posed no alternative to the allocation of power in the traditional class system. It never questioned whether powerful figures should sit in judgement over and dole out favours to ordinary people; it almost invarioubly saw the source of power over other people and valued resources emanating from a bureaucratic hierarchy modelled on the actual government. As Arthur Wolf has pointed out, when revolutionary movements did arise in China, they avoided the traditional gods, utilising instead the images of foreign traditions such as Buddhism and Christianity. In this sense the spiritual realm may have worked to the advantage of those who ruled; the world of spirits did not open the possibility of a radically different kind of world" (ibid., p. 83).

CHAPTER SEVEN
STATE AND RELIGION IN ANCIENT EGYPT

Part One
WATER CONTROL AND THE ORIGIN OF THE STATE

In the previous chapter we considered Marx and Engels's idea that a division of labour in respect of water control could have played a crucial role in the first formation of class and state power in certain dry and deserty regions of the ancient world. They seem to have had in mind particularly, China, Mesopotamia and Egypt amongst other places.

Certainly, if we focus upon the case of ancient Egypt, we can see that archeological evidence does indeed support the idea of a crucial 'hydraulic' dimension to class and state formation, with a general dependence upon collective hydraulic organisation serving to create and sustain the power, first of tribal big men and chiefs and later of kings and bureaucratic ruling class.

The demands of early hydraulic engineering projects seem to have been such as to provide an obvious stimulus to a primordial division of labour, with developing communal dependence upon central organisation and control of planning, construction and maintenance. So that, as Hoffman says, "when viewed as part of a larger functionally interrelated system, irrigation technology was one of the areas most sensitive to manipulation in the game of power politics as well as a focal point of community sentiment and organisation" (HOFFMAN 1984, p. 316).

It is true that the shifting pattern of the Nile flood, the rising water table and the growth of later settlements have left relatively little trace of early Neolithic settlement in the Nile valley. But such evidence as remains seems to indicate a characteristic pattern of early horticulture, initiated by the women (as considered in earlier chapters), of a continuing decline in wild game resources ultimately motivating marginalised male hunters to turn to systematic intensification of agricultural production as an alternative source of income, prestige and power – in precisely the sort of way suggested by Engels in his study of the origin of patriarchy and the state.

Thus, there is general agreement as to a continued, but decreasing, reliance upon large game hunting as a basic subsistence pursuit in the region for some time after the first clear evidence of agriculture round about 5000 BCE. As Butzer points out, "during most of the period between 15 000 and 3000 BCE, the desert supported sufficient game to allow hunting groups at least a seasonal livelihood" while the desert savanna country offered a wide range of edible trees and plants (possibly including wild barley) to serve as the basis for intensive gathering activities, and later also as pasturage for herds of domestic animals.

During late Paleolithic times most of the human settlements in the region were concentrated along levees and riverbanks, and "early farming communities continued to use the forested river banks and desert hill margins for settlement sites, grazing animals in the grass and bush country of the alluvial flats... for eight or nine months of the year and planting their crops on the wet basin soils as the flood receded – rather than moving down to the fertile floodplain" (BUTZER 1976, p. 19).

Frankfort refers to the recent agricultural practises of the camel-herding Bedouin in the Taka country of Nubia as a likely model for such early agricultural practice. As he says,

> "the people appear to be ignorant of tillage. They have no regular fields; and the Dhourra, their only grain, is sown among the thorny trees and tents, by dibbling large holes in the ground, into each of which a handful of the seed is thrown. After the harvest is gathered, the peasants return to their pastoral occupations... they never seem to have thought of irrigating the ground for a second crop with the water which might everywhere be found by digging wells. Not less than four fifths of the ground remain unsown; but the quantity of Dhourra produced is generally sufficient..." (FRANKFORT 1956, pp. 37-8).

And Butzer concluded that

> "this was the early irrigation landscape of Egypt, with natural irrigation... There was no need of drainage to make the valleys habitable. Furthermore, as long as the annual floods were persistently good, the density of Predynastic (i.e. pre-state) population was probably insufficient to warrant artificial irrigation. Given the natural flooding and draining of the Nile floodplain, the average flood would allow a single crop over perhaps two thirds of the alluvial surface" (ibid.).

Due to a lack of geological deposits in the Nile valley north of Aswan which can be dated to between 8000 and 5000 BCE there is disagreement as to exactly how and when plant domestication was first instituted in the region – whether the practice was introduced from elsewhere or whether local species were domesticated autonomously. But there is no doubt that unirrigated farming of emmer wheat, barley and flax was well under way in Egypt shortly after 5000 BCE. By this time there are also clear signs of domestication of sheep, goats, cattle and pigs co-existing with evidence of continued hunting, fishing and gathering.

The arguments of earlier chapters suggest that it would probably have been women who initiated and maintained plant domestication as a development of earlier seed-gathering activities, to supplement a diet in which big game played a decreasing role, while the men continued to hunt or to involve themselves increasingly in animal domestication. And while there is less in the way of mother goddess figurines and other maternal symbols found in early Egyptian sites than in some other Neolithic contexts, it is significant that most of the human representations so far discovered (from Amratian and Badarian times, ie up to about 3500 BCE) are female. And the great Egyptologist Flinders Petrie was of the opinion that the administrative divisions or nomes of early dynastic Egypt had once been matrilineal clan (territories) and that post-marital residence in earliest times was matrilocal.

The suggestion here is that as female-initiated agriculture became more important it shaped social organisation and ideology correspondingly. Communal life became organised on a matrilineal, matrilocal foundation, with the religious life of the community centred upon an Earth Mother Goddess as source of life and fertility.

As Butzer points out, there is no evidence that such unirrigated agriculture or, for that matter, animal herding – of itself led to any very significant population increases. Much more significant in determining qualitative change in the scale and character of social life, according to the Marx-Engels hypothesis, would have been the onset of increasing dessication, leading to diminishing wild plant resources, the extinction of many animal species and drastic reductions in the numbers of others in later Predynastic times. For we can see how this depletion of wild – and probably also domestic – animal resources could have led to an increasing economic marginalisation of the male population. And this could, in turn, have stimulated the entry of the male population into agricultural production – and, in particular, into the development of irrigated agriculture, as a much more productive alternative to earlier, unirrigated forms.

Here again, we do not know if the ideas of irrigation of reclaiming land and setting oxen to work ploughing it, were brought in from outside (probably from Mesopotamia via Sinai) or if they were developed independently in Egypt itself. Certainly increasingly marginalised men would have had plenty of time and incentive for such developments. But whether or not they were re-invented locally or were ideas from outside, we can see how the 'big men' who first proposed them could have quickly received the active support of increasing numbers of their brethren, anxious to re-establish their self-esteem, economic autonomy and, indeed, superiority over the female population. We can see how, like the plough amongst the Iroquois males, the new technologies could have been seized upon as a new source of male power.

Here, Egyptian mythology of the Dynastic period is particularly suggestive, with the first act of the first God being to raise up new land out of the waters, as the first imposition of order on primordial chaos. Thus, in the *Book of Apophis* the Sun-God Re is quoted as saying "Only after I came into being did all that was created come into being. Many are the shapes that come forth from my mouth. The sky had not come into being; the earth had not come into being... I found no place where I could stand". And Frankfort points out that

> "this last sentence indicates what was to be the first act of the sun-god. Within the expanse of the primeval waters he created dry land, the Primeval Hill, which became the centre of the earth, or at least the place round which the earth solidified. Local tradition differed as regards the details; but everywhere the site of creation. the first land to emerge from chaos, was thought to have been charged with vital power" (Frankfort 1978, pp. 151-2).

Here we see a profound shift away from the creative power of the female womb to that of the male idea – the word that sets in motion the collective activity of organised groups of men. And the activity in question appears to be none other than the drainage of the fertile floodplain of the Nile to create new farming land under the direction of a typical male big-man prophet (retrospectively seen as) incarnating the divine (paternal) power of the sun.

As Butzer says,

"the advantages of artificial irrigation were to increase the area of the annual cropland in relation to variable flood level, to retain water in the basins after undesirably brief flood crests, to allow planting of new ground along the perimeter of the floodplain, and to permit a second or even a third crop in intensively utilised garden plots. These are then refinements on a natural system of irrigation, the efficiency of which can be greatly improved by a relatively limited input of labour. This first level of improvement would include the annual dredging or deepening of the natural, diverging overflow channels; the digging of short ditches to breach the low points of natural levees; blocking off the gathering streams by earthen dams; and the use of buckets to raise water manually from residual ponds in natural channels to adjacent fields." (BUTZER 1976, p. 19)

As Hoffman observes, "it is logical to suppose that the manipulation of [such] irrigation technology... required the patronage of a big man on a local level and the skills that he or his clients possessed. This person would have possessed the knowledge and the managerial and juridical expertise to make the decisions that even a simplified irrigation system required". And he could have mobilised previously increasingly marginalised men to create such a system with the promise of a new economic role, and new wealth and power acquired with "a relatively limited input of [extra] labour" (HOFFMAN 1984, p. 316).

Here, indeed, is a new, specifically masculine – rational – politico-economic order of hierarchy and control, superimposed upon – and increasingly displacing – an earlier – 'natural' – feminine order. This 'primal', feminine order was based upon sensitivity and accomodation to the varying contingencies of the pre-existing ecology, rather than attempted subordination of such natural forces to a separate system of social priorities. And it is easy to see how masculine ideology could characterise this transition as the imposition upon male 'order' upon earlier 'chaos'.

In contrast to a likely earlier (typical Neolithic) representation of the earth as Goddess, gestating the new crop of wheat and barley in her womb, we find the land newly raised by Re identified with the earth god Ptah-Ta-Tjenen – Ptah the Risen Land, or with Geb – the male 'ka' or creative energy of all the Gods. Thus, barley is grown 'on the ribs of Geb' and the harvest is 'what the Nile causes to grow on the back of Geb'. And the cycle of planting, growth, and harvesting of the grain was equated with the cyclical birth, death and rebirth of Osiris, son of Geb and Nut, the sky Goddess. It is the male god Osiris who is the spirit of the grain, animating its growth and its nutritional properties and even the 'pure water' or 'young water' of the Nile bringing new silt for the parched fields was 'thought to be brought by Osiris or to emanate from him or take its power from him'. As Frankfort concludes, "vitality emerging from the earth, either in plant life or in water of the Nile, was a manifestation of Osiris, son of Geb" (FRANKFORT 1978, p. 190).

This is a radical transformation of the 'usual' cosmology, presumably driven by the radical nature of the change in agricultural production – where the men – in a sense – really do create new land. As such land 'absorbs' the masculine identity of its creators – and particularly that of the big man who first initiates its creation – so does the earth father god presumably also 'absorb' a proportion of the nurturing and protecting qualities of the Earth Mother Goddess.

Here we can see how the specific requirements of such 'basin' agriculture – in terms of integrated group co-operation in creating and maintaining the necessary ditches, dams, artificial levees etc. would discourage the development and accumulation of independent familial private property in land. On the other hand, we can see how the increasing scale of such projects – and the increasing reliance of an expanding population upon the productivity increases achieved by them – could have increased the power of the big-men who organised them. And we can see how such big-men and their descendants could have become hereditary chieftains, presiding over increasingly hierarchical social systems.

Such practises, along with later elaborations and extensions (including subdivision of the flood basins by dams into special purpose units, controlling water retention in the basin subunits by cuts in the levees or dykes, by networks of short canals and masonry gates etc.) seem – in this way – to have sustained the steady expansion of a number of (tribal) chiefdom structures in various regions of the Nile valley, with a positive feedback of increasing productivity, population and social hierarchy.

These developments seem to have proceeded more rapidly in the south than in the north, most likely because of a more rapid rate of desiccation and lesser resources of large game to start with, because of the smaller size of the basins south of Abydos, making it easier to modify them so as to retain flood water for longer, and because of the greater proximity of settlements – all linked together by water transport on the Nile making possible the rapid spread of people and ideas, rather than strung out and isolated on separate tributaries like those of the delta.

It was in the south also that, chiefly in the region between the Nile Valley and the Red Sea, that the main gold deposits of Egypt were located, quite possibly attracting the attention of traders from the more advanced Mesopotamian city-states, either sailing direct through the Red Sea or travelling south from the delta "but tending to bypass the area because it did not produce the expensive and easily transportable luxury goods for which they were looking".

Most important for present purposes, we can follow Trigger in suggesting that "efforts to control this trade and to exploit the eastern desert more effectively were probably important factors encouraging the further development of powerful chiefdoms centred at certain strategic locations of Southern Egypt". As he says, the nuclei of such developed chiefdoms "appear to have been communities near to points of easy access to the desert, developing into 'large towns or small cities' as their power and wealth increased" (TRIGGER 1983, p. 39).

Here, a solid foundation in irrigation-intensification and centralised control would have paved the way for such developments, creating military-political-economic structures capable of taking advantage of such foreign trade, provisioning from central grain reserves, applying new ideas and imported technology, perhaps attracting expert foreign craftworkers etc. And such developments, in turn, would have reacted back to increase and consolidate such central power.

It is significant that it was the eastern desert also that supplied the malachite and chrysocolla ores which were (probably) the major source of copper in Egypt during this period. Quite possibly, contact with the more advanced Mesopotamian culture contributed new knowledge and skills in processing such ores and in the production of copper weapons. And certainly, effective control of significant deposits of copper could have provided a crucial advantage in conflicts with other, less well supplied local chiefdoms.

Thus, it is in the south that we find the largest and most developed Late Gerzean (i.e. pre-state) settlements, with brick houses, a temple and sophisticated tombs – with elaborate decoration and grave goods as evidence of increasing social stratification, and satellite villages, at Naqada and Hierakonpolis. Most likely they were the administrative centres of the two most developed chiefdoms of the time. And warfare between them, motivated by population pressure on – and competition for – scarce resources – of water, land, minerals etc. – (in a situation with limited scope for geographical expansion) and control of foreign trade, could well have played a central role in the formation of a unified Egyptian state structure, taking in all the territory of the Nile Valley north of Aswan at the end of the Predynastic Period. We see this conflict represented in mythological form in the battle of Horus (falcon god of Hierakonpolis) with Seth (god of Naqada).

Certainly in later Egyptian ideology the formation of such a unified Egyptian state is equated with the conquest of Lower Egypt (identified with Seth) by Upper (identified with Horus). And Hoffman suggests that in late Predynastic times Naqada and Hierakonpolis were already capitals of proto-state structures formed by the conquest of a number of other chiefdom-level groups in the north and south. Here, the assumption is that Hierakonpolis was victorious, while Naqada remained significant as regional capital within the extended state structure.

As Hoffman says,

> "if, indeed, Egypt had coalesced into two contending kingdoms shortly before unification, as most traditions staunchly maintain, it is then possible that the northernmost kingdom was based at Naqada, and had already subdued an area extending into the delta, bringing with its dominance the appropriate symbols of kingship. When the bellicose southerners finally achieved the conquest claimed by Narmer on the famous palette from Hierakonpolis, they would have taken over another, larger Upper Egyptian kingdom that included part of the delta. In the process of political consolidation that accompanied the rules of Scorpion, Narmer and Aha it would have been possible to recast Lower Egypt in terms of its geographically most alien component – the delta." (HOFFMAN 1984, p. 324)

The picture is complicated by the early appearance of royal tombs at Abydos, suggesting that either the rulers of Hierakonpolis may have moved their capital down river to Abydos or that a third power may have subordinated both Naqada and Hierakonpolis. And Trigger raises the further possibility that alliances between the rulers of a number of advanced chiefdoms of Upper Egypt could have been as important as conquest in "establishing a basis of power in Southern Egypt which allowed the conquest of the whole country" (TRIGGER 1983, p. 49).

Part Two
SUBSEQUENT DEVELOPMENTS

However, the precise details of the final unification are not really of very great significance for our present purposes (of testing out the materialist theory of state formation with particular reference to the role of religious ideas). It makes little difference which particular southern chiefdom actually emerged victorious and whether it conquered and incorporated an already largely unified northern kingdom or a number of separate, smaller northern chiefdoms or independent tribal settlements – as Frankfort, e.g., argues. Much more important is the evidence of an increasing scale of hydraulic engineering in Late Gerzean times and for the active involvement of a new ruling class of state functionaries in further extending such hydraulic intensification in the period following the creation of a unified Egyptian state – in early Dynastic times.

Here is clear evidence of a feedback of increasing hydraulic intensification, population expansion and centralised power, leading to competition between a number of developed chiefdoms – confined within narrow geographical limits within the valley – with further accelerated hydraulic intensification, population increase and hierarchical control. Such competition culminates in conquest and incorporation of all such separate chiefdoms into a single, extended state structure. But the basic feedback of intensification and population increase continues for some time – prior to eventual population stabilisation – as the new rulers and their descendants seek to maximise available surplus product (from the total arable land area at their disposal) and extend their control of the rest of the population.

Thus, Butzer cites evidence from a variety of sources (including the considerable concentration of labour required to regulate water intake or drainage in times of flood, to build the great dykes, and to participate in the "great pyramid and temple building efforts of the Old Kingdom Pharaohs") to support his contention that "population would appear to have quadrupled in the 1500 year period preceding the apex of the Old Kingdom" (round about 2500 BCE). And Trigger cites "a reference to 120,000 men, as either prisoners or part of a grant to a temple, on a mace head of king Narmer" to suggest a considerably faster rate of population expansion from as little as 200,000 inhabitants of the Nile Valley in Late Predynastic times to two million or more at the beginning of the early Dynastic period.

As Butzer points out, "irrigation technology appears to have been repeatedly improved" following "the shift from natural to artificial flood irrigation by Late Predynastic times". And Trump, e.g., is in no doubt that the "rapid rise in population" noted above, along with a general "revolution" in "economy and society" was primarily "a result of [the] irrigation works which opened up the immensely fertile valley floor of the Nile to intensive farming" (TRUMP 1981, p. 62-3).

The active involvement of the central power in instituting such hydraulic intensification is clearly attested by the mace-head representation of Scorpion, one of the last of the Predynastic kings (round about 3100 BCE) ceremonially cutting an irrigation ditch. And Herodotus attributes to Menes, the legendary first king of a unified Egypt (quite possibly the same person as the first Dynastic king Narmer, round about 3000 BCE), a large scale hydraulic engineering project of diverting the Nile so as to create an area of new land for the construction of the city of Memphis, and its main temple, dedicated to the god Ptah.

For later periods, Butzer mentions an "unambiguous allusion to Pepi I (c. 2390-2360 BCE) cutting a canal to place a tract of land under water" (BUTZER 1976, p. 45). And Hoffman refers to the boasts of the tenth dynasty monarch, Kheti I, concerning a new canal he has constructed to suggest that at this time, at least, (shortly before 2100 BCE) "the establishment and maintenance of local irrigation networks were the duty of anyone aspiring to legitimate regional political hegemony and did involve the application of special technical and administrative expertise" (HOFFMAN 1984, p. 315).

It is true that Butzer himself, as a leading expert on the subject does argue "that there is no evidence for a centralised bureaucratic apparatus that might have served to administer irrigation at the national, regional or local level", and that "ecological problems were pre-eminantly handled at the local level, at least until the opening up of the Faiyum in the Middle Kingdom". He maintains that artificial constructions were small-scale and consisted primarily of strengthening and enlarging pre-existing natural levees and dikes

separating each of the natural basins of the flood plain from one
another and from the river.

Yet, as Harris shows, Butzer's arguments are actually contra-
dicted by much of the data he himself provides. Thus,

> "Butzer admits the formidable technical requirements" of early
> irrigation technology, frequently demanding the "mass input of the
> total able-bodied rural population of a basin unit, but supposedly of
> only one unit at a time. This conclusion is clearly false since each
> 'basin unit' had at least two neighbours, one upstream and one
> downstream. At high-water, failure to maintain the between-basin
> dikes and the return drainage channels in proper condition would
> result in the uncontrolled flooding of the downstream basin. When
> the Nile flood was higher than usual, a break in an upstream levee
> would threaten not only the adjacent basin, but the next basin as
> well, since the uncontrolled pressure could easily sweep away the
> between-basin dykes. The need for co-ordinating the response of
> several basins was equally great when the Nile flood failed and the
> amount of water diverted by the upsteam basins affected the
> amount that reached those further downstream. Butzer himself
> paints a stark picture of the 'famine, poverty, mass burials, rotting
> corpses, suicide, cannibalism, anarchy, mass dislocations, civil war,
> mass plundering, roving bands of marauders, as well as looting of
> cemeteries' that resulted from a failure of the annual flood. While
> there were occasions when the crests were either so high or so
> low that no power on earth could render assistance, a government
> capable of putting 100,000 men to work building artificial moun-
> tains out of stone blocks in the desert surely did not refrain from
> attempting to moderate the effect of too much or too little water
> under emergency conditions." (HARRIS 1978, p. 179)

Here it is important to add also James observations to the effect
that "the best evidence of years of famine comes from texts of those
periods when central administration was weak or even non-existent,
like the First Intermediate Period" when increasing devolution of

power to provincial governors led to the fragmentation of the Egyptian state. "At times of good government things were automatically better, and it is striking that there are no statements about the occurrence of hunger and bad Niles during the 18th Dynasty" following the destruction of the system of hereditary nomarchs (or regional governors) and its replacement by a strongly centralised bureaucratic machinery "the operators of which owed their allegiance directly to the king in his residence". (JAMES 1985, p. 51)

Here James refers to documentary evidence clearly implicating the vizir, as head of this central bureaucracy and chief minister to the king (and probably also a close relation) in the day-to-day organisation of local irrigation. "By regular reports from all over the country the vizir should know the state of affairs at every season... It is he should dispatch mayors and district governors to [arrange] the cultivation in the summer." He oversees the fixing of district boundaries, and looks into cases involving estate boundaries. "It is he who should examine water supplies on the first day of every ten-day period." (JAMES, 1985, p. 115)

I have, indeed, argued that control of irrigation at the level of the individual basin/nome dates back to prehistoric times as an integral part of the political infrastructure for the military ventures that led to unification. In this context, it is hardly likely that the stabilisation of central power, following unification, should leave this vital element of social organisation (involving the mass input of the total able-bodied – and potentially rebellious – rural population of a basin unit) outside the scope of its detailed planning and control.

Logically, the same officials responsible for other aspects of regional administration (and, in particular, other large-scale mobilisations of regional manpower) would be responsible also for overseeing regular irrigation work within particular basins. And here, there are clear signs that such officials were, at first, very closely bound to the central power – precisely because of the possibility of rebellion and fragmentation of the state structure – along with the functional necessity for central control of inner-regional co-operation in time of crisis, prior to the consolidation of extended functional and ideological control.

In the Old Kingdom there was already

> "a large, well-organised [central] bureaucracy which collected taxes in kind throughout the country, stored these goods in government warehouses and supervised their distribution to those who were privileged to receive royal largesse. The height of the Nile flood was carefully recorded each year and probably served as the basis for computing annual rates of taxation on crops, while a biennial royal tour of inspection allowed for a general census of taxable resources." (TRIGGER 1983, p. 58)

By the time of the Old Kingdom, Butzer himself admits that "Pharaohs power appears to have been virtually absolute", with "national projects such as pyramid building" suggesting the "development of some form of government controlled program to collect, store and, in times of need, redistribute food" (BUTZER 1976, p. 88). And Kemp suggests that pyramid building itself, requiring, as it did, regular mobilisation and integration of large numbers of men from a number of different regions, might have contributed to a situation in which all senior regional officials remained particularly tightly bound to the central power, limited in their responsibilities and periodically circulated from one region to another.

According to James, mass mobilisation for "digging out the canals and smaller channels, the repair and elevation of dikes and other land dividers" and "the ordering of water sluices and estate boundaries in the quickest possible time after the flood before the drying of the land" was accomplished in exactly the same way as mobilisation for pyramid construction – through "the standard Egyptian practise of corvee; statute labour, or the raising of gangs by decree". And the necessity for co-ordinating such large-scale mobilisation for pyramid construction, very strongly suggests that the same high officials (as e.g. Netjer-aperef, "overseer of commissions in the nomes of Coptos, Hu and Dendara") would have been in control of both – with more or less direct involvement of the Pharaoh himself.

Butzer himself recognises an integral involvement of strong central government in vast hydraulic projects in later periods (after 2000 BCE) – including the regulation of the level of the Fayum Lake and the drainage of large portions of the Delta region. And this, anyway, takes us far beyond the initial creation and stabilisation of state power which is the major focus of concern here.

Far more significant, for present purposes, is the fact that these considerations already go a long way towards demonstrating that, in Early Dynastic and early Old Kingdom times, at least, we are actually dealing with a structure quite close to what Marx and Engels call an 'Asiatic despotic' state, formed in much the manner they suggested. Here, the bulk of social surplus is extracted from the primary producers – the peasant farmers – as tax (or tax as a specific form of 'ground rent' for use of state land) in kind and in corvee labour. "The whole state is organised as a machine for the collection, storage and disposal of a massive agricultural surplus." And, over and above extension of the irrigation system and preservation of grain for general consumption in time of crisis, such social surplus functions to sustain the luxury consumption of a substantial ruling class of state personnel – in massive construction projects (temples, palaces, pyramids, tombs), elaborate cult activities, luxury craftwork, foreign trade in the materials for such production, along with prospecting expeditions, mining and warfare. (See MARX AND ENGELS 1979)

Certainly the social structure does appear to have retained specific features in common with a developed – tribal – chiefdom organisation. But this is precisely what we should expect if it came into being through functional transformation of productive intensification, conquest and incorporation of advanced chiefdom structures by one such structure – as considered above. And signs of preservation of a kinship hierarchy at the heart of the (early) Egyptian bureaucratic ruling group – including regular 'strategic' marriage arrangements and a correspondence of kinship roles with specific bureaucratic offices are quite straightforwardly explicable in terms of the preservation of – at least the higher echelons of – the hierarchical 'clan' structure of the particular chiefdom which happened to be victorious in this case.

For the same reasons, we should not be surprised that the characteristic Egyptian ideology of divine kingship – touched upon in the last chapter – is, basically, an extension of the typical ideology of developed chiefdom structures, centred upon the divine ancestry and consequent magical productive powers of the chief. Here, recognition of the true 'functional' role of the central bureaucracy in developing and maintaining necessary irrigation systems is intimately interwoven with the ideology of divine kingship in legitimating the ownership of all cultivated land by the Pharaoh (who 'creates' land for cultivation, who 'waters' and 'nourishes' it, protects and nurtures it and 'watches over' its vital seasonal cycle) and the payment of tax as rent by the primary producers. Similarly, the Egyptian cult of the dead is distinguished primarily by the massive scale of the surplus available to sustain it (at least on the part of the rulers), rather than by its specific form and function.

However, hierarchical kinship bonds seem to have been confined to the bureaucratic administrative hierarchy. They did not extend down into the mass of the primary producers of the conquered populations, but, rather, were decisively severed by class division. By all accounts, very little surplus was actually redistributed back across this divide to the people who actually produced it.

Disarming the conquered people would have been a first priority for the leaders of the victorious chiefdom in order to minimise the threat of rebellion and facilitate their continued appropriation of social surplus product. And in this case we can associate the more aggressive, martial representations of the earlier kings – flail in hand, striking down their enemies etc. – with the necessity for maintaining a tight rein upon still potentially rebellious provinces. But it is conspicuous that in much later periods, while Pharaoh is represented as increasingly benevolent and benign (as protector of the weak etc.), and can apparently call upon little in the way of a standing army, corvee labour is still conscripted, and taxes gathered, under threat of violent physical force, with dire consequences for those who try to evade them. And all state documents dealing with the labour of the primary producers make it quite clear how far those primary producers have gone in losing control of their own labour power (at least as far as substantial periods of corvee are concerned). So that, as James notes, "in terms of treatment, it is unlikely that there was much discrimination between the conscripted freeman and the prisoner or slave when duties were allocated and control exercised" (JAMES 1985, p. 118).

Reference to this particular process of state formation also goes some way towards explaining the presence of feudal-type elements in Egyptian society – even during periods of maximum state control – in the form of large, semi-autonomous agricultural estates at various points throughout the country, free from central taxation and with their own 'tied' labour forces, exempt from central corvee. In particular, we can see how such centres primarily took the form of extended temple organisations devoted to the maintenance of pre-existing local religious cults – which had presumably served a crucial ideological integrative and legitimatory role in the previous development of local chiefly power. We see how the maintenance – and indeed extended elaboration – of such cults (with regular, large scale festivals etc.) could therefore continue to serve as a focus for local identity and integration – and for the legitimation of continued central appropriation of significant social surplus product – following the overthrow of such chiefly power, and the disintegration of hierarchical kinship structures.

Perhaps we see here how senior military and religious leaders of the victorious chiefdom are inserted into pre-existing structures of power, with their own, independent productive facilities, to reward them for their contribution to victory, to divert them from pursuit of central power for themselves and to allow for the stabilisation of class power over a wide area. Perhaps we see rather the rewards of indigenous collaborators – allowed to retain a foothold in their old power bases.

Most important for present purposes, there is clear evidence that "provincial temples were the subject of central government decrees concerning their condition and maintenance". And apart from actual material support, there is also plenty of evidence for a very strong central involvement in re-shaping and implementing local cult practises as vehicles for the legitimation and extension of central state power. As Trigger says,

> "ultimately, the dogmas served to reinforce the historical process by which a central authority had come to exercise its control over a long-established network of community politics, and were themselves continually reinforced in provincial association by ritual and by the iconography of ritual which, e.g., made the king responsible for the ceremonies of provincial temples" (TRIGGER 1983, p. 73).

Thus, we find that the pivot of the new ideology, created by the priesthood of the new capital of Memphis, is the god Ptah, conceived as the spiritual matrix for the integration of the various antecedent cults of the major chiefdoms incorporated into the unitary Egyptian state. In the new system the earlier gods became functioning members in this larger body or totality, who dwells in them as their eternal vital force, their '*ka*', emphasising the primacy of the state over its various regional centres.

> "Therefore it is said of Ptah: 'It is he who made all and brought the gods into being'. He is verily the Risen Land that brought forth the gods, for everything came forth from him, sustenance and food, the offerings of the gods, and every good thing. Thus it was discovered and understood that his strength was greater than that of all the gods. And Ptah was satisfied when he had made all things and every divine word.
> He had fashioned the gods, made the cities, founded the nomes, installed the gods in their shrines, established their offerings and equipped their holy places. He had made likenesses

of their bodies to the satisfaction of their hearts, and the gods had entered into these bodies made of every wood, stone and clay thing that grows upon him, wherein they were taken from."

At the same time, the heart of Ptah, thought of as the seat of will and intelligence, with "mastery over all the other (bodily) members" and capable of creation (ex nihilo) through the word of Ptah's mouth (itself identified with the ancient moon god Thot of Hermopolis), is identified with Horus, "the living son and resurrection of the creative power of Osiris" – and thus also with the living Pharaoh, as pinnacle of the central ruling hierarchy.

"And in this way all the gods and their *'ka's* are at one with (Ptah), content and united with the Lord of the two lands" (from the Pyramid texts c. 2350-2175 BCE). As Campbell says, "the whole pantheon, as well as the world, thus becomes organically assimilated to the cosmic body of the creator" (CAMPBELL 1979, p. 87); in other words, all the regions find their place within the unity of the Egyptian state, subordinated to the political power of Pharaoh, whose word is law.

CHAPTER EIGHT
THE POLITICS OF EARLY CHRISTIANITY

Part One
CONTEMPORARY EVIDENCE OF CLASS RELATIONS

The starting point for a materialist analysis of early Christianity must be consideration of the economic conditions of first century Palestine; in particular of the principal relations of control of material production and structures of class power and inequality of the period. And given the still predominantly rural and agrarian character of the economy, questions of land tenure are of central importance here.

We must take account also of the economic demands of the Jewish state, and of the occupying Roman forces insofar as Israel – as the homeland of the Jewish people – was, at this time, under the imperialistic domination of the Roman state.

There were apparently significant changes in patterns of land tenure at this time.

"Under Herod I (37-34 BC) much of the land had been administered by the King's own estate. Subsequently, his lands were sold off and this led to the increase of large estates, often with absentee landlords (see Matt 21; 33-41). Archaeological evidence shows the existence of such estates with a central settlement and dependent villages. These estates were, in part, sublet to tenant farmers paying rent either in kind or in cash. Labour on the estate proper was provided either by tenants or by day labourers (paid very low wages) (cf., Matt. 20: 1). Under these circumstances the possibility of amassing debts and of shortage of employment was a real one, as the Gospels show (Matt. 18: 25, 20: 6)" (RICHES 1990, p. 24).

There were probably substantial regional variations in prosperity, depending on the quality of the land, population pressure, Roman imperial domination and other considerations. And, as Riches suggests,

"two things suggest that conditions in Galilee away from the coastal strip were (particularly) demanding. In the first place Roman General Pompey's 'liberation' of the coastal cities from the control of the Jews in the first century BCE (Ant. XIV 75-6) probably impelled a sizeable population into the Galilean hinterland who had then to compete for land and work. Second, archaeological evidence shows that the land in the Galilean mountains was intensively farmed and parcelled up into very small lots. The methods of farming were often very laborious; damming streams to stop top soil running off, the use of a form of terracing and so forth. All this indicates that farming was difficult and that pressure of population made it imperative to get as much from the land as possible." (ibid., p. 25)

Thus there are good grounds for supposing that life in rural Palestine generally was far from easy for the peasant farmers and day labourers who made up the bulk of the population. Work in the fields was difficult and heavy, with land, markets and wages largely under the control of a few wealthy landowners. Taking account also of demands for taxes and tithes from both the Romans and the Temple in Jerusalem, we can see that, as Riches says, "none of this made for great security or an easy life. Debt, loss of tenancies, and ultimately slavery threatened (large sections of the population)" (op. cit.).

All of this explains why significant sections of the rural population – particularly in the Galilean regions – should have been drawn to begging, or to "more violent ways of resolving their problems" as thieves, brigands and resistance fighters.

Here, as Karl Kautsky observes,

"The petty peasants and shepherds were being exploited to the utmost by the pressure of taxation and usury, and were thrown into servitude or expropriated, as they were everywhere in the empire… As in other areas of the empire… the more energetic elements amongst [them] resorted to violent insurrection, to banditry. The proximity of the desert, still a home for Bedouin customs and habits, facilitated their struggle by offering numerous hiding places known only to those acquainted with the country. And Galilee itself, with its irregular soil and many caves, offered conditions that were no less favourable to the trade of the bandit… Bandit chieftains declared themselves to be the Messiah [the saviour sent by God] or at least his forerunner, and enthusiasts who felt themselves called to be the prophet or the Messiah, became bandit chieftains." (KAUTSKY 1972, p. 298)

This explains also why rural workers should have been motivated to migrate to the wealthy Hellenistic cities of the region, in search of a better life and better opportunities for work, charity, social revolution or robbery.

There were apparently more than thirty sizeable cities in Palestine at this time. They were centres of wealth, trade and industry and home bases for many of the major landowners. The coastal cities, in particular, were important centres of trade and commerce, with a substantial merchant class. Such cities were controlled by councils of Greek speaking merchants, officials, and landowners, entitled to make their own laws, and exercising control over surrounding agricultural areas. At the same time, they paid taxes and supplied military forces to Rome. (See RICHES 1990, Ch. 1.)

The major city of Palestine was Jerusalem, distinguished by its size and by the presence of the Temple as traditional centre of the Jewish nation. As Riches says,

> "For most Jews, Jerusalem was first and foremost where they came to worship at the major pilgrimages of Passover and Weeks and Tabernacles. This meant that it was the focus of Jewish unity, both for Jews in Palestine and for those living in other cities around the Mediterranean... Traditionally Jerusalem was the centre of Jewish power. God was king of the Jews and his presence resided in the Temple. The high priest represented the people to God and God to the people." (RICHES 1990, p. 22-3)

The High Priest "was also subject to the jurisdiction of the Sanhedrin. This was a court or council made up of priestly families and experts in the Law over which the high priest presided" (ibid., p. 23). Together, these authorities administered the Law and governed the people.

The Sadducees were the priestly aristocrats who had control of the Temple. And this meant they had control of the yearly (double drachma) poll tax supposed to be paid by every male Jew, rich or poor, over two years of age, wherever they lived. They controlled the massive wealth in regular gifts delivered to the temple every year by pilgrims from all over the Roman Empire. They controlled much of the material offered by the worshippers as sacrifices, and the payment of the tithes – the tenth part of all agricultural produce, as well as the payment of the first born of every animal.

In the first century CE the Sadducees had to accept that the temple was overseen by Roman soldiers. After this the high priest was appointed by the Roman Governor, and a roman garrison monitored the Temple courts. But rather than pursue active rebellion against such foreign domination, the Sadducees seem to have chosen instead to collaborate with such occupying forces, in the interests of avoiding conflict which could destroy the Temple. It was, of course, the Temple cult that provided the foundation for their own wealth and power.

Clearly they had a lot to lose from any radical social disruption. "They were apparently pragmatists, not popular with the people, anxious to avoid radical solutions to Israel's predicament." (ibid., p. 46) In this – and other things – they were opposed by the Pharisees, who had more support amongst the mass of the population.

Nonetheless, the Temple itself continued to be supported by the majority of the Jewish people, as the central focus of the Jewish nation and the Jewish faith. It did oversee some redistribution of wealth to those in need. It did serve as a focus for national identity and it did create employment. As Riches observes, "Under Herod the Great a large program of rebuilding had begun that provided employment for many" (ibid., p. 23).

Pilgrims brought wealth to the city. As noted earlier, Jews everywhere paid tax to the Temple; tithes were supposed to be brought to Jerusalem. Around the Temple were a number of small industries catering for the aristocratic priestly families, for the wealthy landowners who made the city their base, for visitors to the city and for the craftworkers and petty merchants themselves. As Riches says, the city "boasted fine craftworkers in glassware, stone carving, and pottery and offered less sophisticated goods for the many thousands employed on public building works" (ibid., p. 20).

At the same time, Jerusalem would presumably also have sustained a substantial 'underclass' or 'lumpenproletarian' population of dispossessed, unemployed or underemployed beggars and street people. And, indeed, the Bible clearly testifies to the significant number living by begging and public charity – particularly those prevented from working through illness or physical disability – throughout Palestine.

Materialist historian Karl Kautsky highlights the potentially revolutionary role of the masses of poor, oppressed and dispossessed Jews living hand-to-mouth in the streets of Jerusalem, and increasingly desperate in their opposition both to the Roman imperialists and the wealthy priestly nobility (the party of the Sadducees) who controlled the Temple and collaborated with the Romans.

As he points out, the ranks of such 'lumpenproletarians' were continually swelled by those whose business ventures had failed (in uncertain times), by poor Jewish handicraft workers, shopkeepers, freed slaves (including freed slaves from Rome) and others fallen on hard times, who congregated in Jerusalem, where they felt themselves at home, and struggled to survive on the charity of their better-off brothers.

He continues, "after Rome, Jerusalem probably contained the largest proletariat of this description, at least relatively. For in both cities this rabble was recruited from the whole empire". And he highlights the close links that continued to exist between such desperate beggars and the poor artisans and domestic workers of the period.

"Whenever such penniless classes of the population congregated in great numbers, they become particularly aggressive. Unlike the possessing classes, they have nothing to lose; their social position is intolerable, and they have nothing to gain by waiting. They are emboldened by the consciousness of number. Furthermore, the military power (of the state) could not easily employ its strength in the narrow and winding streets of those days. Little as the city proletarians were fitted for military service in the open field... they nevertheless were equal to the requirements of street battle." (KAUTSKY 1972, p. 297)

In normal times the proletarians apparently accepted the leadership of the Pharisees – the scribes and rabbis who were the 'orthodox' intellectual opposition to the aristocratic collaborators. "But as the oppositions between Jerusalem and Rome were sharpened, as the decisive moment came nearer and nearer, the Pharisees became more and more cautious and timid, and thus frequently came into conflict with the advancing proletarians." (op. cit.) The latter found a powerful support in the country population of Galilee.

"The bandits of Galilee and the proletarians of Jerusalem were in close co-operation with each other, supporting each other, and finally constituting a common party opposed to the Sadducees, namely the party of the Zealots, or those full of zeal."

As first century Jewish historian Josephus says, such Zealots showed a "stubborn love for liberty, and declared that God alone should be recognised as Lord and prince...". They fomented one war after the other. They were constantly resorting to violence; anyone who expressed himself against such violence had to pay for it with his life. And "from (4 BCE onwards) the fires of insurrection were never completely extinguished in Judea and Galilee until the destruction of Jerusalem".

Part Two
THE SUPERSTRUCTURE

As far as political and ideological superstructures are concerned, we can see that all such groups shared common Jewish beliefs to the effect that the Jews were God's chosen people – sustained by a mutually binding contract between God and themselves. If they obeyed his law he would bless them, and this blessing was specifically connected with the promise of a land flowing with milk and honey. (Deut. 6: 1-3)

Virtually unique in the ancient world, the Jews were monotheists, believing in a single supreme God (Deut. 6: 4) – a stern patriarchal sky-father god, who had created the world and continued to exercise control over it. They believed that the terms of the Covenant were set out in Scripture as the basis of the Law. The practices and institutions prescribed by the Jewish Scriptures – circumcision, dietary laws, observance of certain days and feasts, tithing, paying Temple Tax, the priesthood – were believed to be divinely ordained.

Within this common framework, however, different emphases, different interpretations, and different priorities reflected the particular interests of different social groups. No doubt the Sadducees regarded strict observance of the great festivals, the daily sacrifice (purchased from the Temple) and the ritual of Yom Kippur as the central elements of Jewish life. For it was upon these practices that their wealth and power depended. (See RICHES 1990, p. 59)

They rejected the Pharisees belief that God had given Moses not only the written Law but also the oral law that contained the key to its interpretation. They rather concentrated their attention upon the specific prescriptions of the Pentateuch – the first five books of the Old Testament – as related to the central institutions and structures of the Temple state. As their opponents would say, they clung to the letter of Moses's Torah rather than its spirit and denied the traditional belief in resurrection of the body.

By contrast, the Pharisees were apparently experts in traditional scriptural interpretations who, despite their special learning, remained close to the ordinary people, working alongside them as tailors, shoemakers and other craftsmen – but also educating children, founding regional synagogues and developing an oral tradition of Jewish wisdom which continued into present day Jewish orthodoxy. Unlike the Sadducees they believed that the bodies of dead Jews would physically rise from their graves at the end of time, and for that reason insisted that the dead should be buried, not cremated, and all the bones left intact. The Pharisees seem to have had substantial popular support. And although they do not generally appear to have been directly involved in military operations against the Roman regime they apparently made clear their opposition to it. (Quite possibly they provided some support for, and in a few cases even actively participated in, the military struggles of the Zealots.)

As Riches says, in a situation of social crisis, with the erosion of traditional values and institutions, "the Pharisees stressed the need to intensify efforts to uphold the Law. Amongst them, "the written laws of the Pentateuch were supplemented with a more detailed set of requirements contained in the oral tradition of the law, which were seen to protect the true principles of the law".

Thus, "the study of the Torah became central to the life of the community" and the Pharisees developed their own tradition of interpretation through ongoing teaching, discussion and debate. We can see them as a sort of privileged liberal, middle class opposition to the monopoly power of the Sadducees.

The Sadducees were more actively opposed by various Zealot (and Sicarii) groups, who made regular attempts at insurrection in the name of a return to old values and priestly legitimacy – in the line of Aaron and Mattathias Maccabeas. They were 'zealous for the law' of Moses, and – as noted earlier – carried on a continuous guerilla war against the Romans and all whom they saw as collaborating with the Romans and betraying the old values.

In modern terminology the Zealots might be called Messianic revolutionary fundamentalists and nationalists, carrying on a long established tradition of violent resistance to the loss of Jewish autonomy through integration or conquest. (Though to the Romans, of course, they were terrorists, outlaws and brigands.) And, while some seem to have accepted the traditional Jewish idea of the resurrection of the body, others seem to have believed in the life of the soul in heaven – at least for those who died in the struggle.

Another – fundamentalist – group identified by Josephus is that of the Essenes, who lived in all-male (or principally male) monastic communities sharing productive forces – and even personal possessions – in common, in desert regions apart from other communities. They "called people out of the existing order of things into a community that saw itself as wholly distinct from everyone else, Jew and Gentile alike".

Such communities were supported by farming – with everyone working together, But they were also structured in terms of a 'strict hierarchy' of degrees of spiritual knowledge and enlightenment, culminating in a council with ultimate responsibility for the regulation of community affairs. According to Josephus, indeed, accidental physical contact between persons of different rank led to 'pollution' such that the senior member had to take a bath "as after contact with an alien".

In psychoanalytic terms this suggests a powerful reaction formation against repressed homosexual and/or anal desires. And, indeed, they seem to have been neurotically obsessed with questions of dirt and cleanliness, organising their lives around frequent rites of ritual washing and purification, and concentrating upon intense study of their sacred texts. And the Essenes seem to have seen all other groups as more or less 'polluted' by sin and headed for destruction in a forthcoming 'new age'.

They saw themselves as the true sons of the covenant, summoned by God. Only they fully understood the Law – through lifelong study of the Scriptures and the special interpretations of their own prophets. Only they therefore lived lives fully in accord with the Law. And only they would be saved to inherit the earth with the coming of 'a new age'.

Josephus presents the Essenes as essentially pacifist and on good terms with the Temple hierarchy. But some of the Dead Sea Scroll material from the Essene settlement at Qumran suggests rather a militant, Zealot-like hostility to Roman rule and to all those who collaborate with it, and a preparedness to take up arms to expel the foreign imperialists.

Part Three
JESUS THE MAGICIAN

When we come to consider the specific case of the life and message of Jesus, where exactly Jesus fits into this complex political, economic and ideological framework, we find plenty of evidence to place him on the side of conservatism

It is easy to see his line on the Law (rigorous adherence to the laws of Moses) and on divorce (that women be denied the right to divorce) as far from radical. And there are some indications that when it came to the relation between the Jewish people and the occupying Roman imperialists his position was basically conservative, both directly – in his demand that the Jews, "render unto Caesar that which is Caesar's", and indirectly (in his calls for his followers to love their enemies, turn the other cheek, abjure all violence, get their reward in heaven etc.).

There is a tradition that emphasises the role of Jesus as a clever magician or hypnotist – rather than a religious or political reformer. One of the earliest sources of information about the life of Jesus and his followers outside of the Christian tradition itself is the Platonist philosopher Celsus whose work survives in quotations from the early Christian church father and apologist Origen. And as Morton Smith notes, "the popular picture of Jesus that Celsus knew was primarily one of a miracle worker" (SMITH, M. 1978, p. 58).

> [Celsus] "accused Jesus of having made up the story of his birth from a virgin, whereas actually he came from a Jewish village and from a poor country woman who lived by her spinning. She was thrown out as an adulteress by her husband, a carpenter. Wandering about in disgrace, she secretly gave birth to Jesus, whom she had conceived from a soldier named Pantera. After growing up in Galilee, Jesus went as a hired labourer to Egypt. There he learned some of the magical rites upon which the Egyptians pride themselves. He came back [to Palestine] hoping for great things from his powers and because of them proclaimed himself a god." (op. cit.)

Celsus reported that Jesus had ten disciples who were "tax collectors and sailors of the worst sort, not even able to read or write, with whom he ran, as a fugitive, from one place to another, making his living shamefully as a beggar".

Celsus's account accords closely with those of a number of other early commentators, particularly Rabbinic commentators and others generally hostile to the developing Christian tradition. But as Morton

Smith argues, there are many elements of the New Testament itself which seem to point in a similar sort of direction.

As he says, "Mark equates 'Messiah' (= 'Christ') with 'Son of God' and 'Son of Man' (14: 61f). From then on the equation has been customary. But 'Son of God' was not, in Judaism, a customary Messianic title, nor a common way of referring to the Messiah. Nor is it often connected within the Messiahship in the synoptic gospels. Instead it almost always appears with miracles. As 'Son of God' Jesus casts out demons (Mark 3.11: 5.7p; Luke 4.41), walks on the sea, and knows the Father (Matt. 11.27p; 14.33). Because he claims to be the 'Son of God' the devil demands miracles from him (Matt. 4.3,6p) and the Jews mock him when he is unable to perform them (Matt. 27.40-43). Because he was a 'Son of God' miracles attended his death (Mark 15.38fp)" (ibid., pp. 100-1).

These considerations strongly suggest that the expression 'Son of God' specifically implied "a supernatural being in human form who performs miracles by his own divine power". More specifically, 'Son of God' actually implied 'God'. But the gospel story still has to be explained. It tells of a man made a god by a rite of purification followed by the opening of the heavens and the coming of a spirit..."

In fact, as Morton Smith points out, the New Testament accords closely with contemporary accounts of how magicians "got spirits as constant companions and servants whom they could order about at will so as to perform miracles without elaborate rites or spells" (ibid., p. 97). In particular, such spirits were often represented as descending in the form of a bird.

After Jesus baptism and deification, Mark describes the spirit driving him out into the wilderness. "And he was in the wilderness forty days, being tempted by Satan, and was with the wild animals." (Mark 1.12f) As Smith points out, this nicely fits the standard pattern of a magician's life, especially a shaman's.

> "Compare Eliade's report that a shaman, at the beginning of his career, commonly 'withdraws into solitude and subjects him-

self to a strict regime of self torture'. He is supposed to be tested, subjected to terrible ordeals, or even killed by evil or initiatory spirits, but is helped by friendly spirits who appear in the form of animals. The statement that the spirit drove Jesus into the wilderness accords with Rabbinic reports of demonic compulsion and suggests that Jesus was 'possessed', although elsewhere it is claimed that he 'had' the spirit... this alternation between 'possessing' and 'being possessed' ...is characteristic of shamans in general". (ibid., p. 104)

It is true, of course, that Jesus repudiation of the typically magical power of flying through the air and turning stones into bread was, in one sense, a repudiation of magic. But while Jesus rejects the assistance of devils in performing such feats, he nonetheless returns from the wilderness with the power to call upon angels – as good spirits – to do his bidding. And it was "after his shamanic session in the wilderness that Jesus came, Mark says, to Galilee (1.14), and miracles began to happen" (ibid., p. 106).

"The first miracles reported are of the most credible sorts, and occur in the most plausible succession; winning disciples, exorcisms, and cures. We should expect a miracle worker to get his start in this way; making a few disciples, developing a reputation and self confidence, demonstrating in public his power to control hysteria, and eventually curing... psychosomatic ailments – (like) fever, paralysis, (hysterical blindness) and so on." (op. cit.)

As Smith argues,

"The miracles with which Mark represents Jesus as beginning his career in Galilee are drawn entirely from the (traditional) magician's repertory (cures for fever, blindness, lameness, paralysis, catalepsy, haemorrhage, and wounds). This should not be taken as discrediting their claim to historicity; rather the contrary; it is evidence that such 'cures' did occur. The cure of Peter's mother-in-law is completely plausible. An old lady suddenly recovered from a fever when her son-in-law came back from synagogue bringing as a guest an attractive young holy man who had just healed a demoniac in the presence of the congregation and was doubtless accompanied by half a dozen of the congregation's most prominent members (who would expect hospitality and see the condition of the house)." (ibid., p. 107-8)

"Jesus is pictured not only as having himself controlled spirits, but as having given twelve of his disciples the power ('authority') to expel demons and having sent them out to live as itinerant exorcists." And "...magic was (indeed) a technique that could be taught – as can hypnosis, acting, and pharmacology, (which are) probably its most important ingredients." (ibid., p. 113)

Morton Smith summarises the evidence from the Gospels and from other sources indicating the opinions of hostile 'outsiders' on the Eucharist and the 'mystery' of the Kingdom of God.

"Although (Jesus) pretended to follow Jewish customs, he formed a small circle of intimate disciples whom he taught to despise the Jewish Law and practice magic. These he bound together and to himself by ties of 'love', meaning sexual promiscuity, and by participation in the most awful magic rites, including cannibalism; they had some sort of ritual meal in which they ate human flesh and drank blood." (ibid., p. 114)

From the point of view of this tradition, Jesus as religious reformer (whether committed to a re-assertion or renewal of traditional Jewish values in face of the immanent coming of the Kingdom of God, or to the creation of a new religious movement transcending the boundaries of the Jewish people and the Jewish state) is very much a later construction – by the authors of the New Testament Gospels and others.

And, of course, Jesus actual accomplishments as itinerant healer are 'built up' into increasingly fantastic miracles in order to lend support to the ideas – and the movements – in question. As Kautsky says,

> "the further we advance in time [from the earlier gospels to the later] the more miraculous do these Gospels become. To be sure, miracles already occur in St Mark, [probably the oldest Gospel] but they are quite innocent when compared with the later ones. Thus, in the case of the awakening of the dead, Mark (Ch. 5) has Jesus summoned to the bedside of Jairus daughter, who is at the point of death. All believe she is already dead, but Jesus says, 'the damsel is not dead but sleepeth' and lays his hand upon her, and she arises" (KAUTSKY 1972, p. 31).

Presumably Jesus is quite correct in this case; she was not really dead at all.

In Luke, we have in addition the awakening to life of the youth of Nain. He has been dead long enough to be on his way to the cemetery when Jesus meets him; the latter causes him to arise from his bier. (Luke, Ch. 7)

For St John, these items are not strong enough. In his eleventh chapter he records the awakening of Lazarus, who "has been dead four days", and "by this time stinketh". John thus beats the record. (op. cit.)

And Ranke-Heinemann notes,

> "As for the credibility of the miracle of Lazarus, misgivings are in order from the very fact that the other three Evangelists, who [probably] wrote before John, say nothing about the event. It is unthinkable that the writers of the [earlier gospels], which recount so many of Jesus's miracles, would have ignored this most staggering of wonders if they had known of it. The only possible conclusion is that they never heard of it. This means... that the story did not come into circulation until later, that it was a late vintage fairy tale." (RANKE-HEINEMANN 1994, p. 91)

Part Four
JESUS THE REVOLUTIONARY

But there is another interpretation of Jesus's life and message. If we consider the classical texts of the founding fathers of materialist theory we generally find a very different sort of assessment. In particular, Engels, increasingly interested in the origins and early development of Christianity towards the end of his life, notes that,

> "The history of primitive Christianity presents remarkable coincidences with the modern workers movement. Like the latter, Christianity was originally a movement of the oppressed, it first appeared as a religion of slaves and freedmen, of the poor, the outcasts and the peoples subjected to or dispossessed by Rome. Both Christianity and socialism preach the approaching redemption from servitude and misery." (Quoted in KAUTSKY 1972, p. 462)

He describes early Christianity as "a dangerous revolutionary party... undermining religion and all the foundations of the state. It denied point blank that the Emperor's will was the highest law; it was without a fatherland, international." However, at the same time he denies that the movement had ever aspired to real political-economic revolution on earth. "Christians assign redemption to a future life in heaven after death... whereas socialism would attain it in this world by a transformation of society." (op. cit.)

Karl Kautsky, in his classic materialist analysis of *The Foundations of Christianity* (first published in 1908) goes much further. Carefully dissecting the Gospels so as to separate out original materials from what he takes to be the distortions, reconstructions and fabrications of later, much more conservative forces, he concludes that the early Christian congregation was indeed a proletarian organisation, characterised by intense class hatred against the rich and strongly communistic ideas and practices -- of collective ownership and control of basic material resources.

Referring to Jesus's demands that his disciples forsake their family relations in order to follow him he suggests that such communistic principles might have included collective sexual relations – with complete sexual 'freedom' within the early Christian congregation. Certainly, there is ample evidence of Jesus hostility to the orthodox family structures of his day. ("Whoever does not hate father and mother cannot be a follower of me, and whoever does not hate brothers and sisters... will not be worthy of me", "from now on five in one household will be divided..." etc.) And we have already seen how unsympathetic outsiders accused Jesus and his followers of promiscuity.

Most significantly, Kautsky argues that Jesus and his disciples anticipated the coming of the kingdom of God as a radical political-economic re-organisation of earthly life – with the abolition of poverty, exploitation and inequality (rather than some afterlife of the spirit in heaven). And that they themselves planned to play a very active role in bringing about such a change through inciting the masses to violent revolution.

Here, of course, the Jewish tradition of the Messiah was very much a tradition of a military leader who would liberate the Jewish people from all foreign oppression and domination, and, indeed, lead them to military world-domination. In identifying with such a Messiah, Jesus must have known that it would be, first and foremost, these sorts of hopes and expectations he would raise in his audiences.

Kautsky argues that we can really only make sense of the contradictions and heavily edited material of the Gospels by reference to the general social-political situation in Jesus's lifetime, as revealed in the writings of Josephus and other non-Christian sources. In particular.

[Given the] "rebellious character of those strata of the Jewish people that were waiting for the Messiah, particularly the proletarians of Jerusalem and the roving bands of Galilee, [as] the very elements from which Christianity took its origin... we must therefore assume at the outset that [it] was characterised by violence from its beginnings... This assumption becomes a certainty when we discover traces of this condition in the Gospels, in spite of the fact that their later editors were most solicitously ambitious to eliminate any element that might give offence to those in power." (ibid., p. 364)

"Gentle and submissive though Jesus may appear as a rule, he occasionally delivers himself of a statement of an entirely different kind, a statement forcing us to assume that... he was, in the original tradition, a rebel who was crucified as an unsuccessful leader of an insurrection." (op. cit.)

Jesus asks "Suppose ye that I am come to give peace on Earth?" And he replies, "I tell you, nay, but rather division; for from henceforth there shall be five in one house divided, three against two, and two against three." (Luke XIII 49). And in the Matthew Gospel the situation is clearer still; "Think not that I come to send peace on earth; I came not to send peace, but a sword." (X 34).

Entering Jerusalem at the time of the Passover he presumably relies upon the support of a substantial body of followers in driving out the merchants and bankers from the Temple. As Baigent and Leigh argue,

"Neither moneychangers nor bystanders, nor Jesus's own followers are likely to have stood idle, or engaged in theological debate, while loose coins rolled in all directions. Given the size and importance of the Temple, and the prominent role of the moneychangers, Jesus's overturning of their tables must have resulted in a full scale riot. Nor can Jesus himself possibly have expected anything else. Here again he is adopting a course of confrontation, a course of deliberate challenge to established authority."

"In two prominent instances – [of entry into Jerusalem on an ass and overturning the moneylenders tables] perhaps the two most public acts of his career – Jesus behaves in a way which must provoke violence, It is in these two instances that the Gospels probably come closest to vouchsafing a portrait of the historical Jesus. a man who, in a flagrant, even flamboyant fashion stages public spectacles which implicitly assert his claim as Israel's fore-told and rightful Messiah. And these spectacles are acts of calcu-lated provocation, which reflect an undisguised militancy, an obvi-ous preparedness to countenance force. What is more, both inci-dents make it clear that Jesus had a sizeable following. It clearly includes more than the original twelve disciples." (BAIGENT AND LEIGH 1987, p. 75)

Not long after the attack on the merchants and bankers, at the last supper, immediately before his arrest, Jesus says to his disciples, "Now, he who has a purse, let him take it and also a pocket. and he who has it not, let him sell his cloak, and buy a sword. For I say unto you it must now be fulfilled in me what is written, namely and he will be counted amongst the lawless *(anomon)* For what is written of me shall be fulfilled."

Immediately thereafter, on the Mount of Olives, the conflict takes place with the armed power of the state. Jesus is about to be arrested. "And behold one of them which was with Jesus stretched out his hand, and drew his sword, and struck a servant of the high priests, and smote off his ear."

"But in this Gospel Jesus is represented as being opposed to all bloodshed, consents peaceably to be chained, and is thereupon, executed, while his companions remain absolutely unmolested. In the form in which we have it, this story is a most remarkable one, full of contradictory statements that must originally have been quite different."

"Jesus calls for swords as if the hour of action had come; his faithful set out armed with swords – and at the very moment when they encounter the enemy and draw their swords, Jesus suddenly declares that he is opposed in principle to all use of force..."

"But if Jesus was opposed on principle to any use of force, why did he call for swords? Why did he permit his friends to bear arms when they went about with him? We can only understand this contradiction by assuming that the Christian tradition in its original form must have contained a report of a carefully planned coup d'état for which the time had seemed to be ripe after he had successfully driven the bankers and sellers out of the temple [presumably only with substantial popular support]. The later editors did not dare to throw out the report, deeply rooted in tradition, in its entirety [instead] they mutilated it by making the use of force appear to be an act undertaken by the apostles against the will of Jesus." (KAUTSKY 1972, p. 366)

Kautsky is less than entirely clear as to the precise aims of such a coup. However, he is presumably assuming that Jesus aimed to mobilise the poor, downtrodden, dispossessed Jewish proletarians and peasants to take control of the Temple and the city, removing both the Roman occupying forces and the collaborating Jewish (Sadducee) aristocracy in the name of a return to the 'true spirit of the Law'. From there they might even have aimed to carry the revolution to the surrounding regions, perhaps abolishing radical inequality and exploitation – perhaps dispossessing the wealthy absentee landlords and dividing the land amongst the primary producers.

Kautsky is not alone in this interpretation. More recently, S.G.F. Brandon, H. Maccoby and J. Carmichael have all argued that Jesus alleged pacifism was invented by the Gospel writers in order to make him more acceptable to Gentiles.

"In reality he was an ardent Jewish nationalist in the mould of fellow Galilean Judas the Galilean who had staged the uprising against the Romans in 6 CE. Jesus talk of the Kingdom of God was an appeal to nothing less than the overthrow of the Romans and the establishment of a new, independent Jewish state." (WILSON 1985, p. 96)

"As represented by Joel Carmichael, Jesus attempts to bring this about nearly succeeded. He managed to capture the Jerusalem

Temple with an armed force powerful enough for him to seize this vast edifice and hold it for some time. Equally, the gospel mention of the fall of the tower of Siloim (Luke 13: 4) was a reference to siege operations that the Romans were obliged to resort to in order to regain control of the city." (op. cit.)

Further support for this interpretation comes from the biblical details of Jesus's arrest, particularly in respect of the number of men who came to arrest Jesus in the garden. As Baigent and Leigh point out, the original Greek expression 'cohort' is very misleadingly translated in the authorised version of the Bible as a 'band of men'. In fact, "for the writers and early translators of the Bible it was a very precise term, denoting a very exact figure... the Roman army was organised into centuries, cohorts and legions. A Roman legion was... six thousand troops. A cohort was one tenth of a legion – six hundred soldiers. If, that is, they were regular Roman soldiers. A cohort composed of auxiliaries, as those in the Holy Land were, would number at least five hundred troops."

They suggest that sending

"upwards of five or six hundred troops to Gethsemane for the role purpose of arresting one man – a solitary prophet extolling love, who was attended by twelve disciples would have been a ridiculous example of overkill... an open invitation to civic disturbance. Unless, of course, such a disturbance already existed, and the cohort had been mustered to quell it."

"It would seem clear that there was a civil disturbance of substantial size in the 'Garden'. There may well have been fighting. But whether there was actual fighting or not, the situation was obviously perceived as a military threat by the Roman administration, who reacted to it with a large scale military response." (BAIGENT AND LEIGH 1987, p. 77)

And finally, of course, there are the circumstances of Jesus death to consider. To quote Baigent and Leigh once more,

"whatever Jesus's association with the Zealots, he was certainly crucified by the Romans as a political revolutionary. This much is
stated by the Roman chronicler Tacitus, and thus constitutes the
one assertion about Jesus to issue from a non-biblical, yet contemporary, source. There is no question but that the Romans perceived
Jesus as a military and political figure, and dealt with him strictly
according to this perception. Crucifixion was a penalty reserved for
transgressions against Roman law. and Rome would not have both-
ered to crucify a man preaching a purely spiritual message, or a
message of peace. Jesus was not executed by the Jewish Sanhedrin – which could, with permission, stone to death a man who
had trespassed against Jewish law – but by the Roman administration. And the two men allegedly crucified with him are explicitly
described as 'Lestai', Zealots. They are not, despite tradition, common criminals, but political revolutionaries – or 'freedom fighters'."
(ibid., p. 73)

Part Five
PROBLEMS WITH BOTH INTERPRETATIONS

Here then are two apparently radically different interpretations –
each with quite substantial support from the available material; how
do we decide between them? Of course, they need not be wholly
incompatible. Jesus the Magician could also have become Jesus the
revolutionary leader.

Lately, interest in the idea of Jesus as Zealot leader has been
stimulated by the publication of Baigent and Leigh's (1991) book
on the Dead Sea Scrolls. Traditional orthodoxy (largely emanating
from the Catholic Church) has seen the scrolls as mainly products of
an Essene community of the first century BCE. But, as Baigent and
Leigh point out, a number of scholars – including Cecil Roth and
Godfrey Driver – have argued that they are actually the work of
militant Zealots of the first century CE and thus 'more or less contemporary with the New Testament'.

More recently, Robert Eisenman has gone a step further. While agreeing with Roth and Driver's interpretation (on the basis of a number of archaeological and textual considerations), he argues that the Qumran community that produced the scrolls was in fact a community of early Christians, led by Jesus's brother James, in the period following Jesus's execution by the Romans – a community increasingly at odds with the heresies of Paul, as the latter developed his own brand of non-Jewish, Jesus-worshipping 'Christianity' owing very little to the teachings of Jesus himself.

If Eisenman is right in this regard then early (orthodox) Christians and Zealots would seem to be indistinguishable. And Eisenman draws precisely this conclusion, arguing that Palestinian Christians, Essenes, Zealots and Sicarii are really just "variations on the same theme; manifestations of the same movement" of revolutionary Jewish nationalism (BAIGENT AND LEIGH 1991, p. 292).

However, there are problems with these ideas (over and above the problems of interpreting the precise significance of the Dead Sea Scrolls). And there is also quite a lot of evidence suggesting other dimensions of Jesus life and message not really compatible with either of these interpretations. In particular, there seem to be too many consistent and coherent details of the gospel accounts at odds with the picture of Jesus as a straightforward Jewish fundamentalist revolutionary and guerilla leader.

Certainly there seems to be little doubt that Jesus himself always saw his ideas as part of a continuing tradition of Jewish thought – as a reaffirmation or development of the original Laws of Moses, intended for Jews alone. And after his death his original followers, based in Jerusalem under the leadership of his brother James, apparently continued to live according to his prescriptions, owning everything in common, giving to each according to need, going together to worship in the Temple, eating together, and sharing their food with each other. So did they radically oppose Paul's attempt to turn Christianity into a non-Jewish religious movement based upon abandonment of the Law of Moses and deification of Jesus himself.

As Wilson points out, Jesus's commitment to the Law of Moses (as evidenced for example by Matthew 56: 17-18) could have meant, amongst other things, "a strong accent on humanity, and sympathy towards the poor, the widowed and the oppressed; a rejection of artistic representation of God – as a limitation of his universality; support for the circumcision of every Jewish male child as a mark of his people's covenant with God; and a prohibition on eating certain – unclean – meats".

Nonetheless, the gospels also provide good evidence of Jesus introducing some quite new and radical modifications of Jewish orthodoxy, quite counterpoised to the violent fundamentalism of Maccabean Zealots. In particular, the God of Jesus comes across as a quite different character from the God of the Old Testament, imparting quite a different sort of tone to the New Testament as compared with the Old.

Thus, as noted earlier, the God who appears throughout the Old Testament 'is a jealous God' (Exodus 34.14), as well as a 'God above all other gods'.

"This is a god who constantly sought to demonstrate his power and authority, often through acts of violence, vengeance and murder that recur throughout the accounts of the history of the Hebrew people. Jehovah punished when enraged and jealous, not hesitating to kill and destroy those he considered disobedient to his commands and will. This God clearly was not himself bound by the commandments he had given to Moses and the Israelites." (GREVEN 1992, p. 46)

By contrast, Jesus's God seems to be a god of love rather than of jealousy, violence and war. And Jesus's manner of referring to God is instructive.

Wilson tells us that even highly sceptical commentators have recognised that those of Jesus's utterances that have been left in Aramaic have the greater claim to authenticity and, of these, un-doubtedly one of the most striking is his habit of addressing God as

Abba, meaning 'father'. For most Jews, the awesome power and authority of God were reflected in the fact that "the very name of God carried such mystique that it could not be uttered, nor set in writing". That Jesus could address God so directly – and familiarly – as 'father', indicates that a much more friendly and approachable sort of god is involved in this case. (WILSON 1985, p. 75)

While Jesus was quite clear that the Mosaic Law still formed the proper basis for human conduct his parables, in particular, suggest that "he seems to have believed that there were all sorts of circumstances in which Love should transcend the Law to embrace individuals whose sinfulness had in (orthodox) eyes rendered them unclean, and thus unfit to worship God".

> In conventional Jewish society anyone who had indulged in immoral behaviour, such as a prostitute, or who had collaborated with the Romans, such as a tax-collector, would be considered an outcast, Jesus, though, is represented as deliberately seeking out such people. In this he seems to have followed in the footsteps of John the Baptist who, as Jesus himself remarked, attracted his own following of tax-collectors and prostitutes. (ibid., p. 78)

When Jesus preached the coming of God's Kingdom – the intervention of God in earthly affairs to finally establish his rule – he clearly indicated a radical upheaval in the power structures of his day, which would 'restore to the mainstream of life' all those suffering poverty, exploitation and marginalisation. As Riches points out, "the Beatitudes, at least in their Lucan form (Luke 6.20-3), suggest that it is the disinherited, the physically poor, who will inherit the Kingdom" (RICHES 1990, p. 121). But this change was apparently not associated with ideas of a violent overthrow and expulsion of Roman power.

By sharing meals with tax-collectors, prostitutes and shepherds, in the context of proclaiming the coming of God's Kingdom, Jesus

> "was countering the popular belief that the coming of the Kingdom would be attended by the judgement and destruction of

God's enemies. The Kingdom would not be achieved by military action against the Romans; God would not require the destruction of sinners, but would seek them out and welcome them into the Kingdom." (ibid., p. 120)

It is true, as Wilson says, that many of Jesus's apparently most characteristic ideas actually have clear antecedents in earlier Jewish thought. Jesus's 'communism' (living, owning and sharing necessary resources in common) "is no different from what we are told of the Essenes by Josephus; each man's possessions go into the pool, and as if with brothers, their entire property belongs to them all. Similarly, just as Jesus sent his disciples on their missions with no haversack for the journey or spare tunic or footwear ...so we are told that the Essenes... 'when they travel carry no baggage at all, but only weapons to keep off bandits... Neither garments nor shoes are changed till they are dropping to pieces or worn out with age'." (WILSON 1985, p. 77)

But, as Wilson also points out,

"Time and time again, Jesus gave an existing idea a new twist, and not always in the same direction. John the Baptist asked for the man with two tunics to give away the one he did not need; Jesus asked him, if called upon, to give away both. The book of Leviticus ruled, 'You must love your neighbour as yourself' (Leviticus 19.18); Jesus urged, 'Love your enemies, and pray for those who persecute you' (Matthew 5.44). Such precepts, so far as can be ascertained, were utterly new and exclusive to the gospel Jesus. They have no obvious counterparts in the teachings of either the Pharisees or the Essenes." (WILSON 1985, p. 78)

Certainly these considerations do not sit well with the image of Jesus as militant Zealot leader. And they raise the obvious question of the source of his new teachings. Why and how was Jesus able to transcend the barbarity and violence (the sexism and prejudice) which were so deeply embedded in the dominant theories and practices of his age? But before we try to answer this question, there is more to say about the particular uniqueness and significance of Jesus message.

Part Six
PERSONAL POLITICS

While it is true that, in broad outline, Kautsky's basic picture of class relations seems to be substantially confirmed by contemporary evidence, it is also clear that there still remain crucial dimensions of class relations radically neglected by Kautsky's account. As in so many 'classical' Marxist analyses, Kautsky has considered only relations within the adult male population, without taking account of the social roles and life circumstances of women and children.

To properly understand the social situation – and the particular significance of Jesus life and message – however, we must consider also the patriarchal social relations which gave adult males very substantial power and control over women and children in First Century Palestine – as in other surrounding societies.

Thus, we learn from the Old Testament that in earlier times the Jewish male adult had absolute ('patriarchal') authority over the members of his family. The wife was expected to call her husband *'baal'* or 'master' and in the Decalogue the wife is listed amongst a man's possessions, along with his servants, his ox and his ass (Ex. 20: 17). In this period the father could also sell his daughter into slavery or prostitution.

The patriarchal head of the family had effective control of family property (as the then predominant form of landholding) which was passed on by inheritance to the oldest son. If there was no son it could fall to the daughters but they had to marry within their tribe (or 'clan') so their portion could not be transferred out. If the owner died childless, the inheritance went his brother, uncle or nearest kinsman.

"Thus, descent was reckoned patrilinearly, with the eldest son succeeding the father in authority after the fathers death. All the sons and their wives lived in the fathers household until his death. The father contracted marriages for his children; in the case of sons by paying a bride price. In the case of daughters the father would furnish her a dowry, which took the place of her share of the inheritance. (Thus the daughters of wealthy citizens had some measure of protection from abuse, since the return of her dowry in case of divorce might be to the economic disadvantage of her husbands family.)" (LERNER, G. 1987, p. 169)

All Israelite women were expected to marry and thus passed from the control of fathers (and brothers) to that of husbands and fathers-in-law. When the husband died before his wife, his brother or another male relative assumed control over her and married her, while in earlier times "Hebrew men enjoyed complete sexual freedom within and outside of marriage" including "free sexual use of his concubines and slave women. Polygamy which was widespread amongst the patriarchs, later became rare except for royalty, and monogamous marriage became the ideal."

"Virginity was expected of the bride at the time of marriage, and the wife owed her husband absolute fidelity in marriage. Punishment for adultery was the death of both parties (Lev. 20: 10) and the Jewish wife had little protection against false accusations of adultery. Divorce was obtainable by the husband, with an economic penalty, but it was never obtainable by the wife... Jewish law forced a rapist to marry the woman he had raped and specified that he may not divorce her. Implicitly, this forced a woman into an indissoluble marriage with her rapist (Deut. 22: 28-9). (ibid., p. 170)

In marriage, the wife was expected to produce offspring, namely sons. Barrenness in a wife, which was interpreted to be failure to bear sons, was a disgrace to her and cause for divorce... Adoption of kin, strangers or even slaves was as prevalent in Hebrew as it was in other Near Eastern societies, as a means of

providing a man with an heir in case of childlessness and assur-
ing care for himself in old age. Or, a man might add wives or
concubines to his household, if his first wife did not bear a son."
(op. cit.)

Looking beyond explicit statements of 'biblical law' to the specific details of Old Testament stories, Lerner, Eisler and other feminists highlight the appalling values and ideologies implicit in many
such stories.

"Perhaps the most striking example... concerns the biblical
treatment of rape. In the Book of Judges, Ch. 19, the priests who
wrote the Bible tell us of a father who offers his virgin daughter to
a drunken mob. He has a male guest in his house, a man from the
high caste tribe of Levites. A bunch of rowdies from the tribe of
Benjamin demand to see him outside, apparently with the intention of beating him up. 'Behold' the father says to them, "here is
my daughter, a maiden, and his (the guests') concubine; them I will
bring out now, and humble ye them, and do with them what
seemeth good unto you, but unto this man do not so vile a thing".
"We are told this casually, as a matter of little importance.
Then, as the story unfolds, we are further told how 'the man took
his concubine, and brought her forth unto them, and they knew
her, and abused her all night until the morning', how she crawled
back to the threshold of the house where 'her lord' was sleeping;
how when he woke up 'and opened the door of the house, and
went out to go his way' he stumbled on her and commanded 'up
and let us be going', and how finally, finding that she was dead, he
loaded her body on his ass and went home." (EISLER 1990, p. 99)

Clearly the earlier tribal structure (with inalienable clan property) had been significantly undermined by the developing class
structures of Jesus time. But, as Witherington points out, the evidence of the Mishnah in particular, suggests that "a woman's (and
we can add here also a child's) position and privileges... during and

beyond New Testament times differed little from their status and rights in Old Testament times" (WITHERINGTON 1990, p. 8).

Certainly, as Lerner notes, in later periods (by the time of the monarchy), "the father's power of life and death over his family members was no longer unlimited and unrestrained. In this respect we note an improvement in the position of daughters (and sons) over the earlier period" (LERNER 1987, p. 168). But as Witherington points out, "there can be little doubt that the family (remained) the exclusive sphere of influence of Jewish women in the first century CE".

> "The laws of inheritance, betrothal and divorce [remained] heavily biased in the males favour [with only a few checks and balances such as the wife's divorce price and the daughters 'right of maintenance']. A woman was [still] passed from her father to her husbands sphere of authority, usually without being consulted. Since a woman changed families when she married, she could not be expected to preserve the family's name or keep property in the same family." (WITHERINGTON 1990, p. 4)
>
> "For this reason, the laws stated that she was entitled to 'maintenance' rather than inheritance in most cases. That Rabbi Ishmael can bemoan the poverty of Israel's women is perhaps an indication of how hard and rare it was for a woman to inherit property." (op. cit.)

When a girl was underage (under twelve years), she had no right to her possessions, and the fruit of her labour or anything she found belonged to her father. If she was sexually violated, compensation money for the indignity was paid to the father.

A woman's security in her husbands family was limited by the fact that the husband could divorce her if she caused an 'impediment' to the marriage. This privilege was rarely extended to the wife. A husband could divorce his wife without her consent for reasons ranging from her unchastity, to her burning a meal, or to finding another woman fairer than his own wife. A wife's security was also threatened in some cases by the fact that polygyny was permitted in New Testament times as it was in Old Testament days.

"In the family, the wife's duties included grinding flour, baking bread, washing clothes, breast feeding the children for eighteen to twenty-four months, making the beds, working with wool, and washing her husbands face, hands and feet."

It is true that a woman's position depended to some extent upon the class – or 'caste' – position of her family and that of her husband. As Witherington says, "the extent of a wife's household duties depended on how many servants she brought into the marriage" (ibid., p. 5). And "a woman of priestly stock (a descendent of Levi or Aaron) had certain priestly rights and privileges" (ibid., p. 8).

Furthermore, as Ranke-Heinemann points out, the inclusion of 'evidently well-off' and independent women amongst Jesus disciples in the New Testament accounts, providing financial assistance for the others, provides evidence that not all Jewish women of the period were under the complete financial and moral control of men.

However, as John's Gospel testifies, women were still being stoned to death for alleged adultery in first century Jewish society. Women were still very much second class citizens, banned from the inner courts of the temple, banned from any part of the temple during their monthly periods. The devout male would not even speak to a woman outside his immediate family. (WILSON 1985, p. 80)

As Ranke-Heinemann confirms, in Jesus's day, the general practice was that if a woman so much as spoke to a man on the street, she could be repudiated by her husband without repayment of the marriage portion – roughly equivalent to our alimony. And, conversely, it was considered outrageous for the student of a rabbi (his disciple), not to mention for the rabbi himself, to speak with a woman on the street.

This segregation, domination and restriction of women could also have rebounded upon young children, creating psychological problems for later life. For it could have encouraged a situation in which the mother 'idealised' her son as an alternative love object to the patriarchal husband. So too could she have envied and resented him as a potential patriarchal oppressor in his own right.

Such ambivalent, and potentially stifling responses on the part of the mother can encourage a comparable ambivalence on the part of the son, including powerful Oedipal feelings of desire for the mother and hostility towards the father, possibly persisting in only thinly repressed form into later life.

In the light of these sorts of considerations we can perhaps go someway towards explaining the practice of circumcision of young boys as a hostile attack upon the body – and specifically the genitalia – of the infant boy by a jealous father. His own poorly resolved Oedipal feelings lead to his seeking to monopolise the attentions of his wife – as surrogate mother – and resenting the relationship of mother or son as he resented the relationship between his mother and his father. He inflicts upon the son in reality the punishment he only imagined inflicting upon the father. At the same time, his continuing jealousy and hostility towards the son contribute to the perpetuation of such Oedipal problems across the generations.

The Old Testament also offers substantial support for, and evidence of, high levels of paternal abuse and violence against older male children, in the interests of enforcing total subservience of such children to patriarchal authority. As Greven points out; "sons obedience to fathers is a recurrent biblical theme... Consider the advice Moses gave his people after having delivered Jehovah's commandments to them". As Moses declared,

"Thou shalt also consider in thine heart that, as a man chasteneth his son, so the lord they God chasteneth thee. Therefore thou shalt keep the commandments of the Lord thy God, to walk in his ways and fear him." (Deuteronomy 8.5-6) And Moses added this threat to his admonitions: "As the nations which the Lord destroyeth before your face, so shall ye perish; because ye would

not be obedient unto the voice of the Lord your God." (Deuteronomy 8.28)

Subsequently, when Jehovah spoke through his prophet Nathan
his message to King David was: "I will be his father, and he shall be
my son. If he commit iniquity, I will chasten him with the rod of
men, and with the stripes of the children of men; but my mercy
shall not depart away from him…" (11 Samuel 7: 14-15).

Jehovah's punishments thus provided the paradigm for parental
discipline of children, a model that became most explicit in pro-
verbs attributed to Solomon, the (most wise) King of Israel:

> He that spareth the rod hateth his son; but he that loveth him,
> chasteneth him betimes
> Foolishness is bound in the heart of a child; but the rod of
> correction shall drive it far from him
> The rod and reproof give wisdom; but the child left to himself
> bringeth his mother to shame

Presumably the fundamentalist Maccabeans and their later
followers took such ideas very seriously in their dealings with their
own children. Indeed, from what we read about them it seems
likely that they would have gone all the way with Moses in the
murder of the rebellious son (who does not respond to 'chasten-
ing') through stoning by "all the men of his city" (Deuteronomy
21.18-21).

And finally, on the subject of oppressed groups ignored or side-
lined in the traditional materialist interpretation, it is important to
include reference to the appalling discrimination against the sick,
the infirm and the handicapped (and their relatives) apparently also
characteristic of the period.

As Ranke-Heinemann points out,

> "Ancient Jewish theologians drew up catalogues in which guilt
> and sickness were juxtaposed as cause and effect. E.g. 'there are

three kinds of dropsy; when it results from lewdness, the body is hard; when it results from hunger, the body is bloated; when it results from a magic spell, the body is emaciated'. 'Every judge who accepts a bribe and twists justice will not die at an advanced age without his eyes going blind.' (See Exodus 23.8) 'And you shall take no bribe, for a bribe blinds the officials.' Rabbi Jochanan (d. AD 270) said 'the plagues of leprosy come about from seven things; calumny, bloodshed, perjury, fornication, pride, robbery and envy'. A rabbi said 'Whoever engages in intercourse by the light of a lamp will have epileptic children'. Rabbi L. Jochanan ben Dahadai (c. AD 180) asks 'Why do children become lame? Because the parents turn their table upside down (that is, woman on top, man underneath). Why do they become deaf? Because the parents talk during intercourse'." (RANKE-HEINEMANN 1991, p. 83)

Crossan argues that the terms translated as 'leprosy' in the New Testament actually refer to scaley or flaking skin conditions like psoriasis, eczema or fungus infections of the skin. But there is no doubt that those suffering such conditions were indeed 'lepers' in the sense of being rejected, feared and ostracised by the rest of the (Jewish) community.

Here, indeed, Crossan follows Mary Douglas in identifying the long history of foreign invasion and conquest to which Palestine had been subject as crucial in establishing particularly strong feelings of fear and anger in relation to anything interpretable as a boundary violation amongst the Jewish people – including bodily conditions of breakdown of the skin surface.

As he says,

"The leprous person is not a social threat because of medical contagion, threatening infection or epidemic, as we might imagine, but because of symbolic contamination, threatening in microcosm the very identity, integrity, and security of society at large..." (CROSSAN 1994, p. 79)

Part Seven
JESUS AS RADICAL EGALITARIAN AND HUMANIST

In sharp contrast to these currents of oppressive patriarchal thought and action, Jesus seems to have believed in – and struggled for – radical social equality. We have already touched upon his hostility to the established family structures of his day. In particular, he identifies the family as an arena of struggle between and within the generations, and actively supports the struggle against patriarchal power. In this connection, Crossan observes;

> "The family is society in miniature, the place where we first and most deeply learn how to love and be loved, hate and be hated, help and be helped, abuse and be abused. It is not just a centre of domestic serenity; since it involves power, it invites the abuse of power, and it is at that precise point that Jesus attacks it. His ideal group is, contrary to Mediterranean, and indeed, most human familial reality, an open one equally accessible to all under God." (ibid., p. 60)

Jesus seems to have respected women as equals, regularly "entering into deep conversations with women". And "although the Gospels gloss over the fact, according to Luke, Jesus appears to have had nearly as many women followers as men" (including Mary Magdalene, Joanna the wife of Herod's steward, Susanna and several others) (WILSON 1985, p. 79).

Riches says: "Jesus ... longed for a world in which it would be possible for people to deal openly with one another, respecting each other fully as persons. Even his teaching on marriage and divorce" – while apparently less 'liberal' than that of contemporary Pharisaic authorities like Hillel (in actually forbidding divorce altogether) – "should be seen not as introducing harsh regulations to torment the unfortunate, but as emphasising the potential of the marriage relationship for allowing people to develop deep trust and mutuality. What he was objecting to was the right of a man to dispose of his wife if she offended him." (RICHES 1990, pp. 113-4)

And, along the same lines, Witherington notes that: "The net effect of Jesus's views is that various stereotypes of women as temptresses are countered, and at the same time a woman is given greater security in marriage by making the man responsible for its continued maintenance and by prohibiting the man from using his power to cause its dissolution" (WITHERINGTON 1990, p. 45).

Similarly, Jesus seems to have had a deep love and respect for young children, radically at odds with the Old Testament beliefs and prescriptions quoted earlier. Greven notes,

> From the Gospels it is clear that Jesus loved children and used children often in his parables and speeches as models for others to follow. When children were brought to him to be touched and prayed for, his disciples rebuked him. But Jesus said: "Suffer little children and forbid them not, to come unto me; for of such is the Kingdom of Heaven. And he laid his hands on them and departed hence" (Matthew 19.13-15).
>
> For many [Christians], the crucial text concerning Jesus's attitudes towards children is this: "At the same time came the disciples unto Jesus, saying, Who is the greatest in the Kingdom of Heaven? And Jesus called a little child unto him, and set him in the midst of them, And said, Verily I say unto you, Except ye be converted, and become as little children, ye shall not enter into the Kingdom of Heaven. Whosoever therefore shall humble himself as this little child, the same is greatest in the Kingdom of Heaven. And whoso shall receive one such little child in my name receiveth me. But whoso shall offend one of these little ones which believe in me, it will be better for him that a millstone were hanged about his neck, and that he were drowned in the depth of the sea" (Matthew 18.1-6). (GREVEN 1992, p. 51)

Along the same lines Jesus adds that his disciples and others should "take heed that ye despise not one of these little ones; for I say unto you, That in Heaven their angels do always behold the face of my Father which is in heaven. For the Son of man is come to save that which was lost... Even so it is not the will of your Father which is in heaven, that one of these little ones should perish" (Matthew 18.10-11-14).

Greven adds that Jesus never endorsed the brutal 'punishment' and 'control' of the Old Testament. "Nowhere in the New Testament does Jesus approve of the infliction of pain upon children by the rod or any other implement, nor is he ever reported to have recommended any kind of physical discipline of children by any parent." (ibid.)

Nor, finally, did Jesus accept that the sick were to blame for their own illnesses, and should be rightfully excluded from society. On the contrary, he spent substantial time communing with them and trying to help them. As Crossan says, in respect of Jesus's healing of the leper in Mark 1: 40-44,

> "I presume that Jesus, who did not and could not cure that disease... healed the poor mans illness by refusing to accept the diseases ritual uncleanliness and social ostracisation. Jesus thereby forced others either to reject him from their community or to accept the leper within it as well. Since, however, we are ever dealing with the body politic, that act quite deliberately impugns the rights and prerogatives of society's boundary keepers and controllers. By healing the illness without curing the disease, Jesus acted as an alternative boundary keeper in a way subversive to the established procedures of his society." (CROSSAN 1994, p. 82)

Perhaps Crossan too swiftly dismisses the possibility of cure of skin conditions by (hypnotic) suggestion (see next chapter). But his basic point remains valid.

Here we begin to see what was really uniquely radical about Jesus's life and message. Not only did he challenge class divisions, inequality and oppression in the Marxist sense. He was also a campaigner for the rights of women and children. His egalitarianism extended to include all people – women, children, beggars and the sick, as well as the oppressed workers and peasants. He was a humanist in an age that all too easily radically devalued human life.

But there is still some way to go to the contradictory heart of the Christian message. We have still to explain just why and how he was able to develop such ideas, so radically out of kilter with the prevailing orthodoxy of his day.

CHAPTER NINE
CHRISTIANITY *cont.*

Part One
THE PROBLEM OF EVIL

To outside observers of Christianity, one of the most interesting problems arising from Christian belief concerns the believers themselves: what psychological mechanisms are at work which would allow, or encourage, people to have faith in the Christian God? What sort of psychological role is served by belief in such a being? These questions become all the more compelling once we consider the profound contradictions in what Christian theology has to say about this 'perfect' God.

On the one hand, the Christian God is alleged to be a loving God, an infinitely good God, a God who is omnipotent and omnipresent. On the other hand, history, and the Scriptures themselves, give an account of human existence which, from the beginnings of recorded time, has been characterised by incredible degrees of misery, poverty, cruelty, exploitation, brutality and inequality. For the non-believer, this apparent and inherent discrepancy, of an all-powerful God of Love who allows his people to suffer so horribly, would seem sufficient cause to doubt the entire edifice of Christian ideology.

And yet Christians themselves, those driven by whatever psychological causes to embrace Christian belief, are able both to reconcile the ideas of a loving God and a miserable humanity, and also to proffer arguments explaining away this contradiction. As one such argument runs: God moves in mysterious ways. Suffering occurs in the world of men in order that some 'ultimate' and worthwhile purpose may be achieved and revealed. The idea here is that Good develops in and through the struggle against Evil. The main problem with this argument, however, for the non-believer, is that if God is truly so mysterious there is no way that we could possibly ever know for sure that He is good and omnipotent.

A second argument explaining the co-existence of a Good God and an Evil world is slightly more sophisticated than the first. This explanation states that God gives humans 'free will'. It is this human free will which causes suffering, and not God himself, who would prefer that humans choose to be Good – rather than Evil – without his direct intervention. Again, this argument raises further questions for the non-believer: if God is omnipotent, then surely free will is also subject to God's direction? And if it is not, then why did God fail to 'program in' sufficient intelligence, goodwill and foresight to enable humans to avoid millennia of anguish – generated by, among other things, campaigns of mass slaughter, and by chronic instances of exploitation of the many by the few? Why did God not provide His people with a benign earthly environment, such as to enable humans to avoid competition and warfare over limited resources, and to avoid, too, episodic bouts of mass starvation?

Perhaps the most bizarre aspect of Christian theology, from the outsider's point of view, concerns the notion that God has actually programmed in original sin to ensure the perpetuation of suffering. It would seem, to the non-believer, that if this Christian God did exist, then – far from being a loving God, as Christians claim – He is in fact a cruel god, a sadistic being who enjoys human misery and brutality. Or a best, this Christian God is either incompetent, or else radically out of touch with his own feelings, and the feelings of others.

Why, then, are Christians able to sustain their faith, despite these considerable theological dilemmas? Why are they drawn to this omnipotent father figure, who is believed to be both infinitely good, and yet also seen to be brutal and alienated from his 'family' – the Family of Man?

Part Two
CHRISTIANITY, CHILD ASSAULT AND
PSYCHOPATHOLOGY

When we put the dilemma of Christian belief in these terms, it is not too difficult to see the relevance of psychoanalytic theory in explaining the attraction, for some, of Christian ideology. Christian ideology may, in short, serve as a social sanction for those specific sorts of infantile fantasy defence mechanisms which tend to be deployed by those trying to cope with the experience of childhood abuse. Or, to put the same point another way, fundamentalist Christianity may serve to sustain, to extend, to ameliorate – but not, ultimately, to heal – the guilt and self-loathing arising from parental, or guardian, abuse. If we are to understand how and why this may be so, we should first clarify the relevant aspects of psychoanalytic theory.

Let us first consider the most psychologically problematic instance of violent abuse, that which is inflicted by the parent upon the very young child who has not yet developed clear ego boundaries – a clear sense of their own separate existence. It is at this stage that the child is most vulnerable to outside forces. Violence inflicted upon a very young child can, therefore, have considerable, and considerably disastrous, psychic consequences. The most profound of these is the child's subsequent inability to distinguish between powerful emotions: forever afterwards, victims of early childhood abuse tend to conflate and to confuse love and violence, love and hate, love and pain. Abuse of the young child establishes in the child's mind a fundamental equation of love and violence, and leads to that individual's inability in later life to love others without recourse to violence in speech and behaviour. In other words, those who have suffered abuse as very young children will express their own love through violence, or else will accept love from others only if this love is accompanied by violence.

There is a primitive and fundamental (unconscious) psychic defence mechanism which is at work here: identification with the aggressor. This psychic mechanism is built upon a primordial splitting of the personality. As Sándor Ferenczi points out, young children subjected to violent abuse from those adults upon whom they are completely dependent for care and love, feel physically and morally helpless. The personalities of very young children are "too insufficiently consolidated for [them] to be able to protest even if only in thought... The overwhelming power and authority of these adults renders [them] silent. Often [they are] deprived of [their] senses. Yet that very fear, when it reaches its zenith, forces them automatically to surrender to the will of the aggressor, to anticipate each of his wishes and to submit to them; forgetting [themselves] entirely, to identify totally with the aggressor."

Here we are discussing a world of extremes, a world in which there can be no middle ground between, on the one hand, the totally powerless and abused victim, and on the other the all-powerful and merciless abuser. The only defence available to the child-victim is this process of psychic splitting and identification with the aggressor. And with identification comes emotional fixation and a tendency to respond in a similar way to similar situations throughout later life. (This is what Freud called the repetition compulsion.) This is to say that victims of early childhood abuse tend to respond with violence to demands emanating from beings who are smaller and weaker than themselves (split off from their own empathic feelings of weakness); they also respond to violence against themselves with a similar psychic splitting process. Indeed, such individuals may even encourage violence against themselves – so as to experience the sense of 'release' brought about by their identification with the absolute power of the abuser.

Early and extreme abuse, perpetrated by the loved parent or guardian, may interfere profoundly with the establishment in later life of clear-cut ego boundaries and a coherent sense of self. This being so, such abuse can also contribute to serious psychotic delusional states, including an inability to differentiate between external realities beyond the self, and internal processes such as thoughts, memories and feelings. Early childhood abuse can contribute also to multiple personality disorders, in which the intolerable feelings and impulses generated by the abuse become split into separate 'selves'. Suicidal despair, anger, murderous rage and fear – for example – thereby come to exist within different 'selves', possibly without continuity of experience or memory.

The situation is somewhat altered in the case of a child being older, or when the intensity of the abuse itself is mitigated. For then a space exists for the victim to respond without radical disintegration of the self. Fear, shock and anger – directed towards both his or her own weakness, and also the loved one's betrayal – may be expressed, together with violent and aggressive revenge fantasies. Again, however, even when the abuse situation is somewhat less drastic, there can still be powerful psychic forces at work. In this case, the forces will be directed towards preserving the ideal fantasy of the loving parent, as well as protecting the child-victim from having to face the horrible reality of abuse and cruelty suffered at the hands of those the child is looking to for love, care and acknowledgment. Hence, this need to block out the reality of the abuse may motivate a psychic splitting process, whereby such feelings as weakness, anger and aggression are denied and repressed.

All children old enough to recognise that they exist as separate, albeit weak and dependent, beings have a strong need to believe that their parents are ultimately good and kind. Parents appear to the child to be omnipotent, omnipresent super-beings – God-like figures who, in comparison to the child, have everything: all the food, warmth, love, mobility and so forth. The child desperately needs to feel that these God-like parents are devoted to his or her particular needs and well-being: the consequences of the reverse, for the weak and utterly dependent child, are simply too terrible to contemplate.

Those children whose parents are, in actual fact, truly devoted to their care and well-being do not need to employ extensive wish-fulfilling fantasy. Generally, such children are confident of their parents' love for them, and confident, too, of their own worth, and so are increasingly able to recognise and accept their parents' (real) imperfections. In contrast to this, those children unfortunate enough to have aggressive and unloving parents require a good deal of fantasy in order to maintain the illusion of their parents' perfection. And, while this need not involve repression of the memory of specific episodes of abuse, such children must repress their memories of the negative feelings arising from the abuse. Such feelings are, after all, radically incompatible with the idea of parental perfection.

Although having repressed their feelings of desperation and weakness, of vengeful anger, in order to preserve their fantasy idealisation of the (perfectly) good and kind parent, child sufferers do not simply experience the vanishing of their emotions. Instead, such victims of abuse tend to turn these negative feelings against their own selves. As Freud expresses the point, feelings of anger and desperation are taken up by the parental super-ego – or, in other words, by the child's own conscience. As a result, child victims of abuse blame themselves for their suffering, which they see as punishment for their own, intrinsic, weakness and sinfulness. Moreover, these children become trapped in a downward spiral of guilt, repression and fantasy – a spiral brought upon by the fact that abuse lowers the self-esteem of the individual child, and hence heightens his or her need for love and approval. This enhanced need for love leads to an even more intense idealisation of the parent, which, because the child grows weaker by comparison as the parent becomes stronger, leads to the further undermining of the child's own self-esteem and autonomy.

Repressed aggression not thus taken up by the parental super-ego perpetually threatens to force its way back into conscious awareness

and conscious action ('the return of the repressed'). As a means of
attempting to prevent this, the ego deploys unconscious fantasy
defences of projection and displacement. In the first case, anger and
aggression are projected onto others; consequently, this projected
anger tends to foster within sufferers paranoid fears that they will be
attacked by those upon whom they have projected their aggression.
In the case of displacement, anger and aggression are displaced by
sufferers away from the abusive parents and on to some other, more
accessible, or acceptable, object. (Clearly, these two processes can go
hand in hand: the object of projection may become also the object of
displaced aggression – as in racist attacks, or holy wars.)

Returning to Christian ideology and to those believers who
uphold it, we are now in a better position to consider the likely role
played by parental abuse in the persistence of the more virulent, fundamentalist strains of Christianity. In regard to the most extreme
instances of abuse, in which violence is inflicted upon the child
whose ego boundaries are not yet clearly developed, it seems apparent that the very primitive, schizoid modes of thought engendered
and fixated by this treatment have been at work within particular
Christian congregations during certain historical periods. A case in
point is the European witchcraze, which occurred during the sixteenth and seventeenth centuries. In the name of God's love, fundamentalist Protestant clerics tortured and murdered many thousands
of European women. The activities of these clerics, and the excitement amongst those who endorsed their action, serves to demonstrate a radical confusion of love and hate; and demonstrates, too,
the splitting associated with indifference to pain, on the one hand,
and identification with the aggressor, on the other.

In our own times we may consider the behaviour of those fundamentalist sects which continue to torture and abuse their own
children. We may consider, too, the activities associated with the charismatic and Pentecostal congregations: speaking in tongues, altered
states of consciousness, spirit possession, and so forth. It appears that
these latter sets of rituals serve to foster and develop dissociative 'abilities' which originate, and are nurtured, in the childhood traumas pro-

voked by parental abuse. These childhood dissociative 'abilities' are fostered and developed, somewhat ironically, in the name of spiritual enlightenment, and liberation (reliving Christ's passion, for instance).

Despite these modern examples of primitive, schizoid modes of thought, it is generally the case that the sorts of behaviours which such thinking gives rise to are more closely associated with the ethos and values of the Old Testament, rather than with those of the New. It is the Old Testament God who shows his love for his chosen people by subjecting them to generations of misery, exile, insecurity, shame and degradation. It is Jehovah who flies regularly into fits of rage, leading to merciless violence, vengeance and murder; and it is Jehovah who most respects and loves those of his children who demonstrate equal zeal for mercilessly destroying any who defy his wishes.

The world of the Old Testament is one of half-mad prophets whose disassociated states entail possession by, or hallucinated intercourse with, an array of mystical beings – from the violently aggressive (sky) father-god himself, to various minor demons and angels (the Elohim, Baal and others). With the Old Testament, we are presented with a world in which God's chosen people apparently expect aggression and violence from God as a sign of his 'divine' love.

And indeed, it is the identification with the aggressor father-god – an identification probably engendered – at least in part – by early (and radical) childhood abuse – which sustained the strength of fundamentalist Jews, as God's chosen people, enabling them to strive on through, and despite, their adversities.

It is when we come to consider the second, more neurotic psychological constellation associated with later or lower levels of abuse that we find modes of thought which would appear to be more paradigmatically Christian. The defensive idealisation of the real father (intensified by parental mistreatment), and the low self-esteem which accompanies this fantasy, together pave the way for the idealisation of the fantasy father-in-the-sky. It would seem that the latter idealisation indeed constitutes a 'logical' development of the former. Moreover, it constitutes a social, rather than merely individual, legitimation and extension of the idealisation process. As the 'neurotic' individual moves beyond the family unit, and out into the huge and frighteningly complex world, the Christian congregation and the Christian Church become his or her extended family; the individual is one of the children under the protection of the omnipotent and omnipresent father-god.

Christians themselves, as original sinners, are responsible for their own suffering. And yet they are not without hope of redemption. What is required in order for them to overcome their sinfulness, and attain the salvation of eternal life and happiness, is belief and repentance. In other words, what Christians must do in order to achieve perfection is reinforce the image of the good parent, as embodied in the church, and regress to a state of infantile dependence upon that parent. And yet this narcissistic perfection is brought about by projecting the original burden of guilt onto the sinners who remain, both within and beyond the congregation. Such sinners, via displacement, become the objects of 'divinely' sanctioned aggression by the redeemed, and supposedly all-loving, Christians – in holy wars, witch crazes, festivals of light, anti-abortion campaigns and much more.

These observations, quite plainly, constitute merely the barest of outlines of some of the psychological processes involved in – some – Christian belief. In what follows I will begin to suggest some of the ways in which these ideas may cast light upon the life and work of Jesus himself – as both the inspiration and founder of many subsequent Christian ideas.

Part Three
THE CHILDHOOD OF JESUS

In regard to our previous discussion, the question inevitably arises: Was Jesus himself, as a child, subjected to abuse?

Greven writes: "Since the Gospels are silent concerning so much of Jesus's infancy and childhood, no one knows for certain whether Jesus was subjected to the rod and the pains of physical punishment by his earthly parents", as so many children of his time and place certainly were (GREVEN 1992, p. 50). Alice Miller, however, argues strongly that Jesus's moral vision was possible precisely because he was amongst the few who actually escaped such physical abuse in childhood.

In her words:

> "Much of what Jesus said in the course of his life, and even more, his deeds show that he did not have just one father (God), who insisted on the observance of his commandments (on sacrifice), and was demanding, distant, invisible and infallible (a father whose 'will must be done'). From his early days Jesus also knew another father – Joseph (who never called attention to himself), who protected and loved Mary and the child, encouraged the child, assigned him central importance and served him. It must have been this modest man who made it possible for the child to distinguish what was true and to experience the meaning of love. This is why Jesus was able to see through the hypocrisy of his contemporaries.
>
> A child raised in accordance with traditional principles, who knows nothing else from the start, is not able to detect hypocrisy because he lacks a basis for comparison. Someone who knows only such an atmosphere from childhood will perceive it as normal in all situations, perhaps suffering because of it but unable to recognise it for what it is, If he has not experienced love as a child, he will long for it but will not know what love can be. Jesus did know." (MILLER 1990, p. 97)

Miller clarifies this point later on in her narrative, when she notes that Joseph "served his child because he regarded him as the child of God", adding: "Children who are respected learn respect. Children who are loved for what they are cannot learn intolerance. In an environment such as this, they will develop their own ideals, which can be nothing other than humane, since they grow out of the experience of love." (ibid.)

Miller's line is, so one might think, a logical one to follow in seeking to explain Jesus unique humanity and sympathy. And yet radical contradictions (and obviously mythological elements) in the gospel accounts of Jesus's birth cast serious doubt on the idea that his earthly parents ever saw anything 'special' about him – compared with their other children, for example. Furthermore, given that it is highly unlikely that Jesus was able to escape completely from the brutalising ideology of child rearing which then prevailed, we are obliged to turn from Miller's account, and consider alternative possibilities.

One such possibility is to see Jesus as someone who was subjected to more abuse, rather than less, as compared to other children of his day. Perhaps Jesus was someone so abused in childhood that he was compelled by his psychic suffering to seek some form of radical liberation; a man who, in his quest for psychic relief, acquired unique powers of insight into his own condition, and that of others similarly affected. Perhaps Jesus's insight was both the motive and the means of helping others to follow the same path of liberation.

This explanation places Jesus within one particular tradition of tribal shamanism, as an individual who has suffered, in a particularly intense way, the contradictions of his social milieu. According to this tradition, such an individual has internalised these contradictions in infancy and is in danger of being torn apart by them in adolescence (or later in life). He is saved from torment through the assistance of others, those who have come to terms with their own psychic contradictions, and who are thus able to take the sufferer back through his earlier experiences – and thereby achieve some viable form of reconciliation.

Contemporary or near-contemporary non-Christian references to Jesus's life are few. Nevertheless, those references which we do have take on heightened significance, particularly in view of the unreliable nature of the gospels – which are not only filled with contradictions, but have been subjected to later vetting by the Catholic Church. In regard to the Shamanic connection, Ian Wilson argues that virtually the only information of any relevance is the

Talmudic reference to the 'healing' activities of Yeshu (a) ben Panthera (dating to before 200 CE).

Wilson points out:

> "...the ben Panthera meaning 'son of panthera' patronym ...crops up repeatedly in later Jewish references... They claim Jesus/Yeshu to have been the son of an illegitimate union between his mother Miriam or Mary and a Roman soldier variously called Pandera, Pantera, and Panthera. That a rumour of this kind, whether or not it was soundly based, was at least early in its origin is incontrovertible because the Christian writer Origen tells us that he heard it from the second century pagan philosopher Celsus. Celsus, in his turn, claimed to have heard it from a Jew, so the story seems to have been in circulation around 150 CE.
>
> Christian writers have tended to dismiss the story as a malicious piece of invention, suggesting that 'panthera' may have been a corruption of 'parthenos' or virgin." (WILSON 1985, p. 55)

Wilson continues: "this interpretation fell a little flat with the discovery at Bingerbruck in Germany of the tombstone of one Tiberius Julius Abdus Panthera, a Roman archer from Sidon in Phoenicia... dating from the appropriate early Roman Imperial period."

Adding weight to this alternative reading of Jesus's early life, Bishop Spong notes the way in which the Mark Gospel – generally regarded as being the earliest one, and the basis for much of Matthew and Luke – refers to Jesus as the 'son of Mary'.

> "We know his mother's name was Mary only because one of his critics could not explain his power and wondered how it was that the 'son of Mary' could do these things (Mark 6.3). The name of Jesus's presumed father, Joseph, was never mentioned, adding speculation to the early whispers that Jesus was illegitimate, for designation of one as 'son of Mary' was not done normally unless the name of the father was unknown.

> This same critic also asserted that Jesus was a carpenter. The
> Christian community had trouble with this concept. Perhaps it
> proved to be far too human and therefore too derogatory an image.
> In Matthew's Gospel, written fifteen or twenty years later, this
> biographical note was changed to suggest that Jesus was not a
> carpenter, but 'the carpenter's son' (Matt. 13.55). In one stroke
> Matthew removed the absence of Jesus's father and the human-
> sounding trade of being a carpenter. The power of the myth was
> growing." (SPONG 1991, p. 137)

Interestingly, even the Matthew Gospel itself serves to provide
some possible evidence for Jesus being an illegitimate child. Wilson
draws attention to the "peculiarity of the genealogy ascribed to
Jesus in the Matthew gospel", in that "the only four female ancestors named – Tamar, Rahab, Ruth and Bathsheba – all happen to
have been 'fallen women'. Tamar was a temple prostitute, Rahab
was the madam of a brothel; Ruth, the most moral indulged in
some pretty shameless sexual exploitation; and Bathsheba committed adultery with King David". Wilson asks: "Was the author of
the Matthew genealogy implying something about the only other
women mentioned, Mary herself?" (WILSON 1985, p. 56)

If, indeed, the local Jewish community of Bethlehem had identified Jesus as the illegitimate son of a Roman soldier, this could
certainly have resulted in him being singled out for 'special' treatment. And rather than consisting of the sort of love and respect
imagined by Miller, this 'special' treatment may have been com-
prised of quite the opposite: abuse by Mary herself, by her Jewish
male partner(s), and/or by other members of the community. One
quite possible scenario is that Mary blamed the child Jesus – projected onto him her own guilt – for the hostility to which she, herself, was subjected to from the community for having had illicit
dealings with a hated Roman imperialist.

These ideas may cast a new light on many of the thoughts and
actions of Jesus's later life; in particular, they may illuminate in a
fresh way the very late, and very short, period of Jesus's public min-

istry – possibly covering only one to three years – between his baptism by John the Baptist (possibly in 29 CE) and his crucifiction in 30 CE.

Accepting the Gospels' versions of Jesus's life tends to leave us with a considerable number of difficult, and unanswered, questions: Why do we hear so little of Jesus's early life? Why is Jesus frankly hostile to the 'ordinary' family of his day – calling upon his disciples to leave their families to follow him? And why is he particularly hostile to all child abusers? Furthermore, why does Jesus receive little respect or recognition from his own community when he returns during the period of his public ministry (as described in Mark 6.1-6)? Why, we may well ask, is it the case that the people of Jesus's home town 'would not accept him... and he could work no miracles there? Why is his identification as 'the son of Mary, the brother of James and Joset' enough to disqualify him automatically from having anything worthwhile to contribute, as Mark says?

And why, if Jesus truly does have a healthy self-esteem (the result of a happy childhood) is he willing to take upon himself the sins of all humanity? Why on earth is he so willing to 'turn the other cheek', and actually love those who attack and abuse him? The most rational response upon hearing the chink of Roman armour would have been to slip away from the Garden of Gethsemane with the other disciples, and not to wait to be arrested. Why does Jesus voluntarily give himself up to horrific humiliation, torture and death – all in the name of the Father?

Jesus's perplexing actions make perfect sense if we take into consideration the likelihood that he had suffered terrible abuse in childhood. The silence of the Gospels on the subject of Jesus's childhood is then easily explained: Jesus's early experience of abuse, of disrespect, hostility and violence, does not sit well with his later message, status and personality.

Jesus, growing up in a hostile atmosphere, in a community in which he was reviled because of his illegitimacy, his Roman ancestry, and his mother's (hypothesised) profession as a prostitute, should be expected to suffer from low levels of confidence and self-esteem.

Perhaps Jesus blamed himself for the sins of his parents and of the community, turning against himself the anger and bitterness arising from his abuse by others. Perhaps Jesus was consumed by hatred for the absent father figure – who was not only responsible for all of his own suffering in particular, but was also the embodiment of the evil Roman rule which had caused the suffering of the Jewish people generally. Beyond these psychological consequences, it is possible that (any) such childhood persecution could lead to a psychotic breakdown in later years. We could speculate that the biblical references to Jesus suffering in the wilderness – beset by Satan, prince of demons – refers to just such a breakdown.

The classic case within the psychoanalytic tradition of psychotic breakdown generated as a result of early parental abuse is that of Judge Daniel Paul Schreber (1842-1911), as investigated by Freud, Niederland, Schatzman and others. Schreber, after enduring a childhood marked by extreme and prolonged physical torture at the hands of his father, suffered a schizophrenic psychosis in later life. This psychosis involved a return of the repressed memories of abuse in the form of hallucinations of spirit beings – little men, rays, souls and God continuing to assault him – as well as paranoid fears of persecution, including sexual assault, by various father figures – and especially his doctor.

Ultimately, Schreber 'came to terms' with his condition by means of a spontaneous reframing of the distorted memories of violence and sexual abuse. The memories became an integral part of a process whereby Schreber, so he imagined, was being transformed into a woman – a future bride of the Father God – who was destined to give birth to a new race of humans. These new people would repopulate the earth, following the destruction of the existing populations. In this way Schreber's suffering acquired a positive – indeed a transcendent spiritual – meaning and purpose.

In other cultural contexts such reframing, or reconstruction, of the 'delusions' of paranoid psychotic breakdown may be facilitated by the intervention of shamans, witches, healers or prophets. Typically, these interventions have involved special processes of initiation or rebirth. Through a radical regression, the existing, troubled and contradictory 'self' of the sufferer 'dies', and a new self is 'born' (constructed or liberated). Often, the new self has acquired radical powers of insight and control of self and others. (This, indeed, is an integral part of the typical shamanic election.) Presumably, in the case of Jesus, this 'rebirth' would have been his baptism by the 'wild man' John the Baptist.

As Wilson points out:

> "The John baptism (distinctly different from the routine, self-administered ritual ablutions long commonplace for religious purification amongst Jews of all denominations), was a form of consecration or initiation by which, after repentance, an individual could feel purified from their past sins in preparation for a better life hereafter. According to the Matthew Gospel, John proclaimed the baptism as preparation for the coming of the Kingdom of God." (Matthew 3.2) (WILSON 1985, p. 72)

The similarities between the cases of Schreber and Jesus seem inescapable: just as Schreber came to terms with the return of repressed memories via a radical idealisation of his father (as God), so too did Jesus seem to have come to terms with his repressed memories of horrific abuse on account of his father. Schreber idealised himself as the bride of God, suffering so that the human race could be reborn, just as Jesus idealised himself as the son of God, suffering for the same end.

Wilson continues: "We are told that as he surfaced [from the water] he seemed to receive a vision in the form of a dove accompanied by a heavenly voice announcing: 'You are my son' (Mark 1.11)". It appears that Jesus emerged from this initiation by John the Baptist believing himself to be the son of God (of the Jewish god Jahweh), rather than of a hated Roman soldier. His sufferings now made sense to him as the price of his unique status; they were a part of his struggle to fulfil his unique destiny in bringing his father's word to his people – thereby leading his people back to the path of righteousness, from which they had strayed, and shouldering the burden of all their sins.

It is quite possible to extend the parallels between Jesus and Schreber (and other shamanic initiations) beyond even this. For it is more than likely that the two sufferers of early abuse were also dealing in later life with repressed homosexual feelings.

The indications are that Schreber's father probably experienced strong homosexual feelings in relation to his son, feelings which he equally strongly repudiated, but which nevertheless determined the specific nature of the abuse which he dealt out to his son. For, having thus projected his own intolerable sexual feelings onto the child, Schreber's father then sought to control or destroy these feelings by physically abusing the child's body – abuse which included the boy's genitals. When Freud analysed Schreber, the son, he identified some of the latter's paranoid persecution fantasies as deriving from his own repressed 'positive' homosexual feelings in relation to the father, and father substitutes. The total unacceptability of these feelings led the son to defend himself against paternal (superegoic) persecution by transforming the feelings into their opposites. (Freud called this 'reaction formation'.) Once transformed, the feelings were then projected back onto those who were the original objects of his desires. Schreber's love for other men became – through reaction formation – his hatred of other men. Then, through projection, his hatred of other men became their hatred of him.

Although Freud recognised that the intensity of Schreber's prohibition upon his homosexual desires derived from the father – as a representative of the dominant value system – he failed in Schreber's case to consider the origin of the latter's intense homosexual desire. We can see, of course, that the desire itself derived from precisely the same source as the prohibition against the desire; in other words, both the desire and its prohibition derived from the father. As Miller points out, a very important dimension of childhood sexuality consists precisely of the young child's "constant adjustment to adult desires... and a complete readiness to respond to them" (MILLER 1991, p. 122).

In Schreber's case, the father's very attempts to deny or negate his own 'illicit' desires would have made them a major focus of the son's attention. And we can imagine the boy entertaining fantasies of fulfilling those desires precisely in order to 'make the father happy' – thereby hoping to escape the endless, horrendous 'punishments' to which the unhappy, frustrated and angry father subjected him. The boy would, of course, have been trapped in a classic 'double bind'. He would have been confronted, as well, by his father's absolute repudiation of any such homosexual feelings or relations. This contradiction presumably played a central role in Schreber's later 'schizophrenic' breakdown.

In his discussion of this case, Freud emphasises the way in which Schreber's idealisation of the father – as God – also served to liberate his suppressed (positive) homosexual feelings. The son Schreber was thereby able to escape the paranoid persecution – which was produced, if we remember, by the transformation of his desire for other men into 'hatred and aggression' from other father figures. For if God, the ultimate arbiter of all 'moral values' demands sexual subordination from his son, then homosexual desire must be alright after all.

We must bear in mind, too, that there are other sorts of family relations which may stimulate powerful homosexual desires on the part of young boys and men. Freud focuses his attention upon those situations in which young boys become particularly closely bonded with their mothers. Later, these boys may respond to the loss of the mother as love-object (which occurs typically as a result of particularly intense fears of jealous paternal retribution for Oedipal desires, including castration) by identifying with her – through regression to primitive 'oral' defensive thought patterns. This sort of identification with the mother on the part of the son integrally involves her 'feminine' desire for the father and for other men.

An alternative situation is that which prevails when the 'seductive' or abusive mother, upon failing to establish any fulfilling sexual relations with adult males (or females), turns to her infant son as the source of sexual fulfilment. (Or the mother may, alternatively, blame her son for her own frustration or oppression). The demands of the mother can have the effect of turning her son off all heterosexual relations in later life. This is because the young boy may experience the mature sexual demands of his mother as crushing, overwhelming and castrating – particularly if there are also other forces contributing to low levels of self-esteem (or 'ego-strength') on his part. In cases such as this, the boy may idealise the absent father, and male sexuality, as a 'liberating force' – a liberation from the engulfment and destruction brought about by the intensity of female desire.

If, indeed, Jesus's mother was a prostitute – lacking a stable male partner, and, presumably, also the object of hatred and contempt on the part of the rest of the community – then she may well have developed a seductive (and/or hostile, derisive) relation to her young son, Jesus. And this may well have led to his entertaining fantasies of 'sexual' liberation by an idealised father figure.

While speculating upon this point, it is crucial to recognise that homosexuality was absolutely forbidden by established Jewish law. Homosexuality had, after all, been the crime of the inhabitants of Sodom and Gomorrah. And homosexuality had as its penalty God's ultimate punishment: total destruction. In light of this consideration, we would expect the young Jesus to have been forced, by powerful social pressures, to repress any homosexual desires he may have experienced. It is possible that Jesus may also have employed similar sorts of projected defences to the ones used by Schreber, as a means of maintaining the repression (but at the cost of further paranoid persecution).

What I am suggesting here is that Jesus's initiation may have also liberated repressed homosexual desires, transforming hatred and fear (of other men) back into love. This idea is suggested, too, by Morton Smith's investigations. Smith refers to a letter which had supposedly been written by Clement of Alexandria, an early Church Father living at the end of the second century CE. The letter was addressed to a certain 'Theodore', and it concerned a 'secret' Gospel of Mark. This secret Gospel was based on the normal canonical one, but it contained additions designed for certain 'special' followers of Jesus, variously referred to as 'those who are being perfected', and 'those who are being initiated into the great mysteries'.

Wilson informs us further: "The letter went so far as to quote extracts from the secret version of Mark, revealing it to have contained what appeared to be an account of the 'raising of Lazarus'. Although not directly named as Lazarus, but referred to as the rich young man mentioned elsewhere in the Gospels, he is described as 'dying', being buried, and then brought back to life by Jesus." (WILSON 1985, p. 26)

Most significantly, the quotation refers to a youth 'who loved Jesus'; this youth is apparently Lazarus, whom Jesus had raised from the dead. Jesus rolls the stone away from the door of the tomb, "going in where the youth was, stretching forth his hand and raising him, seizing his hand... But the youth, looking upon him, loved him and began to beseech him that he might be with him". And "going out of the tomb they came into the house of the youth, for he was rich. And after six days Jesus told him what to do and in the evening the youth came to him, wearing a linen cloth over his naked body. And he remained with him that night, for Jesus taught him the mystery of the Kingdom of God..."

As Wilson remarks,

"Clement also fills in an otherwise unexplained gap in verse 46 of the tenth chapter of the canonical Mark Gospel: 'They reached Jericho; and as he left Jericho...' For centuries scholars have puzzled over what might have happened in Jericho. According to the Clement letter, the secret Gospel originally read: 'And the sister of the youth whom Jesus loved and his mother and Salome were there and Jesus did not receive them'." (WILSON 1985, p. 26)

Morton Smith has pointed out that the discovery provides a "powerful explanation for another baffling episode in the canonical Mark Gospel, the fact that at the time of Jesus's arrest in Gethsemane, a young man who followed him had nothing on but a linen cloth. They caught hold of him, but he left the cloth in their hands and ran away naked" (Mark 14.51, 52). (ibid., p. 27) Further supporting the idea of Jesus's homosexuality, Anglican Bishop Hugh Montifiore has referred to two matters of significance. Firstly, the mysterious Gospel reference to the "disciple Jesus loved... leaning back on Jesus's breast" (John 13.23-5); and secondly, the fact that Jesus chose not to marry – and this in an era when Jewish priests and rabbis were very much expected to do so.

In the context of the analysis which I have developed so far, these references are quite suggestive. It seems that many classical initiation ceremonies involved some sort of homosexual intercourse between older men and adolescent boys. In such ceremonies, the transfer of male semen is equated with the transfer of adult male prerogatives and power (liberation from envy of, dependence upon or absorption within the female body and female power), in addition to the assertion of adult male power and authority over the younger generation. What is happening, symbolically, in the course of these initiations is the 'death' of the 'child personality' – which is strongly identified with, or emotionally bonded to, the mother – and the 'birth' of the adult male identity.

The entry of the Holy Spirit, in the form of a dove, into Jesus's body at initiation may well have represented a similar reframing of sexual submission to the father figure (John as God). Once reborn as the son of God, Jesus was then able to take the 'active' role, liberating the repressed 'true' homosexual feelings of other young men who had, like Jesus himself, previously suffered paranoid persecution by such feelings – in what amounted to 'soul murder' – in a violent and patriarchal, homophobic society.

Adding weight to this interpretation, Morton Smith has suggested that Jesus's presence in the Garden of Gethsemane, immediately prior to his arrest and execution, was in fact for the express purpose of instituting a special baptismal 'initiation', and indoctrination, of the scantily clad young man referred to earlier (Mark 14.51). Wilson asks: "Was this one of the occasions on which Jesus took a favoured disciple... on a journey to the Kingdom of God?"

(ibid., p. 101) – a journey which may have involved a physical homosexual initiation, as well as a spiritual one?

It is tempting, furthermore, to surmise that it was the nature of the ceremony which took place at Gesthemene which is the key to understanding why it was that Jesus allowed himself, on this occasion, to be arrested – rather than escaping, as he could have done, with his disciples. Was Jesus too deeply involved with the matter at hand? Or was he suffering recurring pangs of guilt, a result of never having come completely to terms with his own homosexual feelings?

Bishop Spong has explored the more explicit signs of suppressed homosexual desire, and homosexual guilt, on the part of Paul of Tarsus, as revealed in his letters. Spong argues that Jesus's message came to have its urgent appeal for Paul purely because of its emphasis upon God's love and acceptance of all – including those whose feelings or actions (including homosexual feelings or actions) put them beyond the pale of orthodox Judaism. Spong remarks: "this is a hypothesis that makes sense of the data of the Epistles, and accounts for the tone [of the writing], the fear, the passion and the behaviour" (SPONG 1991, p. 119).

It is also possible that part of Jesus's appeal for Paul lay in the latter's recognition (which may have been either conscious or unconscious) that Jesus was a 'kindred spirit' in this regard – another man who loved men, with whom Paul could identify himself.

Proceeding with our analysis, it is important to bear in mind that Jesus was best known, not for secretly initiating young men, but rather for his very open and public healing activities. As Josephus says, Jesus was "a wise man... [who] ...performed astonishing feats" (using the same expression as he used to describe the healings of Elisha). And, as noted earlier, the Talmud refers to Jesus (and his disciples) as healers, seeking to cure a man of snake bite.

What is immediately striking about Jesus's healing activities, details of which are presented in the Gospels, is that he seems to have specialised in conditions of possible psychosomatic, or psychic, origin – rather than, conditions arising from purely physical causes. In particular, Jesus seems to have had the most success in treating, on the one hand, paralysis, blindness, lameness and catalepsy, and on the other, "possession by evil spirits" (associated with violent outbursts, convulsions, etc).

As Wilson points out, we now know that all of the former sorts of conditions can be hysterical in origin – produced, in other words, by repression or hypnotic suggestion. The latter sorts of conditions, meanwhile, seem to correspond to what we would term today multiple personality disorder.

All of these disorders can be identified as possible products of some kind of psychic dissociation process, in which feelings become dissociated from contexts, and in which the sense of self becomes dissociated from the external world. In short, the disorders which Jesus specialised in treating all seem to have involved either repression or 'splitting'. Memories, feelings, desires and so forth are forgotten by the sufferer, excluded from conscious access, leading to the return of repressed mental elements as bodily symptoms; or else the conscious awareness of the patient was 'split' into discrete (possibly context-dependent) elements, lacking in any clear continuity of memory or identity.

Wilson reminds us that dissociation is a product of emotional stress. "Symptoms of this kind are particularly common in wartime and ... there would have been no shortage of causative stresses in Jesus's time" (WILSON 1985, p. 86). What Wilson fails to emphasis is that it is emotional stresses in childhood – as a result of trauma, including abuse by adults – which is most significant in generating dissociation in adult life (as well as in childhood itself). And childhood trauma predisposes individuals to respond to stresses in later life by radical regression to primitive, dissociative defence mechanisms.

Indeed, Greven notes,

"Dissociation is one of the most basic means of survival for many children, who learn early in life to distance themselves, or parts of themselves, from experiences too painful or frightening to bear. Classically, hysterical personalities are rooted in (childhood) dissociative processes; borderline personalities, too, often make use of dissociative means for coping with rage and aggression; and, in the most extreme cases, multiple personalities are created to cope with the emotions generated by intolerable abuses early in life.

Since pain felt and experienced takes many forms and comes in many degrees, from mild to severe to unbearable, children often discover ways to survive their pain through disconnecting and split-ting, in the most extreme cases creating alternative selves and per-sonalities which bear and express feelings that otherwise would have been overwhelming to a small child." (GREVEN 1992, p. 148)

In relation to this last point, it is certainly significant that 'pos-sessed' persons should address Jesus as a single personality speaking for a host of others (as 'us'). A particularly telling example of this is the case of the Gerasene demoniac who, upon being asked his name by Jesus, responds with: "My name is legion... for there are many of us" (Mark 5.10).

Given the 'orthodox' Old Testament ideology of childrearing outlined in the last chapter, together with the major social-political-economic upheavals of the period – and the perceived humiliation and persecution of the Jewish people – we should not be surprised to discover a veritable epidemic of dissociation-based psychosomatic illnesses in first century Palestine. It is certainly not surprising to find Jesus in a particularly good position to help 'cure' others; he himself was, after all, in all probability, an individual who had discovered a means of coming to terms with – and of transcending – many of the dire consequences of his own childhood abuse. As a fellow sufferer, Jesus would have provided empathy and sympathetic identification with his patients – he would have possessed, in other words, a good basis for hypnotic suggestion. For, indeed, it is the case that empathy plays a central role in covert hypnotic induction. The hypnotist 'mir-rors' the subjects unconscious gestures, movements, expressions and so forth back to them, prior to instigating suggestion. (And the success of this form of induction is clearly brought out in the work of contemporary practitioners – that of Milton Erikson, and the so-called 'neuro-linguistic programmers', among them.)

Part Four
CHRISTIANITY AND CHILDHOOD TODAY

Jesus appears to have taken a most significant step away from the Old Testament identification with the all-powerful aggressor, as the basis for the psychic underpinning of inflexible rules – rules, moreover, enforced by violence, child abuse, patriarchy and periodic fundamentalist terrorism and self-sacrifice. (And yet, having said this, we should also acknowledge the influence of those earlier liberal Pharisaic reformers, who sought to temper the more extreme of these practices with tolerance and compassion.)

Jesus radically humanises God and morality. This is seen in his familiar references to his father God; in his flexibility in interpreting the Mosaic Laws; and in his recognition of, and sympathy for, human weakness and frailty. This represents the positive, constructive side of the concept of original sin. Moreover, it is fair to say that this God-parent provides a paradigm of sympathetic acceptance and support – to which all parents and guardians should aspire as a precondition for creating peace and mutual respect on earth. At the same time, however, Jesus remained at least partially trapped in the negative consequences of his own probable childhood suffering. It is apparent that his life continued to involve a destructive oscillation between deep-seated neurotic guilt (self-blame for his own childhood suffering – and adult desire), and a compensatory retreat into narcissistic fantasy (of childhood union with the all-good, all-loving divine parent, always available to look after his special child) employed to escape such guilt, depression and pain. Unfortunately, the latter propensity has all too often been to the fore in the subsequent history of Christian sects and congregations.

Christian thought has been radically depoliticised by the transformation of the active commitment to building God's kingdom on earth into a passive desire to experience God's kingdom in the hereafter. Such a transformation shifts attention to purely individual salvation – and away from understanding the material and psychological underpinnings of oppression, exploitation, misery and fear.

Once Christian thought has transformed the human figure of Jesus into a perfect being – a perfect God become flesh – it is no longer concerned with Jesus's crucial humanisation of God. What is reinforced instead is the dichotomy between divine perfection and human sinfulness. And this dichotomy also, inevitably, reinforces pre-existing neurotic guilt and low self-esteem: the individual blames themselves for their own abuse and suffering.

Meanwhile, what is maintained is the illusion of possible human perfection, as regression to infantile dependence upon the 'perfect' parent – a fantasy of perfection intrinsically dependent upon projection of pre-existing guilt (evil, anger, weakness) onto others, those not among the 'chosen' people.

As I suggested at the beginning of this chapter, early abuse – and the guilt thereby engendered in the victim – may foster this particular interpretation of the Christian message. Crucially, the experience of such guilt provides a potent driving force and motivation for embracing narcissistic regression in order to try to escape the guilt in question.

Established Christian churches have vested interests in furthering the sort of transformation of the Christian message referred to above; churches rely for much of their power and authority on tapping into the guilt prevailing amongst members of their congregations. By promising their congregations a regressive escape, in the form of rebirth as a child of God, churches have won and held people's time, effort and money – things which may have been better directed towards attaining real solutions.

For most Christians, those not choosing the total absorption in fantasy available via monastic seclusion, the church offers forms of temporary release through rituals of mass and confession – perhaps, too, spirit possession or speaking in tongues. All such rituals are, however, followed by an inevitable return of the primary guilt and dependence.

The regressive solutions offered by the Christian churches dissipate the life-energies which may have been directed instead, more usefully, towards real change and growth of the self and society.

More than this, however, such 'solutions' also contribute to the generation of irrational social antagonisms and conflicts – through splitting and projection of hostile impulses. This is not merely a matter of the Christian evangelical impulse, whereby external sources of guilt and pain are tapped into, and 'born agains' are recruited from the great reservoirs of pagan sinners created by exploitative and alienating social structures. On the contrary, such ideologies and practices can serve to perpetuate guilt within already established congregations. For they encourage the violent physical or emotional abuse of young children, which is perpetuated by parents in the name of 'love'.

For there can be no narcissistic perfection – of the parent or the self – without splitting of the self and projection of guilt and sin. And although the entire world beyond the congregation may be available as a repository for split-off 'bad' feelings and parts of the self, these outside forces will generally not be thus employed as a means of acting out or displacing all the suppressed anger and aggression of Christian congregations. For there is little likelihood, in the late twentieth century, that the church will acquire the necessary political authority to organise crusades, or any other large-scale military campaign.

Instead, it is the children within the group who will become the first victims of such projection and displacement. As Alice Miller expresses the point: children are weak, they are small, they are vulnerable, they are loving and beautiful and sexually attractive to repressed adults, they are spontaneous, wilful, instinctual creatures. And above all, they are available. As such, children are the natural vehicles for the projection of parental wickedness, and the displacement of parental anger.

Faith in the divinity of Jesus Christ absolves the parents from their original sin, allowing them to participate in divine goodness – but only through the projection of their sin onto someone else. The classical doctrine teaches the believers that children are born steeped in sinfulness; this aspect of Christian ideology thus marks children out as objects of such projection. Since they are too young for the subtleties of 'faith', they can be saved only by rigorous parental discipline and control. It is all too easy, to put it bluntly, for Christians – and 'born agains' in particular – to fall back on the wisdom of Solomon, rather than on the wisdom of Jesus Christ.

CHAPTER TEN
CATHOLICISM, OEDIPUS AND SEXUAL GUILT

Part One
HATRED OF THE BODY

Catholic Christianity stands out amongst the major religions of the world in its consistent, massive and prolonged hostility towards (hetero) sexual pleasure and its requirement for priestly celibacy. And for many non-believers, and some members of the Church itself this has always been a particularly bizarre and unacceptable dimension of that religion.

In her recent study of Catholicism and sexuality, Uta Ranke-Heinemann refers to "the nonsensical hatred of marriage and the body" which "became so dominant in the Catholic Church that it was widely taken to be the sum total of Catholic teaching" (RANKE-HEINEMANN 1991, p. 6). And she describes this "hostility to plea-sure, leading to hostility to marriage, leading to celibacy" as "a per-version of the work of the man from whom Christianity gets its name" (op. cit.).

Given the strength of instinctual sexual desire, this raises obvious questions of where such ideas could have come from in the first place, and how they have managed to retain their hold for so long. Certainly the Catholic Church did not invent paranoid fear of sex or the idea of sexual abstinence as a necessary condition of 'spiritual' enlightenment or 'favour' with higher – divine – powers. As Ranke-Heinemann points out in her book, these ideas were already established in the 'pagan' Graeco-Roman world within which the Catholic Church first developed.

Menstrual taboos, e.g., involving a temporary abstention from sex, were (and are) widespread in tribal societies, including hunting-gathering and horticultural tribes around the world. Terrible consequences were thought to follow for men exposed to menstrual blood (during sex) – including disease, impotence, damage to the sexual organs and death (and being eaten be sharks in some cases) – depending upon the particular societies concerned. And to avoid this, in some cases, women were segregated from the men (in special women's houses) for some time during their menstrual cycle – with such segregation often backed up by dire threats of punishment by the men for any transgression.

This taboo seems to have become established amongst the patriarchal Jewish tribes. And it makes its appearance in the Old Testament, when, in Leviticus 15: 18-24, God defines a menstruating woman as 'unclean' for seven days, and demands the ostracism of any man and woman who have any sexual interaction during the woman's periods.

By the first and second centuries CE this prohibition had become connected to the recognition of a woman's infertility during menstruation – though there were also confused ideas of damage to children conceived during periods. And the idea remained widespread that 'menstrual blood was, in effect, poisonous'.

Early fathers of the Catholic Church fixed upon all of these ideas – with Clement of Alexandria (d. 218) and Origen (d. 254) claiming that children conceived during menstruation were born impaired. And these ideas persisted right through to the fifteenth century. Similarly, in a work influential for centuries, Isadore of Seville maintained that "after touching (menstrual blood) fruits do not sprout, blossoms fade, grasses wither... iron rusts, brass turns black, dogs that taste it get rabies" (ibid p. 22).

Such ideas presumably contributed to a general climate of fear, hostility and confusion in relation to (hetero) sexuality. Certainly, as we have seen, they seem to have been bound up with more general male – paranoid – fears of women. And we could see sex taboos associated with menstruation as the first step towards total sexual segregation and celibacy.

Another important consideration here is the dualism of mind and body which (in the West, at least) was apparently an original innovation of the ancient Greek world – developing from around the sixth century BCE in the work of the Pythagoreans and others. For this doctrine included also the positive evaluation of the former – mind – at the expense of the latter – body – with sexual feelings and actions associated specifically with the latter.

Whereas other societies – and the earlier Greek society of the eighth century BCE – as evidenced in the writings of Homer – had ideas of 'souls' and 'ghosts' as more attenuated versions of the earthly body (or bodily being) travelling 'out of the body' in trances, sickness or death, it was the Greeks of the classical (or immediately pre-classical) period who seem to have been the first to draw a clear line between a thinking, reasoning, immaterial mind and a feeling, perceiving, desiring, material – and sexual – body.

These ideas are particularly clear in the writings of Plato, where the material world (of sense perception) is seen as a distorted projection of pure – mathematical or geometrical – forms in heaven. The mind as agency of pure (mathematical and logical) thought is seen as the means to lead the individual towards such pure forms, while the body – with its senses and desires – keeps them anchored to the material world.

To turn away from bodily perceptions and desires in life, in favour of the life of the mind is the only way to adequately prepare the soul for its direct experience of the pure forms in heaven at the time of the death of the body. Whereas the properly prepared soul is able to become one with such true – heavenly – reality, others fall back down to earth to be re-incorporated in an endless cycle of re-births, imperfection and suffering.

Amongst the Greek philosophers who first developed these ideas, they were clearly bound up with a general mistrust or hostility towards heterosexual intercourse. As Ranke-Heinemann says, Pytha-goras, Xenophon, Plato, Aristotle and the physician Hippocrates "all look upon… the sexual act as dangerous, hard to control, harmful to health, and draining" (RANKE-HEINEMANN 1991, p. 10). The mind should be focused rather upon the higher spiritual world of heaven, through renunciation of earthly – bodily – pleasures and preoccupations. But the sexual act draws the mind back into the body and distracts it from its higher purposes.

These ideas became integral to – and were further developed by – neoplatonism and the later Stoic philosophy of 300 BCE to 250 CE which profoundly influenced the cultural climate of the Roman Empire during the period of the early development of Catholic Christianity. As Ranke-Heinemann points out,

"While Greek philosophy in general accorded pleasure seeking considerable importance for the humane ideal of life, the Stoics, especially during the first two centuries of the Christian era, changed all that. They (completely) rejected the quest for pleasure… The positive effect of this rejection was the concentration of sexual activity on marriage. But to the extent that carnal pleasures became suspect, marriage was also called into question and celibacy was valued more highly." (ibid., p. 11)

Parallel developments in India included a reformation and re-assessment of the earlier Vedic religion – centred upon the fire rituals and sacrifices presided over by a priestly elite – the Brahmans. From the eighth century BCE, the writers of the *Upanishads* sought to re-direct religious energies towards individual salvation by insight and knowledge rather than ritual action alone.

Whereas previously the emphasis had been upon the reconstruction of the world and of the self through sacrifice, there now developed the idea that it was possible, through study, meditation and concentration to escape the cycle of birth-death and rebirth in the world and achieve a transcendent immortality through merging of the self *(atman)* with the life force of the cosmos *(Brahman)*.

This corresponded with the appearance of a tradition of wandering monks – 'samanas' – who rejected the settled worldly life, preferring to live on the fringes of society. They wandered the forests, living on alms and seeking wisdom through physical – including sexual – renunciation and meditation; laying the foundations of yoga and other, later ideologies and techniques of liberation and salvation.

These developments, in turn, paved the way for new religious traditions and communities. The sixth century BCE, in particular, saw both Gautama and Vardhamana amongst the samanas, establishing new religious traditions which placed particular emphasis upon asceticism and renunciation of the body.

Vardhamana taught the attainment of release of the soul from the material world by extreme asceticism and non-violence. He went about naked, subjecting himself to discomfort and showing his total rejection of worldly possessions. He taught strict vegetarianism and rigorous avoidance of the taking of life in any form. His disciples were the Jains (followers of the Conqueror).

Gautama, the Buddha (563-483 BCE), studied under two masters of yoga, learning disciplines of body and mind which allowed him to systematically withdraw from all ordinary sensory/mental experience and enter into a succession of trance states, He also tried the extreme asceticism of the Jains, punishing his body by fasting.

"Finding no lasting satisfaction in these disciplines, he turned to the practice of what he called 'mindfulness', a kind of self analysis in which, rather than trying to subdue or cut off sensory/mental experience, he simply sat, watching his feelings and thoughts as they arose and reflecting on [their] causal [origins]." (LESTER 1987, p. 22)

Although he later argued in favour of what he called 'the middle way' between the worldliness of traditional Brahmanism and the asceticism of the Jains, he also established a monastic tradition which rejected 'all sexual intercourse, even with an animal'. And the key concept of enlightenment, according to his teachings, was the transcendence of all (bodily) desire. Mindfulness reveals that physical existence is the result of the force of desire. Transcending desire – and finally extinguishing the ego as the true reality of desire – therefore brings about a cessation of the physical and mental suffering inherent in existence.

It is not clear to what extent Greek ideas – or for that matter Indian ideas – influenced the particularly pessimistic Gnostic tendencies, perhaps deriving from Persia, shortly before the time of Jesus, and thereafter spreading rapidly throughout the Near East and Western Roman Empire and developing into a major competitor and influence upon more orthodox Christianity. But the parallels to Pythagorean, Neoplatonic and Indian ideas are plain.

As Ranke-Heinemann says,

> "this movement... believed that it had recognised the worthlessness and baseness of all existing – earthly – being. It preached abstinence from marriage, meat and wine... The body is for the Gnostics the 'corpse with senses', the 'grave that you carry around with you'. The world does not come from the hands of a good god, but from Demons. Only the soul of man ...comes like a spark of light from another world of light. It is captured by demonic powers and banished into this world of darkness. The soul of man thus finds itself in a foreign land, in a hostile environment, chained to the dark prison of the body. Seduced by the clamour and joys of the world it is in danger of not finding its way back to the god of light from which it originated. For the demons try to intoxicate it, because without the sparks of light the world, this creation of demons, falls back into chaos, into darkness." (RANKE-HEINEMANN 1991, p. 15)

Ranke-Heinemann sees Gnostic influences upon the Jewish Essene group based at Qumran, with its monastic asceticism amongst the men and inferior status accorded to women. But generally "Judaism was unreceptive to (Gnostic) asceticism" and hatred of the body.

However, there are already signs of deep Gnostic influences on the early Christian communities of New Testament times – in the idealisation of virginity in the book of Revelation, and in Paul's letter to the Corinthians, where Christians influenced by the Gnostic hatred of the body ask Paul whether it might not be good for "a man never to touch a woman". And such influences seem to have spread and deepened in subsequent centuries.

Marcion, a Church leader from Asia Minor who preached in Rome in the second century, argued that the Church should reject the Old Testament because it was the work of the evil creator-God. Bishop Ignatious of Antioch (d. 110) refers to those within the Church who boast of the higher spiritual value of their virginity. And around 150 Justin Martyr writes of those within the Church who "renounced marriage and remain wholly continent" – including even some who choose to castrate themselves.

As Ranke-Heinemann says, "while Justin (a Church father) cherished marriage – though only for procreation – his disciple Tatian (d. 180) drifted completely away into the Gnostic camp and became head of the 'Abstainers', for whom marriage was 'lewdness'." And at this time "many Christians, especially in Rome and Alexandria, were in danger of being swamped or absorbed by Gnosticism".

Although leading Christians struggled against Gnostic trends, such trends continued to exert a powerful influence, particularly in the life and work of Origen (d. 254) who was a strict ascetic, who never touched meat, wine or women. As Ranke-Heinemann says,

"Origen linked together Jewish-Christian faith in the one, good God as the creator of the body and of matter, of marriage and generation, and Gnostic contempt for the body. Body and matter, he says, do derive from the one, good God (and not from a wicked creator, as in the original, pre-Christian Gnosticism), but the body is not the good God's first thought. According to Origen, it is rather a kind of punishment, a 'chain', a 'prison' that owes its existence to a prior fall of pure souls." (ibid., p. 51)

And in the middle of the third century another leader arose in the east, the prophet Mani, who called himself Apostle of Jesus Christ. Mani taught a full fledged Gnostic message of the struggle between Gods of light and darkness. The God of light had sent messengers to human beings – the most perfect of whom was Jesus, a truly divine being who only seemed to be mortal and material. Thanks to Jesus, the fragments of light in the souls of humans could be caught up after death and returned to the realm of light, Manichean churches were powerful down to the sixth century, and in the eastern regions to the year 1000. And while the 'orthodox' churches eventually succeeded in squeezing out these 'heresies', such orthodoxy was by that time thoroughly permeated by a general Gnostic hatred of the body and of sexuality.

It is highly questionable whether this trend of thought within the Catholic Church derives very much real support from the New Testament (apart from the odd passage in Revelation). However, Ranke-Heinemann shows how the Church hierarchy has, from its earliest days, generated ever more bizarre elaborations and distortions of Biblical material to support its anti-sexual offensive.

As she points out, the virgin birth appears only in (the later Gospels of) Matthew and Luke, and not in the earlier writings of Paul, or the (possibly early) Gospel of John. It therefore seems to be a later construction. And Matthew and Luke use it as a metaphor – like other metaphors in the New Testament – "to express God's special initiative in salvation history... In no way should it be understood as expressing hostility to sexuality and marriage".

Yet this is precisely how it is understood by leading Catholic commentators. "The fact that the New Testament reports the existence of Jesus's brothers and sisters shows ...that the metaphor of the virgin birth was not understood in any sexually pessimistic sense." (ibid., p. 31) "Yet after the New Testament times, from the second century on, Jesus's brothers and sisters were first turned into stepbrothers and stepsisters from the first marriage of Joseph, now a widower, and finally, in about 400, Jerome made the stepbrothers and stepsisters over into male and female cousins" (op. cit.), to 'preserve' the sexual 'purity' of Jesus (earthly) parents.

Part Two
SOCIO-POLITICAL CONSIDERATIONS

We must not see this dimension of Catholic theory and practice in a vacuum. It is an integral part of a global degeneration of early Christian (communistic, revolutionary, egalitarian and feminist) organisation and values; of the creation of a special privileged stratum of supposedly spiritually superior (male) individuals, increasingly in control of church property, organisation and ideology.

As Kautsky points out,

"the first Christian organisations amongst the Jews were saturated with the desire for revolution, for the coming of the Messiah, for social upheaval. Attention to the present moment, the practical detail work, in other words, was probably neglected... But this condition changed after the destruction of Jerusalem. The elements that had given the Messianic congregation its rebellious character had been defeated. And the congregation of the Messiah became more and more an anti-Jewish congregation, within the non-Jewish proletariat, which had neither the ability nor the desire for struggle. But as the congregation became older, it became more and more clear that it could no longer count on the fulfilment of the prophesy still contained in the Gospels, to the effect that the contemporaries of Jesus would live to see the great change. Faith in the coming of the Kingdom of God on earth gradually disappeared. The Kingdom of God, which was to descend from

Heaven, was now more and more transferred to Heaven; the resurrection of the flesh was transformed into the immortality of the soul, which was alone destined to experience all the joys of Heaven or the pangs of Hell... As the messianic expectations of the future assumed more and more this unworldly form, becoming politically conservative or indifferent, the practical interest in the present day necessarily became more and more prominent." (KAUTSKY 1972, p. 409)

And Siegel notes that,

"The destruction of Jerusalem in AD 70 [by the Romans], did away with the base of Jewish [nationalist] revolt. With the defeat of the national hopes of the Jews, Christianity became more and more of a religion not of a revolutionary Jewish Messiah who was to bring the kingdom of god to earth but of a universal Messiah whose kingdom was not of this earth. It more and more dissociated itself from Judaism and made its peace with Rome, becoming a religion that provided solace for the disheartened proletarian masses. In his letter to the Christians in Rome, Paul speaks of personal salvation, not of bringing down kings from their thrones and filling the hungry with good things to eat. The message now is that everyone must obey state authorities, because no authority exists without God's permission, and the existing authorities have been put there by God (Romans 13: 1). With the acceptance of Rome came the rejection of the Jewish revolt against Rome. This is the basis of the antisemitic passages of the New Testament." (SIEGEL 1986, p. 74)

The working class of the Roman Empire consisted of dispossessed small farmers (driven off the soil by the competition of the huge slave-worked estates of the aristocracy), impoverished and uprooted tenant farmers, poor artisans, unemployed former slaves, peddlers and beggars. They congregated in the large cities like those living in third world suburban shanty towns today, maintained by

state hand-outs and entertained by spectacles of cruelty and violence – bread and circuses. And their particular life experience –
their hopes and fears – influenced the further development of
Christianity.

In the first instance, such working class interests sustained earlier
communistic trends of theory and practice within the Christian
Church. This included hostility to wealth and power and a demand
that every member of the congregation sell all of their possessions
and place the proceeds at the disposal of the congregation for distribution to its members. It included also the regular communal meals
shared by all the congregation.

> [The poor] "had succeeded in uniting in order to reduce their
> misery through their united efforts. When they encountered obsta-
> cles to the execution of a perfect communism, they found them-
> selves all the more obliged to expand their charity work which
> would give assistance to the individual in cases of extraordinary
> distress." (KAUTSKY 1972, p. 416)

Times were particularly hard in the second century when barbarian invasions and plagues threatened many cities throughout the
empire. And at this time the Christians' provision for their own
poor, for widows, orphans and the sick offered social and economic
security in an increasingly hostile and unpredictable world. "Other
cults also offered such benefits as life after death or protection from
demons, but they gave far less support to their members during
their earthly lives." (FRANKIEL 1985, p. 16)

However, there were also powerful forces at work tending to
undermine such a communistic orientation. Karl Kautsky argues
that,

> "the common meals and their mutual charity were... the sec-
> urest bond within the Christian congregation, permanently holding
> the masses together... But precisely this practice of charity was
> developing a force destined to weaken and burst asunder the origi-

nal communistic aspirations... As the expectations of the coming of the Messiah in all his glory dwindled, as the congregation became more and more convinced that it was necessary to acquire property in order to carry out its program of assistance, the proletarian class character of the Christian propaganda was violated, More and more efforts were directed to the recruiting of wealthy members whose money could be put to use." (KAUTSKY 1972, p. 417)

"The more money the congregation needed the more diligently did its agitators work in order to prove to wealthy patrons the vanity of all the treasures of this world, their worthlessness compared to the bliss of eternal life, which was attainable by the rich only if they parted with their possessions [for the common good]." (ibid.)

"The more the congregation ceased to be a fighting organisation, the more its charity phase was emphasised, the stronger became the tendencies within the congregation to soften the original proletarian hatred against the rich and enable the latter to feel at home in the congregation, even though they remained rich and clung to (most of) their possessions." (ibid., p. 419) "...the duty to give all one owned was replaced by a voluntary self-imposed tax, often amounting to a small gift." (ibid., p. 420)

The attempt to attract a 'better' class of recruit, and accommodate an influx of wealth and wealthy citizens encouraged an increasing division of labour – and power – within the Church, starting with the creation of a separate congregational office for the administration of income and expenses, and then extending to offices in charge of internal discipline and publicity. And, in the course of time, these offices acquired increasing autonomy and power – exercising authority over the rest of the congregation, rather than responding to their wishes or needs. Not only were the old class antagonisms revived in the Christian congregation, but a new dominant class arose within it, a new bureaucracy and a new head, the bishop.

It is true that for a period the Christians were actively persecuted by the Roman ruling class. As Frankiel says,

> "Christians were under attack as early as Nero's reign (54-68 CE)... [and] by the middle of the third century, Christianity had become strong enough to come into direct conflict with Roman imperial religion, and that was when serious and thorough persecution, as a matter of imperial policy, began. At that time, in face of increasingly serious threats, the empire had to inculcate at least a minimal patriotism to forge some unity among the diverse cultures of the Mediterranean." (FRANKIEL 1985, p. 15)
>
> "The persecutions, especially those of the emperor Diocletian (284-303) shook the Church badly. At the same time they publicised Christian beliefs and added to the Church's list of heroes, exemplars of the true faith; the martyrs. The martyrs followed in the footsteps of Jesus and of the first apostles; their suffering, like his, renewed the spiritual power of the Church." (ibid., p. 16)

However, as Frankiel points out, the significance of such persecutions has frequently been exaggerated. And other historical forces were at work, ultimately bringing the developing hierarchies of Church and state closer together.

A long term reduction in the numbers of independent citizen farmers, displaced from the land in Italy by the expansion of the big-slave worked estates of the wealthy landowners, has been identified by Marxist historians and others as a major factor contributing to the end of the expansion of the Roman Empire, and the eventual 'closing' of its borders. For it was these 'solid' citizens who had originally provided the manpower of the Roman army. This, in turn, meant a radical reduction in the supply of slaves drawn from conquered peoples. A continuous supply of cheap slaves had provided the backbone of the Roman economy and the drying up of supply was the beginning of the end, with the empire eventually faced with internal collapse and barbarian armies threatening from without.

In this atmosphere the Roman ruling class of big landowners, army officers and government officials increasingly lost faith in their traditional beliefs – which identified their leaders with the Olympian Gods – and particularly Mars, the god of war, in their historic mission of military world domination. The ruling classes looked increasingly to philosophies such as Stoicism – touched upon earlier – which advocated a virtuous acceptance of divine providence or fate – the infinite chain of cause and effect. The virtuous individual recognised the meaninglessness of earthly life and its goods and thus rose superior to the vicissitudes of that life. They also, of course, supported the established status quo of hierarchical power, knowing that God, the good father of all things, has ensured that everything is ultimately pre-determined to happen for the best.

At the same time, as Frankiel points out,

> "Christians took the (intellectual) high road by entering into dialogue and debate with the Greek philosophical tradition that dominated the educational system of the empire. In the second century Justin Martyr developed an 'Apology' for Christianity as the true philosophy in the Greek sense... Later, the great scholar Origen of Alexandria, (c. 185-c. 254) argued that Christianity was the culmination of all civilised culture; and Eusebius of Caesarea (263-339), the first Church historian, propagandised for Christianity amongst the educated public – including his friend the Emperor Constantine." (ibid., p. 17)

Christianity, no longer threatening to the rulers, actually began to appeal to the wealthy, powerful and educated, and the Stoical philosophy (in particular) interacted with the new religion. Christianity took from Stoicism the idea of a hierarchical order in society and nature established through the operation of divine and deterministic 'natural law'. "(This) concept of a Law of Nature was to be used by the Catholic Church through the centuries to support a hierarchical social order (in which it enjoyed a position of power and privilege)." (SIEGEL, 1986 p. 75)

These developments, of course, tended to accelerate earlier trends towards specialisation, hierarchy and inequality of power within the Christian Church, as the bureaucracy expanded and increasingly differentiated itself from the mass of the congregation.

> "As the Church grew in wealth and influence, it ceased to be democratic in its internal structure. The power of the bishops increased, and the Bishop of Rome became pre-eminent over the other bishops. Church property was no longer the common property of the Christian community but of a priesthood as a closed corporation. It was administered by the Church bureaucracy, which became quite separated from the masses it nominally served." (ibid., p. 75-6)

The conversion of the Roman Emperor Constantine was the logical culmination of many years of – converging – development of Church and state, allowing the former access to the police-miliary powers of the latter in enforcing orthodoxy, while the latter could exploit the effective ideological control established by the former.

These developments did not prevent the appearance of new religious movements, challenging the power of the Catholic Church. On the contrary, they probably stimulated radical reform movements. Even after Christianity became a state religion, and could call upon the repressive powers of the state to violently suppress opposition, 'heretical' popular sects kept arising, typically in the form of revolts against the corrupting influence of riches in the Church and the monopoly power and wealth of the bishops. Such sects advocated a return to puritan simplicity and austerity or to the original democracy and communism of early church organisation.

Such heretical sects became vehicles for popular nationalist protests and attacks by local African, Egyptian, Syrian and other peoples against oppressive Roman power. And we thus see Christianity coming full circle from a movement of Jewish national liberation, to a peaceful internationalism, and back to militant (anti-imperialist) nationalism.

But as the Roman Church became integrated into the ruling bureaucracy of the Roman state structure its leaders wasted no time in mobilising Roman soldiers to ruthlessly suppress all such revolts and heresies. And its power grew without effective challenge. In Africa, e.g., Augustine, Bishop of Hippo, used Roman imperial troops to suppress the movement of the Circumcellions, who sought to abolish slavery and inequality in the name of a return to 'true' Christian values.

Indeed, the Church hierarchy actively opposed the abolition of slavery, with priests and monasteries controlling substantial slave populations well into the Middle Ages. It was social and economic forces, over which it had no control, that ultimately brought an end to the Roman 'slave mode of production'. The decline in the availability of cheap slaves – following the closure of the borders of the Empire – forced the owners of the large estates to rent parts of their lands to tenant farmers – the *coloni*.

It was these tenant farmers, refugees from the declining towns, freed slaves etc. who were to become the serfs in the new 'feudal' society established by the invading Germanic warriors when the Roman Empire finally disintegrated. In some cases these Germanic peoples had already been converted to Christianity by missionaries sent from Rome, long before they moved in to restore order in the disintegrating empire. As they moved in they arrived at an accommodation with the Church bureaucracy in Rome. Such aristocratic barbarian leaders allowed the Church to retain wealth, power, privilege so long as the Church bureaucracy functioned to help them to establish themselves as the new ruling class – educating the rulers in Roman culture, technology etc. and keeping the peasants in line, passively accepting their lowly status, as workers providing the wealth to maintain lords, ladies, bishops and priests in luxury, while the peasants themselves kept only enough to survive from day to day (if they were lucky). As Frankiel points out,

"while the Eastern church developed its inward spirituality, the Roman branch was developing the political allies it needed to ensure its survival. The Pope sought the help of the Franks, who had converted to Christianity in 496 when their lord Clovis accepted baptism. Their leaders afterwards helped Rome militarily against other societies... and Rome sent, to both Gaul and England, Benedictine monks as missionaries and teachers." (FRANKIEL 1985, p. 26-27)

Official Church doctrine increasingly became a travesty of earlier Christian ideas. The glorification of poverty was now equated with uncomplaining subservience on the part of the mass of the population, slaves, serfs and others. The ideal Christian was the good honest worker who loved his neighbour as himself no matter how exploited he might be by that neighbour or how bad things became for him. Radical inequality and misery had to be accepted as a punishment for the original sin of Adam.

The reward for such uncomplaining acceptance on earth was eternal happiness in heaven. But the punishment for rebellion – once the earthly authorities had finished with the wrongdoer – was eternal pain in Hell.

The idea of charity, derived from the mutual respect and material assistance amongst the members of the early Christian congregation also became radically changed. It ceased to be primarily concerned with helping others and came to centre rather upon buying penance from ones sins and with exalting ascetic self-discipline. The store of grace accumulated by the celibate monks and priests was available for sale to the wealthy, providing them with the keys to heaven and forgiveness for all their earthly sins.

"The Catholic Church, through which donations to the poor were distributed, became unaccountable to those on whose behalf it received donations and bequests." [And in the sixth century it also began to receive tithes, or special church taxes, levied upon every bit of occupied land.] "Their cost was paid for, in the last analysis, by the peasants, upon whom they were a crushing burden." (SIEGEL 1986, p. 77)

And in its own holdings the Church was even more demanding that its serfs fulfil their feudal obligations than the other land-owners.

Some such landowners were monasteries, originally established (from the beginning of the fourth century) as worker co-operatives, attempting to maintain the communistic principles of the early Church. But as the monasteries became increasingly rich and power-ful, so did they turn increasingly to the labour of wage workers, slaves or serfs in place of that of the monks themselves. Monasteries too, therefore, were transformed into their opposites, becoming as ex-ploitative as, and often even more exploitative than, the feudal lords.

The new kingdoms established by the Germanic invaders were themselves relatively shortlived. The absence of efficient military organisation meant that they tended to disintegrate under the attacks of Vikings in the north and Hungarians in the east, giving way to a Dark Age of general lawlessness and breakdown of social order, travel, trade etc. between 800 and 1000 CE. During this period, over much of Europe, the basic unit of social organisation became the fortified stronghold of the local warlord – the knight's castle with one or peasant villages under its protection. The warlords were descen-dants of the military leaders of the invading barbarians, the peasants of Roman slaves, poor farmers etc. And the peasants surrendered half of their time, effort or produce to support the knights and their hangers-on – because they had no swords, horses, armour; no way to effectively protect themselves either from alien raiders or from their own 'nobility'.

By 1000 CE the invasions had more or less ceased, trade picked up, and 1050-1250 saw significant growth in the European econo-my. Some lords formed alliances to conquer others, so that in some areas larger states emerged or revived with more or less centralised and effective power. Old towns revived and new ones formed, sus-tained by the expansion of agricultural production in the country-side. The classical 'feudal' system emerged as a hierarchy of kings, dukes, earls, knights, bailiffs, (craftsmen, apprentices) and – at the bottom of the heap – peasants.

Previously kings had, in theory, raised tax upon all of their land, with all free men liable to do war service under the king. But it had taken too long for the king to raise an army capable of repelling foreign invaders, and the peasants lacked suitable military equipment. At the same time, the taxation system – based upon payment in kind – did not assist the kings in equipping their own standing armies (of properly armed horsemen). In this situation, a form of organisation with origins in the ancient past was gradually developed – called the fief.

"One way in which a fief could be created was by the king giving a part of the crown land in fief to an important military man, often a lord or a rich free peasant. The fiefholder became the lord of the peasants in the fief, and had the right to raise taxes and exercise legal authority. In return he swore allegiance to the king and undertook to take part in the defence of the realm against the enemies of the king and provide a certain number of fully equipped horsemen." [Such lords could, in turn, hand over parts of their land to knights and so on.] "Formally the fief still belonged to the king and reverted to him when the fiefholder died. The Church was generally dependent upon lay protection, so kings could often make fiefs of church land. This system of fiefs enabled kings to secure the equipment and upkeep of an army, and the legal and fiscal administration of the realm; but it also meant that large parts of the kingdom became semi-autonomous." (FINK 1981, p. 7)

During the invasions, the Church had been relatively weak and disorganised. But its power and independence grew in the centuries after 1000 CE. It exerted great influence through its

"monopoly of education of the few who did receive an education and in the communication and interpretation of news and ideas for the whole of society. Internally the structure of the Church was hierarchical, with village priest at the bottom of the pyramid, the Pope at the top and higher Church officials, like Bishops and Archbishops in between. The costs of the Church were covered by the tithes which all peasants had to pay." (FINK 1981, p.13)

But apart from that, bishops and monasteries were also remunerated by holding large estates, with their own masses of 'tied' peasant drudges.

After a series of struggles over the issue, high Church officials came to be appointed by the Church itself, rather than by local Kings. However, they were generally still drawn only from the feudal aristocracy, with the younger sons of noble families appointed as Bishops e.g. And with high posts in the Church – as sources of great wealth and power – effectively accessible only to the nobility, and the Church as the greatest landowner in feudal Europe (holding about one third of all productive land), the Church hierarchy was firmly integrated into the general feudal structure.

Part Three
THE POLITICS OF CELIBACY

In this context, the teaching on celibacy and the evil of sexual pleasure begins to make some sense. As has frequently been pointed out, making the labouring masses – and secular society generally – feel guilty about their most powerful, persistent and insistent desires (and about the actions deriving from those desires) provides a powerful tool of social control and exploitation. On the one hand, such guilt undermines their self-esteem and powers of resistance to exploitation. On the other, in monopolising the means of (temporary) relief for such guilt – via confessions, penances etc. – the Church gains a corresponding power of 'positive' reinforcement for conformity and subservience.

At the same time, the (apparently) successful suppression and transcendence of such desires and actions on the part of the clergy, fosters the illusion amongst the exploited masses that the representatives of the Church had indeed transmuted this powerful 'physical' energy into a higher 'spiritual' form, giving them access to 'higher' powers and possibilities. This, in turn, legitimises the superior social power and privileges of the religious elite, while at the same time sustaining hopes and expectations that they can indeed intercede on behalf of their congregations with such higher spiritual forces.

A nice example here is the letter of Pope Zacharias, written to the Frankish clergy and aristocrats in 745, urging them to accept the reforms of the missionary Boniface, aiming to strengthen Church discipline in relation to priestly celibacy, pagan rites and warfare.

> "It was, he said, because they had false and misleading priests that their enemies had won battles. If the priests would become pure, observing chastity and refraining from bloodshed, the heathen would fall before the Christian armies. Christianity, in short, would provide the support of God for the Frankish warriors; they, in turn, would protect the Church." (FRANKIEL 1985, p. 28)

As Frankiel adds,

> "Undoubtedly it had helped the cause that a Christian leader, Charles Martel, had won a great battle only a short time before, turning back the advance of the Muslim armies at Tours in 732." (op. cit.)

Nor is this perception of the power of re-directed sexual energy necessarily entirely illusory. For (aim-inhibited) sexual energy could indeed be sublimated into more effective political organisation, commitment and unity (amongst men) within the Church – and its organisations – in the service of continued domination and control. Freed from the demands and responsibilities of heterosexuality and family life, the Church hierarchy could devote itself whole-heartedly to maintaining its grip on social power.

The development of the monasteries seems to have played a crucial role here. As Frankiel points out the 'courage and religious dedication' of the early monks was widely recognised. They were both admired and feared as spiritually superior beings.

"In effect, monks and hermits became the new models of martyrdom as the Church conquered the imperial world. The battle against paganism, exemplified by the martyrs, was over. Now a different battle began with less tangible forces of evil, namely the demonic forces that infected people and threatened their souls... Monks exemplified their conquest of the world and their other-worldly powers by their celibacy, eating little and fasting frequently, and living an impoverished life without worldly comforts." (op. cit.)

But there were increasingly powerful economic forces at work here also in promoting the power and appeal of the monasteries with their celibate lifestyle. As Kautsky points out, the economic success of these institutions soon became a factor in encouraging increasing numbers to take up the monastic lifestyle.

"As monastic communities became firm and durable the wealth of the monastery necessarily increased. The monastic industries soon furnished the best products and the cheapest, since the common household rendered the cost of production quite low. Like the oikos system of the great landed proprietors, the monasteries produced themselves almost everything they needed in foodstuffs and raw materials. But the workers (in the monastery) showed far more zeal than had the slaves of the great landed proprietor, for they were members themselves, receiving the entire product of their labour. Besides, each monastery included so many workers, that it might select for each of its industries those workers best fitted for it, thus introducing a far reaching division of labour. Finally, the monastery, as contrasted with the individual, was eternal. Inventions and business secrets which might easily be lost with the death of the inventor and his family (!) became the enterprise of many members of the monastery, being transmitted by them to their successors. Besides, the monastery, being an eternal perso-nage, was not beset with the destructive danger of dissipating its patrimony by inheritance. Its accumulations of property were never divided in the form of bequests... Thus the wealthy of the monastery grew, also the wealth of combinations of monasteries under a single head and under uniform regulations, the so called orders of monks." (KAUTSKY 1972, p. 456)

And Kautsky could also have added that the monastery had the added advantage – over family based production units – that it did not have to devote resources to the upkeep of new generations of – initially – unproductive children.

It is certainly true that in later times monasteries took charge of the care of large numbers of small children – from as early as age five – handed over by their parents (usually from the nobility) – as 'oblates', permanently committed to a monastic vocation. As McLaughlin points out, from the ninth to the eleventh centuries, "the offering of noble children by their parents had been a major, indeed the principle means of monastic recruitment" (quoted in DEMAUSE 1975, p. 129). And the practice certainly did not stop in the eleventh century.

In this case, the financial incentive was clearly that of the parent, rather than the child. The monastic lifestyle – including celibacy – was imposed upon the child from the start, typically with extreme harshness and cruelty. (See DEMAUSE 1975, pp. 130-1.) But, this too, of course, goes some way towards explaining the perpetuation of such an institution during the period concerned. Individuals were subjected to, and socialised into the monastic lifestyle from an early age, with little choice in the matter.

These sorts of considerations are clearly relevant to the Church hierarchy beyond the monasteries also. In the first instance they found themselves in danger of being upstaged by the supposedly greater 'purity' and 'sanctity' of the monks. This provided pressure for them to go down the same path of sexual suppression and celibacy.

Here too, economic considerations became increasingly relevant – both insofar as such supposed spiritual purity became a major factor in extracting gifts and payments from patrons trying to reserve their births in heaven, and insofar as inheritance (within a family) threatened to undermine the increasing wealth and power of the Church.

As Siegel says, celibacy was decreed by the Pope in the eleventh century "in order to keep the wealth of the priesthood within the Church, although it was not effectively instituted until the thirteenth century owing to the opposition of the priests". (SIEGEL 1986)

In fact, this was the culmination of a long struggle going back to the early Church fathers, in which those at the top of the hierarchy sought to impose a celibate lifestyle upon the rank and file of the priesthood, through persuasion or bullying, including threats of violence and imprisonment for priests and/or their partners and children. At the first German Council, convoked by Boniface in 742, e.g., the latter demanded penalties for 'lascivious' priests, monks and nuns including two years in prison for guilty parties, followed by public flogging. "Monks and nuns were to be taken to prison after the third beating to do penance there till a year runs its course." (ibid., pp. 106-7)

The western Church's 'rigourism on celibacy' was apparently a major cause of the split with the eastern Church, based at Constantinople, going right back to the Council of Nicea in 325 CE.

CHAPTER ELEVEN
CATHOLICISM *cont.*

Part One
AUGUSTINE'S NEUROSIS

A key figure in the developing Catholic Christian antipathy towards sexuality is St Augustine (d. 430 CE) – often seen as "the greatest of the Church Fathers". Ranke-Heinemann describes him as the one who definitively "fused Christianity together with hatred of sex and pleasure into a systematic unity". (RANKE-HEINEMANN 1991, p. 75)

"The position taken by Augustine had a decisive influence upon the great medieval theologians including Thomas Aquinas (d. 1274). And his image of God, the world and humanity... is still widely accepted today."

Augustine's major hang-up concerned the idea of 'original sin'. He thought that when Adam and Eve disobeyed God and ate the forbidden fruit of Paradise they became aware of their sexuality and experienced sexual desire. At this point they were ashamed and covered their sexual parts with fig leaves.

The original sin of disobeying God and eating the fruit of the tree of knowledge is equated with the first experience of sexual desire. And, according to Augustine, it is the experience of sexual pleasure in intercourse that 'transmits' this original sin across the generations. The individual who 'succumbs' to such sinful desire thereby 'infects' their children with such sin. Only Jesus was without such sin, having been conceived and born to a virgin mother.

To be burdened with original sin meant eternal misery – damnation for everyone (including unbaptised children) who had not been redeemed by God's grace – through baptism and confession. And, as Ranke-Heinemann points out, "at a time of Aids anxiety we can imagine what it meant to think and feel that sexual pleasure had infected the child with original sin" (ibid., p. 78).

Here too we can see how powerful these ideas could have been in bolstering the power of the Catholic Church. For it was only the Church, with its rites of baptism and confession that had the cure to this horrific infection.

Originally Augustine wavered on the question of whether there was sex in Paradise before the Fall. He thought it possible that children could have been conceived without intercourse – by purely spiritual means. But later, in trying to make sense of God's creation of – otherwise useless – women, he decided that God did indeed create women for the purpose of conceiving, bearing and caring for children (and generally being slaves to men). But such conception was originally without excitement or pleasure. "In Eden the will ruled the sexual organs as it now does the hands and feet." (ibid., p. 89)

According to Augustine, "married couples make good use of the evil of lust only when they wish for the sole purpose of marriage – namely reproduction, before and during the sexual act". As he says, "what cannot occur without lust should not, however, occur because of lust". And Ranke-Heinemann notes that "it is hardly necessary to add that Augustine rejected intercourse with a woman who was menstruating, or pregnant or post-menopausal".

In Augustine's eyes virginity is morally higher than marriage with sex, and marriage without sex is higher than marriage with it.

And following his conversion to (orthodox) Christianity in 387 he himself threw out the woman with whom he had lived for twelve years and thereafter lived a celibate life.

Before his conversion, Augustine was first of all a Platonist, and then a Manichee. As we saw earlier, the Manichees – profoundly influenced by Gnosticism – saw the earth as 'the kingdom of boundless darkness', created by the devil. As a Manichee, Augustine saw procreation as a diabolical act, trapping the particles of light that were human souls in a body and a world of pure evil. And he assiduously practiced contraception in his relations with his mistress so as to avoid such an irresponsible act.

Certainly his general world-view shows clear signs of Gnostic – and Platonic – influence.

> "All worldly states and empires, including Rome, are corruptible and ultimately will die; only the City of God is eternal. Christians therefore reside as aliens in this world; their true home is that eternal city that awaits them after this life. Pagans invest too much in this world, which, beautiful though it is, is transient and full of suffering, marred by the divine punishment of Adam's sin. Christians who long for the other world have as their protector and guard the church and its sacraments, for the church is a shadow here on earth of the true heavenly city." ... "this attitude toward the Church and the world was satisfying to Augustine's generation, troubled by the incursions of barbarians and the economic ups and downs of late imperial society. It also offered a basis for a continued critique of the world, and as such his work has been a resource for theologians down through the centuries. The City of God marked the unification of Christianity as a religion in this world promoting good order on earth, but with aspirations that went far beyond the ordinary round of life." (FRANKIEL 1985, p. 19-20)

And we could see his Christian celibacy as a logical development of Augustines earlier Manichean abstention from procreation. As Ranke-Heinemann says, "in a sense, he turned from a second class Manichee (merely practising contraception), into a first class one".

But yet there seems to be rather more involved in Augustine's radical rejection of sexual pleasure at the time of his conversion than a logical extension of his earlier Manichean commitments. In particular, as Ranke-Heinemann argues, this seems to be more a matter of psychopathology than of conscious, rational decision.

Here she refers to Augustines own comments upon the guilt and anguish he felt upon being forced by his mother to 'give up' his first mistress – who was deemed to be an 'unsuitable' marriage partner for her (teenage) son. "But the rich bride chosen by his mother was, at that stage, not yet of marriageable age, and rather than waiting another two years, the frustrated Augustine took another lover."

As he says,

> "the woman with whom I was in the habit of sleeping was torn from my side on the grounds of being an impediment to my marriage, and my heart, which clung to her, dripped blood. She was returned to Africa after having made a vow to (God) that she would never go to bed with another man. And she had left with me the natural son I had had with her. But I, in my misery, could not follow the example of a woman. I found another woman for myself..."

He called his relationship with the new woman "A mere pact made between two people whose love is lustful..." And he described the pain of loss of his first love as continuing to fester, ...becoming more desperate. As Ranke-Heinemann says,

> "after his conversion, his bad conscience over his own betrayal of his first lover was transformed into a contempt for sexual love in general. As guilty as he may have felt, he thought the fault lay less in himself than in the evil pleasure of the sexual act. Augustine's pessimistic sexual morality is simply a repression of his bad sexual conscience, his aversion to women a continual ferreting out of the culpable cause of his failure." (RANKE-HEINEMANN 1991, pp. 79-80)

Part Two
THE OEDIPUS COMPLEX

But this does not explain the continued appeal of these ideas to all the other Church Fathers right up to the present day, or, indeed, their tight hold upon massive Catholic congregations of thousands or millions of individuals. This seems to suggest a much more pervasive source of sexual guilt, distributed across barriers of class and persisting through massive changes of regime, ideology, and custom.

Sigmund Freud identifies just such a pervasive source of (hetero) sexual guilt in outlining the dynamics of the Oedipus complex. Indeed, he saw the Oedipus complex – and its attendant sexual guilt – as an inevitable concomitant of family life, and the prolonged dependence of the human infant.

Freud assumes that the mother will typically become the first love object of the young boy growing up in a nuclear family "as a result of her feeding him and looking after him". Initially this love centres around 'oral' desires for feeding and fusion with the body of the mother via the mouth – as a means of recapturing the ecstatic, 'oceanic' feelings of the narcissistic symbiosis in the womb. But Freud argues that at a later stage – typically towards the end of the third year of life, the boy becomes increasingly aware of his own genital feelings – and of the likely sexual relationship between his parents. And at this stage so do his desires and fantasies of ecstatic union with the body of mother become increasingly focused upon his penis and upon the idea of some sort of sexual congress with the mother.

It is at this time that the boy's hostility to the father, whom he now perceives as his rival for the – sexual – love of the mother – comes into being or intensifies. "As a result of his wish to possess the exclusive love of the mother the boy develops the wish to kill the father and replace him in his relationship with the mother. (Though, in the mind of the little boy ... to kill means to eliminate, to banish, to be rid of.)"

[Thus,] "according to Freud, basing his description on clinical evidence... the male Oedipus complex is a triangular constellation involving a boy, his father, and his mother, in which the boys sexual desire for the mother, whose love he wishes to monopolise, leads to hostility towards his father (and his siblings) whom he views as a rival for the mother's love" (SPIRO 1982, p. 4).

Of the three parties concerned, Freud himself typically stresses the primary role of the boy as initiator of the Oedipus complex, though he allows that both the sexual and the hostile feelings of the son can be exacerbated by his witnessing of parental intercourse (what Freud calls a 'primal scene'). This experience "simultaneously creates a high degree of sexual excitement" and "the impression that sex is dangerous" (FENICHEL 1945, p. 92).

However, other investigators have argued that there are good grounds for seeing the Oedipus complex as much a consequence of the child's sensitivity to the parents sexual and aggressive impulses as of the child's own 'spontaneous' feelings. Mothers can be 'seductive' towards their sons, thereby arousing their sons sexual feelings towards them. And fathers can view their sons as rivals for the love of the wife-mother and, in expressing their hostility towards the son, so can they thereby arouse the son's fear and hostility towards themselves.

It has been suggested, in particular, that parents who have failed to satisfactorily resolve their own Oedipal feelings (towards their own parents) will tend to encourage or exacerbate the Oedipus complex in their sons. A woman who continues to feel frustrated in her – corresponding – incestuous Oedipal desire for her father may, as a mother, 'put her son in his place' as idealised love object – and behave seductively towards him. A man who continues to feel frustrated in his wish to monopolise his mother's love, may, as a husband, put his wife in the place of the mother and exhibit jealous hostility towards his son.

Freud maintains that the Oedipus complex is typically 'resolved' in the course of the sixth year of the boy's life – or thereabouts. The crucial factor here (according to Freud) is the boy's fear of castration by the father as punishment for his incestuous and patricidal desires. This fear may be a result of actual castration threats from the parents (as threatened punishment for masturbation or exhibitionism e.g.), of the workings of the talion principle (the boy's own fantasy of paternal retribution for his Oedipal desires), or of the boy's perception of the female genitalia (which he may interpret as evidence of the 'reality' of castration).

Anyway, as Freud says, as a result of castration anxiety arising from one or more of these sources, "the child's ego turns away from the Oedipus complex". The boy gives up his wish to kill the father and instead 'identifies' with him – or at least with the child's idea of the fathers values and priorities. The boy 'introjects' the fathers authority as the foundation of his 'super-ego' or the commanding voice of conscience "which takes over the severity of the father and perpetuates his prohibitions against incest…"

His "incestuous wishes are in part desexualised and sublimated… and in part inhibited in their aim and changed into impulses of affection". Having given up his mother as a (sexual) love object, the boy later replaces her with someone who either "resembles her or is derived from her". That is to say, he 'displaces' his Oedipal desires – perhaps onto a sister, a nursemaid, a teacher at school and ultimately onto an appropriate female partner in later life. Perhaps such desires provide the energy for a fantasy of magical union with some sort of divine maternal force in place of the real mother on earth; the individual imagines some sort of ecstatic fusion with a mother goddess in heaven.

The formation of the super-ego 'protects' the ego (the conscious, rational self) from the regressive sexual love for the mother – and its painful social consequences. Ideally this is achieved by the "destruction and abolition" of the boy's incestuous desires. But most likely it will be achieved by repression of such desires, which therefore persist unconsciously (though with reduced intensity), striving to find there way back into conscious awareness and action.

Despite such childhood resolution of the Oedipus complex, it will usually still be revived at puberty – as a result of social and biological – hormonal – pressures and at this stage should be finally resolved. But if it has not been adequately dealt with in childhood, then it is during puberty that its pathological effect will manifest itself. As Freud says, an unresolved Oedipus complex (including persisting, but unconscious longings for the mother) is at the core of most adult neuroses.

Part Three
EVIDENCE

As Melford Spiro points out, evidence for the existence of the Oedipus complex comes from a variety of sources. Psychiatric findings concerning the existence of incestuous desire in clinical populations, and psychological findings concerning the frequency of incest wishes – both overt and disguised – in the dreams of normal populations are clearly of central importance. But such considerations are supplemented by sociological findings of the actual prevalence of incestuous behaviour, anthropological findings concerning the ubiquity of the incest motif in myths, legends and folklore – as well as the universality of nuclear family incest taboos, and ethological findings which indicate a widespread motivation to incest – with young males striving to have sex with their mothers – in more advanced mammalian societies – including those of our closest living relatives the chimpanzees.

Perhaps most significant of all is the cross-cultural evidence of correlation of specific sorts of child-rearing practices with particular consequences, as predicted by the Oedipal theory, in other areas of social and psychological reality. For example, as noted in Chapter Two, there have been quite extensive studies of significant cross-cultural variability in those practices seen as most relevant (from a Freudian perspective) to intensifying or resolving Oedipal desires and conflicts in the early life of the infant. Such variations have then been correlated with predicted outcomes in terms of broader social consequences of such practices, including the necessity for some sort of Oedipal resolution in adolescence, if no adequate resolution has been achieved earlier.

The mythological evidence is particularly interesting in the present context. Consider the case of Greek origin myths. In the beginning, according to Hesiod, there was Chaos. Out of Chaos came Gaia, the Earth Goddess, who parthenogenetically created Uranos, the Sky God. Uranos marries his mother and by her has several children whom he hates and confines to Tartaros – to hell inside the body of the Earth. But Gaia persuades her youngest son Chronos to castrate his father – which he does with a sickle from behind just as Uranos is preparing to have intercourse with Gaia. Out of the drops of blood spring the Giants and the Erinyes – the latter being vengeful cannibalistic female demons.

Chronos, having thus succeeded his father, marries his sister Rhea – who is probably the same person as his mother (and grandmother) Gaia, and in his turn has several children, whom he swallows. But Rhea saves the youngest son, Zeus, by giving her husband a stone wrapped in cloth, which he swallows believing it to be his son. When Zeus grows up he gives his father an emetic so that he vomits up his swallowed children, who emerge none the worse for wear.

As ruler of the sky, Zeus marries his sister Hera, and has a family by her who generally seem to treat him with appropriate respect. The exception is the son Hephaestus, who takes Hera's side in a quarrel with Zeus. But this time the father is victorious; Hephaestus is thrown out of Heaven and lamed by the fall as a symbolic castration by the father. In this generation, in other words, the authority of the father asserts itself in bringing to an end the cycle of Oedipal acting out on the part of mothers and sons.

As Roger Money-Kyrle points out,

"these Greek myths, in which [what Freud calls] the child's 'family romance' is projected upon the gods of sky and earth, are by no means isolated examples. Indeed they are only variants of a type of cosmic myth found amongst the Greeks, Babylonians, and

Egyptians, but also in Africa, India, China, New Zealand and even in America. In these myths the Sky-god and Earth-mother were once locked in a continuous embrace until one of the sons, usually the youngest, separated them, sometimes castrating his father and marrying his mother. In New Zealand, e.g., Tane Mahuta is the youngest son and plays the part of the Greek Chronos."

"Very possibly the story of Oedipus himself – the classical example of parricide and incest – may have originated as a cosmic myth of this kind. But it has been elaborated by the genius of Greek imagination into one of the most powerful dramas of all time." (MONEY-KYRLE 1950, Ch. 2)

Here, as in the myth of Chronos, the fantasy is hardly disguised at all but the criminal intention is repressed. Oedipus kills his father and marries his mother without recognising them. According to Freud, it is this slight distortion that gives the story its dramatic force. Had Oedipus recognised his parents all along, his motives would have seemed too alien to our conscious thought to enable us to identify ourselves with him. As it is, however, our own unconscious Oedipal fantasies are stirred, but not stirred enough to bring their immediate and total repudiation.

Besides explicit Oedipal myths of this kind, in which parricide and incest are undisguised, there are a whole series that display different degrees of distortion, certain elements being repressed and replaced by symbols. Often the characters are disguised. In the Oedipus story itself the father is mistaken for a male stranger. But Freud found that the device of converting a near relative into a stranger is a very common means by which unconscious is converted into conscious fantasy – in dreams, fairy stories, etc.

In the Trobriand Islands, the cannibal monster Dokonikan takes the place of the missing father. He terrorises the islands until he is killed by the culture hero Tudava, living alone with his mother, and aided by her magic in defeating the father-figure.

Moving on to cross cultural investigations of child-rearing practices, we can fairly easily grasp the logic of the classic studies of

Stephens and others, aiming to 'verify' the 'Oedipus complex hypothesis' by focussing particularly upon taboos of various kinds in pre-industrial – and generally tribal – societies.

As Spiro points out, there is considerable cross-cultural variability in respect of both the intensity and the outcome of the Oedipus complex. And "since the implementation of the incest taboo" (or failure of such implementation) in childhood "is a major determinant of its outcome (in later life)" it makes sense to focus upon this area in testing the hypothesis (SPIRO 1987, p. 90).

> "Since sexual desires for the mother may be present... in the nursing infant, the implementation of the incest taboo may be said to begin with weaning, which is also the time when the child is usually banned from the mothers bed and when, in general, he is discouraged from continuing those more intimate forms of physical contact with the mother that she had previously permitted if not actively encouraged." (op. cit.)

Therefore, time of weaning, and any taboos – such as postpartum sex taboos – which keep wives and husbands separated for long periods – and potentially prolong and intensify the physical contact between mother and young child – are relevant variables in determining the likely effectiveness of Oedipal resolution in early childhood. And, if Freud is right, then the use or otherwise of specific castration threats by the parents – as a basis for early compliance with the incest taboo is also relevant.

In Freudian terms,

> "Compliance with the taboo is achieved either by the extinction of the boy's incestuous desire for his mother or by its repression, the latter being accompanied by a 'reaction formation' against the desire, i.e. an emotional aversion to (physical) contact with the mother. If the taboo is internalised the boys incestuous attachment to the mother either disappears entirely (extinction) or, although persisting unconsciously (repression), disappears from conscious

awareness... [But] if, e.g., the implementation of the taboo is only partially successful in promoting its internalisation, the son's sexual attachment to the mother is not extinguished, and although it may be repressed, it undergoes only weak or incomplete repression... [and] a weak or incomplete repression of the Oedipus complex (in early childhood) is one in which repression is insufficiently powerful to preclude the conscious arousal of the boy's incestuous wishes for the mother (and hence his hostile wishes towards the father) under conditions of incestuous temptation (in later life)." (ibid., p. 92)

Psychoanalytic theory predicts various sorts of outcomes arising from such inadequate Oedipal resolution, including persistent castration anxiety on the part of the boy, arising out of his own continuing Oedipal hostility to the father. This could manifest itself in intense male fear of the female genitalia and particularly of the sight of blood in connection with the female genitalia – as apparent evidence of the reality of castration. So that here is another possible determinant of the intense menstrual taboos – and fears of female sexuality in some societies considered in the last chapter.

But most obviously, we can see how the persistence of powerful Oedipal desires beyond infancy could threaten radical social disruption and could therefore motivate appropriate social interventions by the older generation to try to address this problem at a later stage, particularly in face of the intensification of such desires at puberty.

In Freudian terms, there are two obvious forms such intervention could take; on the one hand, reducing the opportunities for incestuous and aggressive temptation by physically separating the boys from their mothers (and sisters) and, on the other, directly strengthening the incomplete repression of the boy's Oedipal wishes by renewed castration (or other) threats. And, indeed, the anthropological record provides abundant evidence of both such solutions.

On the one hand, we see widespread practices of 'child extrusion' whereby boys – and in some societies, girls also – are removed from the parental household, at or before puberty, and, instead, grouped together in some sort of age-graded dormitory, men's house, children's village, or boarding school – or simply placed in some other household. On the other, we see equally widespread practices of painful initiation rites, whereby boys are taught the 'law of the fathers' in a context of isolation, physical torture, ordeals and phallic or other mutilation.

As Spiro points out, in relation to the former sort of practices of extrusion,

> "whatever the conscious motives for these practices might be... they have the consequence (amongst others) of separating the son from his parents, thereby reducing the opportunities for the arousal of his sexual and aggressive Oedipal wishes. When, at some later stage, more frequent interaction with the parents is once again resumed, his libidinal and aggressive impulses have typically been rechannelled." [And he notes in passing that] "son extrusion in human society has its analogue... in the peripheralisation of male juveniles in primate societies" (ibid., pp. 92-3).

Here, of course, the Catholic Church itself has played an integral part in organising such extrusion processes in accepting young boys – often the sons of the nobility – into monastic seclusion as 'oblates'. And Catholic boarding schools have continued the tradition.

As far as painful initiation is concerned, as Spiro says,

> "although the conscious, culturally constituted explanations of these rites only infrequently relate them to the Oedipal issue... the ethnographic descriptions of the practices and of the initiates psychological reaction to them provide strong evidence for the thesis that these rites... constitute an important cultural resource for ensuring compliance with the taboos on incest with the mother and aggression towards the father". (op. cit.)

And he goes on to provide details of the boys initiation rites among the Sambia of Papua New Guinea as a particularly 'blatant' example of the Oedipal significance of such practices.

Here, the older men violently assault the boys, first at the ages of seven to ten, then again at thirteen to sixteen, forcibly bleeding their noses and otherwise terrorising them. At the same time the boys are condemned for 'insubordination' to their fathers and elders, and warned that they must never again so much as touch, hold, talk with, eat with or look at their mothers.

Spiro further points out that in some such tribal societies – particularly in New Guinea – these sorts of rites so "dominate the lives of the (men) of the group" as to constitute the main focus of their interests and actions, absorbing significant social and economic resources. And such a preponderance of 'magical' thinking – as a response to unconscious wishes and fears – can be a major obstacle to evolving "alternative cultural foci based upon realistic thinking". (ibid., p. 96)

Most important for present purposes, Stephens and other investigators have found significant correlations between phenomena associated with early failure of Oedipal resolution, including long post-partum sex taboos, and the predicted long term consequences of such failure – in terms of intensity of menstrual taboos, institutionalisation of extrusion and initiation and other considerations (sexual anxiety, severe kin-avoidance rules etc.). Stephens puts it in these terms "(1) the long post partum sex taboo intensifies the mothers interest in her child; (2) this intensifies the child's sexual interest in her; (3) this in turn intensifies… the effects of the Oedipus complex". (ibid., p. 40)

Fisher and Greenberg point out that,

"Stephens quantitative analysis of vast amounts of anthropological data available to him was largely supportive of the propositions just listed. The results did fit the complex theoretical paradigm he derived from Freud and translated into anthropological terms. If one accepts his initial assumption that the length of the post partum sex intercourse taboo is an index of the degree of intimacy of the mother-son relationship, his findings come across as convincing, Incidentally, he assiduously enumerated a variety of statistical relationships in his data apparently supportive of that initial assumption."
(FISHER AND GREENBERG 1985, p. 216)

Part Four
CATHOLICISM AND SEXUAL GUILT

Now, hopefully, the relevance of these ideas for the Catholic Church's antipathy to heterosexual pleasure – and emphasis upon priestly celibacy – should already be clear. As noted earlier, unresolved Oedipal conflicts provide a very powerful source of guilt and fear in relation to such heterosexual pleasure, potentially very widely distributed in the male population.

One major problem amongst Freud's male patients, e.g., was what he called "the tendency to debasement in love". This refers to the apparent incapacity of such men to achieve any sort of satisfactory sexual relations with their wives – or other women they loved or respected. Many of them were able, on the other hand, to "freely express sensuality" and achieve a "high degree of (sexual) pleasure" in relations with women they "did not need to love", women they could cast into an inferior or generally 'debased' role. As Freud says, "the whole sphere of love in such people remains divided in the two directions personified in art as sacred and profane (or animal) love. Where they love they do not desire and where they desire they cannot love" (FREUD 1977, p. 251).

He traces the split back to the Oedipus complex, when the boy is forced to 'split off' his erotic feelings for his mother from his affectionate feelings for her – under threat of castration by the father. Probably such erotic feelings are to some extent repressed, to some extent displaced onto other models. Such repressed feelings can combine with affection and paternal identification in motivating marriage to a partner modelled on the mother. But then so does sex with such a person once again bring such incestuous desires to the surface – thereby eliciting corresponding punishment or threat of punishment from the paternal super-ego.

The only way to escape the anxiety produced in this situation – and still achieve sexual release – is to seek a sexual partner who can be identified by that super ego as antithesis to the mother as object of love and respect. Here, Freud implies, is one of the psychological foundations of the institution of prostitution – providing just such 'degraded' sexuality to men with such inadequately resolved Oedipal feelings.

Another relevant consideration here, as Freud suggests, is the likelihood that the individuals concerned will also have "retained perverse sexual aims whose non-fulfilment is felt as a serious loss of pleasure, and whose fulfilment, on the other hand, seems possible only with a debased sexual object" (ibid., p. 252).

On the one hand, he is here presumably referring to those – predominantly oral – sexual relations arising directly out of the early 'oral' love and feeding relationship with the mother – still to a great extent tabooed in Freud's day. (See Chapter Three.) On the other, he is referring to the fusion of erotic and aggressive feelings, grounded in early sexualised punishments and in the Oedipal splitting of love and sexuality itself.

Of course, in a patriarchal society, in which women are excluded from public life, and from developing fulfilling extramarital relations of their own, we can see how this sort of attitude on the part of their husbands could be perpetuated across the generations. For such women are more likely to turn to their sons for the sort of emotional fulfilment they are denied in relations with their husbands – and in the wider society – thereby tending to intensify the Oedipal feelings of those sons.

Of course, given the apparent inevitability of the Oedipus complex – and the difficulty of adequate resolution – we should expect that these sorts of problems would actually be very widespread. And, indeed, Freud thought that such a dissociation of love and sexuality was actually 'universal' amongst 'civilised' males – the males of the modern industrialised societies of his own day, though differing in degree between different individuals and social groups.

As we have seen, this sort of split is institutionalised in Catholic ideology with its hostility to sexual pleasure in marriage, (as well as outside it), its images of women as either sexless, sinless madonnas or degraded, loveless whores. Clearly this ideology would receive considerable psychological support from unresolved Odipal tensions

– with men projecting their own sexual guilt onto women as evil seducers. And it could complement such tensions in the parental generation in perpetuating and promoting such problems across the generations – in the sort of fashion discussed earlier.

It suits the Catholic Church to put 'obstacles' in the way of heterosexual fulfilment. As Freud says, this intensifies the excitement and the pleasure and the guilt. The excitement keeps the masses interested in sin (in sex as something peculiarly special). The guilt brings them back to the priest to beg forgiveness and pay their money.

Those males whose guilt is too great cannot go to prostitutes and cannot derive any pleasure from relations with other women. They are obvious candidates for the celibate lifestyle of the Church, where the struggle is transposed to the realm of dream and fantasy, and sanctified as an altogether 'higher' spiritual struggle against temptation.

Here, as with St Anthony e.g., the individual is tempted by demons – in the form of vivid wish-fulfilling dreams and fantasies that become increasingly frequent and powerful in face of 'worldly' frustration. And hopefully, like St Anthony, they emerge 'triumphant' – both in the eyes of their own super-ego and of the rest of the congregation, who are unable to make this ultimate sacrifice.

As Elaine Pagels points out, in the ancient world such 'true ascetics' were renouned as many people today revere certain athletes, men and women who discipline themselves to achieve what their thousands of admirers only dream of doing. "St Anthony and other ascetics spoke of their struggle for self-control in athletic terms, as an attempt to control the body and mind and to maintain both in seemingly effortless mastery." (PAGELS 1990, p. 83)

A more cynical observer might suggest that they had found a way to have their cake of asceticism (and attendant prestige) and eat it too (in sexual fulfilment). With their incestuous sexual fantasies transformed into fantasies of ecstatic fusion with God so do such fantasies become – not just socially acceptable, but signs of ultimate enlightenment, of attainment of a higher state of spiritual consciousness.

Freud identifies the intensity of Oedipal castration fear as a path to a certain sort of male homosexuality. Where such fear is very great, the individual cannot face the penis-less female genitalia – as a reminder of the reality of castration – and turns, instead to the reassurance of the male organ. They possibly turn also to fantasies of ultimate submission to the dominant father figure, to appease his anger and escape his vengeance.

Here again we can see how such fantasies of submission to the father God are institutionalised in the Catholic Church. And we can see how the Church hierarchy and the monastery could provide an obvious refuge for homosexual men who feel threatened by female sexuality.

As for St Augustine, here again we can see deeper Oedipal problems underlying the details of his particular 'neurosis' as identified by Ranke-Heinemann. In particular, we can see many signs of a more than ideal intensity of emotional bonding between the mother Monica (later St Monica) and the son Augustine. The mother's efforts to control the sex life of her son, sending his first mistress back to Africa and arranging another marriage which could not be consummated for years to come, the son's capitulation to these maternal demands, his debasement of his second relationship as a "mere pact for the satisfaction of desire" – without love – all point to the possibility of powerful incestuous desires still linking mother and son, with corresponding problems of deep sexual guilt on the part of the son.

And in this context we can see why Augustine – and others like him – should have experienced his final renunciation of all heterosexual relations as a liberation – a "dying to the world" in order to "raise his own life above the world".

Most important, we can see how powerful psychological forces could have combined with the social forces, considered in the last chapter, to maintain and extend the Catholic teaching on sexuality and celibacy.

CHAPTER TWELVE
PROTESTANTISM AND OBSESSIONAL NEUROSIS

Part One
ANALITY, OBSESSION AND AGGRESSION

Freud's most famous and explicit pronouncements on the subject of religion are those in which he compares religion to mental illness – specifically obsessional neurosis – religions are collective obsessional neurotic conditions. In his first sustained attempt to apply psychoanalysis to religion, his paper on – *Obsessive Actions and Religious Practices,* published in 1907 – Freud highlights the common role of ceremonial in both the activities of pious believers and in the protective devices of obsessive acts. As he says,

"the sense of guilt of obsessional neurotics finds its counterpart in the protestations of pious people that they know that at heart they are miserable sinners; and the pious observances (such as prayers, invocations, etc.) with which such people preface every daily act, and in especial every unusual undertaking, seem to have the value of defensive or protective measures".

It is often assumed that this observation is aimed mainly at
Catholic Christianity. Paul Roazen, e.g., suggests that

> "the resemblance (of obsessive acts) to certain religious prac-
> tices, such as those of the Catholic Church, lies in the pangs of
> conscience, the privacy, and the conscientiousness with which
> both religious rituals and obsessive acts are performed... living in
> Catholic Austria, Freud had less experience with Protestantism,
> which had internalised many of the rites of the Catholic Church"
> (ROAZEN 1970, p. 129).

Without in any way denying the relevance of these ideas for
Catholicism, however, I intend to show that they are just as applicable, perhaps more applicable to Protestantism. And to see how and
why this is the case, we must consider, in some detail, Freud's
thinking about specifically obsessional neurotic conditions.

As Storr says,

> "persons of obsessional personality are meticulous, scrupu-
> lous, accurate, reliable, honest and much concerned with control,
> order and cleanliness". And "some persons with obsessional per-
> sonality are prone to develop obsessional compulsive symptoms.
> These take the form of unwanted thoughts which intrude upon
> the persons consciousness; or of ritual actions which the patient
> feels compelled to carry out against their will". (STORR 1990,
> p. 115)

Here, we think particularly of the compulsive cleanliness of
individuals who feel they must wash their hands a thousand times a
day. And of such cases as the young man so desperate to keep his
flat absolutely clean that he refused to actually let anyone into it –
including himself, and ended up sleeping out on park benches,
becoming increasingly dirty and unkempt.

But of more general significance is the attempt to defend the
self – and other – from aggression and violence. As Storr says,

"for the obsessional personality, both the external world and
the inner world of the mind are places of danger. Only perpetual
vigilance and unrelenting discipline can ensure that neither get out
of hand. In the Ninth Book of the Republic Socrates says that 'in all
of us, even in good men, there is a lawless wild beast nature,
which peers out in sleep'. Obsessionals behave as if the beast
were straining at the leash. Moreover, they are apt to assume that
other people are similarly constituted; and therefore look on the
world as a jungle in which [wild beasts] are forever on the prowl...
The wild beast that obsessionals fear is primarily an aggressive
animal. Although sexual impulses often constitute a part of the
forces which obsessionals are trying to control, aggression plays a
larger part than love in their psychology." (ibid., p. 118)

The compulsive behaviour of the obsessional neurotic is thus
associated with the attempt to 'ward off' the aggression of other
people – or, more likely – to control their own aggression. It typically involves the intrusion of aggressive thoughts and feelings and
the desperate need to escape such thoughts – or ensure that they
cannot be translated into action, by particular sorts of magical, ritual avoidance behaviour.

According to Freud the key to understanding these particular
neurotic conditions lies in understanding what he calls the *anal*
phase of infantile development – as well as understanding the
dynamics of Oedipal conflict, and Oedipal resolution through formation of the parental super-ego.

Freud's ideas of anality are probably the most notorious and
socially unacceptable of all his ideas. Yet some of these ideas at least
(including that of the 'tight-arsed' anal personality) have such a
powerful intuitive appeal that they have also – almost – achieved
the status of contemporary 'common sense'.

The *anal* phase is the second of the psychosexual developmental
stages distinguished by Freud, following on from the *oral* phase of
the first year or so. According to the orthodox Freudian account,
over the next couple of years the child becomes increasingly pre-

occupied with their excretory organs and functions. In particular, Freud believed that during this period, young children derive particular sensual pleasure from excretion – comparable in intensity to the genital pleasure of adults. And "later experience teaches that stimulation of the rectal mucosa may be increased by holding back the faecal mass" (FENICHEL 1945, p. 66). At the same time, children come to see their excrement as their first tangible creation – their first creative achievement.

Previously, their (frustrating) dependence or helplessness has manifested itself in their continuous need to take in the magical products of others bodies. Now they find they can produce an interesting and valuable product of their own, out of their own bodies by their own efforts. And if not prevented from doing so they will be interested to explore the artistic and culinary possibilities of this wonderful new discovery.

If allowed to do so, they will present their excrement as a gift to the parents – both as compensation and recompense for all the parent's gifts to them, and as a narcissistic display of their own achievement and developing autonomy. However, typical parental behaviour in the modern world is likely to preclude any such offering – with young children generally denied access to their excrement, and initiated – at a comparatively early stage – into some form of toilet training.

Freud and his followers associate toilet training, in particular, with a transition from a primary *erotic* phase of anality to a secondary sadistic or retentive phase. Here the emphasis is upon frustration, anger and resistance to such external control. Initially, the parents' negative attitude can be a major blow to the child's self-esteem. But then children discover that they can regain control through withholding their faeces and derive compliments and rewards for appropriate behaviour.

As Borneman says, "this coming together of anal pleasure and the satisfaction of aggression led Freud to call the entire phase 'anal sadistic'". But strictly this characterisation applies only to the secondary phase.

To the extent that toilet training involves the introjection and internalisation of specific parental prohibitions – so that such prohibitions remain effective even in the absence of direct parental intervention, it is also the first step towards the formation of the 'super-ego' (or conscience in the Freudian scheme). After this, the child is involved in the active suppression of particular impulses and desires – in the interest of placating this internalised authority.

According to the orthodox picture, excessive indulgence (or restriction) of primary anal erotic desires can lead to fixation in this stage of development. In adults this is associated with coprophilia – a love of excrement – in the desire for anal intercourse and other anal oriented forms of sexual behaviour. But sublimation or constructive displacement of such desires (involving useful or acceptable symbolic substitutes for the original aims or objects) can contribute to general self-confidence, and pride in creative achievement. Sublimated coprophilia can turn into a pleasure in modelling – sculpting or painting or gardening (digging in the dirt) – or in manipulation of things generally, including people and money. So too is it associated with a pleasure in spending money freely and in bestowing it upon others as a gift.

If such fixated coprophilic desires are repressed – in the sense of being actively shut out of conscious awareness and control of conscious action (in response to parental injunctions) they do not thereby cease to exist but on the contrary, persist, outside of all possibility of further development and modification, and struggling to force their way back, once again, into conscious awareness and fulfilment. In this context, the secondary defence mechanism of *reaction formation* – changing action, lifestyle or personality in such a way as to maximally avoid all possibility of temptation to try to prevent such a breakthrough – can generate a desire, or indeed a compulsion, for cleanliness and order, and a corresponding horror of all things unclean or excremental. So can it encourage and reward activities of indexing, classifying and organising, and generally regimenting, regulating and controlling the self, other people and things.

Fixation in the secondary 'anal sadistic' stage of development – most likely to be produced by early, insensitive or violent toilet training practices – will presumably produce an overly anal sadistic personality type. The unrestrained expression of such anal sadism provides the raw material for the writings of the Marquis De Sade (after whom this developmental stage is named). And the workings of the 'anal sadistic universe' have been mapped out in detail by the French psychoanalyst, Janine Chasseguet-Smirgel.

She says,

> "This, in essence, is the universe of the sacrilege. All that is taboo, forbidden, or sacred is devoured by the digestive tract, an enormous grinding machine disintegrating the molecules of the mass thus obtained in order to reduce it to excrement. The erotogenic zones and different parts of the body become interchangeable and are metamorphosed by a kind of diabolical surgery... the pleasure connected with transgression is sustained by the fantasy that – in breaking down the barriers which separate man from woman, child from adult, mother from son, daughter from father, brother from sister, the erotogenic zones from each other (through acts of incest and perverse sexuality) and, in the case of murder, the molecules in the body from each other – it has destroyed reality, thereby creating a new one, that of the anal universe where all differences are abolished." (CHASSEGUET-SMIRGEL 1987, p. 3)

And she goes on to identify certain classic anal sadistic personalities from history and fiction – in angry rebellion against all parental and social restriction, control or discipline. One particularly obvious case is that of Caius Caesar, nicknamed Caligula, who, in his teens, "could not control his natural cruelty and viciousness; (who) was a most eager witness of the tortures and executions of those who suffered punishment, revelling at night in gluttony and adultery..." He revelled also in monstrously grandiose but futile schemes, in sowing arbitrary dissension, lowering and humiliating the great, he committed rape, incest and murder on a regular basis, he was a transvestite and a bisexual and he tried to turn himself into a god. (ibid., p. 13)

As far as repression or sublimation of such secondary anal impulses is concerned, the symbolic equation of excrement with money is of particular significance. Thus, Freud sees sublimation of such impulses as a causative factor in thrift and avarice. Just as the child withholds its faeces for the sake of more intense anal excitation during defecation – and for the sake of revenge upon and control over adults – so does the adult retain their money (as a symbolic substitute for faeces) for more intense excitement – and for gaining power over others.

The child's pleasures of retention carry over into the adult's pleasures of retention of objects of value (accumulating collections of stamps, antiques etc.) and pleasurable resistance to the demands of others. So here indeed we can see how the accumulation of money puts an individual in a position, not only to gain power over others and thereby incur demands of various sorts (tax demands from government, wage demands from workers, demands from charities etc.) – but also to resist such demands (through tax avoidance schemes etc.). Thus avarice and a thirst for power over others typically go hand in hand. Both derive from the child's anger and aggression directed towards the authoritarian parents for instituting premature toilet training and thus radically challenging the infants self-esteem. And here too Freud identifies adult stubbornness as a substitute expression of the angry child's refusal to empty their bowels when they are placed on the potty.

The equation of money (gold and jewels) with excrement surprised psychoanalytic investigators at first. But they found that it actually fitted in with the peculiar logic of the unconscious and of ego defence. The child first of all thinks that their excrement is the most valuable of products. But adults say that it is the most valueless.

Adults regard money as the substance of all value (particularly anally fixated adults). But the child finds that it just consists of dirty bits of old paper or lumps of metal. Furthermore all money is the same – it is a depersonalised possession, like excrement. Caldwell says,

> "The anal phase provides a set of models based on events and ideas occurring for the first time. During this period the child first experiences demands made of him, both positive and negative. They learn the difference between good and bad, yes and no, dirty and clean. They learn that they must please in order to be pleased, give something in order to get something, and with their faeces (the only possession of convertible value they have) they take their place in the system of symbolic exchange that will govern so many of life's activities.
>
> It is hardly surprising, therefore – with faeces as the currency of these first transactions, that a deep equation should be established in the unconscious mind between faeces and money, or that both the overestimation and underestimation of money in later life may be derived from the ambivalent position of faeces in childhood: on the one hand they are disgusting and abhorrent, but on the other they are supremely valuable as the all-important love to which they are equivalent in a reciprocal process." (CALDWELL 1989, p. 29)

Now we can see that there is a very close relation between the 'obsessional' personality and the 'anal' personality – in the sense of a personality shaped by fixation in the secondary sadistic anal phase – and corresponding (attempted) suppression or repression of such fixated anality. And, indeed, Freud saw his theory of anality as providing an explanation of such neurotic symptoms in terms of childhood 'anal fixation', through harsh and punitive toilet training.

In their comprehensive survey of empirical testing of Freudian theory (up to 1977) Fisher and Greenberg note that

> "the scientific evidence gathered up to this point favours a good part of what Freud said about the anal character. There does seem to be an aggregation of traits and attitudes corresponding to

the anal character image. An impressive tally of studies carried out by investigators with different theoretical perspectives has affirmed that the three major qualities (orderliness, obstinacy, parsimony) that Freud ascribed to the anally oriented do hang together understandably... It is also true that various general measures of anality have proven to be significantly correlated with specific behavioural indices of orderliness, obstinacy and parsimony that have been devised." (FISHER AND GREENBERG 1985, p. 163)

Things are less clear in respect of the actual evolution of anal traits through particular childhood experiences. And this is not surprising considering the greater difficulty of empirical testing in this area. But Fisher and Greenberg do note that "several investigators have identified significant positive relationships between the anality of individuals and intensity of anal attitudes present in their mothers. This obviously suggests that anal traits derive from associating with a parent who treats you in certain ways or provides you with models of how the world is to be interpreted". (ibid., p. 164)

Of course, if the essence of obsessional neurosis is fixated anger and aggression directed against parents in their role as harsh and punitive disciplinarians, then there is no necessity for such aggression to be confined to toilet training. It could also arise from harsh and punitive parenting in other areas. And indeed, Freud certainly recognises this. In his most famous case history of an obsessional neurotic, the case of the Rat Man, he implicates a harsh and aggressive parental response to early childhood masturbation as the originating cause of the patient's later obsessive-compulsive symptomatology (though, of course, there could have been – and the indications are that there probably was – an anal element to such masturbation in this case).

Freud's patient's obsessional symptoms began when he heard a fellow army officer in Vienna defending "the introduction of corporal punishment", which "obliged" him "to disagree... very sharply". The officer then told a story of "a specially horrible punishment used in the East", in which a rat placed in a pot against a person's buttocks would bore into the anus. The patient had thought that similar (anal-sadistic) punishments might be inflicted on both a woman whom he admired and his long-dead father, obsessions that haunted him for a long time.

Ultimately Freud hypothesised that when his patient "was a child of under six he had been guilty of some sexual 'misdemea-nour' and had been soundly castigated by his father. This punish-ment... had put an end to his (masturbation), but... it had left behind it an ineradicable grudge against the father and had estab-lished him for all time in his role as an interferer with the patient's sexual enjoyment."

The patient "had done something naughty, for which his father had given him a beating. The little boy had flown into a terrible rage and had hurled abuse at his father even when he was under his blows".

Freud added that the patient said his father "never beat him again", although the patient "attributed to this experience a part of the change which came over his own character. From that time for-ward he was a coward – out of fear of the violence of his own rage".

Related observations, of particular relevance to considerations of the origins of religious belief are provided by Erik Erikson's famous case history of Martin Luther, *Young Man Luther*. For Erikson speci-fically focuses upon what he takes to be the profound long term consequences of the beatings that Luther experienced as a boy – both for the man himself (in the form of a rigid obsessive-compulsive per-sonality structure), and for the revolution in religious theory and practice in which he played such a key role.

As Erikson observes, "according to the characterology estab-lished in psychoanalysis, suspiciousness, obsessive scrupulosity, moral sadism, and a preoccupation with dirtying and infectious thoughts and substances go together. Luther had them all" (GREVEN 1992, p. 140).

Erikson explores Luther's early experiences in the closely regu-lated world of the monastery as an escape from the anxieties, ten-sions and doubts of his earlier family life. As he says, "it makes psychiatric sense that under such conditions a young man with Martin's smouldering problems, but also with an honest wish to avoid rebellion against an environment which took care of so many of his needs, would subdue his rebellious nature by gradually developing obsessive-compulsive states characterised by high ambivalence". (ERIKSON 1956, p. 137)

Most important, he traces these 'smouldering' problems of the young Luther back to his early experience of betrayal, pain and anger in relation to corporal punishment by his parents. He quotes two comments by Luther himself concerning his experience with corporal punishments as a child; "My father once whipped me so that I ran away and felt ugly towards him until he was at pains to win me back." "My mother caned me for stealing a nut until the blood came. Such strict discipline drove me to a monastery although she meant well." (ibid., p. 64)

Erikson notes that "Martin, even when mortally afraid, could not really hate his father, he could only be sad", and his father, "while he could not let the boy come close, and was murderously angry at times, could not let him go for long". Erikson's clear presumption is that Martin "did hate" his father "underneath", the proof being found "in action delayed, and delayed so long that the final explosion hits non-participants". (ibid., p. 65)

The explosion in question was of course Luther's powerful attack upon the Catholic Church hierarchy. Here, presumably, mother and father church took the place of Luther's original parents.

These considerations point in two directions. On the one hand towards the conflicts of the Oedipus complex. And on the other, towards the idea that it is not so much anality, or even the idea of discipline and punishment per se that are relevant to the formation of obsessional symptoms. Rather it is the much more general phenomenon of parental violence, abuse and disrespect towards the young child, grounded in a general failure of empathy, love and care in respect of that child that lies behind such symptoms. For such hostility and betrayal inevitably generate powerfully ambivalent feelings – including angry and aggressive feelings on the part of that child. So too do they probably engender powerful fears about expressing such feelings.

Part Two
ANALITY AND RELIGION

As far as the influence of anal fixation upon religious beliefs and practices is concerned, two general sorts of phenomena stand out as particularly relevant. First of all there is the ubiquitous phenomenon of religious sacrifice, involving, as it does, gifts from the weaker child-like human to the stronger parent-like God. As Caldwell says; sacrifice in primitive religion is based on the principle of do ut des ('I give so that you will give'); by giving up something of value, the sacrificer tries to ensure that he will receive something of value from the gods. (CALDWELL 1989, p. 28)

Secondly, there are all of those religious practices and rituals specifically concerned with purification of – or deliverance from – a bodily being seen as dirty, corrupt and prone to sin and evil. And this includes both ideas of the body's 'intrinsic' corruption and sinfulness and of 'invasion' or 'possession' of the body by evil influences – including devils and demons of various sorts.

Most obviously there are practices of ritual bathing and baptism (to 'cleanse' the body of sin), practices of prayer – often in extreme discomfort – (for deliverance from evil), 'exorcism' (of supposed demonic forces, in possession of human bodies), and practices of rigorous corporal punishment – of both children and adults – supported by 'divine' or 'sacred' endorsements and encouragements in the name of 'driving out sin'.

In most cases, the centrality of aggression and violence is apparent. Such 'purification' is necessary to appease a punitive father-god. And frequently the process of purification itself becomes an excuse for divinely sanctioned aggression – as in the torture and destruction of alleged witches, or violent exorcisms of various kinds.

The characteristic pessimism of obsessional neurosis is particularly evident in the case of Christianity. As Greven says, "for two millennia, Christians have spent much of their lives anticipating punishments and worrying about how to escape the pains, terrors and tortures of Hell. 'Heaven' has always meant the absence of punishment, as well as eternal life" (GREVEN 1992, p. 122). And the rituals and practices in question are supposedly aimed at avoiding such 'demonic' punishments for the self or for others.

In the case of self-flagellation and scourging, the individual inflicts violence upon themselves – in the interests of 'self-control'. But in other cases it is supposedly the other (the victim) that is the source – or 'repository' of aggression – they are possessed by the devil, polluted by 'original sin' etc. Punishments and exorcisms in this life supposedly save them from worse punishments in the hereafter. In fact, of course, these practices derive from defensive projection of the unacceptable and fearful aggressive desires of the perpetrators themselves, while simultaneously providing a – permissible – outlet for their aggression while also appeasing, placating and serving their anti-aggressive 'conscience'.

For one of the most dramatic demonstrations of the association of anality with religious ideas of sin, evil and the corruption of the human body we can refer once again to Martin Luther's writings. For Luther saw himself as locked in a continuous struggle with the devil or devils. And he saw the devil in specifically 'anal' terms.

For him the devil is black, filthy and smelly and fights with excrement and flatulence. And Luther fights back with the devil's own weapons, threatening to "defecate in his face" or to "throw him into my anus, where he belongs" (BROWN 1968, p. 187). As Norman O. Brown points out, "the devil is virtually recognised as a displaced materialisation of Luther's own anality, which is to be conquered by being replaced where it came from" (op. cit.).

Luther sees the human body – and the material world – including both the power-seeking of capitalist usurers and merchants, and of the Catholic Church, effectively selling forgiveness to sinners, as the province of the devil, of anality. Reason, and even conscience itself, are under the control of the devil. And the devil claims the souls of all sinners, with no hope of escape.

"According to the more merciful Catholic tradition, even those who had made pacts with the devil might, even in the eleventh hour, be saved by some outward act of penance (the 'works' that Luther despised) or by the intercession of the saints." (ibid., p. 192) But for Luther, there could be no such reprieve from ultimate damnation.

As far as he was concerned, life in the material world – and the material body – and the stigma of original sin – inevitably corrupted all of human kind. The only hope of salvation lay in fully recognising the corruption of the world, suffering for all the sins of the world, – as did Jesus Christ – and dying to this world to be reborn with Him. "Satan is the lord of this life, but there is another life where Christ is king, and to have faith in the existence of that other life is to conquer this death-in-life while in it." (ibid., p. 193)

It is while seated on the toilet that Luther receives the "illumination" which became the "fundamental axiom of the Protestant Reformation". As he says,

> "these words 'just' and 'justice of God' were a thunderbolt in my consciousness. They soon struck terror in me who heard them. He is just, there He punishes. But once when in the tower I was meditating on these words, 'the just lives by faith', 'justice of God', I soon had the thought whether we ought to live justified by faith, and God's justice ought to be the salvation of every believer, and soon my soul was revived." (ibid., p. 182)

Presumably it was on the toilet that Luther was most forcefully reminded of the 'material' and 'excremental' nature of bodily being. His father (God) has led him to feel a deep ambivalence about such bodily functions and this situation therefore also triggered powerful feelings of guilt – and terror of divine retribution. The only escape he saw was an escape from such bodily being itself – a complete renunciation of the body, of the world, of reason – in favour of pure 'faith' in the authority and mercy of the father-God.

It is often assumed (following Weber) that the Protestant Reformation paved the way for modern capitalism through 'sanctifying' the operations of merchants and manufacturers, previously condemned by the Catholic Church. For the Catholic Church's 'calling' to a life radically divorced from such earthly pre-occupations as trade and material production, the Protestants substituted a calling to a life of productive endeavour in the material world, with success in business substituted for otherworldly seclusion as a sign of salvation.

But in fact, at least as far as Luther was concerned, the original idea was that all earthly activities were equally tainted by corruption and sin, equally 'dirty'. The Catholic Church was attacked for its hypocritical claims that particular sorts of (essentially pointless and childish) earthly actions (monastic seclusion, fasts, pilgrimages, worship of saints etc.) somehow stood above and beyond such corruption, building up a store of grace from God and guaranteeing direct passage to heaven – no matter what the participants might truly feel in their hearts, and no matter what terrible sins they might otherwise commit.

It is in this context that Luther counterposes justification by faith to the Catholic Church's idea of justification by 'acts'. It is in this context that he contrasts the positive values of participation in trade and manufacture to those of monastic seclusion. As he says, "When the heart is pure... the market is as much esteemed as the monastery". But this does not prevent him, elsewhere, from roundly condemning usury and pursuit of (earthly) power through money as the major problem of his age.

As O. Brown points out, unlike those of later ages, Luther had not yet completely sublimated his fixated anality into unrestricted worship of money and the market. He still recognised the fundamentally excremental nature of nascent capitalism. Here, the angry – capitalist – child, rudely deprived of their faecal materials, amasses and accumulates piles of money as an 'acceptable' substitute, and as a means for gaining a displaced revenge upon the parents through acquiring power over people and things, forcing them into the service of further accumulation.

CHAPTER THIRTEEN
PROTESTANTISM *cont.*

Part One
MATERIAL FORCES IN THE PROTESTANT
REFORMATION

Martin Luther's ideas, and the movements initiated by them, were soon complimented by a variety of other strands of early Protestant theory and practice. And there is no doubt that, taken as a whole, the Protestant Reformation of the sixteenth and seventeenth centuries represents a particularly significant 'intrusion' of anal fixations into religious life. Most relevant here was the emergence of Puritanism, as a particularly virulent strain of Protestantism. For the Puritan mentality is virtually synonymous with the obsessional mentality, as grounded in deep seated anal fixation.

But to further elucidate this connection, it is necessary to step back to gain a basic overview of the major historical forces at work in this situation. Here we recapitulate some of the material of previous chapters.

In the earlier Middle Ages the social organisation of Northern Europe was basically feudal – meaning a predominantly rural economy of local self sufficiency, centred upon the stronghold of the local lord and his soldiers, surrounded by 'tied' villages of peasant serfs. The serfs generated the material wealth to sustain both their own subsistence and the privileged lifestyle of the aristocracy, with surplus appropriated as 'rent' or payment for (protective military) services rendered. Trade was restricted, planned and regulated on a local level by lords, and guilds of merchants and manufacturers in the towns.

In theory, feudal society was hierarchically organised. At the top of a pyramid of secular power was the King, beneath him the Lords and Knights, holding land 'in fief' in exchange for military and other services. But (for a long period of general social dislocation and lawlessness) it was typically at the middle levels – where local lords effectively functioned as absolute authorities within their own lands – that real power often resided.

The Catholic Church was similarly hierarchically organised, with the Pope at the top, Archbishops and Bishops below him, down to the village priest as the bottom. This hierarchy was sustained, not only by its own lands and tied serfs, and gifts from the nobility (to ensure their safe passage to heaven), but also by special taxes, paid by all householders. So too did the Church receive payments from the nobility in its role as sole provider of formal education.

Corresponding to the hierarchical political-economic reality, the Church taught and preached a hierarchical and organic world view, extending the earthly hierarchy up into heaven, as the Pope communed with angels and archangels and ultimately with God himself; and down into Hell, where the Devil and his demons strove to undermine the system (working on its weaker human links – usually identified as peasant women at the very bottom of the power hierarchy).

The Bishops and Lords provided the commanding 'spirit' and 'mind' of this great living system; the peasants the 'working body parts'. At the same time the peasants were presented as 'children' –

incapable of taking serious decisions, and directed, watched over and protected by their natural superiors in all the major transitions and problem situations of life.

Everyone had their 'natural' role and place within this organic hierarchy, determined by birth. And as long as they obeyed God's will, and fulfilled their appropriate function, all would be well. But if they succumbed to the Devil's temptations and efforts to undermine this system (from 'below') through pursuing ideas or practices 'beyond their station' then God would deal with them very severely.

The Church was theoretically hostile to profit-seeking trade. They followed the Aristotelian teaching that such profit derived from buying 'below the true value' and/or 'selling above', i.e. that profit was theft – and hence immoral. And they generally presented a life apart from earthly involvements (in sex, trade, manufacture etc.) as a superior life in the eyes of God. Those who devoted themselves to such a life built up a store of grace from God, which could then be dispensed by the Church as it saw fit (in effect, it could be 'sold' to those seeking a guaranteed place in heaven).

But the period leading up to the Protestant Reformation coincided with an increasing shift to absolute private property, free markets, competitive accumulation and free wage labour. At the individual level this frequently meant increasing fragmentation and isolation, but on a broader political level an opposite tendency was working itself out. In particular, on this broader scale we see a shift from social fragmentation and isolation to the emergence of effective central state power and stable national markets.

As rural production and population expanded, with new technology leading to new prosperity and increased trade in the course of the fourteenth, fifteenth and sixteenth centuries, so did this contribute to the accelerated growth of the towns as centres of trade and manufacture. The towns offered new and (relatively) more free careers for the more adventurous or more disaffected peasants – careers in manufacturing an increasing range of goods which the peasants had previously made for themselves – clothes, shoes, bread etc. and careers in trade – both small scale, supplying peasants with such necessities and large – supplying the lords with luxuries from abroad.

Previously, the hierarchical, organic world view offered by the Catholic Church had probably made a lot of sense to the country-person. For they directly experienced their integration into the various organic cyclical life processes of the natural world; the cycles of the seasons, of the birth, growth and harvesting of the crops, etc. They remained firmly integrated into the protective extended family structure of the village and the feudal estate – protected from alien invasion by the lord's soldiers and from the devil by the local priest, fed from the granaries of the lord or of the church in times of famine, judged and directed by the lord and the Church in every life crisis, conflict or decision.

But this sort of way of viewing the world would have come to make less and less sense to the townsperson, increasingly cut-off from such extended natural and social hierarchy and protection. Indeed, the townsfolk were perpetually struggling against the efforts of the feudal lords in the countryside and the Church officials to try to regulate, restrict, control, manipulate and tax their productive efforts. And we can see how this should particularly have been the case in those more northerly towns of Germany, the Netherlands, Britain and Scandinavia which enjoyed few of the political and economic benefits of Catholic Church domination.

For the money collected as Church taxes from peasants and townsfolk all over Europe was mostly spent in the towns of southern Europe, particularly Italy. During this period it contributed crucially to the great scientific, artistic and engineering achievements of the Renaissance. But things were very different in the north.

Whereas in earlier periods the Roman Church had served a vital social function in these northerly areas as redistributor of wealth to the poor and needy, as guardian of the arts and sciences, and as support for social stability and order in difficult times, it now became increasingly superfluous in all these roles as local wealth increased and local authorities felt able to stand on their own and maintain local stability without benefit of Church interference. Indeed, rather than supporting the poor, the Roman Church made them still poorer through its incessant demands for tax money; rather than leading the developments of art and science it fell behind secular developments in the towns, and rather than supporting local wealth and authority, it increasingly acted to undermine it.

Within the new and expanding towns there were developing new political and economic interests which led to active opposition both to the dominance of the rural feudal aristocracy and to the Catholic Church itself, insofar as secular and sacred powers struggled to stifle or restrict the development of urban commerce and/or drain off the surplus from town to country or to Rome.

Thus, the townsperson stood increasingly alone in face of organised hierarchical power, struggling for autonomy; for the right to pursue their own particular trade or manufacture in their own way – and reap the benefits of their own efforts. This is where Protestantism as a broad and growing religious movement comes in, developing in these more northerly European towns as expression and vehicle of the merchants and manufacturers struggle against Roman/feudal domination.

Thus, the relative isolation of the townsperson, compared to the 'organic' integration of the countryperson (or the direct involvement in Church business and Church wealth in more southerly cities), and their struggle for independence from outside forces, is clearly reflected in the disappearance of the hierarchy of mediation of Catholicism – common to all of the new Protestant ideologies. Now religion becomes a matter of a direct relation between individual human and their God. Individuals become responsible for their own salvation – through their own efforts (or their own 'faith') without the necessary mediation of Church or state.

We have already seen the key role played by Martin Luther (1483-1546) in this regard, with his doctrine of the justification by faith. "Man is normally a sinful creature, but by having faith in God, man's heart is cleansed. It is only in this way that one is saved, not through the good works dictated by the Catholic Church."

332   *Protestantism*

They are purely mechanical actions with no spiritual significance whatsoever.

Thus, Luther and the other Protestant reformers broke the Church's monopoly on God. They radically rejected the idea of the Catholic Church as repository of grace and 'bearer of the keys to heaven'. And in the process they did away with the Church as a necessary intermediary between the individual and their God.

This, of course, tied up the new religious doctrines with radical new ideas of individual freedom which reflect the struggle of the townspeople for freedom from political-economic control by lords and popes. Everyone is really equal in the eyes of God – not 'graded' in degrees of goodness, purity, or intelligence by birth, as Aristotle and medieval Catholic theology had taught. As Martin Luther says, "a Christian is a perfectly free lord, subject to none". And he goes on to describe the Pope as a 'poor stinking sinner', no closer to God than anyone else.

Such a struggle for freedom soon spread beyond the tradespeople of the towns to women and peasants struggling for freedom from patriarchy and feudal domination.

As Siegel points out,

> "the peasant leaders in Germany... read the Bible, communed with God, and did what their hearts told them to do. They found that the peasants, oppressed more heavily than ever by princes, knights, burghers, and the Church, were justified in rising up against their oppression. They demanded the abolition of serfdom 'unless it be shown from the Gospel that we are serfs' and cited the New Testament on the community of goods." (SIEGEL 1986, p. 91)

Luther's ideas of equality had particular significance for women. They had been at the very bottom of the pyramid of power in traditional theory and practice. But it now became increasingly difficult to legitimate their 'natural' subordination. And there was a significant current of women's liberation in some of the new religious movements.

Luther himself, although remaining ambivalent on this point, did, on occasions, argue for equality of husband and wife as joint authorities in the Christian family, and for the extension of women's rights to sexual fulfilment and divorce. And the Swiss Protestant reformer, Ulrich Zwingli (1484-1531) supported the extension of medieval divorce laws to increase the rights of women.

Noblewomen in France "assumed leadership in evangelical reform and were in the vanguard of the Protestant Huguenot movement from 1557 to the 1570's". And the more radical Protestant religious movements "offered women greater opportunities for speaking out on questions of church government". (MERCHANT 1983, p. 147)

> The membership of the early sixteenth century English Lollards (forerunners of the Reformation, who read the Bible in English, stressed scriptural authority and lay governance) was about one third women. (While) the radical Anabaptists, centred on Munster until 1535, whose following came from the lower social classes, allowed women to preach and prophesy [in sharp contrast to established Catholic practice]. (ibid., p. 148)

At the same time, apart from any considerations of freedom and equality, there was also a very straightforward economic rationale for the small business people of northern Europe (and indeed, the leaders of the expanding states of Northern Europe) to reject Catholicism and to opt for the Protestant alternative.

The artisans and small merchants of the towns wanted a cheap church with lower taxes – or ideally no taxes at all. At the same time, as we have seen, while not actually glorifying trade and manufacture as 'pure' and 'godly', Luther at least saw them in a positive light as compared to the otherworldly seclusion advocated by Catholicism. And other, later Protestant reformers went significantly further in this direction.

Such pragmatic – bourgeois – considerations ultimately came into conflict with the new, more radical ideas of freedom, justice and communism. Thus we see conflicts developing within and between the new reform movements themselves.

The other side of the new individualism and the struggle for freedom amongst urban male merchants and manufacturers – turning to the Protestant sects for support – was a radical new insecurity, which ultimately rebounded against other oppressed groups struggling for greater freedom and equality. For the town dweller no longer had the feudal hierarchy, the village community, the traditional organised value system to support them, to protect them, to cushion them. They no longer had the 'daddy' lord or priest or bishop, the all-protective Virgin Mother Mary to turn to. With the greater freedom of urban life came the awesome responsibility of taking control of their own lives in ways their ancestors had never even had to think about.

It is true that originally production and trade in the towns was highly organised and regulated by the guild and corporation systems. This meant rigid local monopolies of raw materials and finished goods controlled by hierarchically organised 'union' structures of merchants and craftspeople, regulating entry to the professions and supply and demand of each commodity.

However, the stabilisation of effective state power (including the rule of law, stable currencies and improved communications) over large areas, coupled with expanding scope and freedom of action of urban merchants, spelled the beginning of the end of the effective local regulation of market relations by guilds and corporations. For in allowing for the possibility of stable and expanding national markets, so did it allow for the expansion of trade beyond the capacity of such institutions to control it.

So that, increasingly, the new middle class of merchants and manufacturers in the towns came into competitive economic conflict with one another, as well as with other class groups outside of the town, to still further intensify their fears and insecurities. And this rebounded against rebellious women and peasants as the townsmen pioneers of the new sects sought stability and protection for what they saw as their own particular interests. For the merchants and manufacturers increasingly saw such liberation struggles as a threat to their own wealth and power.

Another crucial consideration was the ultimate dependence of the new religion – and its new middle class proponents – upon the support of local feudal lords – for protection from the power of the Catholic Church and the Catholic states to the South; – and, indeed, for the Protestant leaders control of their own ecclesiastical organisation. For while such lords increasingly recognised the benefits they could gain from economic development of the towns within their territories, they were hardly sympathetic to peasant revolts that undermined the very foundations of their power.

Martin Luther's thinking seems to have been directly influenced by these sorts of considerations. For, as far as he is concerned, God's truth turns out to be, first and foremost, what is in the interests of stable life for the small business man in the town. As Siegel points out,

"Foremost amongst the principles God has written in the hearts of men, to be perceived when these hearts are pure, is the sacredness of private property. Private property is what raises man above the animals. It is the basis of the social order within which those who have received God's grace perform good works by labouring in their callings in the spirit of serving God... So carried away was Luther by his zeal against the rebellious peasants [challenging this institution] that he proclaimed that those who died fighting against them were 'true martyrs for God' who were assured of salvation. Apparently, killing peasants was a 'good work' so extraordinary that it guaranteed salvation regardless of whether or not it was performed with a pure heart. Moreover, Luther was so fearful of the threat to the social order that he, the upholder of the individual conscience against the Catholic Church, gave the absolutist princes (of Germany) who had the support of the middle class, power over the religion of their subjects." (SIEGEL 1986, p. 91)

Similarly, while the early emphasis was on women's equality, soon enough the male leaders of the new movements argued instead for a 'natural' male domination within such movements, and within society at large. John Calvin, in particular, maintained the necessity for absolute paternal power in the Protestant family. The father must rule with a rod of iron, instilling obedience and fear in wife and children so as to combat their potential for 'depraved' thoughts and actions.

We see this radical insecurity of the middle class male reflected in the Protestant idea of the weakness, wretchedness and sinfulness of the isolated human in face of the stern, patriarchal Protestant God who sees all of the sin in their soul. And we see it particularly in Calvin's grim idea of predestination as a sort of lottery, with some inevitably bound for hell even before they were born, while others were equally inevitably bound for heaven.

This doctrine of predestination is at the heart of Calvinist Protestantism. "A chosen few, the elect, have been predestined by God to salvation, by 'his gratuitous mercy, totally irrespective of human merit'. The rest of humankind have been predestined to damnation, by a just and irreprehensible, but incomprehensible judgement."

And the response of the urban – Protestant – male, their way of coping with this radical new insecurity, was a radical new emphasis upon discipline, self-control, and self-sufficiency; on renunciation of personal pleasure in favour of hard work and (individual) economic success. In other words, they became Puritans.

Now, it might be thought that if a person's fate was predetermined before they were even born, there would have been no point in worrying about sin. They might as well have had a good time while they could. Certainly Calvin's idea was an attack upon the Catholic idea that individual's could 'buy' their way into heaven by good works.

But, in fact, while individuals could not save themselves through particular actions, they could at least reassure themselves. Every day that went by and they had not yet fallen into sin reassured them that up until that point, at least, there was no reason to number themselves amongst the damned. So, perhaps paradoxically, individuals struggled all the harder to avoid any hint of sinful thoughts or actions every day. And, increasingly, this meant working so long and hard at their professions – working so hard making money – that did not have the time or energy for sin.

This meant, in particular, the control of 'bodily' feelings and desires – oral, anal and genital. The body was seen as a tool of the Devil, and it was bodily pleasures that were seen as archetypally sinful. All such pleasures were to be avoided, with the body instead subject to rigid discipline and control as a means to salvation through economic success.

All bodily desires were supposed to be 'sublimated' into long hours of hard work. (But there are plenty of indications that they were often, rather, repressed – giving rise to major neurotic symptoms – and projected into other scapegoat individuals and groups as ego defences. In particular, those women who were identified as witches seem to have become objects of massive projection of anal and phallic desires on the part of the male Protestant clerics.)

"As Adam Smith notes, there is a very close connection between church discipline, Puritan self-discipline and labour discipline. Each was an integral part of the strategy in the war against all evil in which the Puritan was a soldier. The laxness of the Catholic Church, the debauchery of the courtier and the carousing of the country squire, the frequent and irregular festivities during the course of the seasons of an agricultural economy – all of these were not to the Puritan way of thinking. To them the Puritan opposed the discipline of the reformed church, of his sober and methodical life, and of the regular and continuous work rhythms of an emerging urban society that eliminated the Catholic holidays and substituted the strict observance of Sundays, during which one rededicated one's self [and one's workers] to the service of the great Taskmaster." (SIEGEL 1986, p. 92)

In this context we can see how – as Weber claimed – this new Protestant ideology became a major vehicle for carrying forward the development of competitive capitalist market relations. Here, indeed, we can identify a positive feedback process rendering the Puritan attitude increasingly in tune with the actual political and economic reality of urban life. As the individual looked increasingly to their own resources and their own destiny in their struggle against those external forces (of Church, rural aristocracy and state) seeking to subordinate, control and exploit them, so do we see the erosion of the collective restrictions and collective organisation (of urban trade and manufacture) of earlier times, and the emergence of increasing competitiveness and inequality in business life.

And with the individual thus struggling increasingly against their own fellow townspeople in such an individualistic and competitive business environment, as well as hostile external forces, so were they still further motivated to radically discipline and organise their life in pursuit of individual success, in a way increasingly alien to the more layed-back and 'externally' directed lifestyle of the countryperson (whether peasant or lord).

For some, at least, hard work was rewarded with increased revenues. And those seeking to avoid all pleasure were strongly motivated to re-invest all profits back into the business (rather than consuming them in the interests of bodily gratification). Those that accumulated most achieved economies of scale, access to new technology, cheaper raw materials etc. They were therefore more successful in an increasingly competitive environment, made more profits, re-invested more and so on.

Those that fell by the wayside in such a competitive struggle (as well as others displaced from the land by new agricultural technology and organisation) were conveniently available to be employed, and vigorously exploited by their more successful neighbours. And insofar as these neighbours saw their business methods as directly endorsed by God, they had no problems about ensuring that their employees worked just as long and hard, and had just as little pleasure, as themselves.

At the same time, we can see how others might have been attracted to the new religious beliefs as they came to be associated with such success in the market. And how such beliefs might also have gained increasing support from local (Northern) feudal lords, anxious to benefit from such local economic progress and stem the flow of wealth to Rome.

So too, can we see how the Protestant ethic contributed to the scientific and technological revolution of the seventeenth century. For while Catholicism had claimed that human reason partly coincided with the rationality of God, and through so doing provided knowledge of natural law, for the Protestants God had now entered an altogether higher plane where none could claim to have any such direct understanding of his will. And if human reason had no direct access to divine plans, then people would have to find out about the world using their own reasoning and their own senses (in secular fashion) without relying on revelation and ancient opinion.

Whereas the organic Catholic world-view had tended to stand in the way of unrestricted experimental and technological manipulation of the earth — as living expression of God's will and reason, Protestantism provided no such restriction. As God retreated far away from the earth and the graded natural hierarchy through which his order and benevolence had flowed down and permeated the world was swept away, the earth was left as a profane and corrupt place — or a mere inert, soul-less mechanical system — very far from the perfection of heaven.

On the earth all people were equally corrupt. But so too were they equally able to take their lives into their own hands — to do whatever they had to do to gain the approval of daddy-God. And because of the inherent corruption — and materiality — of the earth there was no longer any objection to altering and manipulating it in whatever way they wanted in pursuit of their own individual salvation. Indeed, to the extent that it was corrupt and inert (a place of dangerous evil forces and dirt), such Christian men now had a responsibility to subdue, tame and control it — to subordinate it to their higher cultural — commercial — aims.

Part Two
PSYCHOANALYTIC CONSIDERATIONS

So, from a materialist perspective, there is an obvious political-economic dynamic underlying the development of Protestant ideology and practice. But, looking a bit more deeply into the situation, so too can we see how psychodynamic considerations could also have played a crucial role.

In the countryside – in situations of relatively low population density – with the rhythms of life dictated more by the cycles of the seasons than by any sort of competitive social requirement – (and in small, relatively non-competitively organised towns) it is easy to imagine relatively indulgent practices of childcare. With the comparatively laid-back lifestyle of the feudal peasant, prolonged breast feeding and late and less than obsessive concern with toilet training could well have been the norm – leading to predominantly oral rather than anal fixations.

It is notoriously difficult to get reliable information upon the child rearing practices of the period – given the widespread illiteracy of the population and other problems. And such evidence as we do have makes generalisation difficult. However, in a detailed study of "children and parents from the ninth to the thirteenth centuries", Mary McLaughlin notes that while "the neglect, exploitation and abandonment of children", which characterised earlier epochs 'continued' during this period, nonetheless, "these practices were now more widely and consciously opposed". And while "the idea of the child as the possession and property of its parents continued to dominate attitudes and actions", the "dangers inherent in this conception had achieved wider recognition" and "the proprietary notion had also been joined by more favourable conceptions, by a sense of the child as a being in its own right, as a nature of 'potential greatness' and by a sense of childhood as a distinctive and formative stage of life".

"Tenderness, compassion, the capacity to comprehend the needs and emotions of others... flowered slowly in the hard and sometimes violent lives of this period, especially in the lives of parents who were themselves often literally, as well as emotionally, little more than children. Yet it is in this realm of feeling that the most deeply rooted and fruitful developments of (these) centuries are likely to be found." (DEMAUSE ed. 1975, pp. 140-1)

More concretely, despite a small minority of the noble and prosperous who gave their babies to wet nurses, for all classes the mother who nursed her own children reflected the ideal maternal image. Celebrated in contemporary representations of the Virgo lactans, the Nursing Mother of Christ, and in the poignant Eve nursing her child portrayed on the bronze doors at Hildesheim and later at Verona, this essential maternal function was emphasised and extolled in literary and didactic works of various kinds.

Bartholomew of England, e.g., argued that breastfeeding strengthened crucial emotional bonds between mother and child "for the mother loves her own child most tenderly, embraces and kisses it, nurses and cares for it solicitously". And as McLaughlin observes, "what little can be discovered about the time of weaning in these centuries suggests a variability between one and three years". (ibid., p. 116)

She concludes that, there are clear signs, especially from the twelfth century onwards, of tenderness towards infants and small children, interest in the stages of their development, awareness of their need for love, and active responsiveness to the 'beauty of infancy'.

Apart from its obvious role as a tool of the ruling hierarchy, legitimating hierarchical power and privilege, the 'organic' world view of medieval Catholicism shows clear signs of influence by, and appeal to, a predominantly oral sort of personality structure. In particular, there is the central image of the Virgin Mother Mary, and the 'Mother' Church, always available to love and care for her human children. God and Heaven, as source of spiritual nourishment and love are linked directly (symbiotically) to the dependent, earthly world. And, like a mother's milk, the benevolence, order and love of God flows down, perpetually from Heaven, throughout the extended body of human society and nature.

The Church's promise of ultimate salvation through absolute obedience – through reparative acts deemed appropriate by absolute authority ('works') seems clearly grounded in an oral (depressive) relation to parental love and power. And the Church's Oedipal problems with sexuality – including massive sexual guilt, leading to a radical male 'tendency to debasement in love' (with women identified as madonnas or whores etc) can be traced, in part, back to prolonged breast feeding, and a particularly intense 'oral' relationship of the boy to the mother.

But in the increasingly crowded and competitive environment of the expanding towns there would generally have been less and less time for indulgent breast feeding and an increasing preoccupation with 'order', cleanliness and waste disposal which could well have encouraged earlier and more rigorous toilet training, and a generally more authoritarian and punitive regime of child-rearing. And this could, in turn, have marked an increasing shift from oral (erotic) to anal-sadistic fixation amongst subsequent generations of town dwellers.

Here we can identify another sort of feedback process. For the more competitive, insecure and difficult town life became, and the more the male Protestant tried to cope with such difficulties through puritanical self-control and restraint, the more likely would he be to turn to projection and aggression as means to try to cope. And, in the first instance, it would be his family that would bear the brunt of such projection and aggression.

It is difficult to control what goes on inside your own head; especially if you are consigned to hell for thinking sinful thoughts. Much easier to control what goes on outside it. Hence the tendency to project unacceptable thoughts and feelings out into other people. "It's not me that wants to seduce them; it's they that are trying to seduce me, and I am shocked and appalled at such behaviour and will respond appropriately." In this case it was the townsman's own family – and perhaps also other employees – who became the primary objects of such projected thoughts and feelings – because it was only his family that he had any real power over, and could therefore act 'upon' to counter and punish such thoughts.

Whereas in the countryside, the ideology of male domination tended to be offset by direct co-operation of husband and wife in material production, in the towns women tended to become increasingly economically dependent on their husbands, insofar as the new professions (butchering, baking, etc) were organised in ways that precluded care of – and participation by – young children, and became increasingly dominated by men. And the men could turn this economic advantage into an ideological and emotional advantage in seeking to exercise 'moral' domination of their wives and children.

With the family members as vehicles for the projection of the fathers own unacceptable bodily feelings, so did they threaten to arouse disruptive bodily desires in him and others – and so had they therefore to be rigorously disciplined and controlled. They had to be put to work to serve the father's economic interests (in appropriately non-threatening and subordinate ways) rather than distracting him from pursuit of such interests.

Another consideration here is a likely increase in the male fear of death associated with the new urban and ideological insecurity. With the loss of the organic bond to a wider nature and society and of the confessional as guarantee of safe entry into eternal life in Heaven, with an increasingly vivid awareness of the Devil and demonic persecution, death began to appear an altogether more personal, final and frightening prospect.

One possible response to this intensified awareness of mortality could have been increasingly desperate efforts by the Protestant father to try to live on through 'implanting' himself – or his beliefs and authority – into his first born son (and other children) who would live on after his death, take over the family name and business etc. Through rigorous exercise of paternal authority, so would the father become the stern voice of God within the son's mind, threatening dire punishments if he fails to live up to the father's ideal of himself.

The son will suffer the torments of Hell if he fails to maintain the barriers of repression of his own – unacceptable – desires. To avoid this, he must rather conform to a life of discipline and subordination, repression, sublimation and control of bodily desires, and hard work in pursuit of material success.

Here, the liberation of women could itself have intensified the insecurity and anxiety of the men within the Protestant sects. Women – and children – as vehicles for projection of their unacceptable desires would appear to threaten and subvert the ordered discipline of the male psyche and the male world, and expose the men to the rejection and punishment of their stern father-God. Hence the need to dominate, subordinate and control them with ever renewed vigour and vigilance.

What we see here is the creation (and intergenerational transmission) of an increasingly neurotic – obsessional – male personality structure (compared to earlier rural Catholic culture) – tortured, tempted by devils and women, subject to constant anxiety, always struggling to appease and win the acceptance of the stern, unloving father God by ever greater efforts at self control and renunciation. Always struggling to live up to the impossible ideals and demands of the father-god.

It is in this context that we can best understand the developing reaction against Luther's idea of sexual equality and marriage as partnership for mutual sexual, social and spiritual fulfilment, exemplified by Calvin's call for renewed patriarchal domination. Whereas Luther condemned earthly politics as the work of the devil (as Augustine had before him), Calvin's main concern was for the creation of political structures which would serve to bolster such male power and control within the Church and family life.

The man should function as the ruling intellectual head while the woman is the body that assists him, says Calvin. And in his commentary of the Book of Genesis, he states that "the order of nature implies that the woman should be the helper to man". That she should study to keep the divinely appointed order. Eve's punishment for her sin was to be cast into servitude and subjected to her –

apparently violent – husband's authority and will, whereas before the fall hers had been 'a liberal and gentle subjection'.

In England, male Protestant hostility towards women was particularly intensified by various developments associated with women's domination of the highest positions of state power in the latter half of the sixteenth century. When Mary Tudor came to power in England in 1553 she restored Catholicism and instituted a period of active persecution of Protestants. And in 1558, Mary of Lorraine forbade the preaching of the reformed doctrine in Scotland.

These developments strongly encouraged the paranoia and misogyny of the male leaders of Protestant sects suffering such persecution at the hands of women. Thus, the Scottish Protestant reformer, John Knox, in his *First Blast of the Trumpet against the Monstrous Regiment of Women* (1558) argued that political and economic power in the hands of women overturned God's natural order for the world.

The natural order is now seen as radically polarised between a female, bodily, material, corrupt natural world below and a male, spiritual, pure, divine and virtuous world above. Female nature is identified simultaneously with weakness and passivity and with subversive animal passions and appetites, forever threatening to subvert man's cultural achievements. In a properly ordered universe, the social world should reflect the natural world in which God has created the female of all species to serve and be obedient to the male. The ruling head of human society should be a man, for a woman's rule created a monster. A woman should therefore never be allowed to rule as queen for "the empire of a woman" overturns nature. In allowing a female to rule, men made themselves "inferior to beasts".

When Elizabeth came to the throne in England she restored Protestantism as official state religion and directly aided the Scottish Protestants in their struggle against their Catholic queen. Knox was forced to apologise to Elizabeth for his views and many learned and influential figures in Elizabethan England, including many male Protestants as well as the Queen herself and other women, vigorously disputed such ideas of inherent female inferiority.

However, in part precisely because of the improving status of women under Elizabeth's rule, this developing male paranoia and misogyny – so clearly expressed by Knox – continued to simmer, with many more leading male Protestants supporting and extending Knox's ideas, and thus generating an active ongoing controversy over women's rights that involved women and men of all levels of society throughout the period of Elizabeth's rule.

And, in this context, we can begin to understand why the persecution of women as witches – initially part of the Catholic reaction to the women's liberation inherent in the ideologies and practices of earlier heretical sects – should later have been carried forward with increasing vigour and brutality by the male Protestants themselves.

Here, as frequently been observed, poor women (and particularly women who were seen as posing any sort of challenge to patriarchal power) became scapegoats, blamed for the grinding poverty and famine of the masses, plague, disease, rebellion and heresy and the death and suffering associated with the Counter-Reformation. And the torture and murder of alleged witches was at its most widespread in the more northerly Protestant countries (with the most Puritanical strains of belief and practice) in the hundred and ten years between 1550 and 1660.

The presence of massive projection is glaringly obvious in the fantasies of witches sabots and black masses constructed by the Protestant male clerics. Oral, anal and phallic constructions abound, including the notorious witch's broom handle, protruding from between her legs – a phallus presumably stolen from a man – and all of various alleged sexual interactions with demons whereby women were supposed to acquire their magical – witchly – powers.

In particular, there is a very strongly anal sadistic element to these male phantasies of the witch's sabots. The climax of such get-togethers included the kissing of the Devil's posteriors. And "in the central ceremony of the Black Mass, as the Queen of the Sabbath lay prone, the sacred host was prepared by kneading on her buttocks a mixture of …faeces, menstrual blood, urine, and offal of various kinds" (BROWN 1968, p. 186).

In torturing 'confessions' to such practices from increasing numbers of defenceless women, in situations where the women were stripped naked, their bodies probed and violated by special male 'instruments' the most devout of Protestant male clerics found ways to vicariously indulge all of their most unacceptable, infantile and aggressive desires without suffering the persecution of their stern paternal super-ego. On the contrary, they were rewarded for their zeal and their mercy in trying to save the souls of these poor deluded women.

We have already seen how the dismantling of the hierarchical world view of traditional Catholicism, severed the links between Heaven and Earth and thereby rendered the Earth material and profane. And how this paved the way for scientific experimental investigation and technological subordination and control of natural forces.

We can now see also how material nature, traditionally equated with femininity, similarly absorbed the projections of suppressed male desire, becoming (seen as) a source of chaos, disorder, dirt and threat – a world of violent, untamed forces threatening to overwhelm the beleaguered male ego. And Carolyn Merchant shows how these sorts of ideas also profoundly effected ideas of scientific method and of the nature of technology in the early period of the Scientific Revolution.

As she points out, these influences are particularly evident in Francis Bacon's ideas of nature, society, science and technology, conditioned both by the controversy over women's rights in Britain and by the new development of technology in the service of accumulation of private wealth (and national security).

Brought up in a staunchly Calvinist and repressive Protestant family environment, he seems to have become firmly enmeshed in male paranoia and misogyny, ultimately throwing his full weight and (substantial) political influence behind the anti-feminist position. And while his ideas got short shrift from Queen Elizabeth, her successor, James I was a committed anti-feminist, determined to put women back in their place as household servants to men. When he became King of England he replaced the milder witch laws of Elizabeth (which evoked the death penalty only for killing by witchcraft) with a law that condemned all practitioners of witchcraft to death. And James promoted Bacon to a position of power which directly involved him in organising such persecutions.

It is evident that his experiences in this area coloured his thinking about science and technology. For what is radically new in Bacon's thinking in this area is the equation of experimental investigation of nature with the torture and rape of a strong and independent woman, by men armed with various mechanical devices (of torture), forcing her to give up her secrets and herself to them – with the ultimate aim of permanently enslaving her to their interests; 'binding her into service', 'constraining' and moulding her as a slave to masculine power. And the idea of such technological enslavement of nature as the principle route to social (national) wealth and power.

As Carolyn Merchant points out, Bacon's writings after 1612 reflect the developing sexual dimension of English witch trials – with women accused of 'fornication with the devil' and sexually abused and tortured by their accusers looking for alleged 'witch marks' often within the labia majora.

> "Much of the imagery he used in delineating his new scientific objectives and methods derives from the courtroom, and, because it treats nature as a female to be tortured through mechanical inventions, strongly suggests the interrogations of the witch trials and the mechanical devices used to torture witches. In a relevant passage Bacon stated that the method by which natures secrets might be discovered corresponded to investigating the secrets of witchcraft by inquisition."

> "For you have but to follow and as it were hound nature in her wanderings, and you will be able when you like to lead and drive her afterward to the same place again. Neither am I of opinion in this history of marvels that superstitious narratives of sorceries, witchcraft's, charms, dreams, divinations and the like, where there is an assurance and clear evidence of the fact, should be altogether

excluded... howsoever the use and practice of such arts is to be condemned, yet from the speculation and consideration of them... a useful light may be gained, not only for a true judgement of the offences of persons charged with such practices, but likewise for the further disclosing of the secrets of nature. Neither ought a man to make scruple of entering and penetrating into these holes and corners, when the inquisition of truth is his whole object..." (MERCHANT 1983, p. 168)

The strong sexual implications of the last sentence can be interpreted in the light of the investigation of the supposed sexual crimes and practices of witches. In another example,

"I mean (according to the practice in civil causes) in this great plea or suit granted by the divine favour and providence (whereby the human race seeks to recover its rights over nature) to examine nature herself and the arts upon interrogatories." Bacon pressed the idea further with an analogy to the torture chamber; "For like as a man's disposition is never well known or proved till he be crossed, nor Proteus ever changed shapes till he was straitened and held fast, so nature exhibits herself more clearly under the trials and vexations of art (mechanical devices) than when left to herself.' (ibid., p. 169)

Here too we see evidence of a male envy of the female womb, which provokes the desire to steal the womb and female fertility. In this case, mother-nature's womb is seen to hold secrets, which, through technology, could be pulled from her for use in the improvement of male society. As Bacon says,

"there is therefore much ground for hoping that there are still laid up in the womb of nature many secrets of excellent use having no affinity or parallelism with anything that is now known ...only by the method which we are now treating can they be speedily and suddenly and simultaneously presented and anticipated." (ibid.)

Like the connection between obsession and religion, so has the connection between obsession and science long been recognised by psychoanalysts. But in the next chapter we move on to consider some other, perhaps less obvious connections between science and psychopathology.

CHAPTER FOURTEEN
WOMB ENVY, CREATION AND
THE COPENHAGEN INTERPRETATION

Part One
CREATION AND EXPLANATION

There has been a great deal written lately about the 'wisdom of the ancients' – the supposedly profound cosmological, ecological and social insights of the shamans and elders of pre-literate and pre-industrial cultures. In particular, much has been written about apparent convergences of modern physics with such ancient wisdom.

An obvious place to start in considering such comparisons is with the ideas of pre-industrial societies relating to the origins of the world, human society and the human species. For whatever else the shamans and elders of such societies might have theorised about, they have typically had some ideas in these areas, and quite a lot is known about such 'origin myths' from many different cultures and time periods.

Probably the best known creation myth of all is that of the Hebrew Bible. Here, the making of the world is thought to parallel human actions of building houses and shaping clay. We read that Yahweh founded the earth on pillars, or foundations, that he stretched out the heavens, and that he divided the waters and set a vault between them.

Genesis 2: 4 f.f. presupposes that heaven and earth exist, but it also says that there was (originally) no life on earth. Genesis 2: 5 explains, "Yahweh had not given rain and mankind did not exist to cultivate the earth". But the water came up from the earth and produced fertility. To provide for the cultivation of the earth, first Yahweh like a 'workman' formed a man from clay and dust and then brought his creation to life by breathing his spirit into it. Then He "planted a garden in Eden, in the East, and put there the man whom He had formed".

Moving round to the other side of the world we find central Australian Aboriginal creation stories in which totemic ancestors like Numbakulla first rose out of nothing or out of the earth in the Dreamtime with bodies full of spirit children. They then began their wanderings, introducing form and structure to a previously featureless world. And it was these spirit children or particles of the souls of the adult totemic ancestors (left behind in various natural features visited by these ancestors on their wanderings) which later developed into all the people and animals of the world (entering the wombs of women and female animals when they are near to such objects, to form the souls of new generations).

Clearly there are significant differences between the Biblical and Aboriginal accounts. But there are also obvious similarities between them (and between them and many other such creation stories from around the world). In what follows I want to focus mainly upon such similarities and consider how we might go about assessing their 'wisdom'. How 'rational' are they? And how do they relate to later 'scientific' cosmologies?

In the first instance, both accounts start out with perceived regularities of the everyday world which find no explanation in such everyday perception; the differentiation of earth and sky, local geography, the cycles of the seasons, including the growth and life of plants and animals, the facts of human pregnancy, birth, life and death.

Here we notice also a first and obvious parallel with modern science which similarly starts off from such perceived regularities as material-in-need-of-explanation. And it is important to recognise that this world of everyday perception in ancient society as in modern – is already a world permeated by theory; rather than a world of mere isolated, individual sense data.

Philosopher of science, Rom Harré, calls the sort of theory involved here (which provides the starting point for the formulation of higher-order theory, both scientific and pre-scientific) 'Type 1' theory. Type 1 theories are "Cognitive objects with pragmatic properties". Theories of this type "enable the constitution, classification and prediction of observable phenomena" (HARRÉ 1986).

Such theories derive from direct observation of the phenomena of the world. We classify the objects of our experience in terms of significant similarities and differences – of form, function and behaviour. They derive from so-called 'inductive' reasoning; generalising or extrapolating from specific instances of form or behaviour to whole classes or types of observable phenomena;

> *P1 the sample is of the same category as the population – e.g. this is an apple*
> *P2 the sample has the targeted predicate (property, power or behavioural tendency) e.g. this apple has the power to nourish*
> *C so the population has the targeted predicate – e.g. all apples are nourishing*

Here we note also that as far as explanation is concerned it is the (directly observable) causal powers and developmental tendencies of objects that are most important. We typically explain particular events or states of affairs in terms of the exercise of such powers. Why did object B change its state? Because it was acted upon by object A which – in this situation – has the power to bring about such change (through exerting the appropriate 'pressure' etc). Why did object A thus act upon object B? Because it was 'moved' by agent C or it has an intrinsic tendency to move itself in this sort of way in this sort of situation etc.

However, not everything can be 'explained' or predicted on the basis of such direct observation, classification, and inductive generalisation. Indeed, such generalisations themselves typically raise new problems of explanation; – what is it that makes all apples nourishing? It might indeed be true that the house was destroyed because the river overflowed its banks and swept it away. But why this unexpected overflow? Why does water flow down hill in the first place? How did the river come to be there in the first place?

This brings us onto the second obvious point of similarity between the Palestinian and central Australian accounts; the fact that when they move beyond such type 1 theory – to try to explain these important regularities which find no immediate explanation in terms of directly perceivable facts or forces – they both rely crucially upon analogical reasoning.

Both assimilate the creation of the earth and/or of the first life of the earth to the productive activities of human beings. In particular, both envisage the creation of the world in terms of the productive activities of super-human subjects, shaping and moulding pre-existing (but relatively form-less) natural materials (though in the second case, the ideas of pregnancy and birth also play a central role – as the totemic ancestors place their spirit babies into the natural features they have created or named).

In the case of the Genesis account, the analogical argument in question presumably looks something like this;

P1 the natural world is like a house in ways 1 to n (it has a floor, roof, walls etc., … only it is bigger)
P2 houses are built by human craftspersons for their own purposes (to provide habitation for someone etc.)
C so the natural world was also built by a human-type craftsperson (only bigger) for their own purposes

Now there have certainly been some philosophers of science (and scientists) who have maintained that such analogical reasoning plays no part in modern science. But as Rom Harré points out, this is radically mistaken.

In science, as in mythico-religious creation stories, type 1 theories provide the starting point for further, higher order theories, both in the sense that they provide the raw material in need of explanation by such theories, and in the sense that they provide the raw material for – analogical – construction of such higher order theory.

Harré identifies these new, higher order 'type 2' theories as

> "cognitive objects with iconic properties... Theories of this type enable the representation (including sometimes the simple picturing) of a certain class of unobservable beings. Typical type 2 theories are the bacterial theory of disease, plate tectonics, Hales theory of the motion of the sap and so on. All such theories involve a representation, in some medium or other, of a physical system and its modes of behaviour, which at the time of formulation of the theory, had not yet been observed." (ibid., p. 71)

At this point we move beyond the manifest differentiating properties of things (their colour, size, weight, observed causal dispositions and powers) to look for the underlying 'essence' – "the real constitution of their insensible parts" (or the major environmental forces acting upon them) on which depend, and reference to which thereby explains, such manifest properties. And the mechanism allowing this move beyond appearances, the primary tool for the generation of an initial model of such an underlying essence (provided from within the realm of type 1 theory itself) is the mental activity of analogical reasoning (from observed and understood properties and causal powers).

> "In a great many cases [observation and induction] reveal patterns amongst phenomena for whose explanation the community may be at a loss. It may turn out that these patterns are explained

by processes which are visually unobservable, in that people could not experience them in the same way as they experience the patterns the existence of such processes would explain. Reference to unobservable causal mechanisms and the beings upon whose existence they depend would involve the use of terms which denote beings which are, at the time, beyond experience. In short, the community cannot tell what is producing the phenomena of interest by looking, touching or listening. It is to remedy the lack of microscopical [or macroscopical, ultra fast or ultra slow] eyes [and ears] that the controlled imagining of what these processes and beings might be, begins. The role of source analogies is essential to this cognitive activity. It is from these that the community of scientists draws the images and the conceptual systems, with the help of which the cognitive work of pushing the imagination beyond experience is achieved in a disciplined way." (ibid., pp. 204-5)

There is no doubt that this sort of reasoning has played a central role in the formulations of many famous and influential scientific theories. Here, in addition to the theories referred to earlier by Harré (as classic type 2 theories) we think also of Darwin's theory of evolution, of the planetary model of atomic structure and many others.

P1 the natural world (of living things) is like a farm in ways 1 to n (animals and plants adapted to specific local demands)
P2 in a farm this adaptation is explained by variation and selection — by human agency (changing environment)
C so in nature this adaptation is explained by variation and selection — by changing environmental circumstances.

So apparently, to find the difference between science and myth, we must focus rather upon the criteria for assessing such analogical arguments; for deciding which are good arguments and which are not.

As far as rational assessment of theory is concerned, there are two broad areas to consider; intrinsic plausibility and empirical testability.

The first relates to such things as the internal coherence of the theory, its compatibility with other established truths and its explanatory power in respect of the particular facts it was originally formulated to explain. Is it clearly formulated? Does it seem to be consistent and coherent in itself? Does it properly and convincingly explain those facts? Does it successfully reduce the complex, disparate and diverse to the clear, simple and unitary? Does it explain precisely how the generative mechanism in question gives rise to the surface appearances?

Consider the basic pattern of all analogical argument;

P1 the primary subject (the phenomenon in need of explanation) is similar to the (source) analogue (i.e. some other, already better understood phenomenon) in ways 1 to n, but different in ways x,y,z

P2 the analogue has the targeted predicate (in this case, properties 1 to n are explained by particular aspects of its structure, powers and environment)

C so the primary subject has the targeted predicate (its properties 1 to n are explained by similar aspects of its own structure, environments etc.) – suitably modified by considerations x,y,z (– BURBIDGE, 1990)

As far as intrinsic plausilibility is concerned, its important to consider the relation between the similarities listed in premise one and the causal mechanism identified in premise two. We must consider whether they are closely connected in the object or process concerned (called the analogue). Or are they merely accidental or contingent in respect of this mechanism? If the latter is the case, then clearly any analogical extension of such a mechanism to another entity purely on the basis of its exhibiting similar properties would be quite unjustified. eg.

P1 clouds are like swans insofar as both are soft and white (or black)
P2 swans come from eggs
PC so clouds come from eggs too

In fact, a swan's whiteness has little to do with its 'essential' features as a particular genus of bird – including its birth from an egg. (It has much more to do with the reflective optical properties of its surface features, and the same goes for clouds.)

The second area of rational assessment of theory, that of empirical testability, concerns the power of the theory to generate novel predictions and the production of new knowledge through the verification of such predictions.

The idea here is that science does not just look for plausible explanations of specific phenomena; it looks for explanations that go beyond the phenomena that initially motivated such (type 2) theory construction and actually predict new observations.

As philosopher of science Imre Lakatos points out, theories can be tested only through putting them together with a range of other ideas about the state of the world at the start of the experiment – (other forces bearing upon the system in question, the operation of the experimental apparatus etc.) – generally referred to under the heading of 'initial conditions' and 'auxiliary assumptions' – in order to generate specific – testable – predictions.

In the normal course of events some such predictions will be verified, some refuted. If a theory continues to generate new and interesting predictions (about matters of fact) which are confirmed, then this is a good reason for taking that theory seriously – despite occasional refutations. For the confirmation of novel predictions provides substantial new knowledge about the world; it means that the theory is functioning as an efficient tool of knowledge production.

In this context it is reasonable to assume that refutations are actually due to mistaken auxiliary assumptions (or mistaken ideas about the experimental set-up) rather than the 'core' theory itself.

And we can 'work on' this 'protective belt' of assumptions to try to remove such anomalies in the future.

Broadly speaking, as long as verifications keep ahead of refutations, we have a *progressive* research program – and it is rational to push ahead with the prevailing theory. But once refutations get the upper hand, once the theory ceases to lead the way to substantial new knowledge and rather seems to 'follow after' empirical studies (which necessitate continuous modifications – patching up the theory, after the event), then we have a *degenerating* research tradition and it is rational to look around for some alternative which can better explain the anomalous observations.

Of course, theory-testing can still generate 'new knowledge' – in the sense of unexpected discoveries, even if it contradicts the theory that motivated the testing in the first place. And it is not rational to abandon a theory which has done well in the past if we have nothing better to replace it with in the present.

Nonetheless, we must be suspicious of research traditions that increasingly provide 'explanations' of new discoveries, cobbled together after the event. And if a theory is no longer delivering the goods we should be actively involved in formulating or considering alternatives, rather than resting on our laurels.

Instruments of various kinds will often play a crucial role in such experimental testing – extending the range of human sensory systems. Here indeed the theory (the analogical model) and its novel predictions can often function as a guide for the construction of such instruments.

Via such instruments, the originally unobservable 'underlying' mechanisms or essences identified by the theory can actually become (more or less) directly observable – as a particularly powerful verification of the theory. But even if they do not, the theory can still be strongly supported via confirmation of far-reaching novel predictions (manifesting the causal consequences of the 'operation' of such an underlying essence in the medium of some other – directly perceivable – substance etc.

Here, of course, pre-industrial cultures are again at an obvious disadvantage, in terms of restricted technological resources for such experimental investigations. Even if Yahweh or Numbakulla were precisely located in the sky – or down in the earth – little could be done to effectively test such 'predictions'. As we know, in retrospect, such theories have not faired so well in respect of such direct verification. Nor do they seem to have done much better as far as indirect verification is concerned.

But just because these theories fail as far as generation of new knowledge is concerned, this is no reason for judging them too harshly – as unworthy – of comparison with modern science. In many cases it takes a long period of development and clarification before a theory is put into a form in which it is amenable to empirical testing. There would have been little real scientific progress if researchers had not been prepared to put in such work or development and clarification prior to any effecting empirical verification: so there still remains the question of intrinsic plausibility as an indication that a theory is worthy of such development.

And this brings us onto a third major point of similarity of the two creation stories; the male sex of the major creator god or gods in both cases. In contrast to the obvious empirical fact of the creation of new human life out of the female body – in real historical time – it is a male being or beings that plays the crucial generative role in these first dreamtime creations.

Certainly there can be no doubt about the masculine identity and patriarchal prerogatives of the Hebrew god Yahweh. And in the Central Australian case, indeed, it is particularly striking that we are apparently concerned with pregnant men; the totemic ancestor Numbakulla (and others) 'pregnant' with the souls of humans and animals (though its important to recognise the presence of female totemic ancestors also in the beliefs of many such Australian Aboriginal groups).

Apparently, this inconsistency seriously detracts from the rationality of the accounts in question. And it is therefore tempting to ask what other sorts of considerations might be involved; what sorts of psychological (possibly unconscious, defensive, fantasy wish-fulfilling) and/or political (ideological, power-seeking or power stabilising) forces might be operative in these cases (overriding or substituting for rationality and truth)?

What might make these ideas appear intrinsically plausible or otherwise appealing even when they lack any such real rational foundation? And, in this case, it seems that the very inconsistency they have in common itself holds the key to understanding the major psychological forces involved here.

Ever since the pioneer feminist psychoanalyst Karen Horney first discovered a deep-seated envy of the female womb and female capacity for pregnancy, birth and breast feeding amongst her own male patients and others, there have been attempts to trace back these and many similar myths from all around the world to particular sorts of child rearing and other social arrangements which tend to foster such male envy and insecurity.

The basic idea here is quite straightforward and appealing; in societies where early child care devolves primarily upon women (where men are – indeed – largely absent from the world of women and young children) the young boys dawning realisation of the differences between the sexes can be a major blow to his self-esteem and security. For, in this sort of context, child production and child care become synonymous with adult magic and adult power for the young boy. And the realisation that he can never directly participate in such processes is equivalent to the belief that he can never truly grow up. His male body condemns him to perpetual infancy and dependence.

Such ideas can lead to profound feelings of womb envy and, perhaps, hostile desires to steal or control or destroy the female womb. So can they lead to powerful (manic) psychological defences of denigration and denial of such female powers, of contempt for, and attempted control over such female powers of producing and nurturing children.

On the positive side, such feelings can motivate (compensatory) male creation – of objects, ideas, institutions – to serve as child-substitutes. On the negative side, such creations become vehicles for the exercise of male power over women. And generally, these sorts of thoughts and feelings are implicated in the generation and maintenance of ideologies and practices of male domination – as well as individual acts of aggression and violence against women.

Certainly these ideas seem directly applicable to the ancient Palestinian and Central Australian situations. Here are cultures characterised by quite high levels of sexual segregation and patriarchal power, where the creation stories in question functioned as integral parts of special male religious institutions and ritual practices from which women were (largely) excluded.

In Central Australia, in particular, a classic 'two worlds' sort of situation seems to have prevailed, with men and women radically segregated in economic, political and cultural life – including the care of young children. Here, this fundamental division was actually 'written into' the natural landscape – with specific land areas and sacred sites off limits to each sex. And major rites of passage mediated the adolescent boys transition from the world of women to the world of men.

In many hunting-gathering societies, the sexes are divided in basic materially productive activities, with the men often travelling long distances in pursuit of larger game, while the women travel shorter distances collecting vegetables and smaller game that provide the basis of group subsistence. Prolonged breast feeding and the incompatibility of care of young children with big game hunting ensure that such child care largely devolves upon the women.

Here, perhaps, is a likely foundation for the sort of womb envy described by Horney. And amongst the hunter-gatherers of Central Australia it seems to have contributed to a positive feedback of increasing male insecurity breeding increasing segregation and so on. Thus, it seems that the sort of creation myths referred to earlier played a central role in a whole elaborate constellation of male mythico-religious theory and practice that occupied the adult male population for many months of the year – effectively segregated from women and young children.

Most important here were the initiation ceremonies whereby segregation and major trauma mediated the transition of adolescent males into adult masculinity. Such traumas included threatened and actual physical violence, directly orchestrated by the older males, incarnating the god-ancestors at the time of the creation of the world. Through their actions the boys severed the symbiotic bond with the mothers, maintained through years of breast feeding, living and sleeping with the women.

We can clearly see how the initiation process compensated for the womb envy at the heart of the earlier male identity in providing a new 'ideal' male identity for the boy. For on the one hand, the whole procedure was geared to the affirmation of phallic male power at the expense of female power – in dramatic performance and explicit mythological cosmology. On the other, the whole procedure simultaneously offered the opportunity for the fathers to become mothers to a new generation of men, with much of the typical activity of initiation directly miming that of women in child-birth. For the boys, therefore, to be initiated into manhood was to become an initiator in their own right, and thus a male mother to the next generation of men.

In this context, the most dramatic and obvious expression of male womb envy – and defence against it – is provided by Aranda subincision (six or seven weeks after circumcision of the adolescent males) involving cutting into the underside of the penis through to the urethra, to create an opening similar to the opening of the vagina – and called by the same name. Thus men were directly equipped with an organ for childbirth. And, indeed, the associated myths suggest that the bleeding of subincision corresponds to the girls first period as a necessary sign of male 'fertility'; while the subincision wound is periodically re-opened to mime the woman's later menstruations. The Aranda – in common with other hunter gatherers – saw menstrual blood as the stuff of creation of life. And blood from the subincision wound was seen to be similarly magically powerful – bestowing life or taking it away (curing sickness etc.).

Part Two
QUANTUM MECHANICS

We now shift from mythico-religious thought to the 'highest' realms of contemporary physical science; specifically the famous Copenhagen Interpretation of quantum theory. For not only is this regarded as the jewel in the crown of modern physics, it is also one of the theories (or areas of theory) most frequently cited in respect of the alleged convergence of ancient and modern cosmologies. And it is therefore quite a logical place to commence an assessment of such claims.

It is interesting, in this connection, that it is sometimes claimed that with quantum theory, science has actually moved beyond analogy and picturability, into a world of pure mathematics. As Rom Harré suggests, here we enter the realms of what he calls type 3 theories – (cognitive objects with mathematical properties)

> "Theories of this type enable the representation of non-pictur-able systems of beings and of their behaviour, interrelations and so on. Such systems form a distinct class of unobservables since by virtue of their unpicturability they could never be observed by human beings. The ontology behind such theories is embodied in certain mathematical or quasi mathematical properties of the theoretical discourse." (HARRÉ 1986, p. 71)

Quite a number of physicists (and philosophers – including Harré himself) would claim to favour the Copenhagen Interpretation of such mathematical formulae (as dealing with quantum phenomena only in relation to the 'everyday' reality of macroscopic measuring instruments) precisely because it appears substantially agnostic on the question of the 'true nature' of quantum phenomena. Because they can see no particular empirical test able to clearly distinguish between various other, more 'substantial' interpretations of such phenomena, many physicists declare all such apparently substantial interpretations to be unscientific – mere empty speculation.

As I shall try to show below, I think this sort of idea is doubly mistaken. For, in the first instance, it is simply not true to say that the Copenhagen Interpretation avoids substantial ontological commitments in relation to quantum phenomena 'in themselves'. There can be no physical theory which does not provide some – concrete – interpretation of its mathematical formalism. And the Copenhagen Interpretation (or, at least, the contemporary orthodoxy identified with it) does have substantial – analogical – content in this area insofar as it incorporates certain specific ideas about quantum waves as probability waves and about the nature of the measurement process as interaction between micro and macro worlds.

As such, the theory can be assessed according to the sorts of criteria for assessing analogical arguments considered in Part One. We can still consider the intrinsic plausibility of such ideas, their consistency amongst themselves and in relation to other ideas we take to be true or probable.

In the second instance, it is radically mistaken to dismiss speculation about the 'true' nature of quantum phenomena (as type 2 phenomena) as unscientific just because we cannot – immediately – see how to definitively test such speculations. It is quite possible that it will only be when such theories are further developed that such testing will become possible. And to arbitrarily dismiss such attempts to create a coherent picture of the phenomena in question could therefore stand in the way of further empirical progress in this area.

It certainly seems to be true that the initial attempts to come to terms with the empirical regularities that gave birth to quantum theory generated various mathematical rules whose precise interpretation was unclear. Such rules functioned well in predicting specific observations, but it was far from clear just what was actually going on in the microscopic world, responsible for producing the observed phenomena.

Here, the crucial initial observations concerned the apparently discrete interchange of energy between matter and light.

"Light, which had been known for some time to show distinctly wavelike aspects of diffraction, interference, wavelength and frequency, was now shown to have a particle-like aspect as well. Any detection of light by a material device, say, a piece of photographic film, revealed that light interacted with matter in a very particle-like way. Energy in the light appeared to be contained in discrete packets that could interact with matter only 'one at a time'." (SKLAR 1992, p. 164)

At the same time, matter at the sub-atomic level,

"which was known to be particle-like, showing mass and charge concentrated in a small physical volume, was now seen to have a wavelike aspect too. Electron beams going through small holes in barriers diffracted, as did light beams sent through very small pinholes. Electrons scattered off a crystal lattice exhibited a clear interference pattern analogous to that shown by light scattered off a tradition diffraction grating." (op. cit.)

This duality of apparently incompatible properties posed obvious problems for understanding precisely what was going on at the micro-level. And in this it was complemented by an increasing number of experimental results which seemed to defy all logic or reason.

A classic example here is the famous 'two slits' experiment. In the absence of the intervention of any measuring apparatus capable of detecting which of two closely positioned slits individual electrons fired at the slits actually go through, then the impacts of such electrons registered on a photographic detector beyond the slits appear as elements of an interference pattern such as we would expect from electron waves splitting up to pass through both slits simultaneously, and recombining with interference on the other side (and this applies even if the electrons are fired individually with a time gap, in separate experiments etc.).

But if we set up a device to measure which hole each individual electron is actually passing through, not only do we get a definite result (of one or the other), but if the electrons are also allowed to pass on to the detector screen, the pattern that builds up there is just what we should expect from non-interfering particle impacts.

It is as if, in the absence of measurement, each individual electron is, somehow, coming through both slits at the same time. Physicists came to use the term 'superposition' to describe such a bizarre – and apparently contradictory – situation. But with measurement, the 'superposition' 'collapses' into an ordinary, determinate situation in coming through one slit or the other.

Out of observations of electron diffraction came Erwin Schrödinger's discovery of the appropriate equation whose solution represented the waves associated with both free electrons and electrons bound in various force fields.

Later on Heisenberg, Born and Jordan worked on providing a systematic way of treating the problem of the interaction of atoms and light, and ultimately formulated an entirely new dynamical theory.

"The basic dynamical quantities of position and momentum had previously been mathematically represented by functions that assigned numbers to the particle as a function of time. These were the position and momentum of a particle at a given time. Now, however, the dynamical quantities were represented by mathematical objects called operators. These operators mapped an abstract mathematical entity, the state of the system, from one condition to another. Rules were constructed for determining, given the state of a system and given the operator corresponding to the quantity whose values one was interested in, the possible observed values of the quantity." (ibid., p. 162)

Although these and other equations worked well enough for purposes of prediction questions still remained of what kind of physical world corresponded to this innovative mathematics. "Whereas previously a physical model had led to a mathematical description, here we had a working mathematical structure whose physical interpretation seemed quite problematic." (op. cit.)

Nonetheless, this very situation provided a powerful stimulus for producing some coherent and comprehensive interpretation of the formalism in question. And while various possibilities soon fell by the wayside, (e.g. the wave 'packet') others became firmly established.

A key concept here was Max Born's interpretation of the intensity of the wave function as giving a probability.

"Every wave has an amplitude, the 'height' of the wave magnitude. The intensity of the wave, ...proportional to the square of the amplitude, is what we normally register, for light, as the brightness of the light; it is a measure of the energy in the wave. The amplitudes of the waves of quantum wave mechanics were framed in complex numbers, but their squares were real numbers representing a directly interpretable physical quantity."

"It was Born's insight that these intensities could be taken as representative of the probability with which a physical observable could be found to have one of its possible values if an appropriate measurement were made. The wave function can be represented as a function of different variables, eg, as a function either of the position or of the momentum of the particle to which the wave is associated. Depending on the representation chosen, probability say for finding the particle in a region if a position measurement was made... could be calculated from the appropriate intensity over a region of the quantum 'probability wave' as some began to call it. Probabilities of transition of a particle from one state to another could also be determined from the wave functions and their interactions." (ibid., p. 164)

M.Y. Han e.g. refers to this 'probabilistic interpretation' as the 'culmination' of the quantum revolution and the 'resolution' of particle-wave duality. (HAN 1993, p. 60)

"According to this principle, the 'waviness' and 'particleness' are related to each other by a mathematical recipe for a probability distribution. In other words, a quantum physical entity, be it a photon, electron, proton, or atom is a wave, and its shape controls the probability it will be observed at a particular position; wave > amplitude squared > probability > particle." (op. cit.)

Two other concepts which became firmly established at the foundations of the theory were those of 'superposition' and the 'collapse of the wave function'. We have already encountered the basis for these ideas in considering the results of the 'two slits' experiment. And the idea of 'superposition' finds a fairly direct sort of representation in the mathematical formalism.

Thus, as noted above, there is a mathematical system which describes the production and propagation of quantum particles through the application of force to matter (e.g. electrical force to a light filament.) Depending on how an experiment is set up, such particles start out with certain definite – measured – properties. Indeed, putting the particles through a certain sort of measuring device gives them certain definite properties as measured by that device, which persist unless and until the particle interacts with some other sort of system.

However, the very definiteness of some such properties – established by measurement – seems to render others intrinsically indefinite. So that definite values of some properties are associated with 'superpositions' of others, allowing only probabilistic predictions of those other values – when measured by other – appropriate – measuring instruments.

Of course, when such measurements are actually made, a definite result is achieved. Now there is a definite value where previously there was only superposition and probability. And, at the same time, the value of the original variable becomes indefinite. It has been 'disrupted' by the second sort of measurement.. For this reason, the two sets of properties, say left-right and up-down spin of an electron – or angular momentum spinning about particular directional axes – are described as 'incompatible' properties.

As Sklar says, with measurement 'interference' disappears. And it is a 'rule' of the theory that

> "The wave function describing the system prior to the measurement is to be discarded, and in its place a wave function is introduced corresponding to the value of the observable quantity obtained in the measurement." (SKLAR 1992, p. 182) [This is called the 'projection postulate'.] "If a measurement has just been performed that reveals a given value for an observable, then the state of the system immediately after the measurement is the one appropriate to the systems having that exact value for the measured quantity." (ibid., p. 171)

Putting these various ideas together we have a supposedly coherent sort of account of what is going on e.g. in the two slits experiment – with a key role for the observer. As Gribbin says,

> "the electrons not only know whether or not both holes are open, they know whether or not we are watching them, and they adjust their behaviour accordingly. There is no clearer example of the interaction of the observer with the experiment. When we try to look at the spread out electron wave it collapses into a definite particle; But when we are not looking it keeps its options open. In terms of Born's probabilities, the electron is being forced by our measurement to choose one course of action out of the array of possibilities.
>
> There is a certain probability that it could go through one hole, and an equivalent probability that it may go through the other; probability interference produces the diffraction pattern at our detector. When we detect the electron, though, it can only be in one place, and that changes the probability pattern for the future behaviour – for that electron it is now certain which hole it went through. But unless someone looks, nature herself does not know which hole the electron is going through." (GRIBBIN 1985, p. 171)

Now, despite wide acceptance of these sorts of ideas, they raise at least as many problems as they solve. If we think again about the two slits experiment, e.g., we can see serious problems for the 'probability wave' idea. As Sklar points out, "a simple identification of the wave functions intensity with probabilities as usually understood is fraught with difficulties… if the wave function is just a probability representer and not a physical wave in the world, how can (the observed) interference occur? Normal probabilities just do not 'interfere' with one another" (SKLAR 1992, p. 165).

And, along the same lines, Von Baer says, "if the wave function is sufficiently powerful to direct the electrons path away from the forbidden (i.e. interference) zones (on the detector screen) it must have actual, physical content" – and not just exist as a mathematical abstraction (VON BAER 1992, p. 51).

The concept of superposition seems intrinsically problematic, insofar as it seems to involve the co-existence of contradictory attributes. And the 'collapse of the wave function' raises some particularly intractable difficulties.

According to the mathematical formalism,

> "In ordinary dynamical interaction, the 'interference' effects of the systems originally being in a superposition of states are preserved when the system interacts with some new physical system. The correlations that characterise the interference process are simply transferred to the new joint system." (SKLAR 1992, p. 182)

As far as interaction with some macro-measuring apparatus is concerned, this means that the 'combined' system after interaction has occurred must be in a superposition state. Thus, considering the case of spin measurement by a Stern-Gerlach machine; "the electron is made to pass through a magnetic field which deflects it in different directions according to the different orientations of the spin. If the spin is 'up' the electron goes off one way, if its 'down' the electron goes off the other way (we can place some detecting device

– photographic plates or Geiger counters – which will register whether the electron has arrived at one place or another).

But, of course, the electron – as superposition – is, in a sense, spinning both up and down.

> "If a left spinning particle interacts with an up-down spin detecting apparatus, the particle enters the interaction in a superposition of up and down spin states. The ultimate state of the particle plus measuring apparatus must be, then, a superposition state. It is the superposition of two pure states – 'particle is spin up and machine says spin up' and 'particle is spin down and machine says spin down'." (ibid., p. 188)

The problem is that, in practice, different sorts of measurement give definite (and different) results. With measurement 'interference' disappears. "An electron described by a wave function spread all over space is, after the electron is measured and found to be in a limited spatial region, described by a wave function confined entirely to that region." A photographic plate or other detecting device in the Stern Gerlach experiment registers that each electron has definitely arrived at one place or the other. Each electron is definitely either spin up or spin down. This is described as the 'collapse of the wave function' with measurement.

What is happening here? Hey and Walters speak of the 'delicacy' of quantum phenomena. So that battering an electron with a photon (to see which slit it is emerging from e.g.) "destroys its interference properties – leaving only its particle properties" (HEY AND WALTERS 1987, p. 16).

But yet, according to the theory, the interaction should preserve the superposition of particle and wave. (And, of course, photons are quantum phenomena also.) This is the so-called 'measurement problem', that has bedevilled quantum theory for decades. And the solution is far from obvious.

Part Three
THE COPENHAGEN INTERPRETATION

The probabilistic interpretation – and the 'collapse of the wave function' – became incorporated in Niels Bohr's attempt to frame an overall interpretation of the quantum world and quantum mathematics. And the so-called 'Copenhagen Interpretation' has since become the model favoured by the majority of quantum physicists.

Thus, given that the wave function expresses a mere 'potential' for revealing observable values with specifiable probabilities relative to a chosen (macroscopic) measuring apparatus, it seems logical to take such measurements as primary or primitive concepts within the theory.

In the light of these and other considerations, Bohr draws a clear line between measurements and other sorts of interactions. The results of measurement processes are taken as constituting the real hard facts about the world, and theory is taken as a device whose sole (or essential) role is to provide correlations between the value based on one measurement process that 'prepares' a system in a given quantum state and the value of some observable quantity upon a later measurement.

"Bohr assumed that in our description of these observable results of measurement we will always remain restricted to the typical classical means for describing the world developed by pre-quantum physics. Thus, such things as the position of a particle, its momentum, charge, and angular momentum and so on, are the quantities we read off from our measuring apparatus. A measuring apparatus is something once again characterisable in classical terms. It has definite 'output' states that are correlated to the measured quantities of the microsystems. A deposited mark of metallic silver will e.g. indicate that a photon was absorbed in some limited region of a photographic film, a definite flash of a detector tube may indicate the passage through a region of a charged particle and so on. In our recording of the results of measurement, we will have no place for quantum 'superposition' states, only for states as classically described." (SKLAR 1992, p. 172)

From the point of view of measurement the concepts and mathematical tools of the quantum theory exist so as to allow for probabalistic predictions of the outcomes of the measurement processes.

But what can we say about the quantum world itself – and its true relation to acts of measurement? The answer is that – beyond its essential indeterminateness and potential-for-determination – we cannot say very much. In particular, Bohr tries to evade the problems of making sense of the idea of 'superposition' by keeping ideas of the quantum realm as vague and undefined as possible.

As Rom Harré e.g. says,

"phenomena, observable states of affairs, occur when pieces of material apparatus are physically applied to the 'Ur-Stuff' of the world. ...I prefer to nickname the stuff 'glub', to avoid any metaphysical temptations that arise from the connotations of the word 'stuff'. The way the apparatus is built leads to the shaping up of this glub into this or that displayed phenomenon. If we choose to prod the glub with a bubble chamber and photographic apparatus we force the glub into a particle mode since it must display itself as tracks. Apparatus... is itself constrained by the Newtonian (classical) properties of humanly manipulable and observable matter. All phenomena, then, must be describable in classical concepts. Though the concepts must be classical it may be that there are certain combinations of such concepts that are forbidden. the glub does constrain phenomena in a general way, since there are only certain ways it can be 'shaped up'."

"It turns out that classical physics permits the realisation in physical apparatus of two classes of concepts, particle concepts and wave concepts. The glub is such that the two classes of apparatus cannot be used together, and therefore a description of phenomena in which instances of concepts of each class are paired is unacceptable. Particles and waves are created out of the glub by the use of pieces of apparatus. We should not think of the glub as being either particulate or wave-like in the absence of such an interaction."

Further:

> "any instrument reading is a property of a totality, the indis-
> soluble union of the equipment and just glub. All we know of the
> glub itself is that when prodded with this kind of apparatus it can
> be shaped up this way. In short, we know only its potentials."
> (HARRÉ 1986, p. 305)

But there is still a crucial question of precisely where the line is
to be drawn between quantum measured system – the glub – and
classical measuring apparatus. And here the Copenhagen Interpretation becomes truly bizarre. For nothing in the (formal) theory
makes a hard and fast dividing line between the quantum nature
and the classical measuring device. The division could – in theory –
be drawn at any level. At the same time, on the Copenhagen view,
the very intelligibility of the quantum picture demands that it be
drawn somewhere.

It seems, in other words, as if the Copenhagen Interpretation
has failed to solve the 'measurement problem'. On the contrary, it
has thrown this problem into sharp relief, with its emphasis upon
the qualitative dichotomy of quantum micro-world and classical
macro-world.

Of course, it all depends precisely what we mean by 'measurement'. Clearly the term is ambiguous. Does it refer to a particular
sort of causal interaction of micro and macro system? Or does it
refer to a human action – including also a certain intention and
perceptual experience, interpreted in a particular fashion?

The tendency of the Copenhagen Interpretation is to direct our
thinking very much in the latter direction. Thus, as Sklar says, for
some purposes it is indeed useful to think of the elementary particle
alone as the quantum system and all of the physical world remaining as measuring apparatus. But we could also, consistently, treat
any portion of the measuring apparatus as a physical system in
interaction with the elementary particle, with the whole joint system of particle and that fraction of the apparatus to be characterised

as a quantum system. If we did this, we would narrow the classically described apparatus down to that remaining after the portion initially reacting to the particle had been placed in the quantum realm.

As more and more of the physical system is consigned to quantum indeterminacy, it becomes all the more necessary to find some qualitative 'barrier' through which or beyond which determinism – or determinate properties – set in. And, for dualists, such a barrier is provided by the intervention of the human mind – as the end point of all measurement.

It is easy enough to see where this sort of idea will lead. In particular it points to the notorious 'Schrödinger's Cat' thought experiment, in which (in a recent variant) we imagine a particle generating source locked away in a closed box, inaccessible to human observers. The system is set up such that a particle beam is split with a fifty per cent chance of a particle going in each direction. If the first particle takes one route it triggers an explosion – killing a cat (also locked in the box). If it goes the other way there is no explosion. How should an observer outside the box and unable to know what has happened in it describe the cat after a period of time in which it is certain that at least one particle has gone one way or another?

According to the Copenhagen Interpretation, until they open the box to look inside, the observer should think of the cat not as alive or dead but rather in a superposition of live and dead states (as glub, in other words).

This account leads also to increasingly 'idealistic' sorts of interpretation in which it is the human mind or human consciousness that acquire the crucial role in 'collapsing the wave packet' into some definite classical value. For after all, if there is nothing in the material apparatus 'itself' which does this, then all that is left is apparently 'the mind' of the observer. In some mysterious fashion, mind intervenes in the 'natural order' in order to change the apparatus from superposition to definite classical state. Or alternatively, the collapse itself is 'in the mind' – rather than in the (completely indeterminate) 'things themselves'.

It is also, by now, clear how very closely the Copenhagen Interpretation parallels the creation stories considered earlier (and indeed many other similar mythico-religious creation stories – including Plato's *Timaeus*, the Egyptian primordial hill story – Mother nature as 'formless' etc.).

Before the physicist intervenes there is merely formless stuff (in the microscopic and perhaps even macro world). But by their choice of measuring instruments – and instrumental action – they give form to the stuff – they create a definite macro world of (classical) particles and waves like Yahweh's shaping of the clay. Thus, physicists seem to acquire rather awesome powers as world-creators in this sort of scheme. Only such 'disciplined' observers can create order – or at least, understand what they are doing.

More recently, such powers have been massively increased by the so-called 'many worlds' extension of the Copenhagen Interpretation by Everett and Wheeler. The starting point here is the apparent 'throwing away' of part of a wave function whenever a measurement is performed in the Copenhagen scheme of things.

Everett and Wheeler take it that, in fact, both components of the wave function continue to exist after the measurement has taken place.

"In each measurement the universe splits into a multiplicity of worlds, one for each possible outcome of the measurement process. There is a world in which the particle comes out of the machine in the up-spin state. In that world, the machine also gives a spin up reading, for the detection states of the measuring apparatus are, once again, supposed to be exactly correlated with the value of the measured quantity in question. But along with the world having a spin up particle and a measuring device giving an up reading, there is also a world with a spin down particle and a machine reading spin down etc." (SKLAR 1992, p. 194)

In other words, the god-like physicists, with their instruments, generate – not just a definite measurement – or definite classical reality – in this world; but also whole other worlds (presumably each with their own humans, cities, planets, galaxies and super clusters of galaxies) and they create more new worlds every time they take a measurement (perhaps every time they 'determine' the state of any system).

Here, the parallels with the Aranda creation myth are particularly clear and straightforward. Just as Numbakulla's body is pregnant with spirit children – waiting to be placed into the landscape, and born as people and animals – so is the physicist 'pregnant' with infinite new worlds – infinite alternative realities, just waiting to be born or given life through laboratory measurement.

It is tempting indeed to equate the magical measuring instruments – the photographic plates, Geiger counters, Stern Gerlach machines – with the magical subincised penis of the initiated man – out of which flows the special blood that can create new life – or take life away.

But notice how much greater is the endowment of the physicist than that of the initiated Aranda male. The Aranda just create people and animals (through initiation and 'increase' ceremonies etc, re-incarnating the original totemic ancestors). The physicist creates infinite worlds of possibility, branching off in different directions (imposing form and order upon formless – primordial – nature).

In this context it is, perhaps, hardly surprising that some physicists should come to believe in a physicist god; given the sorts of powers supposedly possessed by the physicists themselves. In some cases, of course, they actually require a physicist god, whose 'final' observation 'collapses' a whole universe of overlapping wave functions into a single, determinate reality (see e.g. Rom Harré's suggestion that while instruments shape the glub, the whole universe shapes the instruments etc.).

For those outside the physics community such a physicist god might explain quite a lot – and avoid some of the logical problems associated with the omniscient, omnipotent and perfectly good and merciful Christian God.

All the centuries of misery, exploitation, persecution, death of innocents etc. might begin to make sense if god is the sort of being who has little interest in, or feel for, human social life and psychology, but is rather much more concerned with the play of particles in the micro or macro worlds. Perhaps he is sceptical of the possibility of any rational understanding of human life and society and uses his scepticism to justify a studious non-involvement.

Perhaps, like Heisenberg, he believes that quantum indeterminism permeates the social world, as it does the micro world, so that there is no more point in fighting Nazis than in joining them, no meaning to moral responsibility etc.

He plays with particles while humans tear each other to pieces – indeed supplies them with the materials to do an even better job. Perhaps he assumes that his knowledge of particles makes him an authority on all things and he acts accordingly. Perhaps he is quite prepared to see the resources of the universe drained away to support his particle 'habit' – his ever greater, but ever more obscure research projects etc.

But are these considerations really relevant? It is true that some, like Einstein, have regarded the Copenhagen Interpretation as irrational myth or religion (Einstein called it 'the Heisenberg-Bohr tranquillising philosophy or religion'). But the majority of physicists have rather accepted its status as 'rational' and presumably objective science. As Gribbin e.g. says:

"Each attack on the Copenhagen Interpretation has strengthened its position. When thinkers of the calibre of Einstein try to find flaws in the theory, but the defenders of the theory are able to refute all the attackers arguments, the theory must emerge the stronger for its trial. The Copenhagen Interpretation is definitely 'right' in the sense that it works; any better interpretation of the quantum rules must include the Copenhagen Interpretation as a working view that enables experimenters to predict the outcome of their experiments..." (GRIBBIN 1985, p. 235)

"Most of the physicists who bother to think about such things are happy with the collapsing wave functions of the Copenhagen Interpretation... The Copenhagen Interpretation is fully vindicated for all practical purposes by the experiments." (ibid., p. 233)

Furthermore, Gribbin vigorously defends the many worlds interpretation as the best and most coherent 'logical' development of the Copenhagen position. It "includes the Copenhagen Interpretation within itself" (ibid., p. 235) and it is "conceptually simple, causal and gives predictions in accord with experience". (ibid., p. 242)

But is the theory really quite as logical and sensible as Gribbin suggests? On the face of it the answer is surely (a resounding) no. We have already encountered some fairly obvious problems with the probability wave interpretation. How can probabilities of future measurement create interference patterns? The waves must have rather more in the way of 'physical reality' than this interpretation suggests.

The obvious problem with the Copenhagen Interpretation itself concerns the great logical gap between the laws of the quantum world and the world of measuring instruments. As Sklar asks, how can there be such things as classically described measuring devices, if, as the theory claims, everything is a quantum system? "And what is the special role reserved for measurement processes? Aren't they just interactions of a system with another physical system? Why should there be a special rule for measurement processes at all, if measurements are nothing but another variety of physical interaction?... How is the system related to a measuring apparatus any different from the system merely physically interacting with some other physical system?"

Clearly, there is indeed a difference if we actually define measurement in terms of human consciousness or the human mind. But then we are back to the idea of a completely mysterious and unexplained wave-function collapsing power of the mind. And this is surely much more problematic than the idea of different 'sorts' of physical interaction.

It is also far from clear that mind exists as anything other than a particular sort of physical system itself. And it is most interesting that otherwise 'hard headed' physicists should so readily entertain such a problematic notion as that of an immaterial (Cartesian) mind.

Here is an apparent logical contradiction between theory and observation. Notice the close parallels with mythico-religious creation stories. There, we are trying to explain the evolution of complex systems out of simpler, less determinate systems. But how do we do it? By presupposing divine forces to shape up the indeterminate stuff which are already at least as complex and determinate as the things to be explained.

With the Copenhagen Interpretation, similarly, instead of trying to explain the first generation of determinate (i.e. apparently classical) large scale systems from 'within' the quantum world (and its laws) we presuppose such classical systems as simply 'given' and irreducible.

Part Four
ALTERNATIVES

By contrast, considerations of consistency suggest that, either we have to find a way of understanding quantum laws which 'purges' them of classical concepts, or we have to develop a fully 'classical' interpretation of the theory – whatever that might look like. Both look far from easy at the present time. But a number of physicists have clearly recognised the need to go down one such path or the other.

Presumably, if we follow the first path, we must acknowledge that all systems are indeed quantum systems subject to quantum laws insofar as they are made up of microscopic constituents. However, certain structural organisations of such constituents exhibit or appear to exhibit new and emergent – in this case determinate – properties – which at first sight appear to defy such quantum laws.

The emphasis here would have to be on appearance. A bird appears to defy gravity; human consciousness appears to transcend mere 'matter'. But, in fact, we know that the bird is just as much a gravitational system as anything else – it utilises rather than defies gravity (along with other forces of wind resistance etc). Humans are just as much physical systems as anything else. Consciousness is an emergent property of a complex system of matter including the human body, brain, sensory systems and external world.

There have been a number of suggestions as to how such determinateness emerges from the indeterminate quantum world – none very convincing. Polkinghorne e.g. suggests that perhaps "the true Schrödinger-like equation... embracing the totality of all that is involved in the measurement process – involves non-linearities which enforce a violation of the superposition principle for very complex systems, while essentially preserving it for the simple systems to which we have actually applied quantum mechanics" (POLKINGHORNE 1990, p. 66). And Sklar suggests that with measurement, perhaps, "the interference correlation has dissipated itself into the vast numbers of degrees of freedom of the innumerable particles that make up the macroscopic apparatus. This dissipation occurs in the amplifying process that reveals the microstate of the particle being measured." (SKLAR 1992, p. 189)

Wherever the solution lies, it is apparent that classical determination is a property of quite simple and small scale systems – just 'above' the quantum level – with no necessary involvement of consciousness. Protons might diffract, but macroscopic objects – like physicists – do not. And there would not be any physicists around at all if quantum systems had not managed – unaided – to generate such determinate systems, and set them off on their own evolutionary pathways long ago.

Notable proponents of the second path – the search for a classical interpretation – include De Broglie, Bohm and Bell. As early as 1952 Bohm developed a theory with more or less the same empirical content and mathematical formalism as 'standard' quantum mechanics but without any such bizarre implications. In this theory every material particle has perfectly determinate and consistent properties of position, momentum etc. Furthermore, the theory explains precisely why such particles appear to lack such properties (when not measured) by reference to the idea of guiding waves that push them about in various ways.

Bohm calls this the 'causal' interpretation, since "the electron or any other elementary particle… follows a causally determined trajectory".

"Unlike the familiar particles of Newtonian physics, the electron is never separated from a certain quantum field which fundamentally affects it… this quantum field satisfies Schrödinger's equation, just as the electromagnetic field satisfies Maxwell's equation… within Newtonian physics, a classical particle moves according to Newton's laws of motion, and the forces that act on the particle are derived from the classical potential V… The basic proposal of the causal interpretation is that, in addition to this classical potential, there also acts a new potential, called the quantum potential Q."

"The quantum potential Q is independent of the strength, or intensity, of the quantum field but depends only on its form. This is a particularly surprising result. In the Newtonian world of pushes and pulls on, e.g., a floating object, any effect is always more or less proportional to the strength or size of the waves. But with the quantum potential, the effect is the same for a very large or a very small wave and depends only on its overall shape." (BOHM AND PEAT 1987, pp. 89-90)

Bohm and Peat use the analogy of a ship that sails on automatic pilot, guided by radio waves.

"The overall effect of the radio waves is independent of their strength and depends only on their form. The essential point is that the ship moves with its own energy but that the information within the radio waves is taken up and used to direct the much greater energy of the ship. In the causal interpretation, the electron moves under its own energy, but the information in the form of the quantum wave directs the energy of the electron." (ibid., p. 90)

"The quantum wave carries 'information' and is therefore potentially active everywhere, but it is actually active only when and where this energy enters into the energy of the particle. But this implies that an electron, or any other elementary particle, has a complex and subtle inner structure that is at least comparable with that of a radio." (ibid., p. 93)

On this model, the electron in the two slits experiment goes through one slit or the other. "But the quantum wave can pass through both. On the outgoing side of the slit system, the quantum waves interfere to produce a highly complex quantum potential which does not generally fall off wit the distance from the slits." The force of this complex field modifies the movement of the electron "to produce the scattered pattern (noted earlier). In this case, the wavelike properties do not arise in any essential duality of the quantum particle but from the complex effects of the quantum potential". (ibid., pp. 90-1)

It is true that Bohm's theory implies a so-called 'non-locality' or ('instantaneous') action at a distance which poses serious problems for reconciling quantum theory with special relativity. But Bell has shown that all other interpretations also imply such non-locality (and Aspect and others have provided empirical verification of the principle) so that this is no reason to reject the Bohm model – especially since it begins to actually explain such action at a distance also. Indeed, Bell himself specifically dismissed the Copenhagen Interpretation – and special relativity also – in favour of a Bohm-type approach.

That physicists have generally rejected the Bohm model in favour of the much more mystical, obscure and apparently incoherent Bohr model – or even more bizarre elaborations based upon ideas of parallel worlds or the mind of God says a great deal about the rationality of some scientists – if not the rationality of science itself.

It is true that the Copenhagen Interpretation has provided the basis for the development of so called 'quantum field theory' – based upon integration with special relativity. Here, ideas about particles are replaced with ideas about infinitely tiny field systems in specific regions of space. And this new theory has achieved significant empirical confirmation – including the prediction and discovery of a number of new subatomic particles (or fields).

However, there remain serious problems with this theory (associated with various, arbitrary manipulations of the mathematics to ensure the 'correct' results, and with the ultimate meaning of it all). The idea of non-locality still implies some 'privileged' or absolute spatio-temporal reference frame, fundamentally at odds with special relativity theory. And it is not yet clear that a Bohm-Bell approach cannot be successfully extended into this area also.

So it looks as if we must return to consider also possible non-rational (psychological and ideological – perhaps unconscious) forces contributing to the widespread acceptance and popularity of the Bohr theory after all. As with the Aboriginal Dream-time mythology we can consider the particular institutional arrangements within which the theory is embedded. And, here again, the parallels are striking, and provide significant confirmation for the womb-envy hypothesis. Certainly at the time of formulation of the Copenhagen Interpretation and to a great extent still today, the community of theoretical physicists had the appearance of a closed male order – nurturing esoteric knowledge, beyond the understanding of the rest of society.

"You can't possibly begin to understand it if you have not mastered the appropriate mathematics. Anything we physicists might say to you ordinary mortals is just a travesty of the truth (we have moved beyond mere analogy etc.)."

But, of course, when you get right down to it, this deep truth turns out to be the Copenhagen Interpretation – closely on a par with the rather pathetic secrets of male pregnancy (or an incoherent amalgam of outdated instrumentalism and idealism, depending on how you look at it).

Here the appropriate highly specialised and mathematised and authoritarian university education – with very little rational discussion but lots of exams constituted the initiation process that mediated the transition of the young men from the world of the women. And note here how attitudes to the Arts – amongst physicists – often still mirror the adult tribesman's attitude to the women's world. The Humanities are denigrated as soft, as inferior, as weak – a pathetic mix of pseudo-science and (arty farty) pretentious nonsense, trying to 'ape' the true hard, pure sciences of the men; but at the same time also vaguely threatening; polluting, having to be kept at arms length to preserve the purity of true male wisdom and male pride.

There is always the sneaking fear that perhaps art and social science are on to something after all. There is always the suspicion that in some sense – in turning away from the arts, the scientists have abandoned the affirmation of life (love, fun) in favour of a preoccupation with dead matter; perhaps as Freud might say, a pure culture of the death instinct. So that it is vital that they keep reminding themselves of the deep knowledge and magical power that is their compensation. It is vital to project their own insecurity, fears, aggression back into the world of the arts, so that it can continue to be denigrated, ridiculed and held up as the foil of pathetic inadequacy compared to their own high calling.

Residual fear and insecurity is compensated by tremendous power over and regular assaults upon the body of mother nature. Her secrets are revealed through spectacular collisions of particles, that rip them apart and spill out their guts. And order is imposed upon her unruly body through appropriate measurements.

Perhaps here, as in the tribal situation, such ideas have thrived and prospered for so long only because of the sort of uncritical credulity fostered by this sort of educational segregation. And only because of the effective insulation of the tradition from the rational judgement and differing values and perceptions of others.

In this context, the recent New Age antics of some leading members of the physics community – discovering God, and ghost particles, strong anthropic principles, many worlds and many minds begins to make perfect sense. It simply represents the culmination of a tendency long inherent in the system. Which is to say, the magic and the mysticism has been there for a long time. But it has been isolated and hedged about with protective ritual and taboo. It has been the preserve only of the 'men of high degree', the shamans of the physics community.

But lately, in a situation of economic, political and cultural crisis, with the degeneration of rational and critical scholarship elsewhere (creation 'science', postmodernism etc.) – a situation in which desperation and disenchantment with traditional ideas has fostered a pervasive relativism and new age mysticism outside of the physical scientific community a fertile climate has been created for sympathetic reception of such ideas.

Now, an increasing number of the elders of the physics community have seen an opportunity to break out of the isolation of the closed order, offering up its deepest secrets to try to win the love and respect of those who previously spurned them, or would previously have had little truck with such magic and mysticism. And they have been received with open arms by the media, by relativistic social scientists, by the religious establishment (eager for 'scientific' endorsement), by New Age mystics, aging hippies and eco-feminists.

Here too, of course, powerful corporate interests are involved. As long as public attention is focussed upon the mystical outer limits of interpretation, it bypasses the significant new technological implications of quantum 'tunnelling' and superconductivity. Here again, new generations of computers and other electronic devices are developed and applied by big business without any sort of public debate, decision, understanding or control.

At the same time, basic theory itself stagnates, as theoretical physicists remain locked into a stifling instrumentalist orthodoxy or become absorbed in wild flights of New Age fancy. It is conspicuous that these new technologies build upon quantum theoretical innovations which are now decades old. Physicist Eric Lerner e.g.

claims that, in recent decades, "the advance of science and technology has radically slowed... while biology remains vibrant, physical technology has been limited to mere quantitative advance for nearly thirty years – a situation unprecedented in over two hundred years" (LERNER 1992, p. 409).

And he is clear in implicating the Copenhagen Interpretation as a central contributor to this 'unprecedented stagnation'. As he says, "the result of this divorce of theory and reality has been... a growing sterility and stagnation of fundamental science" (ibid., p. 358).

CONCLUSION

There is clearly very much more to be said on the subject of religion as ideology and the persistence of 'religious' thought patterns in modern science. Perhaps, most obviously, I have rather neglected the topic of death. Anxieties about death – and attempts to overcome or manipulate such anxieties – would probably be top of most people's list in beginning to provide a social-psychological explanation of the persistence of religious belief.

I agree that this has to be a major focus of concern for any more comprehensive investigation. And I think that materialism and psychoanalysis can contribute much more in this area. The latter, e.g., can begin to trace the origin and nature of the fears and anxieties associated with death – paranoid, depressive or otherwise. Much more can be said from a materialist perspective about the ways in which religious institutions (and states and capitalist corporations) have extended and manipulated such fears for their own ends. Both materialism and psychoanalysis have something to say about the ways in which exploitation and frustration contribute to fear and despair in face of death in later life, as the individual looks back upon missed opportunities and unrealised human potentials with no time left to remedy the situation.

These traditions also have something to say about the potential liberating power of death, as recognition of the true reality of death as the end of life undermines such coercion and manipulation and frees the individual to make the most of this life. They can contribute also to an understanding of the possible role of death – and an individual's control of their own life and death – in a sane and free society.

However, even without any detailed consideration of these issues I think that I have said enough to demonstrate the continued relevance and productivity of materialist and psychoanalytic theories in understanding central aspects of human social life. The task is to build upon the contributions of Marx and Engels, Freud and Klein, rather than simply rejecting them in line with contemporary orthodoxy.

In the modern world, while a crudely materialistic economic rationalism serves to legitimate rampant greed and cruelty in economic life, substantial regions of the intellectual superstructure remain in the grip of postmodern relativism. Far from attacking the former, the latter concentrates its critical energies on the so-called 'grand theories' of historical materialism and [classical] psycho-analysis. Now, we all know that such brand theories have 'failed'.

Little in the way of rational argument is ever produced to support this contention. Indeed, it is far from clear in precisely what sort of way they are supposed to have 'failed'. Such failure is apparently self-evident – or an article of faith, like the ressurrection of Christ – and is repeated like a mantra in ever more derivitive and tedious postmodern tracts.

Plenty of cogent logical criticisms of major tenets of post-modernism (eg its dependence upon outdated and inadequate conceptions of semantics) have been produced – by materialists and others. But now, as ever, rational argument, logical coherence and empirical confirmation are not required of a dominant ideology. So long as it effectively distracts attention from the reality of inequality and oppression, and hooks into some psychic substrate, it will receive support from the powers that be.

It is particularly ironic that postmodernists should make such a big deal of focussing upon the micro-structures of power, when their practice remains so blindly uncritical to the reality of power within the academy itself – let alone in the material world beyond. Thus postmodernism remains congenial to the rapidly expanding bureaucracies that exercise increasing control of intellectual produc-tion throughout the western world.

From a postmodern perspective, the materialist analysis and critique of religion appears 'one-dimensional' and intolerant. The postmodern ontology of diverse language games, discourses and stories can, no doubt, find a place for even the most bizarre and ludicrous of belief systems. After all, as Baudrillard says, "the real is no longer real, no longer exists". There are only appearances, perspectives, choices – and one is as good as another.

But for those not yet quite willing to go all the way with Baudrillard in accepting that Disneyland "is presented as an imaginary in order to make us believe the rest [of the United States] is real, when in fact it is no longer real", for those actually seeking explanatory essences beneath the appearances, I think that the materialist approach, and the materialist theory of ideology, still has much to offer.

There is still much work to be done in applying materialist (and psychoanalytic) theory to be origin and development of postmodernism itself. And, here again, I believe that some of the ideas of this book are relevant and useful.

Of course, it is a mistake to treat materialism and psychoanalysis as 'grand' theories in the sense of theories that provide all possible answers to all possible questions. But few serious students in either tradition have ever made any such claim. Rather, such theories should be judged in terms of their capacity for development and elaboration within specific scientific research traditions, generating cogent and convincing explanations for specific sorts of observations and experiences.

Hopefully this book has gone some way towards demonstrating that such theories still do have something to contribute to our better understanding of the phenomenon of religious belief. And, hopefully, it has therefore also contributed to keeping open   some alternative channels of investigation otherwise blocked by postmodern obfuscation and mystification.

REFERENCES

AHERN, E.M. 1981, *Chinese Ritual and Politics,* Cambridge University Press, Cambridge.

BAIGENT, M. AND LEIGH, R. 1987, *The Messianic Legacy,* Corgi Books Ltd, London.

BAIGENT, M. AND LEIGH, R. 1991, *The Dead Sea Scrolls Deception,* Jonathan Cape, London.

BETTELHEIM, B. 1955, *Symbolic Wounds,* Thames and Hudson, London.

BLACKIE, D. 1990, *Environment in Crisis,* Socialist Workers Party, London.

BLAINEY, G. 1991, *Triumph of the Nomads,* Pan Books, Sydney.

BOCOCK, R. AND THOMSON, K. (eds) 1985, *Religion and Ideology,* Manchester University Press, Manchester.

BOHM, D. AND PEAT, F.D. 1987, *Science, Order and Creativity,* Bantam Books, New York.

BORNEMAN, E. 1976, *The Psychoanalysis of Money,* Urizen Books, New York.

BROWN, N.O. 1968, *Life Against Death,* Sphere Books, London.

BURBIDGE, J. 1990, *Within Reason,* Broadview, Peterborough.

BURNHEIM, J. 1985, *Is Democracy Possible?,* Basil Blackwell, Oxford.

BUTZER, K.W. 1976, *Early Hydraulic Civilization in Egypt,* University of Chicago Press, Chicago.

CALDWELL, R. 1989, *The Origin of the Gods,* Oxford University Press, Oxford.

CAMPBELL, J. 1979, *Masks of God,* Oriental Mythology, Penguin Books, Harmondsworth.

CHASSEGUET-SMIRGEL, J. 1987, *Creativity and Perversion,* Free Association Press, London.

CROSSAN, J.D. 1994, *Jesus, a Revolutionary Biography,* Harper Collins, New York.

DEMAUSE, L. (ed.) 1975, *The History of Childhood,* Harper and Row, New York.

DOWNING, C. 1984, *The Goddess,* Crossroads Publishing, New York.

DRAPER, H. 1977, *Karl Marx's Theory of Revolution,* Vol. 1, Monthly Review Press, New York.

EISLER, R. 1990, *The Chalice and the Blade,* Allen and Unwin Ltd, London.

ENGELS, F. 1977, *The Origin of the Family,* Private Property and the State, Progress Publishers, Moscow.

ERIKSON, E.H. 1958, *Young Man Luther,* W.H. Norton and Co, New York.

FARB, P. 1978, *Man's Rise to Civilisation,* Bantam Books, New York.

FENICHEL, O. 1945, *The Psychoanalytic Theory of Neurosis*, Routledge, London.

FINK, H. 1981, *Social Philosophy*, Methuen, London.

FISHER, S. AND GREENBERG, R.P. 1985, *The Scientific Credibility of Freud's Theories and Therapy*, Columbia University Press, New York.

FRANKFORT, H. 1956, *The Birth of Civilization in the Near East*, Indiana University Press, Bloomington.

FRANKFORT, H. 1961, *Ancient Egyptian Religion*, Harper and Row, New York.

FRANKFORT, H. 1978, *Kingship and the Gods*, University of Chicago Press, Chicago.

FRANKIEL, S.S. 1985, *Christianity*, Harper and Row, New York.

FREUD, S. 1985a, *Civilization, Society and Religion*, Penguin Books, Harmondsworth.

FREUD, S. 1985b, *The Origin of Religion*, Penguin Books, Harmondsworth.

FREUD, S. 1977, *On Sexuality*, Penguin Books, Harmondsworth.

GAY, P. 1989, *Freud, A Life for Our Time*, Dent, London.

GIMBUTAS, M. 1991, *The Civilization of the Goddess*, Harper Collins, New York.

GODELIER, M. 1978, *Perspectives in Marxist Anthropology*, Cambridge University Press, Cambridge.

GODELIER, M. 1988, *The Mental and the Material*, Verso, London.

GREVEN, P. 1992, *Spare the Child*, Vintage Books, New York.

GRIBBIN, J. 1985, *In Search of Schrodinger's Cat*, Corgi, London.

HAN, M.Y. 1993, *The Probable Universe*, TAB Books, Blue Ridge Summit.

HARRÉ, R. 1986, *Varieties of Realism*, Basil Blackwell, Oxford.

HARRIS, M. 1978, *Cannibals and Kings*, Fontana, Glasgow.

HARRIS, M. 1989, *Our Kind*, Harper Collins, New York.

HEY AND WALTERS 1987, *The Quantum Universe*, Cambridge University Press, Cambridge.

HOFFMAN, M.A. 1984, *Egypt Before the Pharaohs*, Routledge and Kegan Paul, London.

HULTKRANTZ, A. 1987, *Native Religions of North America*, Harper and Row, New York.

JAMES, T.G.H. 1985, *Pharaoh's People*, Oxford University Press, Oxford.

KAUTSKY, K. 1972, *Foundations of Christianity*, Monthly Review Press, New York.

KLEIN, M. 1975, *Envy and Gratitude*, Delta Books, New York.

LASCH, C. 1985, *The Minimal Self*, Pan Books, London.

LERNER, E.J. 1992, *The Big Bang Never Happened*, Simon and Schuster, London.

LERNER, G. 1987, *The Creation of Patriarchy*, Oxford University Press, Oxford.

LESTER, R.C. 1987, *Buddhism*, Harper and Row, New York.

LEWIS, I.M. 1971, *Ecstatic Religion*, Penguin Books, Harmondsworth.

LISITSKY, G. 1976, *Four Ways of Being Human*, Penguin Books, Harmondsworth.

LOVELOCK, J. 1991, *Gaia, the Practical Science of Planetary Medicine*, Allen and Unwin, Sydney.

MALLORY, J.P. 1989, *In Search of the Indo-Europeans*, Thames and Hudson, London.

MARX, K. and ENGELS, F. 1955, *On Religion*, Foreign Languages Publishing House, Moscow.

MARX, K. and ENGELS, F. 1979, *Pre-Capitalist Socio-Economic Formations*, Progress Publishers, Moscow.

MAYNARD-SMITH, J. 1986, *The Problems of Biology*, Oxford University Press, Oxford.

MELLAART, J. 1967, *Catal Huyuk – A Neolithic Town in Anatolia*, Thames and Hudson, London.

MERCHANT, C. 1983, *The Death of Nature*, Harper and Row, New York.

MILLER, A. 1988, *For Your Own Good*, Virago Press, London.

MILLER, A. 1990, *Thou Shalt Not Be Aware*, Pluto Press, London.

MILLER, A. 1992a, *Breaking Down the Wall of Silence*, Virago Press, London.

MILLER, A. 1992b, *The Drama of Being a Child*, Virago Press, London.

MONEY-KYRLE, R. 1950 (?) *Superstition and Society*, Hogarth Press, London.

OLSON, C. (ed.) 1985, *The Book of the Goddess*, Crossroads Publishing, New York.

PAGELS, E. 1990, *Adam, Eve and the Serpent*, Penguin Books, Harmondsworth.

POLKINGHORNE, J.C. 1990, *The Quantum World*, Penguin Books, Harmondsworth.

RADIN, P. 1957, *Primitive Religion*, Dover Publications, New York.

RANKE-HEINEMANN, U. 1991, *Eunuchs in the Service of God*, Penguin Books, Harmondsworth.

RANKE-HEINEMANN, U. 1994, *Putting Away Childish Things*, Harper Collins, San Francisco.

RICHES, J. 1990, *The World of Jesus*, Cambridge University Press, Cambridge.

ROAZEN, P. 1970, *Freud; Political and Social Thought*, Vintage Books, New York.

ROHEIM, G. 1945, *War, Crime and the Covenant*, International Universities Press, New York.

ROHEIM, G. 1952, *The Gates of the Dream*, International Universities Press, New York.

ROHEIM, G. 1950, *Psychoanalysis and Anthropology*, International Universities Press, New York.

ROUX, G. 1980, *Ancient Iraq*, Penguin Books, Harmondsworth.

SANDAY, P.R. 1981, *Female Power, Male Dominance*, Cambridge University Press, Cambridge.

SEGAL, H. 1980, *Introduction to the Work of Melanie Klein*, Hogarth Press, London

SEGAL, J. 1992, *Melanie Klein*, Sage Publishers, London.

SIEGEL, P.N. 1986, *The Meek and the Militant*, Zed Books Ltd, London.

SKLAR, L. 1992, *Philosophy of Physics*, Oxford University Press, Oxford.

SLATER, P. 1968, *The Glory of Hera*, Beacon Press, Boston.

SMITH, M. 1978, *Jesus the Magician*, Victor Gollancz Ltd, London.

SMITH, P. AND JONES, O.R. 1986, *The Philosophy of Mind*, Cambridge University Press, Cambridge.

SOBER, E. 1993, *Philosophy of Biology*, Oxford University Press, Oxford.

SOHN RETHEL, A. 1978, *Intellectual and Manual Labour*, Macmillan Press Ltd, London.

SPIRO, M. 1982, *Oedipus in the Trobriands*, University of Chicago Press, Chicago.

SPIRO, M. 1987, *Culture and Human Nature*, University of Chicago Press, Chicago.

SPONG, J.S. 1991, *Rescuing the Bible from Fundamentalism*, Harper Collins, London.

STEPHENS, W.N. 1962, *The Oedipus Complex Hypothesis*, Cross Cultural Evidence, Free Press, Glencoe.

STORR, A. 1990, *The Art of Psychotherapy*, Butterworth-Heinemann, Oxford.

TICKNELL, O. AND HILDYARD, N. 1992, 'Green Dollars, Green Mecace', in *The Ecologist*, Vol. 22, No. 3, May 1992.

TREECE, D. 1993, Why The Earth Summit Failed, in *International Socialism Journal*, No. 56, IS, London.

TRIGGER, B.G. et al. 1983, *Ancient Egypt*, Cambridge University Press, Cambridge.

TRUMP, D.H. 1981, *The Prehistory of the Mediterranean*, Penguin Books, Harmondsworth.

TURNBULL, C. 1961, *The Forest People*, Simon and Schuster, New York.

TURNBULL, C. 1965, *Wayward Servants*, The Natural History Press, Garden City, New York.

VON BAER, M.C. 1992, *Taming the Atom*, Penguin Books, Harmondsworth.

WILSON, I. 1985, *Jesus; The Evidence*, Pan Books, London.

WITHERINGTON, B. 1990, *Women and the Genesis of Christianity*, Cambridge University Press, Cambridge.

INDEX